Frommer's

Niagara Region

by Louise Dearden
with Melanie Chambers

Here's what the critics say about Frommer's:

"Amazingly easy to use. Very portable, very complete."

—*Booklist*

"Detailed, accurate, and easy-to-read information for all price ranges."

—*Glamour Magazine*

"Hotel information is close to encyclopedic."

—*Des Moines Sunday Register*

"Frommer's Guides have a way of giving you a real feel for a place."

—*Knight Ridder Newspapers*

John Wiley & Sons Canada, Ltd.

Published by:

John Wiley & Sons Canada, Ltd

6045 Freemont Blvd.
Mississauga, ON L5R 4J3

Library and Archives Canada Cataloguing in Publication Data
Dearden, Louise
  Frommer's Niagara region/Louise Dearden.
Includes index.
ISBN-13: 978-0-470-83811-2
ISBN-10: 0-470-83811-6
  1. Niagara Falls Region (Ont.)—Guidebooks. 2. Niagara Peninsula (Ont.)—Guidebooks. I. Title. II. Title: Niagara region.

FC3095.N5A3 2006a   917.13'38045   C2006-901252-0

Editor: Robert Hickey
Project Manager: Elizabeth McCurdy
Project Coordinator: Pamela Vokey
Cartographer: Mapping Specialists
Publishing Services Director: Karen Bryan
Publishing Services Manager: Ian Koo
Production by Wiley Indianapolis Composition Services
Front cover photo: The Maid of the Mist
Back cover photo: Grapes in a Niagara Region vineyard

Special Sales

For reseller information, including discounts and premium sales, please call our sales department: Tel. 416-646-7992. For press review copies, author interviews, or other publicity information, please contact our marketing department: Tel. 416-646-4584; Fax: 416-236-4448.

Manufactured in Canada

1   2   3   4   5   TRI   10   09   08   07   06

Contents

List of Maps

Acknowledgements

Heartfelt thanks to my co-author Melanie Chambers, whose boundless energy, professionalism, and dedication never wavered throughout the project. Mel, you're the best. I would also like to extend deepest thanks to my editor, Robert Hickey, who has expertly stewarded the project from conception to completion and resolved numerous challenges with composure and grace.

An Invitation to the Reader

In researching this book, we discovered many wonderful places—hotels, restaurants, shops, and more. We're sure you'll find others. Please tell us about them, so we can share the information with your fellow travelers in upcoming editions. If you were disappointed with a recommendation, we'd love to know that, too. Please write to:

Frommer's Niagara Region
John Wiley & Sons Canada, Ltd. • 6045 Freemont Blvd. • Mississuaga, ON
L5R 4J3

An Additional Note

Please be advised that travel information is subject to change at any time—and this is especially true of prices. We therefore suggest that you write or call ahead for confirmation when making your travel plans. The authors, editors, and publisher cannot be held responsible for the experiences of readers while traveling. Your safety is important to us, however, so we encourage you to stay alert and be aware of your surroundings. Keep a close eye on cameras, purses, and wallets, all favorite targets of thieves and pickpockets.

About the Author

Canadian writer **Louise Dearden** has been an enthusiastic traveler ever since her first trip abroad as a child. She spent the first 15 years of her adult life in the U.K., visiting mainland Europe, particularly France, as often as possible. After an extended period back in her native Ontario, Louise recently moved back to England with her husband and family, where she continues to pursue her writing career.

Frommer's Star Ratings, Icons & Abbreviations

Every hotel, restaurant, and attraction listing in this guide has been ranked for quality, value, service, amenities, and special features using a **star-rating system.** In country, state, and regional guides, we also rate towns and regions to help you narrow down your choices and budget your time accordingly. Hotels and restaurants are rated on a scale of zero (recommended) to three stars (exceptional). Attractions, shopping, nightlife, towns, and regions are rated according to the following scale: zero stars (recommended), one star (highly recommended), two stars (very highly recommended), and three stars (must-see).

In addition to the star-rating system, we also use **seven feature icons** that point you to the great deals, in-the-know advice, and unique experiences that separate travelers from tourists. Throughout the book, look for:

Finds	Special finds—those places only insiders know about
Fun Fact	Fun facts—details that make travelers more informed and their trips more fun
Kids	Best bets for kids and advice for the whole family
Moments	Special moments—those experiences that memories are made of
Overrated	Places or experiences not worth your time or money
Tips	Insider tips—great ways to save time and money
Value	Great values—where to get the best deals

The following **abbreviations** are used for credit cards:

AE	American Express	DISC	Discover	V	Visa
DC	Diners Club	MC	MasterCard		

Frommers.com

Now that you have the guidebook to a great trip, visit our website at **www.frommers.com** for travel information on more than 3,000 destinations. With features updated regularly, we give you instant access to the most current trip-planning information available. At Frommers.com, you'll also find the best prices on airfares, accommodations, and car rentals—and you can even book travel online through our travel booking partners. At Frommers.com, you'll also find the following:

- Online updates to our most popular guidebooks
- Vacation sweepstakes and contest giveaways
- Newsletter highlighting the hottest travel trends
- Online travel message boards with featured travel discussions

The Best of the Niagara Region

There's no doubt about it—the Falls are the main attraction in the Niagara region. And that's as it should be. The breathtaking beauty of the pair of waterfalls—one on American soil and one on Canadian—is an irresistible lure. Charles Dickens poetically captured his first impression of the Falls, declaring, "Niagara was at once stamped upon my heart, an Image of Beauty. . . ." Thousands of visitors before him and millions after him have felt the same awe as they stood facing the majesty of the tumbling water.

If you're a first-time visitor, by all means plan to see the Falls first. But if you have the time to stay more than a day, or you're making a return visit, I strongly encourage you to venture beyond the thundering waters. You'll be pleasantly surprised by the diversity of the Niagara region.

Niagara has much to offer visitors in addition to the Falls. The picture-postcard, tree-lined streets of historic Niagara-on-the-Lake invite you to take a leisurely stroll. The town has gracious inns, great restaurants, a unique upscale shopping district, and world-class live theater. The wine region continues to add new wineries to its prestigious community of award-winning vintners every year, providing visitors with an eclectic variety of wine- and food-tasting experiences. The rich history of the region can be discovered through visits to the Welland Canal, the battlefields and other military sites of the War of 1812, the Freedom Trail of the escaping slaves from the southern United States, and the many museums and monuments. The natural environment is well stewarded, with numerous hiking and biking opportunities along the many pathways, parks, and conservation areas.

1 The Most Unforgettable Niagara Region Experiences

- **The Falls Up Close & Personal** Feel the thunder of the water in your bones and drench yourself in the mist of Niagara Falls for a memory of nature's power and beauty that will never be forgotten. See chapter 7, "What to See & Do in the Niagara Region," p. 111.

- **The Falls by Night** Experiencing the Falls in daylight is memorable, but the most remarkable sight visually is the nightly illuminations. An ever-changing palette of rainbow colors floods the American and Horseshoe Falls every evening at nightfall. See chapter 7, "What to See & Do in the Niagara Region," p. 111.

- **Dining Alfresco in the Vineyards** The Niagara Peninsula serves up some lovely weather in the late spring, summer, and early fall that is perfect for outdoor dining. The only rule is to linger. See chapter 7, "What to See & Do in the Niagara Region," p. 111.

Niagara Region

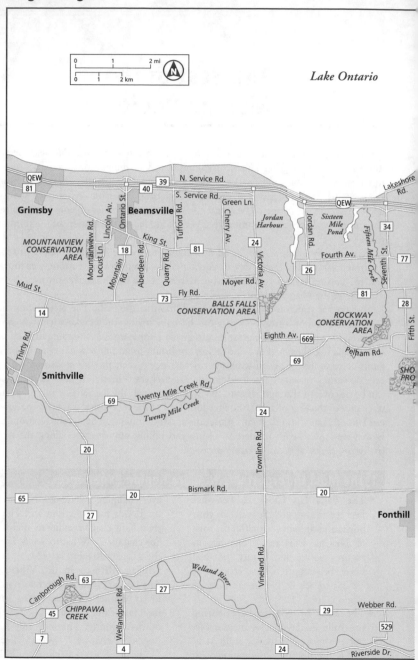

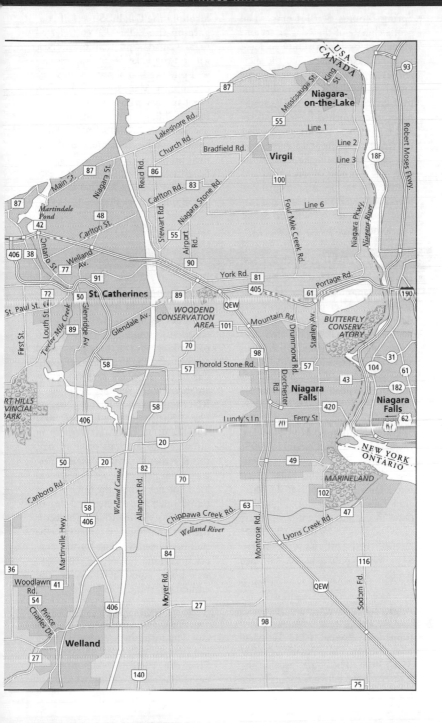

- **Spring Blooms & Blossoms** The gentle climate of the Niagara region, influenced by its proximity to Lake Erie and Lake Ontario and the sheltering effect of the Niagara Escarpment, is particularly favorable for fruit-growing in addition to its abundance of ornamental flowers, shrubs, and trees. Consequently, if you visit the region in spring and summer you will be surrounded by blossom in the acres of commercial orchards, and charmed by the beautiful formal displays in Niagara's many parks and gardens. See chapter 7, "What to See & Do in the Niagara Region," p. 111.

- **Strolling the Quaint Streets of Niagara-on-the-Lake** Often referred to as Canada's prettiest town, Niagara-on-the-Lake is an impressively well-preserved and restored historic community. Many towns have a main street or two with a section of heritage buildings; Niagara-on-the-Lake has an entire neighborhood. Local residents take enormous pride in their properties, and tourists reap the benefits as they stroll along the leafy streets. See chapter 7, What to See & Do in the Niagara Region, p. 111.

2 Best Splurge Hotels

- **Harbour House Hotel,** 85 Melville St., Niagara-on-the-Lake (© **905/ 468-4683**): A serene familiarity settles quite gently upon you at the Harbour House, making you feel like a welcome house guest rather than an overnight tourist. Their feather beds, goosedown duvets and pillows, and fine Egyptian cotton bed linens are the best; it's like being lightly wrapped in a fluffy cloud. See p. 76.

- **Sheraton Fallsview,** 6755 Fallsview Blvd., Niagara Falls, Ontario (© **905/ 374-1077**): For the ultimate sleepover that includes the Falls, check into a fallsview loft suite at the Sheraton Fallsview. Two-story-high windows to capture the entire dramatic view and the chain's signature "Sweet Sleeper" bed (and it's a beauty)— what more could you ask for? See p. 68.

- **Prince of Wales,** 6 Picton St., Niagara-on-the-Lake (© **905/468- 3245**): You could sum up the Prince of Wales as luxury well done. An enormous amount of money and painstaking effort have been directed toward restoring the Victorian splendor of this property, and the results are exceedingly pleasing. See p. 77.

- **Riverbend Inn,** 16104 Niagara Pkwy., Niagara-on-the-Lake (© **905/ 468-8829**): If you're looking for an intimate and gracious place to stay, the Riverbend Inn will please. Rescued from neglect by a well-respected local hotelier family, the Inn has been transformed into a stately and elegant Georgian-style mansion. Service is friendly and polished—many of the staff have been working for the owners since long before the Riverbend was born, and their loyalty and enthusiasm shine through. See p. 77.

3 Best Moderately Priced Hotels

- **Ramada Fallsview,** 6732 Fallsview Blvd., Niagara Falls, Ontario (© **905/ 356-1501**): These are usually the least expensive fallsview rooms in the

city. The furniture is arranged so you can view the Falls from your bed. Just fling the curtains wide-open and enjoy. The retro building, which has a pod of guest rooms perched on top of the concrete elevator shaft, also has an observation deck, a restaurant with a view, and even arranges weddings. See p. 72.

- **Black Walnut Manor,** 4255 Victoria Ave., Vineland Station (© **905/562-8675**): There is nothing with which to compare the Black Walnut in the entire Niagara region. An old farmstead property in the country, equipped with the upscale urban amenities of a downtown boutique hotel. Unique, sexy, gotta go. See p. 82.

- **Alexander Muir,** 43 Dalhousie Ave., Port Dalhousie, St. Catharines (© **905/935-3553**): This is a perfect example of what a traditional B&B should be—cozy, with welcoming, friendly hosts and antique furniture, on a heritage property with pretty gardens for guests to relax in— Alexander Muir has it all. But book ahead—there are only two rooms. See p. 85.

- **Old Bank House Historic Inn,** 10 Front St., Niagara-on-the-Lake (© **905/468-7136**): With such an abundance of intriguing and charming historical properties in Niagara-on-the-Lake, choosing one to highlight seems grossly unfair. However, the Old Bank is a fine example of the type of accommodations you can expect to find in the town. It has a prime location close to the theater, shops, and restaurants, yet on a quiet street steps away from beautiful Simcoe Park and Lake Ontario. Rooms are nicely furnished in period decor, and a picturesque veranda runs along the front of the house. The property's historical secret is that it was the site of the first branch of the Bank of Canada—the original vault (now restored) is still in the house. See p. 79.

4 The Most Unforgettable Dining Experiences

- **LIV,** in the White Oak Conference Resort & Spa, Niagara-on-the-Lake (© **905/688-2550**): Surrender to the tranquillity and serenity of LIV. The spacious, airy dining room is draped with an abundance of soft, sheer, white fabric. Simplicity rules. Food is presented as a work of art, each component thoughtfully placed in relation to the others. See p. 98.

- **Watermark,** in the Hilton Hotel, 6361 Fallsview Blvd., Niagara Falls, Ontario (© **905/353-7138**): The innovative design features of Watermark will leave a lasting impression: aquariums, vaulted ceilings, blue glass accents, cascading waterfalls, a sculpture of Poseidon, and 5m-tall (18-ft.) windows to capture the panorama of the Falls. See p. 92.

- **Stone Road Grille,** in the Garrison Plaza, corner of St. Mary Street and Mississauga Street, Niagara-on-the-Lake (© **905/468-3474**): Even the most jaded urban palate is rejuvenated at Stone Road Grille. You will find yourself alternately nodding with satisfaction at the imaginative dishes and sighing with delight at the depth of the chef's understanding of how to marry flavors and textures. See p. 100.

- **Peninsula Ridge,** 5600 King St. West, Beamsville (© **905/563-0900**): The restaurant is located in a superbly restored red-brick Victorian manor, built in Queen Anne style. A distinctive turret and cedar-shingled roof add to the character of the property. Note the polished cherrywood staircase and red pine floors. Ask for a table facing the lake; you will see the gorgeous sunset as you dine, depending on the time of year. Try the prix fixe lunch or five-course tasting menu paired with Niagara wines. See p. 104.

- **Terroir La Cachette,** 1339 Lakeshore Rd., Niagara-on-the-Lake (© **905/468-1222**): Although Terroir La Cachette's cuisine focuses on regional wines and ingredients, the French Provençal style of cooking that Quebecois chef Alain Levesque has perfected remains at the heart of the restaurant's dishes. And French cuisine is rather thin on the ground in the Niagara region, so it's especially nice to find expertly prepared Provençal-inspired cuisine in a striking dining room, overlooking picturesque countryside, right in the middle of a winery. See p. 106.

- **Vineland Estates Winery Restaurant,** 3620 Moyer Rd., Vineland (© **888/846-3526**): One of the most consistently excellent restaurants in the Niagara region, Vineland Estates' restaurant is also arguably the prettiest of the winery restaurants. The epicurean menu changes seasonally and makes good use of local ingredients. If you wish to indulge in a leisurely summer lunch, reserve a table on the shaded terrace; the view across the vineyards toward Lake Ontario is divine. See p. 104.

5 The Most Romantic Niagara Moments

- **Relaxing in bed in a luxury hotel with a view of the Falls illuminations.** The high-rise hotels on Fallsview Avenue in Niagara Falls, Ontario, have spectacular views of the Falls from many of their rooms. Try the Ramada Plaza Fallsview, which has an angled floor-to-ceiling wall of windows and king-size beds, or the Sheraton Fallsview Hotel & Conference Centre, which has stunning loft suites with a two-story wall of windows. See chapter 5, "Where to Stay," p. 72 and p. 68.

- **Taking a horse-drawn carriage ride.** The historical streets of Niagara-on-the-Lake are a picture-perfect setting for a romantic carriage ride, either in summer when the gardens and hanging baskets are filled to overflowing with colorful blooms, or on a crisp, sunny winter day, bundled up under a blanket. See chapter 7, "What to See & Do in the Niagara Region," p. 111.

- **Hiking along the Bruce Trail on the Niagara Escarpment.** The Bruce Trail is an 850km (528-mile) meandering path. The Niagara Bruce Trail section runs between Beamsville and Queenston, overlooking the Niagara River. The trail passes through countless orchards and wineries, yet feels secluded and wild. Hikers can experience fantastic views, cascading waterfalls, lush fauna and flora, and a kaleidoscope of colors. See chapter 7, "What to See & Do in the Niagara Region," p. 147.

- **Enjoying a leisurely meal on a winery patio overlooking the vineyards.** There is no better way to dine than outdoors in the fresh air. A summer breeze, a glass of fine wine at your fingertips, and your true love—they all add up to a memorable experience. Try Peller Estates on a summer evening, when the terrace twinkles with candlelight, or Vineland Estates on a warm June afternoon, with the rolling vineyards spread out before you. See "Dine among the Vines" in chapter 8, p. 180.

6 The Best Things to Do for Free (or Almost)

- **Viewing the Falls from both sides of the border:** The best views of the Falls are enjoyed in Niagara Falls, Ontario, but you are free to stroll up and down the sidewalks along the Niagara Gorge on both sides of the Niagara River to view both sets of falls. See chapter 7, "What to See & Do in the Niagara Region," p. 111.

- **Enjoying the summer fireworks display over the Falls:** On Friday, Sunday, and holiday evenings at 10pm during the main tourist season (Victoria Day in May to Labour Day in Sept), there is a spectacular fireworks display over Niagara Falls. See chapter 7, "What to See & Do in the Niagara Region," p. 111.

- **Watching a ship go through the locks on the Welland Canal:** Lock 3 and Lock 7 are the best viewing locations. See chapter 7, "What to See & Do in the Niagara Region," p. 124.

- **Tasting wine at a winery tasting room:** Some wineries charge a nominal fee for each sample and a few ask for a donation to charity, but quite a number are free. However, there is a legal limit to the amount of wine a winery can serve a customer. See chapter 7, "What to See & Do in the Niagara Region," p. 111.

- **Strolling the Niagara Parks Commission Botanical Gardens:** These gardens are open all year around. The displays of flowers, shrubs, and trees are deeply inspiring to gardeners and a delight to everyone who enters. See chapter 7, "What to See & Do in the Niagara Region," p. 138.

- **Hiking and biking your way around the Niagara Peninsula:** The Niagara region is rich in hiking and biking trails, conservation areas, and parklands. Take a leisurely stroll through groomed parks with formal flower displays, or visit a designated conservation zone such as Ball's Falls, Beamer Memorial Conservation Area, or Niagara Glen Nature Reserve. If you prefer a less structured environment, explore the 850km (528-mile) Bruce Trail, Canada's oldest and longest hiking trail. The southern terminus of the Bruce Trail is located in Queenston Heights Park. Follow the white blazes as the trail winds along the Niagara Escarpment, a prominent ridge that cuts through the Niagara region from east to west and has been designated a UNESCO World Biosphere Reserve. See chapter 7, "What to See & Do in the Niagara Region," p. 111.

7 Best Activities for Families

- *Maid of the Mist:* From the youngest to the oldest, everyone loves the *Maid of the Mist.* Schedule your visit early in the day (the first sailing is at 9am during peak season), before the lineups begin to form. Put on the voluminous, recyclable blue rain poncho and prepare to be drenched by Niagara water. Head for the upper decks for the best views and the wettest, most authentic experience. The *Maid of the Mist* operates boats on both sides of the border. See p. 112.

- **Cave of the Winds:** A wooden boardwalk takes visitors right to the base of the American Falls. Souvenir non-slip sandals and lightweight recyclable rain ponchos are provided. Tour hours have been extended so that tourists can see the illuminations and fireworks displays from unique vantage points on the boardwalk. See p. 118.

- **Butterfly Conservatory:** The Conservatory, on the Niagara Parkway in Ontario, is a bright and airy rainforest-like environment with a multi-level pathway (stroller and wheelchair accessible) that winds its way through the lush foliage. An amazing 2,000 tropical butterflies, representing 50 different species, live freely in the Conservatory. The trick is to walk slowly and pause often, since the most rewarding sights are usually found through quiet observation. Even boisterous kids will enjoy the soothing atmosphere of this magical jungle. See p. 116.

- **Carousel at Lakeside Park:** One of the largest and best preserved examples of a Looff menagerie carousel, the carousel at Lakeside Park on Lake Ontario in Old Port Dalhousie is a fantastic sight. Built in 1898, there are 69 carousel animals arranged in four rings. And it costs only a nickel a ride! See p. 136.

2

Planning Your Trip to the Niagara Region

Whether your trip planning style leans toward thorough research and meticulous attention to detail or last-minute and anything goes in terms of when, where, and how, taking time to plan will help you make the most of Niagara's extensive choice of visitor attractions, activities, and unique experiences. Moreover, in today's climate of heightened travel security it's in your best interest to ensure that you understand the rules and requirements for transportation and, for those who are arriving from abroad, the entry requirements for Canada.

1 Visitor Information

FROM NORTH AMERICA

Within Canada, your starting point for information on the entire Niagara Region is the **Tourism Niagara** website at **www. tourismniagara.com**. Their e-mail address is info@tourismniagara.com.

You can also access the expertise of the **Gateway Niagara Information Centre**, 424 South Service Rd., Queen Eliza beth Way at Casablanca Boulevard in Grimsby (© **800/263-2988;** www. tourismniagara.com/gatewayniagara; gateway@tourismniagara.com). Travel counselors can be reached between 8am and 8pm daily from July to August. The rest of the year, the phone lines are open between 9am and 6pm daily.

Niagara Falls Tourism, 5515 Stanley Ave., Niagara Falls, Ont. (© **800/ 56FALLS (563-2557)** or 905/356-5567; **www.niagarafallstourism.com** or **www. discoverniagara.com**) has a wealth of information on accommodations, entertainment, events, golf, attractions, casinos, wedding planning, and travel in and around the city of Niagara Falls. Their travel counselors are available Monday to

Friday from 8am to 6pm and weekends from 10am to 6pm year-round.

The **Niagara Parks Commission** is a self-financed agency of the Ontario government. They manage the immediate vicinity of the Falls and the Niagara River corridor, with the mandate of preserving and enhancing the natural beauty of the area. Their website offers valuable information on planning a visit to the area. Visit them at **www.niagaraparks.com** or write for information to The Niagara Parks Commission, P.O. Box 150, Niagara Falls, ON. L2E 6T2.

Another excellent source of information on activities throughout the Niagara region is the **Ontario Travel Centres.** Operated by the Ontario Ministry of Tourism, these centers offer provincial road maps, tourist guides, and attraction brochures. Give them a call at © **800/ ONTARIO (668-2746)** or visit them online at **www.ontariotravel.net**. In the Niagara area, they can be found in **Fort Erie** at 315 Bertie St., just off the Queen Elizabeth Way at the Peace Bridge (© **905/871-3505**), in **Niagara Falls** at

5355 Stanley Ave. (west on Hwy. 420 from the Rainbow Bridge) (© **905/358-3221**), and in St. Catharines on the westbound Queen Elizabeth Way at the east end of Garden City Skyway (© **905/684-6354**).

For tourist information on Niagara Falls, New York, visit **Niagara Tourism and Convention Corporation,** 345 3rd St., Suite 605, Niagara Falls, NY, 14303 (© **800/338-7890**; www.niagara-usa.com). They offer a free comprehensive travel guide that can be ordered online.

FROM ABROAD

Visit the official travel site of the **Canadian Tourism Commission, www.travelcanada.ca,** and click on your country of residence to access customized visitor information, including advice on traveling to Canada and contact information for tour operators and travel agents in your country who specialize in Canada as a destination.

There are more than 300 Government of Canada diplomatic and consular missions overseas, which can provide information on traveling to Canada and direct you to the appropriate sources for tourist information. If your country of residence is other than those listed below, you can access the full directory online at **www.dfait-maeci.gc.ca/world/embassies/menu-en.asp**.

U.K.: The **Canadian High Commission,** 1 Grosvenor Sq., London W1K 4AB (© **0207/258-6600**).

Ireland: The **Canadian Embassy,** 65 St. Stephen's Green, Dublin 2 (© **01/417-4100**).

Australia: The **Canadian High Commission,** Commonwealth Avenue, Canberra, ACT, 2600 (© **02/6270-4000**), or the Consulate General of Canada, Level 5, Quay West Building, 111 Harrington St., Sydney, NSW, 2000 (© **02/9364-3000**). There are also Consulates in Perth and Melbourne.

New Zealand: The **Canadian High Commission,** 61 Molesworth St., 3rd Floor, Thorndon, Wellington (© **04/473-9577**).

South Africa: The Canadian High Commission, 1103 Arcadia St., Hatfield, Pretoria (© **012/422-3000**). There is also a Consulate General in Cape Town and a Consulate in Durban.

2 Entry Requirements & Customs

ENTRY REQUIREMENTS

The following guidelines for entry documents should be followed carefully. Security has been heightened at border crossings and other points of entry since the September 11, 2001, terrorist attacks. Laws, restrictions, and entitlements that affect visitors are subject to change at any time. It's best to check before you travel.

All visitors to Canada must show proof of citizenship. A valid passport is the preferred entry document, and is a requirement for most visitors. U.S. citizens and permanent U.S. residents do not need a passport to enter Canada, though it is the easiest and most convenient method of proving citizenship.

For an up-to-date country-by-country listing of passport requirements around the world, go to the "Foreign Entry Requirement" Web page of the U.S. State Department at **http://travel.state.gov**.

U.S. citizens may present one of the following documents, provided it is accompanied by official photo ID: certificate of citizenship, birth certificate, or certificate of naturalization. U.S. permanent residents must also carry their Alien Registration Card (Green Card).

If you plan to drive into Canada, be sure to bring your car's registration papers and insurance documents. If you are traveling with children, make sure they have identification documents. Parents

---

Tips **Passport Savvy**

Allow plenty of time before your trip to apply for a passport; processing can take several weeks. Keep in mind that if you need a passport in a hurry, you'll pay a higher processing fee. When traveling, safeguard your passport in an inconspicuous, inaccessible place like a money belt and keep a copy of the critical pages with your passport number in a separate place. If you lose your passport, visit the nearest consulate or embassy of your native country as soon as possible for a replacement.

---

who share custody of their children should carry copies of the legal custody documents. If you are not the parent or legal guardian of the children traveling with you, you should carry a written statement from the children's parent or guardian, granting permission for the children to travel to Canada under your supervision.

Citizens of most European countries, Commonwealth countries, and former British colonies, as well as certain other countries, do not need visas but must carry passports. Entry visas are required for citizens of more than 140 countries. You must apply for and receive your visa from the Canadian embassy, high commission, or consulate in your home country. For a complete list of countries and territories whose citizens require visas in order to enter Canada as visitors, visit www.cic.gc.ca.

CUSTOMS
WHAT YOU CAN BRING INTO CANADA

Generally, you are allowed to bring in goods for personal use during your trip into Canada, although there are restrictions and controls on the importation of certain goods, such as firearms, ammunition, fireworks, meat and dairy products, animals, plants and plant products, firewood, fresh fruits and vegetables, and certain food and drug products. Outdoor sportsmen and women should note that fishing tackle can be brought into Canada, but the bearer must posses a non-

resident license for the province where he or she plans to use it. However, there are severe restrictions on firearms and weapons, and visitors are strongly advised to contact the Canadian Firearms Centre, **www.cfc-cafc.gc.ca** (② **800/461-9999** within Canada, or 506/636-5064 from other countries), to verify the declaration process prior to travel.

If you meet the minimum age requirement of the province or territory through which you enter Canada (the age is 19 in Ontario), you can bring in, free of duty or taxes, no more than 1.14 liters (40 fl. oz.) of liquor, or 1.5 liters (52 fl. oz.) of wine, or 24 containers of beer (355 mL, or 12 fl. oz. each). Visitors entering Ontario who are aged 19 or older can also bring up to 200 cigarettes, 50 cigars or cigarillos, 200 grams (7 oz.) of manufactured tobacco, and 200 tobacco sticks duty-free. Dogs and cats in good health can enter Canada from the U.S. with their owners, but you should bring a valid rabies vaccination certificate with you. Check with the Canadian Food Inspection Agency's Import Service Centre (② **800/835-4486**) if you wish to bring other kinds of animals from the U.S., or any animal from another country.

For more information on customs matters, contact your nearest Canadian embassy or consulate, or call the **Automated Customs Information Service** (② **800/461-9999** from within Canada, or 204/983-3500 or 506/636-5064 from outside Canada). Information is available online from the Canada Border Services Agency at **www.cbsa-asfc.gc.ca**. Print publications can be ordered by calling ℭ **800/959-2221**.

WHAT YOU CAN TAKE HOME FROM CANADA

Returning **U.S. citizens** who have been away for at least 48 hours are allowed to bring back, once every 30 days, $800 worth of merchandise duty-free. Be sure to have your receipts or purchases handy to expedite the declaration process. *Note:* If you owe duty, you are required to pay on your arrival in the United States, either by cash, personal check, government or traveler's check, or money order, and in some locations, a Visa or MasterCard.

To avoid having to pay duty on foreign-made personal items you owned before you left on your trip, bring along a bill of sale, insurance policy, jeweler's appraisal, or receipts of purchase. Or you can register items that can be readily identified by a permanently affixed serial number or marking—think laptop computers, cameras, and CD players—with Customs before you leave. Take the items to the nearest Customs office or register them with Customs at the airport from which you're departing. You'll receive, at no cost, a Certificate of Registration, which allows duty-free entry for the life of the item.

With some exceptions, you cannot bring fresh fruits and vegetables into the United States. Also, Cuban tobacco products purchased in Canada cannot be brought back into the U.S. For specifics on what you can bring back, download the invaluable free pamphlet "Know Before You Go" online at www.cbp.gov. (Click on "Travel," and then click on "Know Before You Go! Online Brochure.") Or

contact the U.S. Customs & Border Protection (CBP), 1300 Pennsylvania Ave. NW, Washington, DC 20229 (ℭ **877/287-8667**) and request the pamphlet.

Citizens of the U.K. who are returning from a non–E.U. country have a customs allowance of: 200 cigarettes or 50 cigars or 250 grams of smoking tobacco; 2 liters of still table wine; 1 liter of spirits or strong liqueurs (over 22% volume); 2 liters of fortified wine, sparkling wine, or other liqueurs; 60cc (mL) perfume; 250cc (mL) toilet water; and £145 worth of all other goods, including gifts and souvenirs. People under 17 cannot have the tobacco or alcohol allowance. For more information, contact HM Customs & Excise at ℭ **0845/010-9000** (from outside the U.K., 208/929-0152), or consult their website at www.hmrc.gov.uk.

The duty-free allowance in **Australia** is A$900 or, for those under 18, A$450. Citizens aged 18 or over can bring in 250 cigarettes or 250 grams of loose tobacco or 250 grams of cigars, and 2.25 liters of alcohol. For more information, call the Australian Customs Service at ℭ **1300/363-263**, or log on to www.customs.gov.au.

The duty-free allowance for **New Zealand** is NZ$700. Citizens over 17 can bring in 200 cigarettes, or 50 cigars, or 250 grams of tobacco (or a mixture of all three if their combined weight doesn't exceed 250g); plus 4.5 liters of wine and beer, or 1.125 liters of liquor. For more information, contact New Zealand Customs, The Customhouse, 17–21 Whitmore St., Box 2218, Wellington (ℭ **04/473-6099** or 0800/428-786; www.customs.govt.nz).

3 Money

Setting a budget for a trip to the Niagara region can be a challenge. The spectacular views of the Falls are free for all to see,

but if you want to take a tour boat, ride to the top of an observation tower, and eat a meal or two, the price can quickly escalate. Accommodations throughout the region, whether in the city of Niagara Falls itself, in the nearby town of Niagara-on-the-Lake, or in the wine country, tend to be expensive, although there are plenty of low-rent motels (with the most basic of amenities) in Niagara Falls, if you are willing to go that route. Restaurants show a similar pattern—a great choice of higher-end eateries that in general are worth the price, not too much choice in the middle range, and a slew of chain restaurants at the bottom end. So while it's possible to "do" the Falls on a limited budget, the experience will not even begin to compare with the higher-priced options.

CURRENCY

The currency of Canada is the Canadian dollar, made up of 100 cents. Paper currency comes in $5, $10, $20, $50, and $100 denominations. Coins come in 1¢, 5¢, 10¢, and 25¢ (penny, nickel, dime, and quarter) and $1 and $2 denominations.

U.S. visitors will still find their dollar buys more in Canada than at home, but the heady days of highly favorable exchange rates have passed, and the Canadian dollar is hovering around 83 cents in U.S. money, give or take a couple of points' variation. What this means is that your American money gets you about 20% more the moment you exchange it for local currency. The British pound has been sitting at around $2.16, a little lower than in recent years, but still translating into excellent value for visitors from the U.K. (You might want to visit a website such as **www.xe.com/ucc** for up-to-the-minute exchange rate information.)

Most tourist establishments in Canada will accept U.S. cash, but to get the best rate, change your funds into Canadian currency upon arrival. If you do spend American money at Canadian establishments, you should understand how the conversion is calculated. Often there is a sign at the cash register stating U.S. CURRENCY XX%. The stated percentage, for example 20%, is the "premium," which means that for every U.S. greenback you hand over, the cashier will consider it equivalent to $1.20 Canadian. For example, to pay a $24 tab, you'll need only $20 in U.S. currency. Be aware that the exchange rate may not be as favorable as you would get at a bank or currency exchange booth—you pay a price for convenience.

It's a good idea to bring some Canadian funds to take you through your first day or so, when you'll likely need cash for cab or bus fare and a snack. That way, you can avoid lines at airport ATMs (automated teller machines). In the U.S., you can exchange money at your local American Express or Thomas Cook office or your bank. Most banks in the Niagara region offer currency-exchange services. If you're far away from a bank with currency-exchange services, **American Express** offers traveler's checks and foreign currency, though with a US$15 order fee and additional shipping costs, at www.americanexpress.com or ✆ **800/807-6233.**

TAXES

Be aware that although sales taxes are high in Canada (15% tax is added to retail goods purchased in Ontario, with

---

Fun Fact

The common name for the $1 coin is the "loonie" because of the loon on the reverse side. When the bi-metallic $2 coin was subsequently introduced into circulation, it was instantly dubbed the "toonie."

taxes for restaurant meals even higher), as a visitor you may be eligible to claim a **partial tax refund** for some purchases (see "Taxes" under "Fast Facts: Niagara Region" in chapter 4, "Getting to Know the Niagara Region").

ATMs

The easiest and best way to get cash away from home is from an **ATM** (automated teller machine). The **Cirrus** (© **800/ 424-7787; www.mastercard.com**) and **PLUS** (**www.visa.com**) networks span the globe; look at the back of your bank card to see which network you're on, then call or check online for ATM locations at your destination. Be sure you know your personal identification number (PIN) before you leave home and be sure to find out your daily withdrawal limit before you depart. Also keep in mind that many banks impose a fee every time a card is used at a different bank's ATM, and that fee can be higher for international transactions than for domestic ones. On top of this, the bank from which you withdraw cash may charge its own fee.

You can also get cash advances on your credit card at an ATM. Keep in mind that credit card companies try to protect themselves from theft by limiting the funds someone can withdraw outside their home country, so call your credit card company before you leave home. And keep in mind that you'll pay interest from the moment of your withdrawal, even if you pay your monthly bills on time.

TRAVELER'S CHECKS

Traveler's checks are something of an anachronism from the days before the ATM made cash accessible at any time. Traveler's checks used to be the only sound alternative to traveling with dangerously large amounts of cash. They were as reliable as currency, but, unlike cash, could be replaced if lost or stolen.

These days, traveler's checks are less necessary because most cities have 24-hour ATMs that allow you to withdraw small amounts of cash as needed. However, keep in mind that you will likely be charged an ATM withdrawal fee if the bank is not your own, so if you're withdrawing money every day, you might be better off with traveler's checks—provided that you don't mind showing identification every time you want to cash one.

Visitors from the U.S.: You can get traveler's checks at almost any American bank. American Express offers denominations of $20, $50, $100, $500, and (for cardholders only) $1,000 in Canadian and U.S. currency. You'll pay a service charge ranging from 1% to 4%. You can also get **American Express** traveler's checks over the phone by calling © **800/ 221-7282;** Amex gold and platinum cardholders who use this number are exempt from the 1% fee.

Visa offers traveler's checks at Citibank locations nationwide, as well as at several other banks. The service charge ranges between 1.5% and 2%; checks come in denominations of $20, $50, $100, $500, and $1,000. Call © **800/732-1322** for information. **CAA and AAA members** can obtain Visa checks without a fee at most AAA offices or by calling © **866/ 339-3378. MasterCard** also offers traveler's checks. Call ☏ **800/223-9920** for a location near you.

American Express, Thomas Cook, Visa, and MasterCard offer foreign currency traveler's checks. You'll pay the rate of exchange at the time of your purchase (so it's a good idea to monitor the rate before you take the plunge), and most companies charge a transaction fee per order (and a shipping fee if you order online). However, almost all hotels, restaurants, shops, and attractions accept U.S.–dollar traveler's checks, and you can exchange them for cash at local banks if you show ID, although there may be a charge for this service.

If you choose to carry traveler's checks, be sure to keep a record of their serial numbers (separately from your checks, of course), so you're ensured a refund if they are lost or stolen.

American Express has introduced a **traveler's check card**—a prepaid, reloadable card that is not linked to your bank account. It functions in much the same way as paper traveler's checks; if it's lost or stolen, your balance is replaced within 24 hours in most cases. According to American Express, the card is accepted everywhere that welcomes American Express cards, including ATMs around the world. For a fee, you or someone you authorize can add more funds to the card by calling ☏ **888/412-6945** in Canada and the U.S. or ☏ **801/945-9450** collect from other countries.

CREDIT CARDS

Credit cards are invaluable when traveling—they provide a safe way to carry money, a convenient record of all your expenses, and they generally offer relatively good exchange rates. You can also withdraw cash advances from your credit cards at banks or ATMs, provided you know your PIN. If you've forgotten yours, or didn't even know you had one, call the number on the back of your credit card and ask the bank to send it to you. It usually takes 5 to 7 business days, though some banks will provide the number over the phone if you can provide certain personal information to prove your identity. Keep in mind that when you use your credit card abroad, many banks now assess a 1% to 3% "transaction fee" on all charges you incur abroad (whether in local currency or your home currency). But credit cards still may be the smart way to go when you factor in things like exorbitant ATM fees and higher traveler's check exchange rates (and service fees).

Almost every credit card company has an emergency toll-free number to call if you credit card is lost or stolen. This number is often printed on the card, so it is wise to print the number on a piece of paper that is safely stored separately from the card location. The credit card company may be able to wire you a cash advance from your credit card immediately, and in many places they can deliver an emergency card in a day or two. In

---

⌒Tips **Dear Visa: I'm Off to Niagara!**

Some credit card companies recommend that you notify them of any impending trip abroad so that they don't become suspicious when the card is used numerous times in a foreign destination and block your charges. Even if you don't call your credit card company in advance, you can always call the card's toll-free emergency number (see "Credit Cards" above) if a charge is refused—a good reason to carry the phone number with you. But perhaps the most important lesson here is to carry more than one card with you on your trip; a card might not work for any number of reasons, so having a backup is the smart way to go.

What Things Cost in Niagara	C$	US$	UK£
Shuttle from Toronto airport to Niagara Falls hotel, one adult return	97.00	80.50	44.60
Newspaper	1.00	.83	.46
Local telephone call	.25	.21	.12
IMAX Theatre ticket, one adult	14.00	11.60	6.45
Adult ticket for Shaw Festival Theatre	40.00–80.00	33.20–66.40	18.40–36.80
Taxi fare, typical ride between downtown attractions	6.00–10.00	5.00–8.30	2.75–4.60
People Mover Bus day pass (unlimited travel)	8.00	6.65	3.70
Two-course lunch for one (moderate)* in Niagara Falls	25.00	21.00	12.00
Two-course lunch for one (winery restaurant)	50.00	41.50	23.00
Three-course dinner for one (moderate)* in Niagara Falls	45.00	37.35	20.70
Three-course dinner for one (winery restaurant)	90.00	75.00	41.40
Bottle of Niagara wine at winery shop	10.00–30.00	8.30–25.00	4.60–13.80
Parking meter, downtown Niagara Falls, per hour	1.00	.83	.46
All-day parking lot, downtown Niagara Falls	5.00	4.00	2.30
Skylon Tower entrance fee, one adult	10.00	8.30	4.60
Maid of the Mist entrance fee, one adult	13.00	10.80	6.00
Instant camera, 24-exposure print	12.00	10.00	5.50
Regular latte	3.50	2.90	1.60
Bottle of water	2.00	1.70	1.00
Large takeout pizza	20.00	16.60	9.20

Includes tax, tip, and nonalcoholic beverage

Canada, **MasterCard** holders should call ℂ **800/MC-ASSIST 622-7747,** Visa customers should call ℂ **800/847-2911,** and **American Express** cardholders should call collect ℂ **336/393-1111.** Information is available online at **www.mastercard. com, www.visa.com,** and **www.american express.com.** You can call a toll-free

The Canadian Dollar, the U.S. Dollar & the British Pound

The prices in this guide are given first in Canadian dollars, then in U.S. dollars. Amounts over $5 have been rounded to the nearest dollar. Note that the Canadian dollar is worth about 20% less than the U.S. dollar. At the time of writing, C$1 was worth about US84¢, and that was the equivalency used to convert the prices in this guide. The U.K. pound is included here for your reference, with C$1 worth about £0.46. Note that exchange rates are subject to fluctuation, and you should always check the most recent currency rates when preparing for your trip.

Here's a quick table of equivalents:

C$	US$	UK£	C$	US$	UK£
1	0.83	.46	1.20	1	0.56
5	4.20	2.30	6.00	5	2.80
10	8.40	4.60	12.00	10	5.60
50	42.00	23.00	60.00	50	28.00
80	67.20	36.80	96.00	80	44.80
100	84.00	46.00	120.00	100	56.00

information directory at ☎ **800/555-1212** to get Canadian toll-free numbers. The best and quickest way to get assistance when you are in your home country is to call your card issuer.

4 When to Go

Hotel rooms fill up quickly during July and August, and also during major events such as Canada Day (July 1), Independence Day (July 4), and the Niagara Wine Festival (mid- to late September). If you plan to visit during these times, reserve accommodations several weeks or even months ahead. If you want to avoid the crowds but still maximize your chances of good weather, visit during the last week of August or first week in September. With the kids heading back to school and the Wine Festival not yet begun, this time of year is great for traveling to the Falls if you want to avoid lineups and enjoy a little peace and quiet.

Note that several of the top Falls attractions, including *Maid of the Mist* and Cave of the Winds, operate only during the summer months. They open each year once the ice has melted in April or May, and end their season during the month of October.

THE CLIMATE

Spring in the Niagara region runs from late March to mid-May (although late snowfalls may surprise visitors in April, and frosts are not uncommon in May). **Summer** temperatures are usually enjoyed from mid-to-late May to mid-September. June, July, and August are the hottest months, with average highs of 79°F (26°C) and lows of 59°F (15°C). The **fall** season runs from mid-September to mid-November, although even October can be quite brisk. **Winter** spans November to March, with temperatures varying between 16°F (–8°C) and 39°F (4°C). Snowfall is abundant and winter temperatures have been known to plunge well below –8°C some years.

Tips Nightly Illuminations

The American Falls and the Horseshoe Falls are illuminated nightly throughout the year. All times posted are approximate and subject to change according to light conditions. During the peak tourist season, the Falls are flooded with light May 1 to August 15 between 9pm and midnight. From August 16 to September 30 the lights are switched on between 8:30pm and midnight. April lights go on at 8:30pm and shut down at 11pm. Between May and August 24 lights are on at 9pm shutting down at midnight. From August 24 to September 30, lights are on at 8:30pm (off at midnight) and during October the Falls are lit at 7pm and switched off at midnight.

Keep in mind that the Great Lakes can adversely affect local weather conditions, ranging from high humidity and sudden thunderstorms in the summer to lake-effect snowsqualls and freezing rain in the winter. Having said that, Lake Erie and in particular Lake Ontario are the main influence on the unique microclimate of the Niagara Peninsula, with a tendency to moderate summer heat and winter cold most years. The Niagara Escarpment also acts as a natural shelter against frost in the spring and fall. The weather can be somewhat unpredictable in this region, so I recommend packing some long-sleeved shirts for unexpectedly cool summer days and multiple layers to shed during a warm winter.

Visitors standing close to the Falls can get quite wet from the mist, especially if the wind is blowing in their direction. This can be welcome on a hot summer's day, but be prepared to don rain gear or even change into dry clothing. With the recent high-rise development around the Falls the mist has actually increased in the area, and you don't need to be that close to the water to get wet.

Niagara's Average Temperatures (°F/°C)

	Jan	Feb	Mar	Apr	May	June	July	Aug	Sept	Oct	Nov	Dec
High	–1/31	1/33	6/42	13/55	21/69	25/76	28/82	27/80	22/72	16/60	9/48	3/37
Low	–8/17	–8/17	–4/25	2/35	8/46	13/55	16/61	15/59	11/51	4/40	0/32	–5/23

HOLIDAYS

On most public holidays, banks, government offices, schools, and post offices are closed. Museums, retail stores, and restaurants very widely in their policies for holiday openings and closings, so call before you go to avoid disappointment.

Note that some museums are closed on Mondays and Tuesdays outside of the peak summer months.

The Niagara Region celebrates the following holidays in Canada: New Year's Day (Jan 1), Good Friday and/or Easter Monday (Mar or Apr, dates vary each year), Victoria Day (Mon following the third weekend in May), Canada Day (July 1), Civic Holiday (first Mon in Aug), Labour Day (first Mon in Sept), Thanksgiving (second Mon in Oct), Remembrance Day (Nov 11), Christmas Day (Dec 25), and Boxing Day (Dec 26).

The U.S. has a number of national holidays that differ from Canada. The most notable ones are Martin Luther King, Jr.'s, Birthday (third Mon in Jan), Washington's Birthday (third Mon in Feb), Memorial Day (last Mon in May), Independence Day (July 4), and Thanksgiving Day (last Thurs in Nov). On these dates, the Niagara region on the Canadian side of the border tends to swell with visitors just as it does during Canadian holidays.

NIAGARA REGION CALENDAR OF EVENTS

The following list of events will help you to plan your visit to the Niagara region. Even the largest, most successful events sometimes retire, a few events are biennial, and dates may change from those listed here. In addition to the following events, numerous smaller community and cultural events take place throughout the year. Contact the relevant tourist information center (see listings earlier in this chapter under "Visitor Information") to confirm details if a particular event is a major reason for your vacation.

January

Niagara Icewine Festival. Mid-January, the Niagara region bustles with tours, tastings, and other activities related to harvesting of the grapes to make icewine. © **905/688-0212. www.grapeandwine.com.**

March

Shaw Festival Season opens. The Shaw Festival exclusively produces the plays of George Bernard Shaw and his contemporaries, and plays set during Shaw's (very long) lifetime. The season runs from March to November, on three stages in Niagara-on-the-Lake. © **800/511-7429. www.shawfest.com.**

Maple syrup season. When the daytime temperatures begin to climb above 32°F/0°C in late winter, the maple sap begins to run. Local farms offer tours of the "sugar bush," pancake breakfasts, and maple syrup products for sale. © **905/682-0642. www.whitemeadowsfarms.com.**

May

Niagara Folk Arts Festival. This annual event is billed as Canada's oldest heritage festival, spanning more than 2 weeks in mid- to late May. Multi-cultural music, theater, dance, food, and traditions are celebrated. Held at various sites throughout the Niagara Region. © **905/685-6589. www.folk-arts.ca.**

Spring Festival at the Falls. This festival in Niagara Falls includes fireworks, concerts, sporting events, and gardening seminars. © **877/NIA-PARK (642-7275). www.niagaraparks.com.**

Opening Day at Fort Erie Racetrack. May 1 marks the beginning of the Fort Erie horseracing season. © **800/295-3770. www.forterieracing.com.**

June

Welland Rose Festival. Early June smells sweet as a variety of events lead up to the display and judging of the fairest roses in the land. © **905/735-8696. www.wellandrosefestival.on.ca.**

Niagara New Vintage Festival. Dozens of Niagara wineries present the first taste of the season of their award-winning wines. Events are held in Jordan, St. Catharines, and other sites throughout the region. © **905/688-0212. www.grapeandwine.com.**

Beamsville Strawberry Festival. Strawberry treats, live entertainment, crafters, car show, and more. Third weekend in June. © **905/563-0034. www.strawberryfest.ca.**

July

Friendship Festival. A celebration of shared history and culture and friendship between Canada and the U.S. Events are held in Fort Erie, Ontario, and Buffalo, New York. © **888/333-1987. www.friendshipfestival.com.**

Canada Day. Each July 1, Canadians gather in communities across the country to celebrate the nation's birthday. In the Niagara region, celebrations take place at the Falls and surrounding towns, including Port Dalhousie, Welland, St. Catharines, and Port Colborne.

Two Nations Celebration. This binational event, running from July 1 to

July 4, celebrates the birth of two nations—Canada and the United States of America. Based in Queen Victoria Park, Niagara Falls, Ontario. © 877/NIA-PARK (642-7275). www. niagaraparks.com.

Battle of Chippawa Commemorative Ceremony. On July 5, the anniversary of the Battle of Chippawa is remembered at Chippawa Battlefield, Niagara Falls with a memorial ceremony. © 877/NIA-PARK (642-7275).

Dragon Boat Festival. Held in late July on Martindale Pond, home of the Royal Canadian Henley Regatta in historical Port Dalhousie. Teams from Niagara and across the globe compete and raise funds for the St. Catharines Museum and the United Way. © 905/ 984-8880. www.st.catharines.com/ tourism/festivals_events_summer. asp.

Niagara International Chamber Music Festival. Local churches, wineries, and museums host more than 30 concerts by internationally renowned artists. © 877/MUS-FEST (687-3378). www.niagaramusicfest.com.

Niagara Motorcycle Rally, Niagara Falls, New York. Bike enthusiasts can speak with custom bike builders, listen to live bands, compete in the chili cook-off, and buy swag from bike companies. www.buffalothrills.com/ events/ev-festivalsevents/niagara motorcycle.htm.

August

Canal Days Marine Heritage Festival. On the Civic Holiday weekend (incorporating the first Mon in Aug) Port Colborne hosts this waterfront festival celebrating the community's marine heritage. © 888/PORT-FUN (767-8386). www.city.portcolborne. on.ca.

Royal Canadian Henley Regatta. This annual regatta draws more than 3,500 international competitors. Held on Martindale Pond, Port Dalhousie. © 905/937-1117. www. henleyregatta.ca.

Siege Re-enactment at Old Fort Erie. Re-enactment of the life and times of the battles during the War of 1812. Camps, artillery and musket demonstrations, and drills are featured. Held at the historic fort at Fort Erie. © 905/ 871-0540. www.niagaraparks.com.

September

Niagara Wine Festival. During 10 days in mid- to late September, this major festival boasts winery tours and tastings, concerts, Niagara cuisine, artisan shows, wine seminars, and more. Events held at various locations throughout the Niagara region. © 905/688-0212. www.grapeandwine.com.

Niagara Food Festival. In late September, sample the fare of more than three dozen Niagara region restaurants, complemented by Niagara wines. Held on Merritt Island in downtown Welland. © 905/735-8696. www. niagarafoodfestival.com.

Fort Erie Highland Festival. Celtic dancing and musical entertainment, pipe bands, heavy events, border collie demos, clan tents, and more. Held on the grounds of Old Fort Erie. © 877/ NIA-PARK (642-7275).

October

Ball's Falls Thanksgiving Festival. Outdoor fun for the whole family during the Canadian Thanksgiving weekend (incorporating the second Mon in Oct). © 905/788-3135. www. conservation-niagara.on.ca.

Vineland Thanksgiving Artfest. Billed as one of the best-quality juried shows in Canada, with approximately 130 exhibitors. © 905/563-5626. www.vaxxine.com/vinelandartfest.

November

Winter Festival of Lights. From November until January 2, this is Canada's largest lights festival. Over one million lights on display, almost 100 motion light displays, fireworks, illuminated night parades, and more. Niagara Falls, Ontario. © 800/563-2557. www.wfol.com.

December

New Year's Eve in Queen Victoria Park. Against the dramatic backdrop of the Falls, enjoy an outdoor concert to welcome in the New Year. © 800/563 2557. www.niagaraparks.com.

5 Travel Insurance

Before you buy travel insurance, check your existing insurance policies and credit card coverage. You may already be covered for lost luggage, canceled tickets, or medical expenses. The cost of travel insurance varies widely, depending on the cost and length of your trip, your age and health, and the type of trip you're taking, but expect to pay between 5% and 8% of the vacation itself.

TRIP-CANCELLATION INSURANCE Trip-cancellation insurance helps you get your money back if you have to back out of a trip, if you have to go home early, or if your travel supplier goes bankrupt. Allowed reasons for cancellation can range from sickness to natural disasters to government travel advisories that declare your destination unsafe for travel. Insurance policy details vary, so read the fine print—and make sure that your airline is on the list of carriers covered in case of bankruptcy. Protect yourself further by paying for the insurance with a credit card—you may, depending on the laws of your country, get your money back on goods and services not received if you report the loss within 60 days after the charge is listed on their credit card statement.

Note: Many tour operators, particularly those offering trips to remote or high-risk areas, include insurance in the cost of the trip or can arrange insurance policies through a partnering provider, a convenient and often cost-effective way for the traveler to obtain insurance. Make sure the tour company is a reputable one, however: Some experts suggest you avoid buying insurance from the tour or cruise company you're traveling with, saying it's better to buy from a third-party insurer than to put all your money in one place.

U.S. Citizens: For more information, contact one of the following recommended insurers: **Access America** (© 866/807-3982; www.accessamerica.com); **Travel Guard International** (© 800/826-4919; www.travelguard.com); **Travel Insured International** (© 800/243-3174; www.travelinsured.com); and **Travelex Insurance Services** (© 888/457-4602; www.travelex-insurance.com).

MEDICAL INSURANCE Medical care in Ontario is provided to all residents through the Ontario Health Insurance Plan (OHIP), administered by the provincial government. Visitors from abroad are ineligible for OHIP coverage and should arrange for **health insurance** coverage before entering Canada. For more information, contact a private insurance company directly, or call the **Canadian Life and Health Insurance Association** (© 800/268-8099; www.clhia.ca). Canadian travelers are protected by their home province's health insurance plan for a limited time period. Check with your province's health insurance agency before traveling.

U.S. Citizens: For travel abroad, most health plans (including Medicare and

Medicaid) do not provide coverage, and the ones that do often require you to pay for services upfront and reimburse you only after you return home. Even if your plan does cover treatment, most out-of-country hospitals make you pay your bills upfront, and send you a refund only after you've returned home and filed the necessary paperwork with your insurance company. If you require additional medical insurance, try **MEDEX Assistance** (© 410/453-6300; www.medexassist. com) or **Travel Assistance International** (© 800/821-2828; www.travelassistance. com).

LOST-LUGGAGE INSURANCE If you are a homeowner or have contents insurance for a rental property, see if your policy covers off-premises **theft and loss** wherever it occurs. Ask your insurance agent what procedures you need to follow to make a claim. Be sure to take any valuables or irreplaceable items with you in your carry-on luggage, as many valuables (including books, money, and electronics)

aren't covered by insurance policies. Otherwise, you should take out a separate policy to cover lost luggage.

If your luggage is lost, immediately file a lost-luggage claim at the airport, detailing the luggage contents. For most airlines, you must report delayed, damaged, or lost baggage within 4 hours of arrival. The airlines are required to deliver luggage, once found, directly to your house or destination free of charge.

RENTAL CAR INSURANCE If you plan to rent a car, check with your credit card issuer to see if they pick up the collision damage waiver fee (CDW) in Canada. Many credit card companies cover the CDW, as long as you pay for the entire rental cost with the credit card. If you pre-book the rental, remember to bring the same credit card with you when you pick up the vehicle. The CDW can run as high as C$20 (US$16) per day, adding a considerable amount to the cost of car rental. Check your car insurance policy, too—it might cover the CDW.

6 Health & Safety

GENERAL AVAILABILITY OF HEALTHCARE

Contact the **International Association for Medical Assistance to Travelers (IAMAT)** (© 416/652-0137 in Canada, or 716/754-4883 in the U.S.; or visit **www.iamat.org**) for tips on travel and health concerns in the country you're visiting and lists of local doctors. The **United States Centers for Disease Control and Prevention** (© 800/311-3435; **www.cdc.gov**) provides up-to-date information on health hazards by region or country and offers tips on food safety.

The website **www.tripprep.com,** sponsored by a consortium of travel medicine practitioners, may also offer helpful advice on traveling abroad. You can find listings of reliable clinics abroad at the **International Society of Travel Medicine** (**www.istm.org**).

WHAT TO DO IF YOU GET SICK AWAY FROM HOME

For non-life-threatening emergencies that require a physician consultation, go to a **walk-in clinic.** These clinics operate just as the name implies—you walk in and wait your turn to see a doctor. Look in the Yellow Pages or ask your hotel to recommend one. Payment procedures and opening hours vary among clinics, so call ahead and ask about their billing policy for nonresidents of Ontario or Canada. Most clinics will accept health cards from other provinces, although Quebec residents may be required to pay cash and obtain reimbursement from their provincial government. Out-of-country patients may be required to pay cash—checks or credit cards may not be accepted. Some doctors will make house calls to your hotel.

Avoiding "Economy Class Syndrome"

Deep vein thrombosis, or as it's known in the world of flying, "economy-class syndrome," is a blood clot that develops in a deep vein. It's a potentially deadly condition that can be caused by sitting in cramped conditions—such as an airplane cabin—for too long. During a flight (especially a long-haul flight), get up, walk around, and stretch your legs every 60 to 90 minutes to keep your blood flowing. Other preventive measures include frequent flexing of the legs while sitting, drinking lots of water, and avoiding alcohol and sleeping pills. If you have a history of deep vein thrombosis, heart disease, or other condition that puts you at high risk, some experts recommend wearing compression stockings or taking anticoagulants when you fly; always ask your physician about the best course for you. Symptoms of deep vein thrombosis include leg pain or swelling, or even shortness of breath.

If you are suffering from a serious medical problem and are unable to wait to be seen at a walk-in clinic, visit the nearest hospital emergency room. Emergency rooms operate on a triage system, where patients are assessed upon arrival and those who need care the most urgently are seen first. Hospitals and emergency numbers are listed under "Fast Facts: Niagara Region" in chapter 4.

Ontario emergency rooms are extremely busy and wait times for non-urgent cases are typically several hours. If at all possible, use the walk-in clinics. For minor health problems, consult a **pharmacist.** These professionals are trained in health consultation and will recommend whether you should see a doctor about your particular condition. Many pharmacies are open evenings and weekends and advertise their hours in the Yellow Pages.

If you suffer from a chronic illness, consult your doctor before your departure. For conditions like epilepsy, diabetes, or heart problems, wear a **MedicAlert identification tag** (© **800/668-1507** or www.medicalert.ca in Canada; © **888/633-4298** or www.medicalert.org in the U.S.), which will immediately alert doctors to your condition and give them access to your records through MedicAlert's 24-hour hot line.

Pack prescription medications in your carry-on luggage, and carry prescription medications in their original containers with pharmacy labels—otherwise they may not make it through airport security. Also bring along copies of your prescriptions in case you lose your pills or run out. Don't forget an extra pair of contact lenses or prescription glasses. Carry the generic name of prescription medicines, in case a local pharmacist is unfamiliar with the brand name.

For domestic trips, most reliable healthcare plans provide coverage if you get sick away from home. For travel abroad, you may have to pay all medical costs upfront and be reimbursed later. See "Medical Insurance," under "Travel Insurance," above.

STAYING SAFE

The Niagara region is generally safe for visitors, but be alert and use common sense, particularly late at night. That said, it's never a good idea to take your safety for granted. Take the same precautions you would in any crowded district—women should carry a shoulder bag diagonally across one shoulder and men should carry their wallets in a secure place, not stuffed in their back pocket. Use the neck or wrist strap of cameras and other electronic equipment. Don't flaunt quantities of expensive jewelry or wads of bills. Keep a few small bills handy and put the remainder in a concealed place.

At the hotel, keep the door locked and use the bolt when you're inside. Before you answer the door, make sure you know who it is. If it's an unexpected visit from room service or maintenance, don't be embarrassed to call the front desk to make sure it's legitimate. Remember that the staff have passkeys, and your room is frequently opened when you're not there. Use the in-room safe for cash, traveler's checks, and other valuables. If there's no safe in your room, inquire about using the hotel safe.

In light of global concern surrounding terrorist attacks, unattended bags or suspicious-looking packages in public places should be reported.

7 Specialized Travel Resources

TRAVELERS WITH DISABILITIES

Most disabilities shouldn't stop anyone from traveling. There are more options and resources out there than ever before. To find out which attractions, accommodations, and restaurants in the Niagara region are accessible to people with disabilities, refer to **Accessible Niagara,** an annual guide available from local Visitor Information Centers, or visit their website at **www.accessibleniagara.com**. The guide covers accommodations, tourist attractions, parks, religious facilities, restaurants, shopping malls, retail stores, wineries, and transportation. On the U.S. side find www.oapwd.org, the New York State Commission on Quality of Care and Advocacy for Persons with Disabilities.

Several local taxi services can accommodate travelers with disabilities, including pickup from local major airports. National car rental companies can arrange rental of a vehicle with hand controls if advance notice is given.

Blind and visually impaired travelers can obtain information on how to make the most of their trip to Niagara by calling the **Canadian National Institute for the Blind (CNIB)** Information Centre at © **905/688-0022** or the **American Foundation for the Blind** (© **800/ 232-5463;** www.afb.org).

Other organizations that offer assistance to travelers with disabilities include **MossRehab** (© 800/CALL-MOSS 2255-6677; www.mossresource net.org), which provides a library of accessible-travel resources online, and the **Society for Accessible Travel and Hospitality** (© 212/447-7284; www.sath. org), which offers a wealth of travel resources for all types of disabilities and informed recommendations on destinations, access guides, travel agents, tour operators, vehicle rentals, and companion services. SATH charges an annual membership fee of US$45 adult and US$30 seniors and students.

For more information specifically-targeted to travelers with disabilities, the community website **iCan** (www.ican online.net/channels/travel) has destination guides and several regular columns on accessible travel. Also check out the quarterly magazine *Emerging Horizons* (www.emerginghorizons.com) and *Open World* magazine, published by SATH (see above).

GAY & LESBIAN TRAVELERS

Canada is one of the world's most progressive countries, and the December 2004 Supreme Court of Canada equal marriage decision demonstrated the country's commitment to human rights and strengthened the country's position as a gay-friendly travel destination. For gay-friendly accommodations, bars, and restaurants in the Niagara area, visit www.gaycanada.com or www.gay niagara.com. Details of the region's annual Pride Weekend, held in St. Catharines in June, are posted on the Gay Niagara website. On the U.S. side, see www.gayjourney.com/hotels/us_ny.htm.

The **International Gay & Lesbian Travel Association (IGLTA)** (© 800/ 448-8550 or 954/776-2626; www.iglta. org) is the trade association for the gay and lesbian travel industry, and offers an online directory of gay- and lesbian-friendly travel businesses.

SENIOR TRAVEL

Some attractions and accommodations offer special rates or discounts for seniors, so always mention the fact when you make your travel arrangements. Carry a form of photo ID that includes your birth date. Becoming a member of a senior's organization may earn you a discount on travel arrangements. Consider joining the **Canadian Association of Retired Persons (CARP)**, 27 Queen St. E., Suite 1304, Toronto, ON. M5C 2M6 (© **416/363-8748; www.carp.ca**). The website has a comprehensive travel section for members, which features hotels, packages, transportation, and travel insurance. The U.S. equivalent is **AARP** (formerly known as the American Association of Retired Persons), 601 E. St. NW, Washington, DC 20049 (© **888/687-2277; www.aarp.org**). Members get discounts on hotels, airfares, and car rentals. AARP offers members a wide range of benefits, including *AARP: The Magazine* and a monthly newsletter. Anyone over 50 can join.

Recommended publications offering travel resources and discounts for seniors include the quarterly magazine *Travel 50 & Beyond* (www.travel50andbeyond. com); *Travel Unlimited: Uncommon Adventures for the Mature Traveler* (Avalon); *101 Tips for Mature Travelers*, available from Grand Circle Travel (© **800/221-2610** or 617/350-7500;

www.gct.com); and *Unbelievably Good Deals and Great Adventures That You Absolutely Can't Get Unless You're Over 50* (McGraw-Hill), by Joann Rattner Heilman.

FAMILY TRAVEL

Luckily for visitors with kids in tow, the Niagara region has a good selection of hotels with suite accommodations, which are equipped with kitchenettes or full kitchens and one or two bedrooms; some have two bathrooms. You get the advantage of food-preparation facilities and accommodations for the entire family in one unit, which are important considerations when you have young children with you. When booking your accommodations, always ask if family packages are available.

When you're deciding which time of year to visit, try to schedule your trip during school vacation periods, which in Ontario run for 2 weeks during Christmas/ New Year, 1 week in mid-March, and the months of July and August. Special events and festivals aimed particularly at families are held at various museums and other locations during school holidays.

To locate accommodations, restaurants, and attractions that are particularly kid-friendly, refer to the "Kids" icon throughout this guide.

Recommended family travel Internet sites include **Family Travel Forum** (www.familytravelforum.com), a comprehensive site that offers customized trip planning; **Family Travel Network** (www.familytravelnetwork.com), an award-winning site that offers travel features, deals, and tips; **Traveling Internationally with Your Kids** (www.travel withyourkids.com), a comprehensive site offering sound advice for long-distance and international travel with children; and **Family Travel Files** (www.thefamily travelfiles.com), which offers an online magazine and a directory of off-the-beaten-path tours and tour operators for families.

STUDENT TRAVEL

Students seem to always be on a shoe-string budget. If you're 12 years of age or over and a full-time student, obtaining an **International Student Identity Card (ISIC)** (www.isic.org) will get you substantial savings on rail passes, plane tickets, and entrance fees, and often you'll get discounts on accommodations, food, and retail purchases. It also provides you with a 24-hour help line. The card is available for C$16 (US$13). If you're no longer a student but are still under 26, you can get an **International Youth Travel Card (IYTC)** for the same price from the same people, which entitles you to similar discounts. You can get your ISIC or IYTC card from **Travel CUTS** (*©* 866/246-0762; www.travelcuts.com) or **STA Travel** (*©* 888/427-5638; www.sta travel.com) for both Canadian and U.S. residents. Irish students may prefer to turn to **USIT** (*©* 01/602-1904; www.usitnow.ie), an Ireland-based specialist in student, youth, and independent travel.

Students who would like to attend lectures, seminars, concerts, and other events can contact **Brock University,** 500 Glenridge Ave., St. Catharines (*©* 905/688-5550; www.brocku.ca) or **Niagara College** (*©* 905/641-2252; www.niagarac.on.ca for information on all campuses: Welland, St. Catharines, Niagara Falls, and Grimsby).

Survival Tips for Traveling with Kids

- Don't try to see and do as much as you would if you were traveling without your children.
- Make a list of everything you want to do on vacation, then cut it in half.
- Choose accommodations close to a park or playground.
- Alternate sightseeing or travel days with unstructured play days.
- Bring medication, paper towels, and plastic bags in case of travel sickness.
- Plan meal times in advance and *always* carry snacks to appease hungry tummies.
- If you're traveling to a different time zone, schedule meals and bedtime for the new time a few days before leaving to adjust more quickly.
- Bring a few favorite bedtime stories.
- Bring toys, but avoid ones with lots of small parts that can get scattered or lost.
- Bring an umbrella stroller—it's lightweight, it folds easily, and it can be used as a feeding chair or napping place when necessary.
- Let kids pack their own entertainment backpacks.
- Buy each child a portable cassette player with earphones. You can get stories on tape as well as children's music. The trip will be *so* quiet!
- If you have a long trip, splurge at the dollar store on a few simple toys and treats. Pack them in a bag, and each time you have a rest stop, let the kids take a "lucky dip."
- Give older children their own budget to spend on souvenirs.
- Call your hotel to find out what items they have on hand for infants and small children. You may be able to leave half the kitchen sink at home.
- Finally, if you can swing it, try to schedule some vacation time away from your children.

WOMEN TRAVELERS

Journeywoman (www.journeywoman.com) is a great travel resource for female travelers. The website offers a free monthly e-mail newsletter, message boards, and an extensive library of articles. Women Welcome Women World Wide (5W) (© 1494/465441; www.womenwelcomewomen.org.uk) encourages international friendships by facilitating women from different countries to visit one another. Men may accompany women on their travels, but they cannot join the club. The organization has more than 3,000 members in around 70 countries. *Safety and Security for Women Who Travel,* by Sheila Swan Laufer and Peter Laufer (Traveler's Tales, Inc.), contains travel tips and common-sense advice.

8 Planning Your Trip Online

SURFING FOR AIRFARES

The "big three" online travel agencies, **Expedia.com, Travelocity.com,** and **Orbitz.com** sell most of the air tickets bought on the Internet. (Canadian travelers should try **Expedia.ca** and **Travelocity.ca;** U.K. residents can go for expedia.co.uk and opodo.co.uk.). **Kavak.com** is also gaining popularity and uses a sophisticated search engine (developed at MIT). Each has different business deals with the airlines and may offer different fares on the same flights, so it's wise to shop around. Expedia and Travelocity will also send you **e-mail notification** when a cheap fare becomes available to your favorite destination. Of the smaller travel agency websites, **SideStep** (www.sidestep.com) has received the best reviews from Frommer's authors. The website (with optional browser add-on) purports to "search 140 sites at once," but in reality beats competitors' fares only as often as other sites do.

Also remember to check **airline websites,** especially those for low-fare carriers, whose fares are often misreported or simply missing from travel agency websites. Even with major airlines, you can often shave a few bucks from a fare by booking directly through the airline and avoiding a travel agency's transaction fee. But you'll get these discounts only by **booking online:** Most airlines now offer online-only fares that even their phone agents know nothing about. For the websites of airlines that fly to and from your destination, see "Getting There," later in this chapter.

Great **last-minute deals** are available through free weekly e-mail services provided directly by the airlines. Most of these are announced on Tuesday or Wednesday and must be purchased online. Most are valid for travel only that weekend, but some can be booked weeks or months in advance. Sign up for weekly e-mail alerts at airline websites or check mega-sites that compile comprehensive lists of last-minute specials, such as **Smarter Travel** (smartertravel.com). For last-minute trips, **site59.com** and **lastminutetravel.com** in the U.S. and **lastminute.com** in Europe often have better air-and-hotel package deals than the major-label sites.

If you're willing to give up some control over your flight details, use what is called an **"opaque" fare service** like **Priceline** (www.priceline.com; www.priceline.co.uk for Europeans) or its smaller competitor **Hotwire** (www.hotwire.com). Both offer rock-bottom prices in exchange for travel on a "mystery airline" at a mysterious time of day, often with a mysterious change of planes en route. The mystery airlines are all major, well-known carriers—and the possibility of being sent from Philadelphia to Chicago via Tampa is remote; the airlines' routing computers perform a lot better than they used to. But your chances of getting a 6am or 11pm flight are pretty high. Hotwire tells you flight prices before you buy; Priceline usually has better deals than Hotwire, but you have to play their "name our price" game. If you're new at this, the helpful folks at **BiddingForTravel** (www.biddingfor travel.com) do a good job of demystifying Priceline's prices and strategies. Priceline and Hotwire are great for flights within North America and between the U.S. and Europe. But for flights to other parts of the world, consolidators will almost always beat their fares. *Note:* In 2004 Priceline added non-opaque service to its roster. You now have the option to pick exact flights, times, and airlines from a list of offers—or opt to bid on opaque fares as before.

SURFING FOR HOTELS

Shopping online for hotels, which is much easier in the U.S., Canada, and certain parts of Europe than it is in the rest of the world, is generally done one of two ways: by booking through the hotel's own website or through an independent booking agency (or a fare-service agency like Priceline; see below). These Internet hotel agencies have multiplied in mind-boggling numbers of late, competing for the business of millions of consumers surfing for accommodations around the world. This competitiveness can be a boon to consumers who have the patience and time to shop and compare the online sites for good deals—but shop they must, for prices can vary considerably from site to site. And keep in mind that hotels at the top of a site's listing may be there for no other reason than that they paid money to get the placement.

Visit **www.tourismniagara.com** for detailed contact information for accommodations throughout the region. For the Niagara Falls area, you can also visit **www.niagarafallstourism.com**. If you want to stay in the pretty town of Niagara-on-the-Lake (only a 20-min. drive from the Falls), visit **www.niagara onthelake.com**. You can view photos and descriptions of B&Bs, hotels, inns, and private vacation homes. The local Chamber of Commerce Accommodation Booking Service will make a reservation for you at one of more than 200 properties by calling © **905/468-4263,** or you can book online. Another useful site for B&B accommodations is **www.bbcanada.com.**

Of the "big three" sites, **Expedia** offers a long list of special deals and "virtual tours" or photos of available rooms so you can see what you're paying for (a feature that helps counter the claims that the best rooms are often held back from bargain-booking websites). **Travelocity** posts unvarnished customer reviews and ranks its properties according to the AAA rating system. Also reliable are **Hotels.com** and **Quikbook.com.** An excellent free program, **TravelAxe** (www.travelaxe.com), can help you search multiple hotel sites at once, even ones you may never have heard of—and conveniently lists the total price of the room, including the taxes and service charges. Another booking site, **Travelweb** (www.travelweb.com), is partly owned by the hotels it represents (including the Hilton, Hyatt, and Starwood chains) and is therefore plugged directly into the hotels' reservations systems—unlike independent online agencies, which have to fax or e-mail reservation requests to the hotel, a good portion of which get misplaced in the shuffle. More than once, travelers have arrived at the hotel only to be told that they have no reservation. To be fair, many of the major sites are undergoing improvements in service and ease of use, and Expedia will soon be able to plug directly into the reservations systems of many hotel chains—none of which can be bad news for consumers. In the meantime, it's a good idea to **get a confirmation number** and **make a printout** of any online booking transaction.

Frommers.com: The Complete Travel Resource

For an excellent travel-planning resource, we highly recommend **Frommers. com** (www.frommers.com), voted Best Travel Site by *PC Magazine*. We're a little biased, of course, but we guarantee that you'll find the travel tips, reviews, monthly vacation giveaways, bookstore, and online-booking capabilities thoroughly indispensable. Among the special features are our popular **Destinations** section, where you'll get expert travel tips, hotel and dining recommendations, and advice on the sights to see for more than 3,500 destinations around the globe; the **Frommers.com Newsletter,** with the latest deals, travel trends, and money-saving secrets; our **Community** area featuring **message boards,** where Frommer's readers post queries and share advice (sometimes even our authors show up to answer questions); and our **Photo Center,** where you can post and share vacation tips. When your research is done, the **Online Reservations System** (www.frommers. com/book_a_trip) takes you to Frommer's preferred online partners for booking your vacation at affordable prices.

In the opaque website category, **Priceline** and **Hotwire** are even better for hotels than for airfares; with both, you're allowed to pick the neighborhood and quality level of your hotel before offering up your money. Priceline's hotel product even covers Europe and Asia, though it's much better at getting five-star lodging for three-star prices than at finding anything at the bottom of the scale. On the down side, many hotels stick Priceline guests in their least desirable rooms. Be sure to go to the BiddingForTravel website (see above) before bidding on a hotel room on Priceline; it features a fairly up-to-date list of hotels that Priceline uses in major cities. For both Priceline and Hotwire, you pay upfront, and the fee is nonrefundable. *Note:* Some hotels do not provide loyalty program credits or points or other frequent-stay amenities when you book a room through opaque online services.

SURFING FOR RENTAL CARS

For booking rental cars online, the best deals are usually found at rental-car company websites, although all the major online travel agencies also offer rental-car reservations services. Priceline and Hotwire work well for rental cars, too; the only "mystery" is which major rental company you get, and for most travelers the difference between Hertz, Avis, and Budget is negligible. Members of frequent-flier programs will find it worthwhile to check their airline's website; discounts for frequent-flier cardholders are often on offer.

9 The 21st-Century Traveler

INTERNET ACCESS AWAY FROM HOME

Travelers have any number of ways to check their e-mail and access the Internet on the road. Of course, using your own laptop—or even a **PDA (personal digital assistant)** or electronic organizer with a modem—gives you the most flexibility. But even if you don't have a computer, you can still access your e-mail and even your office computer from cybercafes.

WITHOUT YOUR OWN COMPUTER

It's hard nowadays to find a city that *doesn't* have a few cybercafes. Although there's no definitive directory for cybercafes—these are independent businesses, after all—two places to start looking are at **www.cybercaptive.com** and **www.cybercafe.com**.

Aside from formal cybercafes, most **public libraries** offer Internet access, although you may have to reserve a computer terminal a day or so in advance.

Most hotels now offer in-room wireless Internet access. If it's important to you to have access to your e-mail, make your accommodations reservation by phone and confirm you will have Internet access available. If you use a **hotel business center,** inquire about Internet access rates before using the service; some places charge exorbitant rates, while others offer complimentary access to hotel guests.

To retrieve your e-mail, ask your **Internet Service Provider (ISP)** if it has a Web-based interface tied to your existing e-mail account. If your ISP doesn't have such an interface, you can use the free **mail2web** service (www.mail2web.com) to view and reply to your home e-mail. For more flexibility, you may want to open a free, Web-based e-mail account with **Yahoo! Mail** (http://mail.yahoo.com). (Microsoft's Hotmail is another popular option, but Hotmail has severe spam problems.) Your home ISP may be able to forward your e-mail to the Web-based account automatically.

If you need to access files on your office computer, look into a service called **GoToMyPC** (www.gotomypc.com). The service provides a Web-based interface for you to access and manipulate a distant PC from anywhere—even a cybercafe—provided your "target" PC is switched on and has an always-on connection to the Internet. The service offers top-quality security, but if you're worried about hackers use your own laptop rather than a cybercafe computer to access the GoToMyPC system.

WITH YOUR OWN COMPUTER

Wi-Fi (wireless fidelity) is the buzzword in computer access, and more and more hotels, cafes, and retailers are signing on as wireless "hotspots" from where you can get high-speed connection without cable wires, networking hardware, or a phone line (see below). You can get Wi-Fi connection one of several ways. Many laptops sold in the last year have built-in Wi-Fi capability (an 802.11b wireless Ethernet connection). Mac owners have their own networking technology, Apple AirPort. For those with older computers, an 802.11b/**Wi-Fi card** can be plugged into your laptop. You sign up for wireless access service much as you do cellphone service, through a plan offered by one of several commercial companies that have made wireless service available in airports, hotel lobbies, and coffee shops, primarily in the U.S.

T-Mobile Hotspot (www.t-mobile.com/hotspot) serves up wireless connections at more than 1,000 Starbucks coffee shops nationwide. **Boingo (www.boingo.com)** and **Wayport (www.wayport.com)** have set up networks in airports and high-end hotel lobbies. Available for C$5 (US$4) per day at the Hamilton International Airport. For all Canadian locations check the website.

There are also places that provide **free wireless networks** in cities around the world. To locate these free hotspots, go to **www.personaltelco.net/index.cgi/WirelessCommunities**.

In addition, major **Internet Service Providers (ISPs)** have **local access numbers** around the world, allowing you to go online by simply placing a local call. Check your ISP's website or call its toll-free number and ask how you can use your current account away from home, and how much it will cost.

If you're traveling outside the reach of your ISP, the **iPass** network has dial-up numbers in most of the world's countries. You'll have to sign up with an iPass provider, who will then tell you how to set up your computer for your destination(s). For a list of iPass providers, go to www.ipass.com and click on "Individuals Buy Now." One solid provider is **i2roam** (www.i2roam.com; ℂ **866/811-6209** within Canada and the U.S., or 920/233-5863 from other countries).

Wherever you go, bring a **connection kit** of the right power and phone adapters, a spare phone cord, and a spare Ethernet network cable—or find out whether your hotel supplies them to guests. The electrical current in Canada is the same as the U.S.: 110–115V AC.

USING A CELLPHONE

The three letters that define much of the world's **wireless capabilities** are GSM (Global System for Mobiles), a big, seamless network that makes for easy cross-border cellphone use throughout Europe and dozens of other countries worldwide. In the U.S., T-Mobile, AT&T Wireless, and Cingular use this quasi-universal system; in Canada, Microcell and some Rogers customers are GSM, and all Europeans and most Australians use GSM.

If your cellphone is on a GSM system, and you have a world-capable multiband phone such as many Sony Ericsson, Motorola, or Samsung models, you can make and receive calls across civilized areas on much of the globe, from Andorra to Uganda. Just call your wireless operator and ask for "international roaming" to be activated on your account. Unfortunately, per-minute charges can be high.

That's why it's important to buy an "unlocked" world phone from the get-go. Many cellphone operators sell "locked" phones that restrict you from using any removable computer memory phone chip card (called a **SIM card**) other than the ones they supply. Having an unlocked phone allows you to install a cheap, prepaid SIM card (found at a local retailer) in your destination country. (Show your phone to the salesperson; not all phones work on all networks.) You'll get a local phone number—and much, much lower calling rates. Getting an already locked phone unlocked can be a complicated process, but it can be done; just call your cellular operator and say you'll be going

Digital Photography on the Road

Many travelers are going digital these days when it comes to taking vacation photographs. Not only are digital cameras left relatively unscathed by airport X-rays, but with digital equipment you don't need to lug armloads of film with you as you travel. In fact, nowadays you don't even need to carry your laptop to download the day's images to make room for more. With a **media storage card,** sold by all major camera dealers, you can store hundreds of images in your camera. These "memory" cards come in different configurations—from memory sticks to flash cards to secure digital cards—and different storage capacities (the more megabytes of memory, the more images a card can hold). (*Note:* Each camera model works with a specific type of card, so you'll need to determine which storage card is compatible with your camera.) When you get home, you can print the images out on your own color printer or take the storage card to a camera store, drugstore, or chain retailer.

Online Traveler's Toolbox

Veteran travelers usually carry some essential items to make their trips easier. Following is a selection of handy online tools to bookmark and use.

- **Airplane Seating and Food.** Find out which seats to reserve and which to avoid (and more) on all major domestic airlines at www.seatguru.com. And check out the type of meal (with photos) you'll likely be served on airlines around the world at www.airlinemeals.net.
- **Foreign Languages for Travelers** (www.travlang.com). Learn basic terms in more than 70 languages and click on any underlined phrase to hear what it sounds like.
- **Intellicast** (www.intellicast.com) and **Weather.com** (www.weather.com). Give weather forecasts for all 50 states and for cities around the world.
- **Mapquest** (www.mapquest.com). This best of the mapping sites lets you choose a specific address or destination, and in seconds will return a map and detailed directions.
- **Time and Date** (www.timeanddate.com). See what time (and day) it is anywhere in the world.
- **Universal Currency Converter** (www.xe.com/ucc). See what your dollar or pound is worth in more than 100 other countries.
- **Travel Warnings** (http://travel.state.gov, www.fco.gov.uk/travel, www. voyage.gc.ca, www.dfat.gov.au/consular/advice). These sites report on places where health concerns or unrest might threaten American, British, Canadian, and Australian travelers. Generally, U.S. warnings are the most paranoid; Australian warnings are the most relaxed.
- **Visa ATM Locator** (www.visa.com) for locations of PLUS ATMs worldwide, or **MasterCard ATM Locator** (www.mastercard.com) for locations of Cirrus ATMs worldwide.

abroad for several months and want to use the phone with a local provider.

For many, **renting** a phone is a good idea. While you can rent a phone from any number of overseas sites, including kiosks at airports and at car-rental agencies, we suggest renting the phone before you leave home. That way you can give loved ones and business associates your new number, make sure the phone works, and take the phone wherever you go—especially helpful for overseas trips through several countries, where local phone-rental agencies often bill in local currency and may not let you take the phone to another country.

Two good wireless rental companies are **InTouch USA** (② **800/872-7626;** www.intouchglobal.com) and **RoadPost** (② **888/290-1606** or 905/272-5665; www.roadpost.com). Give them your itinerary, and they'll tell you what wireless products you need. InTouch will also, for free, advise you on whether your existing phone will work overseas; simply call ② **703/222-7161** between 9am and 4pm EST, or go to http://intouchglobal.com/travel.htm.

10 Getting There

BY PLANE

When visiting the Niagara region, you have a choice of arriving in Canada or the United States. The majority of the attractions are on the Canadian side, but the Buffalo Airport is closer to the Falls than either Pearson (Toronto) or Hamilton.

Most flights arrive at Pearson International Airport in northwest Toronto, approximately a 2 hour drive from Niagara Falls. The trip usually takes 30 or more minutes longer during the weekday peak commuter times: 7 to 9am and 4 to 7pm.

Since the September 11, 2001, terrorist attacks, airport security has been enhanced (see "Getting Through the Airport," below). Changes in procedures may cause increased processing times for passengers, both at the check-in counters and the security checkpoints. Ask your airline for recommended check-in times.

If you're traveling with children, ask your air carrier in advance about child safety restraints, transport of strollers, times of meal service, availability of children's meals, and bulkhead seating (which has extra room to stretch out). Mention any food allergies or medical concerns.

Note that the term "direct flight" may include an en-route stop but not an aircraft change.

ARRIVING IN CANADA

FROM THE U.S. Canada's only national airline, **Air Canada** (© 888/247-2262; www.aircanada.ca) operates direct flights to Toronto (Pearson Airport) from most major American cities and many smaller ones. It also flies from major cities around the world and operates connecting flights from other U.S. cities.

There are also a couple of discount Canadian carriers servicing select routes. One is **CanJet** (© 800-809-7777; www.canjet.com), which operates flights to Toronto from New York, Orlando, and Palm Beach. **WestJet** (© 888-WEST-JET; www.westjet.com) has service between Toronto and San Francisco, Los Angeles, and Phoenix.

Among U.S. airlines, **American** (© 800/433-7300; www.aa.com) has daily direct flights from Chicago, Dallas, Miami, and New York. **United** (© 800/241-6522; www.united.com) has direct flights from Chicago, San Francisco, and Washington (Dulles); it's a code-share partner with Air Canada. **US Airways** (© 800/428-4322; www.usairways.com) operates directly into Toronto from a number of U.S. cities, notably Baltimore, Indianapolis, Philadelphia, and Pittsburgh. **Northwest** (© 800/225-2525; www.nwa.com) flies direct from Detroit and Minneapolis. **Delta** (© 800/221-1212; www.delta.com) flies direct from Atlanta and Cincinnati.

The Hamilton International Airport is smaller but closer to the Niagara region—it takes about 45 minutes to drive from the airport to Niagara Falls. WestJet flies into Hamilton from Orlando.

WITHIN CANADA Air Canada, which also operates under the Jazz logo, offers direct flights to **Toronto (Pearson)** from most major Canadian cities. The central reservation number for Air Canada is © 888/247-2262; www.aircanada.com. **CanJet Airlines** serves Halifax, St. John's, Moncton, Deer Lake, Calgary, and Vancouver (© 800/809-7777; www.canjet.com). For a direct flight from Calgary, Winnipeg, Thunder Bay, Montreal, Halifax, Moncton, Charlottetown, and several cities in British Columbia, contact **WestJet** (© 800/538-5696; www.westjet.com).

For flights to **Hamilton International Airport**, WestJet operates a service from

Calgary, Edmonton, Winnipeg, Halifax, and Moncton. Air Canada and CanJet also serve Hamilton.

FROM ABROAD There's frequent service (direct and indirect) to Toronto from around the world.

Several airlines operate from the United Kingdom. **British Airways** (© 0870/850-9850; www.ba.com) and **Air Canada** (© 08705/247-226) fly direct from London Heathrow Airport. Air Canada also flies direct from Glasgow and Manchester.

In Australia, **Air Canada** (© 02/9286-8900) has an agreement with Qantas and flies from Sydney to Toronto, stopping in Honolulu. From New Zealand, **Air Canada** (© 09/379-3371) partners with Air New Zealand, scheduling an average three flights a week from Auckland to Toronto, via Honolulu, Fiji, or both.

From Cape Town, South Africa, **Delta** (© 011/482-4582) operates via New York; **Air Canada** (© 011/875-5800) via Frankfurt; and **South African Airways** (© 011/978-1000; www.saa.co.za) via Miami or New York. Several airlines fly from Johannesburg, including **British Airways** (© 011/441-8600) via Heathrow and **South African Airways** (© 011/978-1000) via Miami or New York.

ARRIVING IN THE U.S.

WITHIN THE U.S. Niagara Falls International Airport is for charter and cargo planes only, so plan to fly into **Buffalo Niagara International Airport** (4200 Genesee St., Cheektowaga, NY; © 716/630-6000; www.nfta.com/airport). The airport is served by a number of airlines including **JetBlue** (© 800/538-2583; www.jetblue.com), which has lots of cheap one-way flights from other parts of New York, **AirTran Airways** (© 800/247-8726; www.airtran.com), **American** (© 800/433-7300; www.aa.com), **Continental**

(© 800/525-0280; www.continental.com), **Comair/Delta Connection** (© 800/221-1212; www.comair.com), **Northwest** (© 800/225-2525; www.nwa.com), **Southwest** (© 800/435-9792; www.southwest.com), **United** (© 800/241-6522; www.ual.com), and **US Airways** (© 800/428-4322).

FROM CANADA Travelers whose departure city is within Canada are advised to fly to Toronto or Hamilton rather than Buffalo.

FROM ABROAD A number of major U.S. airlines fly into Buffalo Niagara International Airport (see "Within the U.S." above). Visitors arriving from abroad can make connections to Buffalo from several major U.S. cities, including Atlanta, Boston, Chicago, Detroit, and New York.

GETTING TO NIAGARA FROM THE AIRPORT

If you land at **Pearson International Airport** in Toronto, renting a car may be your best bet. However, there is an **airport express bus service** that will take you to the bus station and train station in downtown Toronto, where you can get transportation to the Niagara Region. The fare is C$16 (US$13) per adult one-way. Car-rental companies with desks inside the terminals include **Avis, Budget, Dollar/Thrifty, Hertz,** and **National/Alamo.**

Car-rental companies at **Hamilton International Airport** include Avis, Hertz, and National.

Niagara Airbus (© 800/268-8111 for 416 and 905 area codes, or 716/374-8111; www.niagaraairbus.com) offers a flexible shuttle and taxi service from **Toronto (Pearson)** and **Buffalo Niagara International Airport** to any destination in the Niagara region in Canada and the Niagara Falls/Buffalo area in New York State. The one-way fare from Toronto

Pearson Airport to Niagara Falls, Ontario, is C$60 (US$50). The company also serves **Hamilton** airport with individual taxi cabs rather than a shuttle service.

If you arrive at **Buffalo Niagara International Airport,** the closest airport to the Falls, the **ITA Shuttle** (© **800/ 551-9369;** www.buffaloairporttaxi.com) can take you from the airport to the American side of the Falls for C$36 (US$30) per person each way or to the Canadian side for C$48 (US$40) per person each way. Children under 6 years old ride free. Reservations must be made at least 12 hours in advance and can be made online or by phone. If you prefer to rent a car, Avis, Budget, Hertz, and Enterprise all have rental counters at the airport.

GETTING THROUGH THE AIRPORT

With the federalization of airport security, security procedures at Canadian and U.S. airports are more stable and consistent than ever. Generally, you'll be fine if you check in **1 hour** before a domestic flight and **2 hours** before an international flight; if you show up late, tell an airline employee and you may get whisked to the front of the line. To board flights within Canada, a current, government-issued photo ID is required. Most Canadians use a driver's license as ID for domestic flights. Proof of citizenship is required for entry at all Canadian border crossings, including airports, and a passport is the most recommended document to carry. For requirements for U.S. citizens arriving in Canada, see "Entry Requirements" earlier in this chapter. Citizens of most European countries, Commonwealth countries, and former British colonies, as well as certain other countries, do not need visas but must carry passports. Entry visas are required for citizens of more than 140 countries. Keep your ID at the ready to show at check-in, the security checkpoint, and the gate.

E-tickets have made paper tickets nearly obsolete. Passengers with e-tickets can beat the ticket-counter lines by using airport **electronic kiosks** or even **online check-in** from your home computer. Online check-in involves logging on to your airline's website, accessing your reservation, and printing out your boarding pass—and the airline may even offer you bonus miles to do so! If you're using a kiosk at the airport, bring the credit card you used to book the ticket or your frequent-flier card. Print out your boarding pass from the kiosk and simply proceed to the security checkpoint with your pass and a photo ID. If you're checking bags or looking to snag an exit-row seat, you will be able to do so using most airline kiosks. Even the smaller airlines are employing the kiosk system, but always call your airline to make sure these alternatives are available. **Curbside check-in** is also a good way to avoid lines, although a few airlines still ban curbside check-in; call before you go.

Security checkpoint lines are shorter than they were during 2001 and 2002, but at times they can be slow going. If you have trouble standing for long periods of time, tell an airline employee, the airline will provide a wheelchair. Speed up security by **not wearing metal objects** such as big belt buckles. If you've got metallic body parts, a note from your doctor can prevent a long chat with the security screeners. Keep cellular phones, laptops, personal CD players, and other electronics easily accessible, and be prepared to have these items hand-checked by security staff—this may include a request to switch on the item in question. Keep in mind that only **ticketed passengers** are allowed past security, except for folks escorting disabled passengers or unaccompanied minors.

Federalization has stabilized **what you can carry on** and **what you can't.** The general rule is that sharp things are out,

⟨Tips⟩ Don't Stow It—Ship It

If ease of travel is your main concern and money is no object, you can ship your luggage and sports equipment with one of the growing number of luggage-service companies that pick up, track, and deliver your luggage (often through couriers such as Federal Express) with minimum hassle for you. Traveling luggage-free may be ultra-convenient, but it's not cheap: One-way overnight shipping can cost from US$100 to US$200, depending on what you're sending. Still, for some people, especially the elderly or the infirm, it's a sensible solution to lugging heavy baggage. Specialists in door-to-door luggage delivery are **Virtual Bellhop** (www.virtualbellhop.com), **SkyCap International** (wwww.skycap international.com), **Luggage Express** (www.usxpluggageexpress.com), and **Sports Express** (www.sportsexpress.com).

nail clippers are okay, and food and beverages must be passed through the X-ray machine. Bring food in your carry-on rather than checking it, as explosive-detection machines used on checked luggage have been known to mistake food (especially chocolate, for some reason) for bombs. Travelers in Canada and the U.S. are allowed one carry-on bag, plus a "personal item" such as a purse, briefcase, or laptop bag, although if flights are fully booked, the airline may ask you to check your carry-on luggage. The U.S. Transportation Security Administration (TSA) has issued a list of restricted items; check its website (www.tsa.gov/public/index.jsp) for details.

Airport screeners may decide that your checked luggage needs to be searched by hand. You can now purchase luggage locks that allow screeners to open and re-lock a checked bag if hand-searching is necessary. Look for Travel Sentry certified locks at luggage or travel shops and Brookstone stores (you can buy them online at www.brookstone.com). These locks, approved by the TSA, can be opened by luggage inspectors with a special code or key. For more information on the locks, visit www.travelsentry.org. If you use something other than TSA-approved locks, your lock will be cut off your suitcase if a TSA agent needs to

hand-search your checked luggage and you are not available to provide the key or combination.

FLYING FOR LESS: TIPS FOR GETTING THE BEST AIRFARE

Passengers sharing the same airplane cabin rarely pay the same fare. Travelers who need to purchase tickets at the last minute, change their itinerary at a moment's notice, or fly one-way often get stuck paying the premium rate. Here are some ways to keep your airfare costs down.

- Passengers who can book their ticket **long in advance,** or conversely **at the last minute,** or who **fly midweek** or **at less-trafficked hours** may pay a fraction of the full fare. If your schedule is flexible, say so, and ask if you can secure a cheaper fare by changing your flight plans.

- You can also save on airfares by keeping an eye out in local newspapers for **promotional specials** or **fare wars,** when airlines lower prices on their most popular routes. You rarely see fare wars offered for peak travel times, but if you can travel in the off-months, you may snag a bargain.

- Search **the Internet** for cheap fares (see "Planning Your Trip Online," earlier in this chapter).

• **Consolidators,** also known as bucket shops, are great sources for international tickets, although they usually can't beat the Internet on fares within North America. Start by looking in Sunday newspaper travel sections; U.S. travelers should focus on the *New York Times, Los Angeles Times,* and *Miami Herald.* **Beware:** Bucket shop tickets are usually nonrefundable or rigged with stiff cancellation penalties, often as high as 50% to 75% of the ticket price, and some put you on charter airlines, which may leave at inconvenient times and experience delays. Several reliable consolidators are worldwide and available on the Net. **STA Travel** (© 800/ 781-4040; www.statravel.com) is now the world's leader in student travel, thanks to their purchase of Council Travel. It also offers good fares for travelers of all ages. **ELTExpress** (**Flights.com**) (© 312/332-0090; www.eltexpress.com) started in Europe and has excellent fares worldwide, but particularly to that continent. It also has "local" websites in 12 countries. **Air Tickets Direct** (© 800/778-3447; www.airtickets direct.com) is based in Montreal and leverages the relatively weak Canadian dollar for low fares.

• Join **frequent-flier clubs.** Accrue enough miles, and you'll be rewarded with free flights and elite status. It's free, and you'll get the best choice of seats, faster response to phone inquiries, and prompter service if your luggage is stolen, your flight is canceled or delayed, or if you want to change your seat. You don't need to fly to build frequent-flier miles— **frequent-flier credit cards** can provide thousands of miles for doing your everyday shopping.

BY CAR

When driving from the I-90 in **New York State,** take Route 290 to Route 190 to the Robert Moses Parkway—this will put you in downtown Niagara Falls, New York, and you'll see signs for the Rainbow Bridge to Canada. Other crossing points to Canada from the U.S. are between Lewiston, New York, and Queenston, Ontario, and between Buffalo, New York, and Fort Erie, Ontario.

Driving distances from major U.S. cities to Niagara Falls include Boston (774km/484 miles), Chicago (861km/538 miles), Detroit (384km/240 miles), New York (677km/423 miles), and Washington (768km/480 miles).

From **Toronto,** take the Queen Elizabeth Way (signs read QEW) to Niagara via Hamilton and St. Catharines. Driving time is approximately 1½ to 2 hours, depending on traffic. Note that rush hour snarl-ups can considerably lengthen your trip when traveling from Toronto. If possible, avoid driving on major highways in

---

Travel in the Age of Bankruptcy

Airlines go bankrupt, so protect yourself by **buying your tickets with a credit card,** as the Fair Credit Billing Act guarantees that you can get your money back from the credit card company if a travel supplier goes under (and if you request the refund within 60 days of the bankruptcy). **Travel insurance** can also help, but make sure it covers against "carrier default" for your specific travel provider. And be aware that if a U.S. airline goes bust mid-trip, a 2001 federal law requires other carriers to take you to your destination (albeit on a space-available basis) for a fee of no more than $25, provided you rebook within 60 days of the cancellation.

Flying with Film & Video

Never pack film—exposed or unexposed—in checked bags, as the new, more powerful scanners in U.S. airports can fog film. The film you carry with you can be damaged by scanners as well. X-ray damage is cumulative; the faster the film, and the more times you put it through a scanner, the more likely the damage. Film under 800 ASA is usually safe for up to five scans. If you're taking your film through additional scans, U.S. regulations permit you to demand hand inspections. In international airports, you're at the mercy of airport officials. On international flights, store your film in transparent baggies, so you can remove it easily before you go through scanners. Keep in mind that airports are not the only places where your camera may be scanned: Highly trafficked attractions are X-raying visitors' bags with increasing frequency.

Most photo supply stores sell protective pouches designed to block damaging X-rays. The pouches fit both film and loaded cameras. They should protect your film in checked baggage, but they also may raise alarms and result in a hand inspection.

You'll have little to worry about if you are traveling with **digital cameras.** Unlike film, which is sensitive to light, the digital camera and storage cards are not affected by airport X-rays, according to Nikon. Still, if you plan to travel extensively, you may want to play it safe and hand-carry your digital equipment or ask that it be inspected by hand. See "Digital Photography on the Road," earlier in this chapter.

Carry-on scanners will not damage **videotape** in video cameras, but the magnetic fields emitted by the walk-through security gateways and hand-held inspection wands will. Always place your loaded camcorder on the screening conveyor belt or have it hand-inspected. Be sure your batteries are charged, as you may be required to turn the device on to ensure that it's what it appears to be.

the Toronto and Hamilton area between 7am and 10am and between 3:30pm and 6:30pm.

From **Windsor** and **Detroit,** take Highway 401 East to Highway 403, then join the QEW to Niagara. Driving time from Windsor to Niagara Falls is approximately 4 to 4½ hours.

Exit from the QEW at Highway 55 if your destination is Niagara-on-the-Lake, or if you would like to take the scenic route to Niagara Falls, which will lead you along the Niagara Parkway on the west side of the Niagara River. If you want to go straight to the Falls, continue on the QEW to Highway 420 and follow the signs. A third option is to continue on the QEW to Fort Erie, at the southern end of the Niagara River. You can visit the attractions in Fort Erie, then make your way along the southern portion of the Niagara Parkway to the Falls, which is also a pretty drive.

Be sure to carry your driver's license and car registration and insurance documents if you plan to drive your own vehicle. If you are a member of the **American Automobile Association (AAA),** the **Canadian Automobile Association (CAA)** can provide you with assistance if you call **CAA Niagara** (© **905/984-8585;** www.caa.niagara.net).

If you decide to **rent a car,** try to make arrangements in advance to make sure the vehicle you want will be available. If you are traveling from outside Canada, you may obtain a reasonable discount by booking before you leave home. The rental fee depends on the type of car, but a typical fee for a midsize car with automatic transmission is around C$50 (US$41) a day, plus taxes. This price will vary according to season, availability, and length of rental (a full week's rental will often give you a lower price than the daily rate multiplied by seven). The price quoted usually does not include insurance, but some credit card companies offer automatic insurance coverage if you charge the full amount of the car rental to the card (check with your credit card issuer before you travel). Be sure to read the fine print of the agreement and undertake a thorough visual check for damage before accepting the vehicle. Some companies add conditions that will boost your bill if you don't fulfill certain obligations, such as filling the gas tank before returning the car. Note that rental car companies customarily impose a minimum age of 25 for drivers, and some companies have a maximum age of 70 or 75.

BY TRAIN

Amtrak (© **800/USA-RAIL** [872-7245]; www.amtrak.com) and **VIARail Canada** (© **888/VIA-RAIL** [842-7245] or 416/366-8411; www.viarail.ca) operate trains between **Toronto** and **New York,** stopping in **Niagara Falls** and **St. Catharines** but not Niagara-on-the-Lake. Amtrak comes right into the Niagara Falls station in New York State at 27th Street and Lockport Road.

BY BUS

Greyhound Canada (© **800/661-8747**) provides coast-to-coast service with connections to Niagara Falls. The local bus

station is Niagara Transportation, 4555 Erie Ave., Niagara Falls, Ont. (© **905/357-2133**). Book online or obtain schedule and fare information at www.greyhound.ca. **Greyhound Lines, Inc.** (© **800/231-2222**; www.greyhound.com), provides bus service between the U.S. and Canada. The local bus station on the U.S. side is at Niagara Discount Souvenir, 303 Rainbow Blvd., Niagara Falls, NY (© **716/282-1765**).

Traveling by bus may be faster and cheaper than the train, and if you want to stop to visit towns along the way its routes may offer more flexibility. But there's also less space to stretch out, toilet facilities are meager, and meals are taken at roadside rest stops, so consider carefully, particularly if you're planning to bring children with you.

Investigate offers such as unlimited-travel passes and discount fares. It's tough to quote typical fares because bus companies, like airlines, are adopting yield-management strategies, resulting in frequent price changes depending on demand.   11 Packages for the Independent Traveler

Before you start your search for the lowest airfare, you may want to consider booking your flight as part of a travel package. Package tours are not the same thing as escorted tours. Package tours are simply a way to buy the airfare, accommodations, and other elements of your trip (such as car rentals, airport transfers, and sometimes even activities) at the same time and often at discounted prices—kind of like one-stop shopping. Packages are sold in bulk to tour operators—who resell them to the public at a cost that usually undercuts standard rates.

One good source of package deals is the airlines themselves. Most major airlines offer air/land packages, including **American Airlines Vacations** (© 800/321-2121; www.aavacations.com), **Continental Airlines Vacations** (© 800/301-3800;

www.covacations.com), and **United Vacations** (© 888/854-3899; www.united vacations.com). Several big **online travel agencies**—Expedia, Travelocity, Orbitz, Site59, and Lastminute.com—also do a brisk business in packages. If you're unsure about the pedigree of a smaller packager, check with the **Better Business Bureau** in the city where the company is based, or go online at www.bbb.org. If a packager won't tell you where they're based, don't fly with them.

Travel packages are also listed in the travel section of your local Sunday newspaper. Or check ads in the national travel magazines such as *Arthur Frommer's Budget Travel Magazine, Travel & Leisure, National Geographic Traveler,* and *Condé Nast Traveler.*

Package tours can vary by leaps and bounds. Some offer a better class of hotels than others. Some offer the same hotels for lower prices. Some offer flights on scheduled airlines, while others book charters. Some limit your choice of accommodations and travel days. You are often required to make a large payment upfront. On the plus side, packages can save you money, offering group prices but allowing for independent travel. Some even let you to add on a few guided excursions or escorted day trips (also at prices lower than if you booked them yourself) without booking an entirely escorted tour.

Before you invest in a package tour, get some answers. Ask about the **accommodations choices** and prices for each. Then look up the hotels' reviews in a Frommer's guide and check their rates online for your specific dates of travel. You'll also want to find out what **type of room** you get. If you need a certain type of room, ask for it; don't take whatever is thrown your way. Request a nonsmoking room, a quiet room, a room with a view, or whatever you fancy.

Finally, look for **hidden expenses.** Ask whether airport departure fees and taxes, for example, are included in the total cost.

3

Suggested Itineraries for the Niagara Region

Everyone thinks first of the Falls, without a doubt the primary reason why most tourists visit the Niagara region. And if you've never seen them, then certainly they should be your first priority. Second on your list should be Niagara-on-the-Lake, an elegant, small Ontario town with exquisite accommodations, excellent shopping and dining, and the renowned Shaw Festival Theatre. The Niagara region is also the proud home of a well-respected wine industry, and those with a penchant for good food and wine could spend anything from an afternoon to a week exploring the wine country. Sidling up to the accessible locks of the Welland Canal is another worthwhile experience. In between, there are villages, bicycle trails, and nature preserves that will add variety to your schedule and allow you to discover delights of the Niagara region you might otherwise never realize were on the doorstep of the world's best-known waterfalls.

Note: These itineraries have been set up for visitors who come to Niagara during the prime tourist season between April and October. Many, but not all, of the attractions are open in the winter months, and Niagara under snow can be a magical winter wonder. However, please call ahead (or check chapter 7, "What to See & Do in the Niagara Region") if you are planning to visit outside the main tourist season and there are specific attractions or itineraries you wish to include.

1 The Best of Niagara Falls in 1 Day

Seeing the sights of Niagara in 1 day requires an early start, discipline, and stamina, but it's quite doable. Start on the Canadian side, since it is on this side of the river that you will get the gorgeous panorama of both the American and Horseshoe Falls. First, park your car in an all-day parking lot, then buy one of the tourist passes. The large lot on the Niagara Parkway south of the Horseshoe Falls in Canada is recommended because you can purchase your **Great Gorge Adventure Pass** at the kiosk there and take the People Mover (unlimited transport for the day is included with the pass) right from the parking lot to the Falls and other attractions. **Start:** *Maid of the Mist on the Canadian side.*

● The *Maid of the Mist*

Although your first instinct will be to rush to the side of the river and stare at the Falls, head straight for the *Maid of the Mist* for two reasons. First, during the boat trip you will immediately feel the immense power of the water and get a deep appreciation of the size and grandeur of both the American and Canadian Falls. Second, you will avoid the lineups, which get longer as the day goes on. Grab a spot on the starboard side of the boat (that's the right-hand side, for you landlubbers)—you'll get closer to the Horseshoe Falls and will still have great views of the American Falls on your return to the dock. See p. 112.

❷ The Falls by Day

After you alight from the *Maid of the Mist*'s dock, walk south along the edge of the Niagara River to Table Rock Point. Now is the time to drink in the views and marvel at the thundering waters of Niagara from the safety of the shore. Get out your camera—and don't be shy to ask a fellow tourist to take a picture of you with the Falls in the background. You'll probably be asked to do the same thing yourself!

❸ Journey Behind the Falls

Now it's time to plunge down into the gorge on foot. Use your Great Gorge Adventure Pass in Canada and enter Table Rock House to take the Journey Behind the Falls. Walk through tunnels bored into the rock behind the Horseshoe Falls and emerge onto the lower balcony at the northern edge. This is where you will feel the power of the Horseshoe Falls at its mightiest.

☕ TAKE A BREAK

Take a food/beverage break at the **Table Rock Restaurant**, 6650 Niagara Pkwy., Niagara Falls (✆ **905/354-3631**), or cross the street to **Edgewater's Tap & Grill**, Queen Victoria Park, Niagara Pkwy., Niagara Falls; ✆ **905/356-2217** (p. 93) (upper floor; great views of the Falls).

---

❺ White Water Walk

Jump on the People Mover and ride north to the White Water Walk attraction. An elevator takes you on a deep plunge to the bottom of the Niagara Gorge. A boardwalk along the edge of the base of the gorge brings you face to face with one of the world's wildest stretches of white water. See p. 117.

❻ Butterfly Conservatory

Take the People Mover to the Butterfly Conservatory, a delightful place to spend an hour or so. The Conservatory doubles as the display greenhouse for the Niagara Parks Botanical Gardens and is blessed with an abundance of natural light. The butterflies spend a considerable amount of time resting, so it's a great place to bring your camera. See p. 116.

❼ Skylon Tower or Konica Minolta Tower

Take the People Mover to the Incline Railway, situated opposite Table Rock House terminus. If you have a Great Gorge Adventure Pass the trip is free, otherwise you will have to pay a small fee to ride up the cliff. Once at the top, walk farther up the hill to Fallsview Boulevard, turning right (north) for the Skylon Tower (p. 115) or left (south) for the Konica Minolta Tower (p. 114). Both towers are only a couple of minutes' walk away and both will give you a terrific aerial view of the Falls.

❽ IMAX Theatre

Take in the IMAX movie, which gives those who are unfamiliar with the Falls and their history a broad appreciation of this famous wonder of the natural world. The Niagara Daredevil Gallery, which holds an impressive collection of objects that have carried people over the Falls and through the rapids, is inside the IMAX building, and entry to the exhibit is free. See p. 204.

☕ TAKE A BREAK

In the Fallsview Boulevard area, you can choose from a variety of dining options. For casual fine dining, go to **Wolfgang Puck's** or head upstairs to **TuTu Tango's** funky atmosphere, both at 6300 Fallsview Blvd, Unit A, Niagara Falls, Ontario; ✆ **905/354-5000**. See p. 92. There are several family-style and roadhouse restaurants in the immediate area, if your tastes run more to that type of food.

Niagara Falls Itineraries

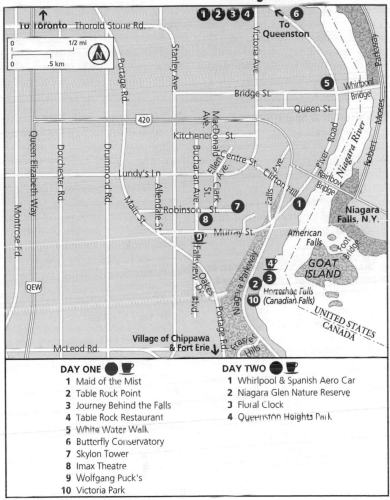

DAY ONE 🔴 ☕
1 Maid of the Mist
2 Table Rock Point
3 Journey Behind the Falls
4 Table Rock Restaurant
5 White Water Walk
6 Butterfly Conservatory
7 Skylon Tower
8 Imax Theatre
9 Wolfgang Puck's
10 Victoria Park

DAY TWO 🔴 ☕
1 Whirlpool & Spanish Aero Car
2 Niagara Glen Nature Reserve
3 Floral Clock
4 Queenston Heights Park

⑩ The Falls by Night

When darkness falls, both falls will be magically illuminated in a flood of rainbow colors. Take another tower trip, or walk down into Victoria Park and view the light show from the Canadian shore of the Niagara Gorge.

2 The Best of the Niagara Region in 2 Days

Head north on the Niagara Parkway by car or the Niagara-on-the-Lake Shuttle (see chapter 4, "Getting to Know the Niagara Region"). Marvel at the whirlpool in the Niagara Gorge, and then enjoy the beauty of the public areas of the Niagara Parks Commission by exploring the Botanical Gardens or taking a leisurely ramble through the Niagara Glen Nature Reserve before heading to historic Queenston Heights Park, scene of one of the most famous battles of the War of 1812. Explore the beautiful town of Niagara-on-the-Lake, including the quaint shops and restaurants along Queen Street. Fill your afternoon with a visit to Fort George, live theater at the Shaw Festival, or a thrill ride along the Niagara Gorge Rapids on a jet boat. *Start: Niagara Parkway alongside Victoria Park.*

---

❶ Whirlpool & Spanish Aero Car

A vintage metal carriage, suspended on cables above the whirlpool phenomenon in the Niagara Gorge, takes passengers on a hair-raising 1km (½-mile) round-trip. If you like thrill rides, and the lineup is short, then go for it. Otherwise, take a gander at the whirlpool from the safety of the shore and move on to the next stop. See p. 116.

❷ Niagara Glen Nature Reserve or Niagara Parks Botanical Gardens

On the east side of the Niagara Parkway, a short drive north of the whirlpool, you'll find the Niagara Glen Nature Reserve, which features a series of seven linked trails, ranging in length from .4km (¼ mile) to 3.3km (2 miles). Note that all of the paths, or access to them, are steep in places—River Path is the flattest, but you need to descend the cliff to reach it. Alternatively—or in addition, if you just love to be outdoors—you can stroll the beautiful Niagara Parks Botanical Gardens, just a little farther north on the west side of the Parkway. See p. 138.

❸ Floral Clock

Visitors flock to take photos of their friends and family standing in front of this Niagara landmark. The 12m-diameter (40-ft.) clock face is filled each summer with 16,000 bedding plants, carefully arranged in artful patterns that change annually. In spring, the clock is planted with a profusion of pansies. See p. 137.

❹ Queenston Heights Park

Queenston Heights Park has a variety of facilities and attractions for visitors. View Brock's Monument (under repair with no set reopening date at press time) and the Laura Secord Monument. Take a 45-minute self-guided walking tour of the battleground of the War of 1812's Battle of Queenston Heights, or enjoy the mature shade trees and grassy open spaces of the park, perfect for ballgames and family fun. See p. 139.

> ### ❺ TAKE A BREAK
> If you're looking for an early lunch, **Queenston Heights Restaurant,** located right in the park, enjoys beautiful open vistas looking north along the Niagara River toward Lake Ontario. Lunch, afternoon tea, and dinner are served, and a children's menu is available, 14184 Niagara Pkwy, Queenston, Ontario; ✆ **905/262-4274** (p. 89). If you have a picnic hamper with you, enjoy lunch on one of the many picnic tables throughout the park.

❻ Shaw Festival Afternoon Performance

I recommend booking tickets in advance if you wish to see a performance at the world-renowned Shaw Festival. The Shaw has three theaters in Niagara-on-the-Lake, and presents plays written by George Bernard Shaw and his contemporaries along with plays set during the period of Shaw's lifetime. See p. 200.

Niagara Parkway

To Queenston →

Niagara River

Niagara River

Niagara-on-the-Lake

To Niagara-on-the-Lake ←

Queenston St.

Niagara

To Niagara Falls →

Queenston

Pkwy.

1/4 Mi

0   .25 Km

York Rd.

Portage Rd.

405

9

Queen's Parade

Melville St.

6

Ball St.

Delatre St.

Ricardo St.

Wellington St.

7

Byron St.

Picton St.

Davy

Platoff St.

St.

Castlereagh St.

Nelles St.

Christopher Ct.

Weatherstone Ct.

Pafford St.

Park Ct.

King St.

10

Regent St.

Front St.

Prideaux St.

8

Queen St.

Johnson St.

Gage St.

Centre St.

Victoria St.

Anre St.

Lake Ontario

Gate St.

10

Simcoe St.

John St.

N

1/4 mi

.25 km

0

0

DAY TWO
5 Queenston Heights
    Restaurant
6 Shaw Festival Theatre
7 Simcoe Park
8 Queen Street
9 Fort George
10 Niagara-on-the-Lake Visitor
    & Convention Bureau
11 Zee's Patio & Grill

❼ Simcoe Park, Niagara-on-the-Lake
If you are not going to the theater, you will have time to relax in Simcoe Park. This park, with its rolling landscape, mature trees, shady playground, and paddling pool, is a haven for families traveling with children. There are benches tucked away from the giggling and chattering for those who would like to rest quietly. If you stroll two blocks northeast on King Street,

which borders the park, you will reach Queen's Royal Park, which has a pretty gazebo overlooking Lake Ontario—it's a popular spot for weddings.

❽ Queen Street Shopping
The best boutique shopping in Niagara is to be found along Queen Street in Niagara-on-the-Lake; the shops spill onto the side streets along the route. The street

gets crowded in the summer months, but the shops are quaint, unique, and entertaining. Don't miss this. See chapter 9, "Shopping."

TAKE A BREAK
There are plenty of places to buy a tasty bakery treat, ice cream, or cold drink along Queen Street. Or take the time to enjoy afternoon tea—try the **Prince of Wales Hotel**, 6 Picton St., Niagara-on-the-Lake (*©* **888/669-5566**) (p. 77) or the **Charles Inn**, 209 Queen St., Niagara-on-the-Lake (*©* **866/556-8883**) (p. 96) for an elegant experience.

---

❾ Fort George or Jet Boat Tour

Fort George is a reconstructed British fort that served as military headquarters in the past and played a key role in the War of 1812. Highlights of the fort include the reconstructed guardhouse, officers' quarters, flag bastion, blockhouses, and Brock's bastion, the fort's most strategic artillery battery (p. 121). If you'd rather immerse yourself in water than history, go for a jet boat tour, leaving Niagara-on-the-Lake dock at the foot of Melville Street several times daily. Note that you'll need a complete change of clothing unless you plan on a Jet Dome tour, which has a covered deck (p. 133).

❿ The Leafy Side Streets—by Foot or Horse & Carriage

The graceful and pleasant streets of Niagara-on-the-Lake's Heritage District—the "Old Town"—are laid out in a grid fashion, making it simple to find your way around. Just head down any side street off the main shopping district on Queen Street and you will find quaint streets lined with impressively restored historic homes. You can pick up a map of the town at the Niagara-on-the-Lake Visitor & Convention Bureau, at 26 Queen St. Sentinel Carriages will take you around town in a horse-drawn carriage, passing by places of historic interest on the way.

⓫ TAKE A BREAK
If you have tickets for an evening Shaw performance, then make a reservation for an early dinner for around 5:30pm, which will allow you time to walk to the theater afterward without having to rush. If you *aren't* going to the theater, then wait until around 7pm, when the pre-theater crowds have thinned out; you will enjoy a more peaceful and relaxed meal. Try **Zee's Patio & Grill**, right across the street from the main theater, 92 Picton St., Niagara-on-the-Lake (*©* **906/468-5715**) (p. 100). If you are looking for a quiet place for a drink in the evening, try one of the hotel bars.

---

3 The Best of the Niagara Region in 3 Days

On the third day, you can really begin to get to know Niagara, and make your itinerary more personal. Start your day with a tour of the local wineries. The Welland Canal is well worth a visit, but only if you have your own vehicle to drive to one of the two main viewing locations *and* a ship will be entering or leaving the lock you choose to view at a convenient time. See chapter 7, "What to See & Do in the Niagara Region," for how to find the shipping traffic schedule for the day of your visit. Finally, drop in to the pretty villages of Old Port Dalhousie or Jordan, and enjoy life at a slower pace for the afternoon. *Start: Niagara Peninsula Wine Route.*

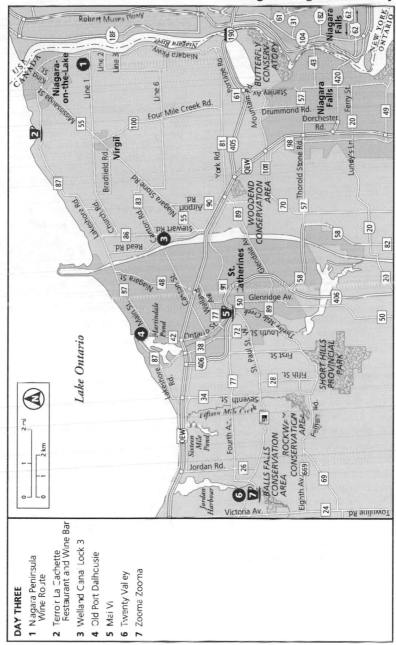

DAY THREE

1 Niagara Peninsula
  Wine Route
2 Terroir La Cachette
  Restaurant and Wine Bar
3 Welland Canal Lock 3
4 Old Port Dalhousie
5 Mai Vi
6 Twenty Valley
7 Zooma Zooma

❶ The Niagara Peninsula Wine Route

Visit the wineries in the morning (10am is the almost universal opening time), before the crowds arrive. Remember, you're tasting 1-ounce samples, and it's perfectly acceptable to spit the wine out after tasting, so don't get in a twist about drinking before noon. You are likely to have the tasting bar staff all to yourself, which means you can linger, ask questions, and generally have a more relaxing time. Check out chapter 8, "The Wine-Country Experience," for more details.

> ☕ **TAKE A BREAK**
> If you're looking for a winery lunch, **Terroir La Cachette Restaurant & Wine Bar** at Strewn Winery, 1339 Lakeshore Rd., Niagara-on-the-Lake (✆ **905/468-1222**) (p. 106) offers excellent Provençal cuisine at reasonable prices and tends to be a little more casual than most of the region's winery restaurants.

❸ Welland Canal Lock 3 or Lock 7

Viewing complexes have been created for the public to watch the "salties" (ocean going ships) and "lakers" (those ships that sail the Great Lakes) at Thorold Lock 7 Viewing Complex, where you can watch the ships climb up and down the Escarpment at a series of three twinned locks and get a close-up view of Lock 7 in operation. There is a tourist information center and small cafe at this location (p. 124). The Welland Canal Centre is located at Lock 3, which is also home to the St. Catharines Museum (p. 125).

❹ Old Port Dalhousie

Browse the village shops and take a stroll along the waterfront. If you have kids in tow, do not miss the antique carousel in the park along Lake Ontario's shoreline.

> ☕ **TAKE A BREAK**
> By now you'll probably be ready for lunch—try **Mai Vi,** 55 St. Paul's St., St. Catharines (✆ **905/988-1426**) (p. 107). Or **Spice of Life,** 12 Lock St., Port Dalhousie (✆ **905/937-9027**) (p. 109).

❻ Twenty Valley

Shop in the boutiques of Jordan Village, enjoy the rolling hills, woodlands, and meandering streams of the countryside, or experience the hospitality of the many wineries in this area. The Bruce Trail blazes through the Twenty Valley's southern end, circumventing Ball's Falls and passing within sipping distance of several wineries.

> ☕ **TAKE A BREAK**
> Enjoy a light meal at **Zooma Zooma Café,** 3839 Main St., Jordan Village, Ontario (✆ **905/562-6280**) (p. 107). If you want to experience an authentic wine-country dinner, call for reservations at **On the Twenty Restaurant,** 3836 Main St., Jordan Village, Ontario (✆ **905/562-7313**) (p. 103). Be adventurous and ask whether a tasting menu is on offer. Typically presented as a series of five to seven smaller courses paired with wines, this type of menu is often found only in wine regions.

4

Getting to Know the Niagara Region

The name Niagara is synonymous with the Falls, and indeed the extraordinary power of the seventh forgotten wonder of the natural world is often the biggest draw for visitors to the Niagara region. But the Niagara region has much more to offer. Once you have gazed in awe upon the physical beauty of Niagara Falls—whether from below, behind, alongside, or above—you can step into the commercial maze of Niagara Falls, Ontario, and its sister city Niagara Falls, New York, or escape along the Niagara River Parkway into an oasis of groomed greenery.

For those exhausted by the force of the Falls and the city's exuberant tackiness, a journey of discovery to the rest of the Niagara region will provide welcome relief. The pretty town of Niagara-on-the-Lake, the rolling vineyards and fragrant orchards of Niagara's agricultural heart, and the friendly communities strung along the mighty Welland Canal are waiting to delight the traveler who ventures beyond the Falls.

1 Orientation

VISITOR INFORMATION

In the city of Niagara Falls, Ontario, visit **Niagara Falls Tourism** at 5515 Stanley Ave. (© **800/563-2557;** www.discoverniagara.com). Other major tourism offices include **Niagara-on-the-Lake Visitor and Convention Bureau,** 26 Queen St., Courthouse Building, Lower Level, Niagara-on-the-Lake (© **905/468-1950;** www.niagaraon thelake.com); **St. Catharines Tourism Information Centre,** 1932 Government Rd., St. Catharines (© **800/305-5134;** www.stcatharineslock3museum.ca); and **Thorold Lock 7 Information & Viewing Centre,** 50 Chapel St. S., Thorold (© **905/680-9477;** www.thorold.com).

If you are traveling by car, drop in to one of the **Ontario Travel Centres:** the **Niagara Falls** location at 5355 Stanley Ave. (west on Hwy. 420 from the Rainbow Bridge) (© **905/358-3221**), **Fort Erie** at 315 Bertie St., just off the Queen Elizabeth Way (QEW) at the Peace Bridge (© **905/871-3505**), or **St. Catharines** on the westbound QEW at the east end of Garden City Skyway (© **905/684-6354**). If you are arriving in the Niagara region along the Queen Elizabeth Way, you can also visit **Gateway Niagara Information Centre** at 424 S. Service Rd., QEW at Casablanca Boulevard (at the Grimsby exit).

On the American side, the **Niagara Tourism and Convention Corporation** is at 345 Third St., Suite 605, Niagara Falls, NY (© **800/338-7890** or 716/282-8992; www.niagara-usa.com). Office hours are Monday to Friday from 8:30am to 5pm.

PUBLICATIONS & WEBSITES

The daily newspapers are *Niagara Falls Review, St. Catharines Standard, Fort Erie Review, Port Colborne Tribune,* and *Welland Tribune.* Several smaller communities publish weekly newspapers. *Niagara This Week* is a free local paper that carries local news and a listing of community events in its "It's Happening" section. Also published is the smaller *Free Daily Press.* Both are available at tourist information centers. On the U.S. side you'll find two dailies: *The Niagara Gazette* and *The Tonawonda News. The Current* is a free weekly. Online sources of information on the Niagara region include **www.tourismniagara.com**, **www.niagarafallstourism.com**, **www.info niagara.com**, **www.niagaraparks.com**, and **www.niagarapeninsula.com**. For information more closely tied to specific areas and towns, visit the websites of the tourist information centers listed in "Visitor Information," above.

LAYOUT OF THE REGION

The **Niagara region** is a peninsula bordered by **Lake Ontario** to the north, the **Niagara River** to the east, and **Lake Erie** to the south. A ridge of land known as the **Niagara Escarpment,** characterized by a steep face on one side and a gentle slope on the other, rises from Queenston on the Niagara River and runs east to west through the region. The other major physical structure in the landscape is the **Welland Canal,** which connects Lake Ontario with Lake Erie via a series of eight locks and roughly divides the region in half. At the head of the Canal sits the port city of **St. Catharines.** Moving south along the Canal, **Thorold,** with its Lock 7 Viewing Complex, is the next major place of interest. Farther south is the city of **Welland.** Finally, at the connection with Lake Erie lies the marine city of **Port Colborne.**

The **Falls** are situated midway along the Niagara River, which connects Lake Ontario and Lake Erie. They consist of two main waterfalls. The **American Falls** (which are, appropriately, located on U.S. soil) dramatically cascade onto tons of fallen rock that lie at the base of the waterfall. The **Horseshoe Falls,** located across the border in Canada, send clouds of mist into the air from their concave center. Afternoon sunlight creates a rainbow in the swirling droplets of water.

The cities of **Niagara Falls, Ontario** and **Niagara Falls, New York,** cluster around the Falls on either side of the border, connected by the **Rainbow Bridge** just downstream from the American Falls. Farther downstream, the **Lewiston–Queenston Bridge** provides another span across the **Niagara River.** Where the Niagara River flows into Lake Ontario proudly sits the town of **Niagara-on-the-Lake,** once the capital of Upper Canada.

At the opposite end of the Niagara River, the city of **Buffalo** lies on the southwestern edge of Lake Erie and the Niagara River, with the town of **Fort Erie** across the river in Canada. The **Buffalo–Fort Erie Peace Bridge** transports vehicular and foot traffic at this border crossing.

The major highway in the region is the Queen Elizabeth Way (QEW), which runs along the southern shore of Lake Ontario from Toronto, turning south as it makes its way through St. Catharines and eventually linking with I-190 across the border in Buffalo. Feeder highways siphon traffic off the QEW into St. Catharines (Hwy. 406), the Lewiston–Queenston Bridge to the U.S. (Hwy. 405), and Niagara Falls, Ontario (Hwy. 420).

The **winegrowing area** in the Niagara region is the sheltered section of land between Lake Ontario's south shore and the Niagara Escarpment, running from just west of Grimsby all the way to the Niagara River. An official **Wine Route Map** is available and the route is clearly marked with signposts along the roadways.

The Niagara Escarpment

The **Niagara Escarpment** forms the backbone of the Niagara Peninsula. The unique natural features of the escarpment and its ecological importance have been recognized by the United Nations Education, Scientific and Cultural Organization (UNESCO) and the escarpment has been duly designated as a **Man and the Biosphere Reserve.** The designation has elevated the escarpment's significance, joining the growing ranks of Biosphere Reserves that include the Galapagos Islands, the Serengeti National Park, and the Florida Everglades.

The Niagara Escarpment is a 1,050km (650-mile), crescent-shaped *cuesta*—a ridge formed by inclined rock strata, with a gentle slope on one side and a steep slope on the other. Its origin lies in New York State, south of Rochester. The ridge extends into Canada, running through Queenston on the Niagara River, bisecting the Niagara region from east to west, then traveling north before plunging into Lake Huron. It eventually ends at the Door Peninsula in Wisconsin in the midwestern United States.

The southern part of the escarpment, which contains the section that is found in Niagara, is located in Canada's warmest region, the **Carolinian Canada Zone.** It is a fragile ecosystem containing roughly one-quarter of the country's population and half of the endangered species—in an area that represents less than one-quarter of one percent of Canada's total landmass. This region is one of the most threatened of all Ontario's natural areas, and numerous organizations are involved in the preservation and conservation of the Niagara Escarpment's natural and cultural heritage.

The **Bruce Trail** follows the Niagara Escarpment through Ontario from Queenston Heights in the south to Tobermory at the northern tip of the Bruce Peninsula. The trail, which is marked by white blazes painted on trees, fence posts, and rocks, links parks and conservation areas along the route. The path is steep and rocky in places, but its rugged beauty, accented by waterfalls tumbling over the dolostone cliffs, is worth the effort. The trail offers a welcome escape from the urban landscape and agricultural development that cover much of the Niagara region.

THE REGION IN BRIEF

Niagara Falls, Ontario, Canada

The Niagara Falls area is the hub of the region. This is where you will find the mighty "thundering waters" of the powerful American Falls and the spectacular Canadian Horseshoe Falls. In a district that welcomes a mind-boggling 14 million visitors each year, it is no surprise that the City of Niagara Falls is geared to tourists like no other place on earth. Skyscraper hotels look over dozens of eateries on top of the hill in the area now officially known as the Fallsview District. Anchoring the hotel district, Clifton Hill exudes a boisterous carnival atmosphere. A protected strip of land lies between the Falls and the commercial mayhem of the city of

Niagara Falls. The Niagara Parks Commission is the steward of this beautiful oasis, which provides a delightful mix of immaculately groomed lawns and flowerbeds along the edge of the Falls and the Niagara Gorge. The world-famous *Maid of the Mist* tour boat can be boarded here. Traveling north along the western bank of the Niagara River, the scenic Niagara Parkway links Niagara Falls and Niagara-on-the-Lake by road, passing by the Niagara Parks Botanical Gardens, Butterfly Conservatory, Niagara Glen Nature Area, Floral Clock, McFarland House, Queenston Heights, Sir Adam Beck 2 Generating Station, and other places of interest.

Niagara Falls, New York, U.S.

You can take in the view of the Falls from the American side and also see the pre-falls rapids. The district includes the Niagara Falls State Park, the oldest state park in the United States. There are a number of other tourist attractions on the American side, including the *Maid of the Mist* (which launched here in 1846), Cave of the Winds, a boardwalk constructed next to the American Falls, and an observation tower. The infrastructure for tourists is not as well developed in Niagara Falls, New York, as it is in Niagara Falls, Ontario, however, so if you start your Niagara visit on the U.S. side of the border it's well worth crossing to Canada.

Niagara-on-the-Lake

Only a 1½-hour drive from Toronto, Canada's largest city, lies one of North America's prettiest and best-preserved 19th-century villages. The tranquil streets of Niagara-on-the-Lake are lined with mature trees. Dozens of immaculately restored and maintained historical brick and clapboard homes grace the town. The town center is home to the Shaw Festival, the best

boutique shopping in the Niagara region, B&Bs, inns, and a choice of fine restaurants. On the edges of the town you'll find a number of wineries, as well as Fort George National Historic Site. If you like tranquillity and elegance, base yourself in Niagara-on-the-Lake and tour the region from here.

Wine Route

The Niagara Peninsula is home to more than 60 wineries and is the largest designated viticultural area in Canada. The region is divided into three areas, each of which offers a variety of accommodations, primarily in B&Bs and inns, and restaurants ranging from exquisite winery cuisine to cozy tea shops and delicious ethnic fare.

Grimsby and Beamsville are the farthest west. This plateau of fertile land, which lies between the escarpment ridge and Lake Ontario, runs from Grimsby to just west of St. Catharines.

Jordan and Vineland is the next region you will meet as you travel east. This area offers art galleries, unique shopping in quaint villages, and the Bruce Trail, which at 850km (528 miles) is Ontario's longest footpath. The Bruce Trail can be accessed from several wineries that back onto the Niagara Escarpment. (Grimsby, Beamsville, Jordan and Vineland are all part of an area known as "The Bench.")

Niagara-on-the-Lake is the third viticultural area in Niagara (see above).

Welland Canal Corridor & Fort Erie

St. Catharines is the largest city in the Niagara region. The city has two main heritage districts—downtown St. Catharines (encompassing Queen Street Heritage District and Yates Street District, which feature fine examples of historical residential architecture) and

Fun Fact

Scientists speculate that at the present rate of erosion the Falls will no longer exist in 50,000 years, although a river will still flow between Lake Erie and Lake Ontario.

the lakeside village of Port Dalhousie. St. Catharines is known as the "Garden City" due to its surrounding vineyards, gardens, nurseries, and farmland. The Welland Canals Centre is located at Lock 3 along the Welland Canal.

Thorold, south of St. Catharines, offers another visitor-friendly viewing point, the Lock 7 Viewing Complex. The Twinned Flight Locks, which raise and lower ships up and down the Niagara Escarpment (42m/140 ft.), are also located in Thorold.

Welland is the next city along the canal. Canada's Rose City, Welland hosts a Rose Festival each summer. Recreational trails run alongside the canal here. Merritt Island, a haven for outdoor enthusiasts, is a highlight of the area.

Port Colborne is the community situated at the mouth of the Welland Canal and Lake Erie. The city's signature event is the Canal Days Marine Heritage Festival.

Fort Erie lies on the banks of the Niagara River, overlooking Buffalo and just a few minutes from the Peace Bridge. Attractions include Historic Fort Erie, Fort Erie Historical Museum, Ridgeway Battlefield Site, Fort Erie Railroad Museum, Mahoney Dolls' House Gallery, The Slave Quarters, and Fort Erie Racetrack.

2 Getting Around

BY CAR

A car is necessary if you wish to tour the entire region during your visit, but you do not need a car to get around in Niagara Falls. Public transit is not available between Niagara Falls and Niagara-on-the-Lake, but a shuttle bus runs between the bus terminal and certain hotels in Niagara Falls to Fort George in Niagara-on-the-Lake (© **800/667-0256** or 905/358-3232). The bus leaves in the morning and returns in the late afternoon. Niagara-on-the-Lake is small enough that you don't need a car. Wine country tours can be arranged through tour companies; see chapter 8 for details.

DRIVING RULES   In Ontario, a right turn on a red light is permitted after coming to a complete stop unless posted otherwise, provided you yield to oncoming traffic and pedestrians. Wearing your seat belt is compulsory. Fines for riding without a seat belt are substantial. Speed limits are posted and must be obeyed at all times. Always stop when pedestrians are using the crosswalks, and watch for pedestrians crossing against the lights. Radar detectors are illegal. American drivers should note the difference in speed limits—Canadian signs are calculated in kilometers, while U.S. are miles. To convert, divide the kilometers by 1.6 to obtain the mileage.

PARKING   Parking meters generally accept quarters, loonies, and toonies. Always read the signs posted near parking meters to find out if there are any parking restrictions. If you must leave your vehicle on a city street overnight, ask hotel staff or your B&B host whether there are parking restrictions. Parking meters are available in the city of Niagara Falls, New York, but I recommend that you park your vehicle in the Niagara Falls State Park. Meters are plentiful on both the U.S. and Canadian sides. Meter payment is required 7 days a week.

For **parking at the Falls,** you can leave your vehicle at the **Rapids View Parking Lot** for C$6.50 (US$5.40) (south of the Horseshoe Falls on the Niagara Parkway). The price includes a free shuttle to and from the Falls. Other options include purchasing a **People Mover Pass** at the parking lot (see below), which allows you unlimited on/off privileges on the People Mover transit system that runs between Table Rock at the Horseshoe Falls and Queenston Heights, north of the Niagara Gorge along the Niagara Parkway. The People Mover stops at most of the major tourist attractions along the route, including the *Maid of the Mist,* American Falls, Whitewater Walk, Whirlpool Rapids, Botanical Gardens & Butterfly Conservatory, and the Floral Clock. You can also elect to purchase a **Niagara Falls and Great Gorge Adventure Pass** at the parking lot (C$38/US$32 adult, C$24/US$20 children 6–12). This pass includes entry to major attractions and access to the People Mover for a single, discounted price. Additional parking is available opposite the Horseshoe Falls (all day for a single fee ranging between C$12 (US$9.95) and C$18 (US$15), and at the Niagara Parks Greenhouse south of the Horseshoe Falls (Apr–Nov C$3/US$2.50 per hour to a maximum of C$12/US$9.95; free in the winter). You will find a number of all-day parking lots with the reasonable fee of around C$5 (US$4) in the Fallsview district at the top of the escarpment. From here, you can take footpaths down to the Falls (ask your parking attendant for directions, since these paths are not well signposted), or travel on the **Incline Railway** (see below for details).

RENTAL CARS   If you decide to rent a car during the high season (generally May–Sept), try to make arrangements in advance to ensure the vehicle you want will be available. If you are traveling from outside Canada, you may obtain a reasonable discount by booking before you leave home. The rental fee depends on the type of car, but the starting point is around C$30 to C$50 (US$25–US$41) a day for a compact or midsize vehicle, plus taxes. This price does not include insurance, but some credit cards offer automatic coverage if you charge the full amount of the car rental to the card (check with your credit card issuer before you travel and bring the credit card you used to book your rental car with you when you pick up the vehicle). Be sure to read the fine print of the agreement and complete a thorough visual check for damage before accepting the vehicle. Some companies add conditions that will boost your bill if you don't fulfill certain obligations, such as filling the gas tank before returning the car. *Note:* If you're under age 25 or over 70, tell the rental company when you book— most companies have a minimum age policy, and some have implemented a maximum age as well.

Car rental insurance may not cover liability if you cause an accident. Check your own auto insurance policy, the rental company policy, and your credit card coverage

---

(*Fun Fact*

The brilliant green color of the Niagara River comes from dissolved minerals and finely ground rock, mostly from the limestone riverbed but also from the shale and sandstone under the limestone cap at the Falls.

Fun Fact

In the mid-1800s, Frederic Church, a talented landscape artist, painted a gigantic 2m-wide (7½-ft.) canvas of the Horseshoe Falls. Thousands of people flocked to view the painting when it was displayed in London, England. They were amazed by the power of the landscape, which Church had painted without the foreground in an attempt to give viewers the impression they were standing on the brink of the precipice. You can view a life-size reproduction of the painting behind the main service desk at the Niagara Falls Public Library, 4848 Victoria Ave., in Niagara Falls, Ontario.

for the extent of coverage. Is your destination covered? Are other drivers covered? How much liability is covered if a passenger is injured? (If you are relying on your credit card for coverage, you may want to bring a second credit card with you, as damages may be charged to your card and you may find yourself stranded with no money.)

BY PUBLIC TRANSPORTATION

BUS   Niagara Transit operates throughout the city of Niagara Falls and surrounding communities, including service to Brock University and Niagara College. The bus station is located at 4555 Bridge St., Niagara Falls, Ont. (© 905/356-1179; www.niagaratransit.com). The buses operate on an exact-fare basis: C$2.25 (US$1.87) adult, C$2 (US$1.68) student and senior, and C$1 (US83) child. Buses run regularly until midnight. Welland Transit has regular routes and the last run is 10:30pm (160 E. Main St.; © 905/732-6844, ext. 6; www.city.welland.on.ca/Transit/wTransit.html). The City of St. Catharines Transit Commission has regular bus routes and also services Thorold, with limited services in Niagara-on-the-Lake (© 905/687-5555; www.yourbus.com). The last St. Catharines bus leaves at 11:45pm. Niagara Falls, New York, runs buses via the Niagara Frontier Transportation Authority (© 716/855-7300; www.nfta.com). Rates depend on zones crossed starting at C$1.75 (US$1.50) within one zone to a maximum of C$2.63 (US$2.25) for four zones.

THE FALLS SHUTTLE   Owned and operated by the Niagara Transit Commission, the Falls Shuttle passes by tourist accommodations properties in the Lundy's Lane and River Road district. The **Red Line** serves Lundy's Lane, Via Rail Station, Bus Terminal, the Falls, and points of interest along the Niagara Gorge. The **Blue Line** serves the Fallsview area, including the Konica Minolta Tower, Skylon Tower, and Clifton Hill, traveling as far as Marineland. When the fireworks display over the Falls is in operation, every Friday and Sunday (10pm) and holidays from May 24 until September, a special **fireworks shuttle** takes tourists to the brink of the Falls. Fare is C$5 (US$4.15) per adult and tickets are available from shuttle bus drivers, the Niagara Bus Terminal, and most lodgings.

PEOPLE MOVER   This public transportation system, operated by the Niagara Parks Commission between April and October, is highly recommended for visitors to Niagara Falls. The spotless and air-conditioned buses shuttle between the main terminal beside Table Rock Plaza to the Horseshoe Falls and Queenston Heights Park along the Niagara River. Buses operate daily between April and October, although first and

Getting Married

If you want to join the ranks of millions of romantic couples who have gazed at the splendor of the Falls, there are dozens of organizations eager to help you and your beloved tie the knot in Niagara. If you've done the deed elsewhere and you're considering a post-wedding getaway, the Honeymoon Capital of the World awaits, complete with heart-shaped tubs in a plethora of motel rooms (see chapter 5, "Where to Stay," for a look at the region's coziest love nests). And for same-sex couples, the Niagara region is quickly becoming a popular destination.

Wedding Services   Niagara Falls Tourism has compiled a list of local photographers, wedding planners, florists, limos, and other wedding services. You can access this list at www.discoverniagara.com/play/main.

Same-sex couples   After you have obtained a license from City Hall, head to the Sheraton Fallsview Hotel & Conference Centre (6755 Fallsview Blvd.; ✆ **800/618-9059**) for a ceremony, reception, or honeymoon. For more information, visit www.gayniagara.com.

Venues   The **Niagara Parks Commission** (5881 Dunn St., Niagara Falls, Ont.; ✆ **877/642-7275;** www.niagaraparks.com) offers six beautiful outdoor locations for wedding ceremonies. **Oakes Garden Theatre** features graceful architecture and beautiful gardens, with the Bridal Veil Falls in full view across the Niagara Gorge. The Victorian-style lattice **wedding arbor** in the **Botanical Gardens** is a popular spot, as is the secluded **willow pond,** with its quaint wooden bridge. The elegant **Niagara Parks Greenhouse Garden,** surrounded by tall grasses and ponds, is the newest venue. Reservations can also be made for indoor wedding photos at the Greenhouse. Farther from the Falls, you will find the **Laura Secord Monument** at Queenston Heights and the **Mather Arch** in the town of Fort Erie. Weddings are also held at the **Queenston Chapel,** an 1862 white clapboard chapel that features oak pews and stained-glass windows.

Other popular wedding venues include **Niagara Fallsview Weddings,** located at the top of the Konica Minolta Tower overlooking the Falls. With

last trip times vary by season. All-day passes are available, which allow visitors to hop on and off at will. For more information call ✆ **905/357-9340.** Departs every 20 minutes. C$7.50 (US$6.20) adults, C$4.50 (US$3.70) children 6 to 12. Children 5 and under free. Pass includes unlimited rides on the Incline Railway.

INCLINE RAILWAY   This open-air car transports pedestrians up and down the cliff between the Fallsview tourist area and the Horseshoe Falls. The cost is C$2 (US$1.70) per trip or unlimited access with the purchase of a People Mover Day Pass.

BY BICYCLE

If you are fit and healthy, getting around rural Niagara (the wine country, Niagara Parkway, and Niagara-on-the-Lake) can be very enjoyable during the summer and the Pinnacle Restaurant and the Ramada Plaza Hotel located in the same tower, you can arrange the ceremony, reception, and honeymoon all in one location. You'll find the Tower at 6733 Fallsview Blvd., Niagara Falls, Ont. (✆ **866/325-5785** or 905/356-1501). **Niagara Fallsview Casino Resort** (6380 Fallsview Blvd., Niagara Falls, Ont. ✆ **888/325-57883**) offers a choice of two wedding chapels, or can arrange a wedding on their outdoor terrace overlooking the Falls. The **Little Wedding Chapel** (7701 Lundy's Lane, Niagara Falls, Ont.; ✆ **800/463-0884** or 905/357-0266) features candlelit services performed by licensed ministers and elegant white pews with seating for 40 people. **Niagara Weddings Canada** (5669 Main St., Niagara Falls, Ont.; ✆ **866/645-1714**) performs wedding ceremonies in various locations in the Niagara area, including the gazebo in **Niagara-on-the-Lake,** overlooking Lake Ontario. They also operate the **Wayside Chapel,** a tiny chapel beside the Niagara Parkway that holds a maximum of 8 people. **Two Hearts Wedding Chapel** (5127 Victoria Ave., Niagara Falls, Ont.; ✆ **866/251-1115** or 905/371-3204) is close to the Falls and City Hall. Religious and civil candlelit services are available. **The Wedding Company of Niagara** (6053 Franklin Ave., Niagara Falls, Ont.; ✆ **877/641-3111** or 905/371-3695) offers services in their chapel and off-site. If you would like to hold your wedding ceremony or reception in wine country, many of the wineries now host weddings. Make your inquiries directly with the wineries. See chapter 8 for contact information.

Marriage licenses   Licenses must be obtained prior to the ceremony and are valid for 3 months from the date of issue. You can apply in person for a marriage license at City Hall, Clerks Department, 4310 Queen St., Niagara Falls, Ont.; ✆ **905/356-7521.** The fee is C$100 (US$83), although the price is subject to change, and must be paid in cash. Both parties must be 18 years of age or over to obtain a license. Applicants who are 16 or 17 years of age must have parental consent. Two pieces of identification (original documents only) must be produced. Note that while same-sex marriages are recognized in Canada, they may not be accepted as legal in other countries.

early fall months. As a tourist, riding a bicycle is not practical in the larger towns, since the roadways heavily favor vehicular traffic. For bicycle rental information and tips on touring, see chapter 7, "What to See & Do in the Niagara Region."

BY TAXI

You can hail a taxi on the street, but you'll also find one readily at taxi stands in front of major hotels. You can also summon a taxi by phone: ✆ **905/357-4000** for Niagara Falls Taxi or ✆ **905/685-5463** for 5-0 Transportation. Other cab companies are listed in the Yellow Pages. On the American side, call LaSalle Cab Dispatch Service (✆ **716/284-8833**). Cabs will cross the Canada–U.S. border.

Fun Fact

The name "Niagara" has evolved from the North American Native word *Onguiaahra,* most often translated as "the strait," although the more poetic phrase "thunder of waters" is frequently attributed.

5-0 SHUTTLE   For service between Niagara Falls and Niagara-on-the-Lake, you can use the 5-0 Taxi shuttle bus. Pickup is at major hotels in Niagara Falls and the Niagara Falls Bus Terminal. One-way fare is C$10 (US$8.30) adult and C$5 (US$4) child. For more information call ℂ **800/667-0256** or 905/358-3232; www.5-0taxi.com.

FAST FACTS: Niagara Region

Airport For general inquiries, and for information on flights, baggage, and air freight, call the appropriate airline company; see "Getting There" in chapter 2. You can also obtain general information from the airport switchboards and on the relevant websites. **Toronto (Pearson) Airport** ℂ **866/207-1690** for all terminals or locally 416/247-7678 for Terminals 1 and 2 and 416/776-5100 for Terminal 3; www.gtaa.com. **Hamilton International Airport** ℂ **905/679-1999;** www.hamiltonairport.com. **Buffalo Niagara International Airport** ℂ **716/630-6000;** www.nfta.com. **Niagara Falls International Airport** is located at Niagara Falls Boulevard at Porter Road, Niagara Falls, New York (ℂ **716/297-4494;** www.nfta.com/nfairport). For information on transportation from the airports to Niagara, see "Getting There" in chapter 2.

Air Travel Complaints The Canadian Transportation Agency handles unresolved passenger complaints against air carriers. Information and complaint forms are available at www.cta-otc.gc.ca. For more information call the Canadian Transportation Agency (ℂ **888/222-2592**). You can also contact the Travel Industry Council of Ontario, a provincial government authority that deals with consumer matters including travel, at ℂ **888/451-8426** or 905/624-6241; www.tico.on.ca. In the United States, contact the Aviation Consumer Protection Division to file a complaint: www.airconsumer.ost.dot.gov or ℂ **202-366-2220** to complain about U.S. airline service.

American Express For card member services, including traveler's checks and lost or stolen cards, call ℂ **800/528/4800** or 363/393-1111 collect (only if your card is lost or stolen). There is an American Express Affiliated Travel Agency, which provides travel and financial services, at World Wide Travel One, 3714 Portage Rd., Niagara Falls, Ont. ℂ **905/353-8400.**

Area Codes The telephone area code for the Niagara region is 905. The area code in Niagara Falls, New York, is 716.

ATMs Walk-up cash machines that link to the Cirrus or PLUS networks can be found every few blocks at various bank branches. You can also get cash advances against your MasterCard or Visa at an ATM, but you'll need a separate personal identification number (PIN) to access this service, and will likely be charged interest from the time of withdrawal. ATMs generally charge a fee for each withdrawal unless the machine is operated by your own banking institution. Various convenience stores (U.S. and Canadian) also have ATMs.

Babysitting Hotel concierge or front desk staff can usually supply names and phone numbers of reliable sitters.

Business Hours Most **stores** are open Monday to Saturday from 9:30 or 10am to 6pm, and many have extended hours one or more evenings. Sunday opening hours are generally from noon to 5pm, although some stores open at 11am and others are closed all day. **Banks** generally open at 10am and close by 4pm, with extended hours one or more evenings; some are open Saturdays. **Restaurants** generally open at 11 or 11:30am for lunch and around 5pm for dinner, although many stay open all day. Hours for **attractions and museums** vary considerably depending on the season; refer to chapter 7, "What to See & Do in the Niagara Region," for individual opening hours. **U.S. banking** hours are generally 9am to 5pm Monday through Thursday, 9am to 6pm Friday, and Saturday 9am to 1pm.

Car Rentals See "Getting Around," earlier in this chapter.

Climate See "When to Go" in chapter 2.

Currency Exchange Generally, the best place to exchange your currency is at a bank or by obtaining local currency through an ATM. The Table Rock House Plaza, located on the Niagara Parkway, near the lip of the Horseshoe Falls, has a currency exchange center open 7 days a week (© **905/358-3268**). There is a currency exchange facility at **Niagara Clifton Currency Exchange** (4943 Clifton Hill, Niagara Falls, Ont.; © **800/668-8840**).

Dentists For emergency dental care, ask the front desk staff or concierge at your hotel for the name of the nearest dentist, or call the Ontario Dental Association Monday through Friday 8:30am to 4:30pm (© **416/922-3900**). In the United States, contact the American Dental Association for information: (© **312/440-2500**).

Directory Assistance For numbers within the same area code, call © **411, in the U.S. and Canada.** For other numbers, call © **555-1212,** prefixed by the area code of the number you're searching for. There is a charge for these services. In the U.S. call "0" for the operator to get a long-distance number.

Disability Services Many of Niagara's museums and public buildings, as well as many theaters and restaurants, are accessible to travelers with disabilities. For details, refer to *Accessible Niagara,* a free publication for mobility-impaired visitors and residents, or visit www.accessibleniagara.com. For more information, see "Travelers with Disabilities" in chapter 2.

Doctors Ask hotel staff or the concierge to help you locate a doctor. Some physicians will visit hotels. Walk-in clinics are available to out-of-province and international visitors, but be prepared to pay for services on the spot with cash. You will find walk-in medical clinics listed in the local Yellow Pages directory. For more information, see "Health & Safety" in chapter 2.

Documents See "Entry Requirements" in chapter 2.

Driving Rules See "Getting Around," earlier in this chapter.

Drugstores **Shopper's Drug Mart** has two late-night locations. Both are open until midnight 7 days a week: 6240 Lundy's Lane in Niagara Falls, Ont. (✆ **905/354-3845**) and 111 Fourth Ave. (Ridley Sq.) in St. Catharines (✆ **905/641-2244**). If you are a U.S. resident wanting a prescription filled, you must obtain a prescription from an Ontario licensed doctor. In Niagara Falls, New York, **Walgreens Drug Store** (1202 Pine Ave.; ✆ **716/285-0281**) is open 8am to 10pm Monday through Friday, Saturday 9am to 6pm, and Sunday 10am to 6pm. Visit Tonawanda—a 15-minute drive from Niagara Falls—for a 24-hour Walgreens (2601 Sheridan Dr.; ✆ **716/835-3346**).

Electricity It's the same as in the United States—110 to 115 volts, AC.

Embassies & Consulates All embassies in Canada (more than 100 in total) are located in Ottawa; consulates are primarily located in Toronto, Montreal, and Vancouver. Embassies include the **Australian High Commission,** 50 O'Connor St., Suite 710, Ottawa, ON K1P 6L2 (✆ **613/236-0841**); the **British High Commission,** 80 Elgin St., Ottawa, ON K1P 5K7 (✆ **613/237-1530**); the **Embassy of Ireland,** 130 Albert St., Ottawa, ON K1P 5G4 (✆ **613/233- 6281**); the **New Zealand High Commission,** 727–99 Bank St., Ottawa, ON K1P 6G3 (✆ **613/238-5991**); the **South African High Commission,** 15 Sussex Dr., Ottawa, ON K1M 1M8 (✆ **613/744-0330**); and the **Embassy of the United States of America,** 490 Sussex Dr., Ottawa, ON K1N 1G8 (✆ **613/238-5335;** www.usembassycanada.gov for general inquiries).

Emergencies Call ✆ **911** emergency services for fire, police, or ambulance. For the **Ontario Regional Poison Information Centre,** call ✆ **800/268-9017.** For the **Western New York Regional Poison Control Center,** call ✆ **800/222-1222.** When in Ontario, call **Telehealth Ontario** ✆ **866/797-0000** to speak with a registered nurse and have health questions answered, including whether your health situation should be deemed an emergency, urgent care, or regular consultation.

Eyeglasses For same-day service (perhaps as quick as 1 hour) on most prescriptions, try **Precision Optical,** Niagara Square, 7555 Montrose Rd. N., Niagara Falls, Ont. (✆ **905/356-5955**) or **Lenscrafters** in the Pen Centre shopping center at 221 Glendale Ave., St. Catharines (✆ **905/682-8000**). In New York, visit **Sterling Optical** (8962 Porter Rd.; ✆ **715/297-4994**).

Hospitals Emergency services are available at **Greater Niagara General Hospital,** 5546 Portage Rd., Niagara Falls, Ont. (✆ **905/358-0171**) and **St. Catharines General Hospital,** 142 Queenston St., St. Catharines (✆ **905/684-7271**). Ontario hospital emergency rooms are extremely busy and wait times for non-urgent cases are typically several hours. If at all possible, use a walk-in clinic; for more information see "Health & Safety" in chapter 2. On the U.S. side, **Niagara Falls Memorial Medical Center** offers emergency services (621 10th St.; ✆ **716/278-4000,** or **716/278-4394** emergency room).

Internet Access New wireless hotspots are popping up all over the place, so if you're equipped with the technology you should find it fairly easy to go online. Otherwise, try the public library. See "Libraries," below. **UPS Stores** offering paid Internet access include locations in St. Catharines at the Pendale Plaza 210

Glendale Ave. (✆ **905/682-5310**; in Niagara Falls at the Doubletree Resort Lodge & Spa (see chapter 5) and 4025 Dorchester Rd. ((✆ **905/357-4348**) and in Fort Erie 1243 Garrison Rd. ((✆ **905/994-8339**) and at the Welland Plaza 200 Fitch St. ((✆ **905/788-9993**).

Kids Help Phone Kids or teens in distress can call (✆ **800/668-6868** for help.

Laundry & Dry-Cleaning Most hotels provide same-day laundry and dry-cleaning services or have coin-operated laundry facilities.

Libraries In Ontario, the main branch of the Niagara Falls public library is located at 4848 Victoria Ave. ((✆ **905/356-8080**; www.nfpl.library.on.ca). The main branch of the St. Catharines public library is at 54 Church St. ((✆ **905/688-6103**). In Niagara-on-the-Lake, you'll find the library at 10 Anderson Lane ((✆ **905/468-2023**). Online databases, local history materials, and local photo galleries are just some of the resources available. In the U.S., visit the Niagara Falls Public Library (1425 Main St.; (✆ **716/286-4899**).

Liquor You must be **19 years of age or older** to consume or purchase alcohol in Ontario. Bars and retail stores are strict about enforcing the law and will ask for proof of age at their discretion. The **Liquor Control Board of Ontario (LCBO)** sells wine, spirits, and beer. Beer is also available through the Beer Store, with numerous locations in the Niagara region. Niagara wines may also be purchased at individual wineries by the bottle or case. You must be **21 years of age or older** to consume or purchase alcohol in the United States. Beer, and sometimes wine, can be purchased at local convenience stores. Liquor is sold through private proprietors.

Mail Mailing letters and postcards within Canada costs C51¢ (US44¢). Postage for letters and postcards sent from Canada to the United States costs C89¢ (US77¢), and overseas C$1.49 (US$1.30).

Newspapers & Magazines The daily newspapers are the *Niagara Falls Review, St. Catharines Standard, Fort Erie Review, Port Colborne Tribune,* and the *Welland Tribune.* Several smaller communities publish weekly newspapers. For entertainment listings in the St. Catharines area, pick up a copy of *The Downtowner* or *Pulse St. Catharines. The Brock Press* is Brock University's student newspaper. There are two local dailies in Niagara Falls, New York: the *Niagara Gazette* and the **Tonawonda News.** *The Current* is a free weekly.

Police In a life-threatening emergency or to report a crime in progress or a traffic accident that involves injuries or a vehicle that cannot be driven, call (✆ **911.** Non-emergency inquiries should be directed to (✆ **905/688-4111.** The Niagara Falls Police Department in New York can be reached at (✆ **716/286-4711** for non-emergency inquiries.

Post Offices Many convenience stores and drugstores offer postal services, and some have a separate counter for shipping packages during regular business hours. Look for the sign in the store window advertising such services. You will also find **Canada Post** outlets at 4500 Queen St. in Niagara Falls ((✆ **905/374-6667**), 4 Queen St. in St. Catharines ((✆ **905/688-4064**), and 117 Queen St. in Niagara-on-the-Lake ((✆ **905/468-3208**). For general information and delivery inquiries call (✆ **800/267-1177.** For postal code information call (✆ **900/565-2633** (there is a charge for this service). On the U.S. side, there are more than a half-dozen United States Postal Service locations in Niagara Falls—look for the blue-and-red storefront signage. For general information, as well as zip codes, visit **www.usps.com.** Central locations include 2020 Pine Ave. (front A) and 615 Main St. Call ✆ **800/ASK-USPS** for hours and other locations.

Public Transit Information For information on public transit, see "Getting Around," earlier in this chapter.

Radio The **Canadian Broadcasting Corporation (CBC)** broadcasts on **99.1 FM. CFLZ 91.9 FM** is operated by the Niagara Parks Commission and provides information about events, attractions, and bridges. Soft rock tunes are played on **CHRE FM-Light 105.7**. For news and talk radio, tune in to **AM610 CKTB**. Adult contemporary music features on **CHSC AM1220** and **CKEY FM 101.1.** For country music fans, there's **Spirit 91.7 FM/CHOW.** Fans of sports and '70s music should check out **CJRN AM 710.** Album-oriented rock takes the stage on **97.7 HTZ-FM.** Tune in to **AM930 WBEN** from Buffalo for news, traffic, weather, and sports. **WBFO FM88.7** plays jazz, the blues, and news. The local rock station is **KISS FM 98.5.**

Safety The Niagara region is generally safe for visitors. That said, it's never a good idea to take your safety for granted. In a region that welcomes 14 million visitors each year, it's wise to be alert and use common sense, particularly late at night. Keep a look out for pickpockets and thieves.

Taxes Canada's national Goods and Services Tax (GST) is 7%. In Ontario there is a provincial retail sales tax (PST) of 8% on most goods; certain purchases, such as groceries and children's clothing, are exempt from provincial sales tax. The accommodations tax is 5%.

In general, nonresidents may apply for a tax refund. They can recover the GST for nondisposable merchandise that will be exported for use, provided it is removed from Canada within 60 days of purchase. The following do not qualify for rebate: meals and restaurant charges, alcohol, tobacco, gas, car rentals, and services such as dry-cleaning and shoe repair.

The quickest and easiest way to secure the refund is to stop at a duty-free shop at the border. You must have original receipts with GST registration numbers. You can also apply through the mail, but it will take several weeks to receive your refund. For an application form and information, write or call the **Visitor Rebate Program** Enquiries Line (✆ **800/668-4748** within Canada, or 902/432-5608 outside Canada). The forms are available at tourism kiosks around town and in some shops. You can also get information and an application form online at www.cra-arc.gc.ca/visitors.

In Niagara Falls, New York, sales tax is 8% on all goods and accommodations. There are no duty-free stores in the U.S. To receive a tax refund on goods, visitors can receive tax-free purchases only if they ship their purchases home at the time of purchase. For more information visit www.tax.state.ny.us or call ✆ **800/972-1233**.

Taxis See "Getting Around," earlier in this chapter.

Telephone A local call from a telephone booth costs C25¢; Canadian and U.S. coins are accepted at face value. Watch out for hotel surcharges on local and long-distance phone calls; often a local call will cost at least C$1 (US85¢) from a hotel room. Canada and the United States are on the same long-distance system—to make a long-distance call between the two countries, use the area codes as you would at home. Canada's international prefix is **1**. Phone cards can be purchased at convenience stores and drugstores.

Time Niagara is on **Eastern Standard Time. Daylight saving time** is in effect from the first Sunday in April (clocks are moved ahead 1 hr.) to the last Sunday in October (clocks are moved back 1 hr.).

Tipping Basically, it's the same as in major U.S. cities—15% in restaurants (up to 20% in higher-end restaurants or for exceptional service and food, 10%–15% for taxis, C$1 (US85¢) per bag for porters, C$2 (US$1.65) per day for hotel housekeepers.

Weather For the weather forecast, check the daily newspaper, catch a radio broadcast, or tune in to the weather channel on TV. Some hotels post this information at the front desk.

Moments A Little Peace, Please

It can be quite a challenge to escape the crush of people jostling for prime viewing positions alongside the Falls, but there are a couple of places where you can avoid the crowds and still drink in the beauty of the rushing water.

On the Canadian side, head to **Navy Island,** located opposite Ushers Creek in Chippawa, at the northern tip of Grand Island closest to the Canadian shore. Home to French, British, and Canadian rebels and farmers, Navy Island was considered for both the 1960 World's Fair and the home of the United Nations, although neither plan came to fruition. The island now serves as a refuge for many species of wildlife, including deer. It's a popular spot for fishers, nature lovers, bird-watchers, and campers. The vegetation is lush, and in the summer you may be rewarded by the discovery of wild raspberries and grapes. The wide variety of trees includes pawpaw, oak, hickory, and blue beech. Be careful when venturing on a hike, though—the island also plays host to poison ivy. (Navy Island is only accessible in your own personal watercraft—there are no boat rentals or public transportation to the island.)

On the American side, head to **Three Sisters Islands,** tiny islands that jut out from Goat Island. You'll be close enough to the swirling rapids to dip your toes in, but take care near the water's edge, and keep children with you at all times. Looking out over the rapids in this spot, it's easy to forget the crowds of people behind you.

5

Where to Stay

Visitors looking for a place to stay in the Niagara region will find accommodations in a range of styles, although places tend to be a bit pricey unless you plump for one of the dozens of bargain-basement motels. (You should inspect these establishments in person before deciding whether they're right for you, even if you are on a shoestring budget, since the least expensive motels are extremely basic.) Whether your idea of the perfect place to call home during your vacation is a top-of-the-line high-rise tower, a romantic B&B, or a chic boutique hotel, you'll find a listing in this chapter to meet your needs.

For those traveling with children I strongly recommend staying in a one or two-bedroom suite with kitchenette facilities if your budget will allow, or hunt down a self-contained cottage in Niagara-on-the-Lake or along the shores of Lake Ontario. In return for your investment, you'll get a comfortable base with space for everyone to spread out, a place to make meals on your own schedule (you'll also save money by not having to eat out all the time), and usually more than one TV. You may even get some private time once the kids are asleep, when you can enjoy a glass of wine with your spouse as you watch the spectacular nightly illumination of the Falls. Couples looking for a more romantic getaway will do well to base themselves at an inn or B&B in Niagara-on-the-Lake or in the wine country and tour the region by car or bicycle.

Many of the properties listed in this chapter are clustered around the Falls themselves, or in the beautiful serene setting of Niagara-on-the-Lake. Wine-country choices abound, with everything from luxurious inns to cozy cottages for two and friendly B&Bs. If you are looking for somewhere off the beaten tourist path, head for Port Dalhousie or watch the majestic lakers and ocean-going freighters glide past your balcony alongside the Welland Canal.

PARKING If you have a vehicle with you, remember to factor in parking charges when estimating the cost of your accommodations if you plan to stay at one of the larger properties close to the Falls. Hotel parking rates at these locations vary from C$5 (US$4.15) to C$20 (US$17) per night.

AN IMPORTANT NOTE ON PRICES The prices quoted in this chapter are generally a range from the cheapest low-season rate up to corporate or rack rates (rack rates are the highest posted rates, although rooms are rarely sold at the full rack rate). In each listing, the prices include accommodations for two adults sharing. Discounts can result in a dramatic drop in the rate, typically anywhere from 10% to 50%.

Almost every hotelier I spoke with mentioned that weekend specials or family packages are available at various times throughout the year. Note also that 5% accommodations tax and 7% GST (Goods and Services Tax) are required by law to be added to your bill, but the GST is refundable to nonresidents upon application (see "Taxes" under "Fast Facts: The Niagara Region" in chapter 4).

A NOTE TO NONSMOKERS Happily, many of the properties in the Niagara Region are entirely or almost entirely non-smoking, partly due to a reduced demand for smoking rooms and partly due to the increasing trend toward smoking by-laws that prohibit smoking in public places. Typically 10% of the rooms in any given hotel are reserved for smokers. However, people who want a smoke-free environment should make that clear when reserving a room. Rooms for smokers are often clustered together at one end of the hallway, and the rooms and even the hallways adjacent to those areas tend to smell strongly of tobacco smoke, even in the cleanest hotels. Never assume that you'll get a smoke-free room if you don't specifically request one.

A NOTE ABOUT POOLS Please be aware that hotel pools are almost always **not** supervised by hotel staff. If you have children with you, make sure they are under your direct supervision in pool areas at all times.

BED-AND-BREAKFASTS The Niagara region, in particular Niagara-on-the-Lake and the River Road district in the city of Niagara Falls, has an abundance of gracious, older homes, many of which have been transformed into charming B&Bs. For the most part, B&Bs are located in quiet residential neighborhoods with tree-lined streets. If you're traveling solo or as a couple, then a B&B presents an economical and delightful alternative to a hotel room, but families will usually need to rent two rooms to secure enough sleeping area and that must be taken into account when estimating costs. Also, be aware that B&Bs and inns are usually geared to adult visitors. Many homes have expensive antiques on display and guests are expecting a quiet, restful stay. If you have children with you and they're young, boisterous, or both, then you're better off in a family-oriented property.

There are a number of resources available to assist you in the selection of a B&B or guesthouse property. In **Niagara-on-the-Lake,** you can contact the Chamber of Commerce Accommodation Booking Service at the Visitor and Convention Bureau (© **905/468-4263;** www.niagaraonthelake.com). They will search for availability using your personal criteria (price, type of accommodations required, number of guests in your party) and make a reservation for you at one of more than 200 bed-and-breakfast homes and cottages. A nominal booking fee is charged. If you are in the **Twenty Valley** region in the vicinity of Jordan and Vineland, in the heart of wine country, visit www.20valley.ca to view more than two dozen bed-and-breakfast and guesthouse accommodations. Another great online source is **niagarabb.com**, the home of **Niagara Bed and Breakfast Official B&B Directory** (© **905/988-3588**).

REDUCING YOUR ROOM RATE *Always* ask for a deal. Corporate discounts, club memberships (CAA, AAA, and others), and discounts linked to credit cards are just a few of the ways you can get a lower price. Rates between June and August are decidedly higher than the rest of the year and fluctuate wildly depending on the particular week; if any events are scheduled which increase the rates, try the following week. Weekend rates and getaway packages for couples and families are often available. Packages may include golf, spa treatments, attraction tickets or discounts, restaurant coupons, or other money-saving deals.

Saving on Your Hotel Room

The **rack rate** is the maximum rate that a hotel charges for a room. Hardly anybody pays this price, however, except in high season or on holidays. To lower the cost of your room:

- **Ask about special rates or other discounts.** Always ask whether a room less expensive than the first one quoted is available, or whether any special rates apply to you. You may qualify for corporate, student, military, senior, or other discounts. Mention membership in AAA, AARP, frequent-flier programs, or trade unions, which may entitle you to special deals as well. Find out the hotel policy on children—do kids stay free in the room or is there a special rate?

- **Dial direct.** When booking a room in a chain hotel, you'll often get a better deal by calling the individual hotel's reservation desk rather than the chain's main number.

- **Book online.** Many hotels offer Internet-only discounts, or supply rooms to Priceline, Hotwire, or Expedia at rates much lower than the ones you can get through the hotel itself. Shop around. And if you have special needs—a quiet room, a room with a view—call the hotel directly and make your needs known after you've booked online.

- **Remember the law of supply and demand.** Resort hotels are most crowded and therefore most expensive on weekends, so discounts are usually available for midweek stays. Business hotels in downtown locations are busiest during the week, so you can expect big discounts over the weekend. Many hotels have high-season and low-season prices, and booking the day after "high season" ends can mean big discounts.

1 Niagara Falls, Ontario & New York

With 14 million visitors to the Falls every year, you would expect the vicinity to be awash in hotels and motels—and you'd be right, at least on the Canadian side. There are fewer choices on U.S. soil.

Accommodations range from huge chains to quaint B&Bs to seedy motels. In general, hotels are much nicer on the Canadian side, although the Canadians have their share of dodgy digs (thankfully, these are easy to spot by their general outward appearance). In Niagara Falls, New York, your best bet is to pamper yourself at the elegant Red Coach Inn adjacent to the Niagara Falls State Park and within view of the Niagara River rapids. If that is too much of a squeeze on the finances, head up Niagara Falls Boulevard (Hwy. 62), where a number of chain hotels have staked their claim. The **Super 8,** 7680 Niagara Falls Blvd. (② **716/283-3151**) and **Econolodge,** 2000 Niagara Falls Blvd. (② **716/694-6696**) on this stretch of road are good choices—both properties are relatively recently built and are clean and bright.

The Niagara Falls area caters well to families, and the major hotels in town on the Canadian side woo honeymooners with packages galore. Staying in Niagara Falls means a lot of chain restaurants and nightlife, which centers on the carnival atmosphere of

- **Look into group or long-stay discounts.** If you come as part of a large group, you should be able to negotiate a bargain rate, since the hotel can then guarantee occupancy in a number of rooms. Likewise, if you're planning a long stay (at least 5 days), you might qualify for a discount. As a general rule, expect 1 night free after a 7-night stay.
- **Avoid excess charges and hidden costs.** When you book a room, ask whether the hotel charges for parking. Use your own cellphone, pay phones, or prepaid phone cards instead of dialing direct from hotel phones, which usually have exorbitant rates. And don't be tempted by the room's minibar offerings: Most hotels charge through the nose for water, soda, and snacks. Finally, ask about local taxes and service charges, which can increase the cost of a room by 15% or more. If a hotel insists upon tacking on a surprise "energy surcharge" that wasn't mentioned at check-in or a "resort fee" for amenities you didn't use, you can often make a case for getting it removed.
- **Book an efficiency.** A room with a kitchenette allows you to shop for groceries and cook your own meals. This is a big money saver, especially for families on long stays.
- **Consider enrolling in hotel "frequent-stay" programs,** which reward repeat customers who accumulate enough points or credits to earn free hotel nights, airline miles, complimentary in-room amenities, or even merchandise. These are offered not only by many chain hotels and motels (Hilton HHonors, Marriott Rewards, Wyndham ByRequest, to name a few), but individual inns and B&Bs. Many chain hotels partner with other hotel chains, car-rental firms, airlines, and credit card companies to give consumers additional ways to accumulate points in the program.

Clifton Hill and the glitz of the casinos—if that excites you, then the Falls is the place to be. Otherwise, you will find the much quieter atmosphere of Niagara-on-the-Lake or the tranquillity of the wine country more attractive.

VERY EXPENSIVE

Hilton Niagara Falls Fallsview 🏔🏔 *Kids*   Family focused, this monstrous 512-room hotel has an Adventure Pool, which includes a 10,000-square-foot pool complete with a waterslide and cascading waterfall. Above the pool, parents can work out in a fitness area. Kids can also play in the neighboring arcade. Rooms are generously proportioned—the idea is that each room can hold a good-size family if needed. Choose from rooms offering city views, or a view of the Canadian or U.S. falls—these are the real attraction, not the plain decor in the rooms. A unique feature in all suites is a two-person Jacuzzi tub with French doors opening up into the main bedroom. Watch TV from the tub! For families who travel en masse, a family suite offers two adjoining rooms (one king-size bed in one room and two queen-size beds in the other) with a connecting door. And with a couple of restaurants, there's something to please everyone. For the parents, the Watermark is an intimate dining experience with an in-wall sculpture of Poseidon, blue glass accents, and cascading waterfalls a must-visit.

For drinks afterward, the Blue Martini is on the top floor—33 floors up—a bird's-eye view of the Falls! And if you're feeling lucky, take a walk along the catwalk to the casino across the street, which offers a plethora of shops, more restaurants, and a spa. Room prices are cheaper when booked online or by phone in advance.

6361 Fallsview Blvd., Niagara Falls, Ont. ℂ **888/370-0325** or 905/354-7887. Fax 905/374-6707. www.niagarafalls hilton.com. 512 units. C$99–C$400 (US$82–US$332) double; suites from C$129 (US$107). Weekend packages. AE, DC, MC, V. Valet and self-parking C$20 (US$17). **Amenities:** Restaurant; bar; coffee shop; pool; golf nearby; hot tub; exercise room; spa; Jacuzzi; sauna; arcade; concierge; separate tour/activity desk; business center; shopping arcade; limited room service; massage; babysitting. *In room:* A/C, TV w/pay movies, dataport, coffeemaker, hair dryer, iron.

Marriott Niagara Falls Fallsview & Spa ✵✵✵ *Kids*

The amenities at this hotel are plentiful—so much so that you may never want to leave the hotel. Families traveling with children will love the entertainment possibilities—a pool, a PlayStation in the rooms, a game room, a clear view of the Falls from the rooms (including the fireworks display held on summer weekends), and much more. Holiday packages for families may include popcorn and movie night, complimentary tickets to one or more local attractions, and a magician's workshop. There are family shows in the on-site live theater and a kids' club to keep the little darlings busy. The hotel is only 90m (300 ft.) from the Falls and built in a curving design that allows virtually every room an unobstructed view. Even the standard rooms are generously sized with large bathrooms; upgraded rooms let you take a whirlpool bath with the Falls just a glance away.

6740 Fallsview Blvd., Niagara Falls, Ont. ℂ **888/501-8916** or 905/357-7300. Fax 905/357-0490. www.niagarafalls marriott.com. 427 units. C$99–C$399 (US$82–US$331) double; suites from C$189 (US$157). Packages available. AE, DC, DISC, MC, V. Valet parking C$13 (US$11). **Amenities:** Restaurant; lounge; large indoor pool; exercise room; spa; 2 Jacuzzis; sauna; children's programs; game room; concierge; tour desk; courtesy car; business center; limited room service; massage; babysitting; laundry service; same-day dry cleaning; executive-level rooms. *In room:* A/C, TV w/pay movies, dataport, minibar, coffeemaker, hair dryer, iron, safe.

Sheraton Fallsview Hotel & Conference Centre ✵✵✵

At the far end of Fallsview Boulevard, away from the hustle of the casino area, lies the Sheraton Fallsview. The hotel expanded in recent years, bringing the total number of rooms over the 400 mark. Rooms on the upper floors have the best views of the Falls and are better appointed. All rooms feature the signature Sheraton "Sweet Sleeper" beds, which are among the most comfortable, luxurious beds anywhere. For a honeymoon, book one of the loft suites. With their two-story bank of windows overlooking the Falls, contemporary earth-tones decor, fireplace, and bedroom on the upper level, they are a luxury worth splashing out on. Take advantage of in-room candlelight dining for the ultimate romantic evening. Families are also welcomed here, with several packages; during Christmas and March breaks, a kids' club operates daily from noon to 9pm.

6755 Fallsview Blvd., Niagara Falls, Ont. ℂ **905/374-1077.** www.sheraton.com/fallsview. 402 units. C$99–C$349 (US$82–US$290) standard double; C$209–C$609 (US$174–US$505) suite. Children 18 and under stay free in parent's room. AE, DC, DISC, MC, V. Self-parking C$10–C$20 (US$8–US$17); valet parking C$25 (US$21). Dogs up to 36kg (80 lb.) accepted, C$25 (US$21) per stay. **Amenities:** 3 restaurants; bar; indoor pool; golf course nearby; exercise room; hot tub; sauna; limited children's programming; concierge; shuttle for local area; business center; limited room service; massage; babysitting; laundry service; dry cleaning; executive floor. *In room:* A/C, TV w/pay movies, dataport, coffeemaker, hair dryer, iron.

Sheraton on the Falls ✵✵

Before the building boom on Fallsview Boulevard a few blocks away, the Sheraton on the Falls was the most upscale hotel in the area. Right in the heart of the touristy Clifton Hill neighborhood, this high-rise hotel faces the American Falls. Kids can enjoy the enormous pool and amusement park, while parents can dine at nearby restaurants including the Hard Rock Cafe and Planet Hollywood. Get

Niagara Falls Accommodations

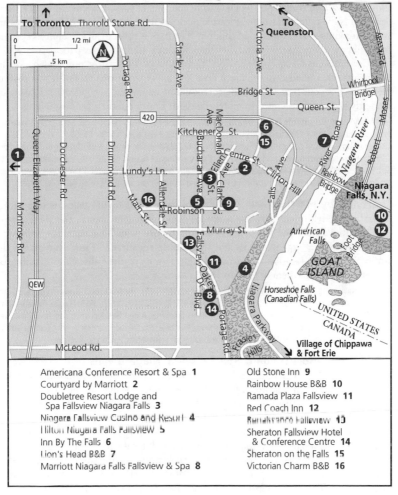

Americana Conference Resort & Spa **1**	Old Stone Inn **9**
Courtyard by Marriott **2**	Rainbow House B&B **10**
Doubletree Resort Lodge and	Ramada Plaza Fallsview **11**
Spa Fallsview Niagara Falls **3**	Red Coach Inn **12**
Niagara Fallsview Casino and Resort **4**	Renaissance Fallsview **13**
Hilton Niagara Falls Fallsview **5**	
Inn By The Falls **6**	Sheraton Fallsview Hotel
Lion's Head B&B **7**	& Conference Centre **14**
Marriott Niagara Falls Fallsview & Spa **8**	Sheraton on the Falls **15**
	Victorian Charm B&B **16**

a splash of the mist on your face from some coveted rooms that have balconies facing the Falls.

5875 Falls Ave., Niagara Falls, Ont. ⓒ **888-229-9961** or 905/374-4445. Fax 905/371-0157. 670 units. Nov–Apr double C$99–C$399 (US$82–US$331); May–June and Sept–Oct double C$129–C$399 (US$167–US$331); July–Aug double C$199–C$499 (US$165–US$414). Packages available. AE, DC, MC, V Valet parking C$19 (US$16). **Amenities:** 4 restaurants; lounge; 2 pools (indoor, heated outdoor); health club; spa; sauna; children's programs in summer; concierge; tour desk; small business center; shopping arcade; 24-hr. room service; massage; laundry service; dry cleaning. *In room:* A/C, TV w/pay movies, coffeemaker, hair dryer, iron.

EXPENSIVE

Americana Conference Resort & Spa *Kids* Head west on Lundy's Lane, past dozens of insignificant strip motels, and you will eventually land at the Americana, a re-vamped two/three-story motel that has recently aspired to resort status through the addition of a spa, conference center, and indoor water park. It seems to be the water park that is the main attraction, at least at peak vacation periods when the hallways are awash in swimsuit and towel–clad children. The park is open to all ages, but its size and amenities are more suited to children than teens or adults. Water-park passes, which retail for C$20 to C$30 (US$17–US$25) for a mere 4 hours for nonresidents of the Americana, are included in the room rates and allow unlimited access. If you plan to spend most of your time in the park, this could be construed as good value. Rooms are modestly sized and decorated to motel standard. Entire building is nonsmoking.

8444 Lundy's Lane, Niagara Falls, Ont. ℂ 800/263-3508 or 905/356-8570. Fax 905/356-9233. www.americananiagara. com. 209 units. C$119–C$299 (US$99–C$248) room with 2 queen-size beds; C$199–C$399 (US$165–US$331) 2-room suite. Up to 4 water park passes included in rates. Up to 2 children age 16 and under stay free in parent's room. Additional room occupants around C$30 (US$25) each, depending on season. AE, DC, MC, V. Free parking. **Amenities:** Restaurant; bar; indoor water park; exercise room; spa on-site; hot tub; sauna; arcade/game room; business center; limited room service; massage; babysitting; washers and dryers. *In room:* A/C, TV, coffeemaker, hair dryer.

Courtyard by Marriott ☆☆
Presidential suites offer luxury and comfort with a Jacuzzi, while whirlpool king-size suites are also a decadent choice. But there's room for the entire family and more in a two-room family suite. This tastefully decorated, newer hotel has a large pool area and fine-dining restaurant to suit everyone in the family. It's a great location next to all the attractions of the Falls without being too immersed in the mayhem of Clifton Hill.

5950 Victoria Ave., Niagara Falls, Ont. ℂ 800/321-2211 or 905/358-3083. Fax 905/358-8720. www.nfcourtyard.com. 258 units. June–Aug C$99–C$399 (US$82–US$331) double, C$159–C$399 (US$132–US$331) suite. Packages available. AE, DC, MC, V. Self-parking June–Aug C$8 (US$7), other times free. **Amenities:** Indoor/outdoor pool; small exercise room; Jacuzzi; sauna; children's programs; game room; tour desk; limited room service; laundry; coin-op laundry; same-day dry cleaning. *In room:* A/C, TV w/pay movies, dataport, coffeemaker, hair dryer, iron, safe.

Doubletree Resort Lodge & Spa Fallsview Niagara Falls ☆☆
The foyer of this hotel has a ski-lodge-resort feel—expansive ceilings decorated with wooden beams and an abundance of fieldstone. Continue the opulent feeling at the Five Lakes Spa AVEDA. Enjoy a herbal body masque, Dead Sea mud body wrap, or rosemary and mint body wrap. Departing these elegant touches the rooms are standard hotel fare—but spacious and warmly decorated in cherry and burgundy wood furniture. And despite its big-hotel feel, each room is decorated with local fallsview art and black-and-white photos of Ontario from days gone by. Unfortunately, the complimentary breakfast at Buchanan's isn't on a par with the rest of the hotel; the basic breakfast is similar to diner food. The pool is separated in two: a two-lane, 11m (35-ft.) pool sits above a shallow pool for the kids. There's an outside hot tub in the summer surrounded by trees from Ontario's Algonquin Park. A new art gallery called the Ochre Gallery features beautiful Canadian landscape art and totem poles from British Columbia.

6039 Fallsview Blvd., Niagara Falls, Ont. ℂ 800/730-3817 or 905/358-3817. Fax 905/358-3680. www.niagarafalls doubletree.com. 224 units. C$99–C$299 (US$82–US$248) double; suites from C$119 (US$99). Children 18 and under stay free in parent's room. Weekend packages. AE, DC, MC, V. Self-parking C$10 (US$8). **Amenities:** Restaurant; coffee pub; indoor pool; golf nearby; exercise room; spa; seasonal hot tub; sauna; arcade; concierge; seasonal activity desk; business center; limited room service; massage; babysitting; same-day laundry/dry cleaning Mon–Fri only. *In room:* A/C, TV w/pay movies, dataport, coffeemaker, hair dryer, iron.

Niagara Fallsview Casino Resort ☆☆
If you want to be pampered, try this upscale Canadian version of Las Vegas. Shop at swanky stores like Swarovski, play your luck at the expansive gambling casino, or treat yourself to a pedicure—this recently opened casino is a self-contained biosphere of hedonism. The Diplomat suite

has a spectacular view, overlooking both the American and Horseshoe Falls. Parlour suites have an enclosed TV/sofa area with desk to keep work and sleep time separate. The bright, white-tiled pool area, with large tropical plants and glass window, feels like an exotic spa. To get the full spa treatment, walk down the hall from the pool for pedicures and therapeutic massages. Next door is an impressive workout room—all new machines facing four large flatscreen TVs. Staff come by frequently with fresh towels for guests' use. Jacuzzis are located in all suites, plus the spa and pool areas. Everything feels new and flashy throughout the resort as sun beams through the glass entrance onto shiny silver fixtures. In the main lobby stands an enormous water fountain fashioned with giant steel mechanical parts overflowing with surreal blue water. Several times a day the "Hydro-Teslatron" comes alive for a seven-minute show simulating an electrical disaster: lasers, LED, electricity, and loudspeakers reveal the true power of water. Many of the casino guests are baby boomers and can be seen ambling around the expansive lobby and trendy shops. But there's also a younger crowd courting Lady Luck in the casino, looking to make a few bucks. Romantics can get married in the on-site chapel and take advantage of a wedding package with all the trimmings. Choose from 10 different restaurants—ranging from gourmet pan-Asian, Pinto Dolce (an Italian ice-cream parlor), or The Famous, a 24-hour retro diner serving breakfast all day. If you want Vegas-style amusements, the 365 Club offers up live entertainment.

6380 Fallsview Blvd., Niagara Falls, Ont. ☏ 888/FALLSVU or 905/358-3255. Fax 905/371-7952. www.fallsviewcasino resort.com. 374 units. C$129–C$169 (US$107–US$140) double; suites from C$229 (US$190). AC, DC, MC, V. Self-park C$10 (US$8). Small pets accepted (cage). **Amenities:** 10 restaurants; 4 bars; pool; golf nearby; hot tub; exercise room; Jacuzzi; sauna; bike rental (summer); concierge; business center; shopping arcade; hair salon; 24-hr. room service; massage; babysitting; laundry service; same-day dry cleaning; executive floor. *In room:* A/C, TV w/pay movies, dataport, coffeemaker, hair dryer, iron, safe.

Old Stone Inn   Sporting thick wooden beams and stone walls, this motel-style inn was once a turn-of-the-century flourmill and attracts mainly a quiet, mature crowd and corporate clients. The late Former Canadian prime minister Pierre Trudeau and the late actor Christopher Reeve have been a few of the distinguished guests to visit over the years. See their pictures on the way into the dimly lit, high-ceilinged restaurant, which has a real wood burning fireplace and simple chandeliers. Or for something more intimate, have a seat in a plush chair beside the fire in the Rendezvous Lounge. Rooms are spacious, clean, and cozy but the decor, even in the updated rooms, is slightly old-fashioned, with white bedspreads and brass-accented furniture. A portion of the rooms are under renovation, due for completion in 2006. The entire property is nonsmoking. Located just a short walk from downtown, it's situated on a busy commercial street.

5425 Robinson St., Niagara Falls, Ont. ☏ 800/263-1234 or 905/357-1234. Fax 905/357-9299. www.oldstoneinn.on.ca. 111 units. C$85–C$199 (US$70–US$165) double; suites from C$177–C$399 (US$147–US$331). Children 12 and under stay free in parent's room. Weekend packages. AE, DC, MC, V. Free parking. **Amenities:** Restaurant, lounge; pool (indoor, outdoor); golf nearby; hot tub; Jacuzzi in some rooms; limited room service; massage; babysitting; same-day cleaning; executive floor. *In room:* A/C, TV w/pay movies, dataport, coffeemaker, hair dryer, iron.

Red Coach Inn   This 1920s-era Tudor-style hotel with its distinctive gabled roof is the most luxurious property on the American side of the Falls by a nautical mile, and its individuality is worth crossing the border for. The prices are set at a reasonable level for the high standard of service and room amenities, and the restaurant is worth eating in. Located just across the street from the Niagara River rapids, you're at the gateway of Niagara Falls State Park's attractions. The standard rooms are rather small compared with the suites, which are more like apartments, with full kitchens, dining tables, and comfortably upholstered furniture for relaxing in. Suites also enjoy a view of the rapids, separate bedroom, and spacious bathrooms. The feel of the place is like an English country house.

2 Buffalo Ave., Niagara Falls, NY. ℂ **800/282-1459** or 716/282-1459. www.redcoachinn.com. 19 units. C$119–C$215 (US$99–US$179) double; C$155–C$431 (US$129–US$359) suite. Packages available. AE, DISC, MC, V. **Amenities:** Restaurant; lounge. *In room:* A/C, TV/VCR, dataport, fridge, coffeemaker, hair dryer.

Renaissance Fallsview *↔*   Bright reds and yellows liven up this large hotel, which is a good bet for families. Adjoining rooms mean parents can have some peace and quiet, while kids can talk all night. Rooms are very spacious, particularly the Executive Fallsview, with two doubles (or a king-size) in one room adjoined to a room with another two queen-size—not to mention a great view of the Horseshoe Falls. Or for the adults, choose from a spacious deluxe room with Jacuzzi (heart-shape tubs are optional) and king-size bed. Kids 12 and under receive half price on meals, and 5 and under eat free. Cribs and rollaway beds are complimentary. Squash and racquetball are available beside the small gym, which is in need of better ventilation. Located in the heart of Niagara Falls, there is a convenient catwalk attached to the casino, which is loaded with more restaurants, shops, and spa services.

6455 Fallsview Blvd., Niagara Falls, Ont. ℂ **800/363-3255** or 905/357-5200. Fax 905/357-7487. www.renaissance fallsview.com. 262 units. C$89–C$299 (US$74–US$248) double; suites from C$129 (US$107). Children 18 and under stay free in parent's room. Weekend packages. AE, DC, MC, V. Valet, self-parking C$18 (US$15). **Amenities:** 2 restaurants; lounge; pool; golf nearby; exercise room; hot tub; Jacuzzi; sauna; children's programs; game room; seasonal concierge; business center; shopping arcade attached via catwalk to casino; limited room service; massage; babysitting; same-day dry cleaning; executive floor. *In room:* A/C, TV w/pay movies, fridge available C$10 (US$8), coffeemaker, hair dryer, iron.

MODERATE
Ramada Plaza Fallsview *↔* *Value*   A landmark of Ontario's Niagara Falls skyline for decades, the Ramada Plaza Fallsview Hotel features a mere 42 guest rooms, all in a pod at the top of the Konica Minolta Tower Centre. This gives the property a distinctive boutique hotel feel. It's a great place for a quiet weekend getaway—just try not to think about the fact that all the rooms are suspended hundreds of feet above the lobby, with only a concrete elevator shaft linking them to the ground.

The lobby has been recently refurbished in a minimalist style. The rooms, which are quite comfortably appointed, will be given a similar face-lift beginning in 2006, with a switch from patterned quilted bedspreads to neutral colors and boutique-hotel touches. The fallsview rooms have fabulous views, but the quirky room shapes, with their outward-leaning windows, can give you quite a dizzy turn. The location on Fallsview Boulevard is convenient for walking to the Falls, riding the Incline Railway to the base of the hill, or heading out for dinner or to one of the casinos. Guests have access to the exercise room and pool at the Radisson Hotel. Weddings are a specialty. Staff are courteous and efficient.

6732 Fallsview Blvd., Niagara Falls, Ont. ℂ **866/325-5784** or 905/356-1501. Fax 905/356-8245. www.niagara tower.com. 42 units. Double C$89–C$199 (US$74–US$165). AE, DC, MC, V. Valet parking C$10 (US$8). **Amenities:** Restaurant; bar; golf course nearby; limited room service; massage; same-day laundry and dry cleaning. *In room:* A/C, TV w/pay movies, dataport, fridge, coffeemaker, hair dryer, iron, safe.

Victorian Charm B&B *Value* *Kids*   Starched embroidered linens, a piano in the foyer, and a turret combine to make the name appropriate. The Garden Room—my favorite—has a terrace overlooking the garden, a remote-controlled fireplace, and an air-jet therapeutic tub. Decorated with white wicker furniture and yellow walls, it's an airy and fresh room. The Grande Room has a mini–living space with sofa and bath-tub in the room, while the bathroom is located immediately outside the door. Add some lavender salts to your bath, which are provided free, or have a massage from a local masseuse on the fold-up massage table. Or stay in and watch your VCR, with a large selection of movies to choose from. Owner Anne Marie, the mother of five children, is happy to cater to the little ones—there is a brand-new crib, and a carriage and stroller are ready to go for a jaunt through the quiet residential area, only a short walk from the casino and Falls. For breakfast, try the Belgian waffles with fruit from Anne Marie's organic garden (or preserves in the winter), or savor the crepes with whipped cream and maple syrup. Wireless Internet access available.

6039 Culp St., Niagara Falls, Ont. ℂ 877/794-6758 or 905/357-4221. Fax 905/357-9115. www.victoriancharmbb.com. 5 units. C$120–C$185 (US$100–US$154) double. Rates include breakfast. Weekly rates 1 day free. AE, MC, V. Free parking. Kids welcome. **Amenities:** Golf nearby; spa available in room; Jacuzzi; free train station pickup/drop off; massage; babysitting; washers/dryers. *In room:* A/C, TV/VCR, dataport, fridge, coffeemaker, hair dryer, no phone. No smoking.

INEXPENSIVE

Inn by the Falls *(Value*   Simply decorated, good prices, and a central location make this hotel a great place to sleep but not necessarily to linger. Rooms are furnished in a basic manner, but they're clean and spacious. Want the authentic Niagara Falls motel experience? This is one of the places you can jump into a heart-shaped Jacuzzi tub. In the summer enjoy the open courtyard and pool area, set back from the hustle and bustle of Clifton Hill. Rooms closer to the front of the hotel tend to be noisy—get one farther back near the courtyard. Ask about packages that include breakfast and casino vouchers.

5525 Victoria Ave., Niagara Falls, Ont. ℂ 800/263-2571 or 905/374-6040. Fax 905/374-7715. www.innbythefalls.net. 80 units. C$50–C$199 (US$42–US$165) double. Packages available. AE, DC, DISC, MC, V. **Amenities:** Outdoor pool; Jacuzzi. *In room:* TV, coffeemaker, hair dryer.

Lion's Head B&B *✿✿*   This historical bed-and-breakfast hasn't changed structurally since 1910. Overlooking the gorge, it's a cozy retreat from the bright lights and tall

---

Family-Friendly Sleepovers

Where can you take the kids and have fun at the same time? You'll find a warm welcome at **Victorian Charm B&B**, 6039 Culp St., Niagara Falls, Ont.; ℂ **877/794-6758**. Crib, carriage, and stroller are waiting for your little one. Crepes and Belgian waffles will put a smile on sleepy faces. If your kids like nonstop entertainment, head for the **Marriott Niagara Falls Fallsview & Spa**, 6740 Fallsview Blvd., Niagara Falls, Ont.; ℂ **888/501-8916**. With a pool, game room, kids' club, live family theater, PlayStation, and movie and popcorn nights, your children will play hard and sleep well. For a country vacation, experience the charm of the farm at **Feast of Fields Organic Vineyard B&B Cottage**, 3403 11th St., Jordan, Ont.; ℂ **905/562-0151**. This self-contained two-bedroom cottage with full kitchen is part of a restored farmhouse (ca. 1835). The surrounding paddocks are inhabited not only by horses and cows, but also llamas and a peacock or two.

buildings of downtown Niagara Falls, which is only a 10-minute walk away. Each room is decorated in keeping with its artist namesake—the coral pink walls and dark wood furniture in the Georgia O'Keeffe Room are decidedly bohemian, while the luminescent yellows of the van Gogh are as bright as a sunflower. The third-floor French Quatres room offers privacy for a couple with its own entrance, while friends can be accommodated in an adjacent room.

The eclectic, funky decor throughout the home reflects owner Helena Harrington's effervescent personality and world travels, as does her breakfast menu, which is constantly changing—recent dishes include stuffed tomatoes with asiago cheese and her signature poached pears with orange spice glaze and yogurt topping. And don't expect plain old table sugar—hers is imported from France, and the maple syrup hails from Quebec. More added touches in the rooms include goose-down bedding and Italian ceramic tiles—all handpicked by Helena, who goes to painstaking lengths to get the color and feel of every room exactly to her liking.

5239 River Rd., Niagara Falls, Ont. © **905/374-1681**. www.lionsheadbb.com. 5 units. C$95–C$125 (US$79–US$104) double. Rates include gourmet breakfast. AE, MC, V. Free parking. **Amenities:** Golf nearby; massage. *In room:* A/C, hair dryer, iron. No smoking.

Rainbow House B&B   A historical Victorian home with wrought-iron beds, embroidered doilies, stained-glass windows, and heaps of charming clutter. Think whitewashed wicker furniture and lots of collectables. Owner Laura Lee takes pride in her cozy home and has made it extremely cheery and welcoming. Standard rooms offer better value than the suite. If you get the urge to get hitched in the honeymoon capital of the world, there is a wedding chapel conveniently located on the premises. This property is best suited to adults and older children.

423 Rainbow Blvd. S., Niagara Falls, NY. 14303 © **800/724-3536** or 716/282-1135. Fax 716/292-1135. www.rainbow housebb.com. 4 units. C$66–C$174 (US$55–US$145) double. Packages available. Rates include breakfast. MC, V. Free parking. *In room:* A/C, hair dryer, iron. No smoking.

2 Niagara-on-the-Lake

Niagara-on-the-Lake, with its historical streets, fine choice of restaurants, and boutique shopping, is an attractive place to spend a night or two. Adult vacationers without children in tow will find the town to be a welcome contrast to the razzmatazz of Niagara Falls.

There are literally hundreds of B&Bs in Niagara-on-the-Lake, and the majority of them are located in meticulously restored historical properties. In addition, there are a number of luxurious inns from which to choose. Don't let the plethora of accommodations lull you into thinking you can breeze into town and find somewhere to stay on a whim, though. Niagara-on-the-Lake is highly popular for overnight stays, particularly in the summer months, and there is often no room at the inn (or the B&B, or the guest cottage). Although you are strongly advised to book ahead, the consistency of the quality of properties in this area is quite remarkable, and you are extremely unlikely to be disappointed wherever you end up staying. You'll find that proprietors and staff are experienced in hosting guests and eager to share knowledge of the area that will enhance your vacation, whatever your special interests and needs may be.

VERY EXPENSIVE

Charles Inn   Built shortly after the War of 1812, this grand Georgian-style inn, with sweeping verandas and stately gardens, takes you back to a simpler time, nicely

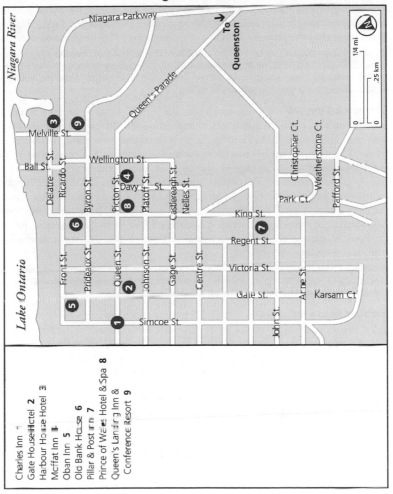

Niagara Parkway

Niagara River

To Queenston

Queen's Parade

Melville St.

Wellington St.

Ball St.

Christopher Ct.

Weatherstone Ct.

Pafford St.

Delatre St.

Ricardo St.

Byron St.

Picton St.

Davy St.

Platoff St.

Castlereagh St.

Nelles St.

Park Ct.

King St.

Regent St.

Lake Ontario

Front St.

Prideaux St.

Queen St.

Johnson St.

Gage St.

Centre St.

Victoria St.

Arne St.

Gale St.

Karsam Ct

John St.

Simcoe St.

1/4 mi

.25 km

Charles Inn **1**
Gate House Hotel **2**
Harbour House Hotel **3**
Moffat Inn **4**
Oban Inn **5**
Olde Bank House **6**
Pillar & Post Inn **7**
Prince of Wales Hotel & Spa **8**
Queen's Landing Inn & Conference Resort **9**

overlaid with modern amenities. The Verandah Room backs onto the porch, once the kitchen of the homestead—the large fireplace and cast-iron bake oven remain, and you can still smell the bread cinders if you take a good whiff inside. Most rooms have a fireplace (gas or wood-burning) to add to the ambience, although the smaller rooms (Magnolia, Renoir, Apple, and Sunflower) do not. The Verandah Room and the Richardson Room feel like a step back in time, with four-poster beds and antique furniture, whereas other rooms such as the Magnolia, Safari, and Poppy feature modern, elegant decor. Bed linens are 300-thread-count Egyptian cotton, while the duvets and pillows are down-filled. Creaking floors and wooden antique furniture throughout the property add to the experience—you could swear former owner Charles Richardson is smiling down at you. After supper in the fine-dining restaurant, sip cognac on a bar stool at the newly constructed oak bar in the lounge. If you want to be active, the backyard spills onto the Niagara-on-the-Lake golf course, one of the oldest in North America. Breakfast includes seasonal freshly squeezed orange juice from gigantic Osage trees surrounding the property. Wedding ceremony services are available on-site.

209 Queen St., Niagara-on-the-Lake, Ont. L0S 1J0 Ⓒ **866/556-8883** or 905/468-4588. www.charlesinn.ca. 12 units. Double C$99–C$325 (US$82–US$270). Weekend packages. AE, MC, V. Free parking. **Amenities:** Restaurant; lounge; enclosed veranda dining year-round; golf course next door; limited room service; massage; babysitting. *In room:* A/C, dataport, coffeemaker, hair dryer, iron, no phone. No smoking.

Gracewood Inn 𝕰𝕰   If you're looking for the perfect romantic getaway, this could be it. Set back from the Niagara Parkway and surrounded by mature pine and deciduous trees, this red-brick 1819 heritage home is decorated with warm, rich colors and fabrics. The property features two sitting rooms for guests, each with a fireplace. Two of the three guest rooms are large enough to incorporate a sitting area with comfortable upholstered furniture. The opulent bathrooms merit a special mention. Breakfast consists of a buffet or three-course breakfast and is included in room rates. On the extensive grounds, you'll find an outdoor pool, romantic walking paths, and formal English gardens with clipped boxwood hedges and perennials. Just minutes away by car from Niagara-on-the-Lake, and within walking distance of parks, recreational trails, and wineries.

16052 Niagara Pkwy., Niagara-on-the-Lake, Ont. L0S 1J0 Ⓒ **905/468-9658.** Fax 905/468-7479. www.gracewood.ca. 3 units. C$200–C$295 (US$166–US$245) double. Not suitable for families with young children. **Amenities:** Outdoor pool; bike rental. *In room:* A/C, TV in lounge, dataport, hair dryer, iron, no phone.

Harbour House Hotel 𝕰𝕰𝕰   Harbour House is tucked away on a quiet street close to the marina and Lake Ontario, yet an easy walk to the center of the historical district of Niagara-on-the-Lake and the Shaw Festival Theatre. A refined tranquillity settles upon you from the moment you enter the main door. Check in with ease at the unobtrusive front desk, with two upholstered chairs thoughtfully supplied so you can rest your weary feet during the registration process.

The rooms are well-appointed, with boutique hotel–quality amenities: Frette robes, soft throws to cuddle up in next to the fire, and Judith Jackson bath products. And the best treat of all is that you will experience one of the most comfortable beds you have ever slept in, thanks to the Mount Orford feather bed (filled with hypoallergenic duck feathers) laid on top of the mattress. Lightweight white goose-down duvets and pillows and 300-thread-count Egyptian cotton linens complete the slumber kit. Note that those with feather allergies can request that a room be converted to non-feather bedding.

There is a cozy sitting room with fireplace, an intriguing selection of books, and a complimentary DVD lending library. At the cocktail hour, sample wines from local wineries, accompanied by Harbour House potted cheese. A hearty and healthy buffet breakfast is served in a pretty room overlooking the secluded patio. What sets Harbour House apart is its friendly yet impeccable service, its serene atmosphere, and those heavenly beds.

85 Melville St., Niagara-on-the-Lake, Ont. L0S 1J0 Ⓒ **866/277-6677** or 905/468-4683. Fax 905/468-0366. www. harbourhousehotel.ca. 31 units. C$199–C$335 (US$165–US$278) double; C$310 (US$257) and up suite packages available. Rates include breakfast. AE, MC, V. Free parking. Pets allowed in two specific guest rooms, C$25 (US$21) per day. **Amenities:** Bike rentals; concierge; courtesy shuttle; business services; limited room service; massage; babysitting; same-day laundry, dry cleaning. *In room:* A/C, TV, dataport, coffeemaker, hair dryer, iron. No smoking.

Pillar & Post Inn 𝕰𝕰   The phrase "rustic charm" comes to mind as you stroll the corridors of the Pillar & Post, with its expanses of exposed brick, post-and-beam structures, and original windows, which have been preserved where possible. The inn's rooms are laid out in a U-shape around a central courtyard with lovely gardens. The inn features an indoor saltwater pool, separate outdoor pool, and a splendid indoor/outdoor hot spring with cascading waterfall that is open year-round—luxury with a casual twist.

Guest room decor is classic Canadiana, featuring Windsor-style chairs, pine cabinets, and historical engravings. Some rooms have bay windows and flower boxes. Rooms in some wings have larger bathrooms than others; request a more spacious one if that's important to you.

The dining room is heavy on wood; the food and service are more than satisfactory (see chapter 6, "Where to Dine," for more details). The inn is popular with families and also hosts a lot of weddings. Wireless Internet is available.

48 John St., Niagara-on-the-Lake, Ont. L0S 1J0 ⓒ 888/669-5566 or 905/468-2123. Fax 905/468-3551. www.vintage inns.com. 122 units. From C$225 (US$187) double; from C$425 (US$353) suite. AE, DC, DISC, MC, V. Free parking. **Amenities:** Restaurant; bar; indoor and outdoor pools; spa; Jacuzzi; sauna; bike rental; concierge; shuttle available; business center; babysitting; same-day dry cleaning. *In room:* A/C, TV w/pay movies, minibar, hair dryer, iron, safe.

Prince of Wales Hotel & Spa ☆☆☆

Much admired and highly photogenic, this is the flagship property in the old town of Niagara-on-the-Lake, standing in prime position at the southeast corner of Picton Street and King Street, the crossroads at the head of Queen Street, Niagara-on-the-Lake's shopping mecca. The hotel was renovated and restored to its original Victorian glory in 1999. Rooms are individually decorated, drawing their inspiration from days gone by, with an abundance of floral fabrics and attractive antiques, complemented by reproductions and 21st-century amenities. Partake of English afternoon tea in the gracious Drawing Room, nibble on appetizers in the Tapas Wine Bar, or relax in the Churchill Lounge with a bar meal. The ultimate in luxury dining can be found at Escabeche. The Secret Garden Spa is available for those who live for self-indulgence.

6 Picton St., Niagara-on-the-Lake, Ont. L0S 1J0 ⓒ 888/669-5566 or 905/468-3246. Fax 905/468-5521. www.vintage inns.com. 110 units. From C$225 double. Packages available. AE, DC, DISC, MC, V. Valet parking C$5 (US$4), free self-parking. Pets accepted. **Amenities:** Restaurant; cafe; bar; lounge; indoor pool; health club; spa; Jacuzzi; bike rental; concierge; shuttle available; business center; 24-hr. room service; babysitting; same-day dry cleaning. *In room:* A/C, TV w/pay movies, dataport, minibar, hair dryer, iron, safe.

Queen's Landing Inn & Conference Resort ☆☆

Queen's Landing is a property with stature. Georgian architecture, magnificent sweeping staircase, unique stained-glass ceiling, marble floors—all of these elements combine to present guests with stylish sophistication. The fresh flower arrangements in the lobby are beautiful. Rooms are spacious and elegantly furnished to a high standard; many have fireplaces and Jacuzzis. The fitness center is in pristine condition. For relaxation, take a soak or leisurely swim in the indoor saltwater pool. Enjoy a meal on the terrace overlooking the marina and the Niagara River, or choose a table in the Tiara Dining Room. The food here is very good—no need to eat out.

155 Byron St. (at Melville St.), Niagara-on-the-Lake, Ont. L0S 1J0 ⓒ 888/669-5566 or 905/468-2195. www.vintage inns.com. 142 units. From C$225 (US$187) double; from C$425 (US$298) suite. AE, DC, DISC, MC, V. Free parking. **Amenities:** Restaurant; lounge; indoor pool; health club; Jacuzzi; sauna; bike rental; concierge; shuttle available; business center; 24-hr. room service; babysitting; same-day dry cleaning. *In room:* A/C, TV w/pay movies, dataport, minibar, hair dryer, iron, safe.

Riverbend Inn & Vineyard ☆☆☆

The Riverbend Inn, an intimate and gracious property with only 21 guest rooms, opened in spring 2004. The inn is owned and operated by John Wiens and family, who are well known and respected locally as hoteliers, having previously owned the legendary Prince of Wales Hotel in Niagara-on-the-Lake. The Inn has a fascinating history, culminating in its rescue from decay by the Wiens family and its subsequent restoration and reconstruction. The process has been chronicled in a photo album proudly on display in the lobby. The transformation of the building into an elegant and charming stately Georgian-style mansion is quite remarkable.

Rooms are larger than average and all have fireplaces. Corner rooms have several windows, offering different views over the vineyards and surrounding greenery; a few rooms have private balconies. Due to its semi-rural location on the Niagara Parkway at the southern edge of Niagara-on-the-Lake, views are lovely from all rooms. Bathrooms are spacious. A magnificent chandelier hangs in the front foyer. Riverbend has 17 acres of vineyards, and its neighbor Reif Estates Winery manages the maintenance of the vineyards and production of the wine—the first vintage is expected to be released in 2006. The dining room has won praise for its cuisine, and rightly so. Open for breakfast, lunch, and dinner for nonresidents as well as inn guests, the restaurant offers an eclectic cuisine in the expert hands of resident chef Chris Smythe, blending local products with Southern style. Service in the restaurant and at the front desk is friendly and polished—many of the staff have been working for the Wiens family since long before the Riverbend was born, and their loyalty and enthusiasm shine through. If you're looking for a romantic getaway, this place will please.

16104 Niagara River Pkwy., Niagara-on-the-Lake, Ont. L0S 1J0 ℂ 905/468-8866. Fax 905/468-8829. www.riverbend inn.ca. 21 units. C$255–C$325 (US$212–US$270) double; C$370 (US$307) suite. Kids 10 and under stay free in parent's room. C$25 (US$21) per extra person 11 years and over in room. AE, MC, V. Free parking. **Amenities:** Restaurant; bar; bike rental; business services; limited room service; massage; babysitting. *In room:* A/C, TV, dataport, hair dryer.

Rivervine B&B ℱ   Facing the gorge and overlooking the New York neighbors, this modern home is ornately decorated, giving it an old-home feel. Rooms are lavishly decorated with such details as roll-top desks and grand armoires. Every room has an en-suite bathroom with jet bathtub. Second-floor rooms have their own terraces with French doors opening up to the well-manicured lawns—with the exception of the Champagne Room, which enjoys an expansive view of the gorge. Guests are invited to use the billiards table in the lower-level recreation room, which also has an armoire of board games and a TV with movies. And for those who have purchased a few vintage bottles of local wine, feel free to store your wine in the temperature-controlled wine cellar. The outdoor pool area is decorated with wrought-iron chairs and encircled with grand trees. Owner Lynn Legallais offers up a five-course gourmet breakfast, featuring dishes such as fresh herb soufflé and apple cinnamon French toast. This property is best suited to adults.

15639 Niagara Pkwy., Niagara-on-the-Lake, Ont. L0S 1J0 ℂ **905/468-0001** or 905/468-5534. www.rivervinebb. com. 3 units. C$210–C$250 (US$174–US$207) double. Rates include 5-course breakfast. MC, V. Free parking. **Amenities:** Outdoor pool; golf nearby; tennis next door; jet bathtub; in-line skate/bike rental; game room; limo service available; gift boutique; massage. *In room:* A/C, hair dryer, no phone. No smoking.

White Oaks Conference Resort & Spa ℱℱ   Striving to be the ultimate in a combined resort/spa/conference center, White Oaks has a list of facilities, amenities, and activities as long as your arm. Their spa offers skin-care treatments, massage, hydrotherapy, and a variety of retreat packages. Self-indulgence is the order of the day. Fitness nuts will lap up private sessions with personal trainers and Pilates instructors. Rooms are spacious, swathed in muted earth tones, and all have either sunrise or sunset view. Ask for a room facing the nicely landscaped gardens rather than the parking lot. The entire property whispers urban sophistication. Wear black.

253 Taylor Rd., Niagara-on-the-Lake, Ont. L0S 1J0 ⓒ 800/263-5766 or 905/688-2550. www.whiteoaksresort.com. 220 units. C$149–C$279 (US$124–US$232) double; C$169–C$429 (US$140–US$356) suite. Children 12 and under stay free in parent's room. AE, DC, MC, V. Free parking. **Amenities:** 2 restaurants; indoor pool; golf course; indoor tennis courts; health club; spa; hot tub; sauna; bike rental; children's center; concierge; business center; shopping arcade; limited room service; massage; babysitting; same-day laundry and dry cleaning; executive rooms. *In room:* A/C, TV w/pay movies, dataport, minibar, coffeemaker, hair dryer, iron, safe. No smoking.

EXPENSIVE

Gate House Hotel 🕊️   European marble accents, black lamps, leatherette sofas, and Italian light fixtures—this Italian-style hotel is a refreshing change from standard hotel decor. On-site is the excellent Italian restaurant Ristorante Giardino (see the review in chapter 6). Dinner and accommodations packages are available, which saves you money and at the same time provides the convenience of a great restaurant literally on your doorstep. Situated at the top of Queen Street, at one end of the main shopping district.

142 Queen St., Niagara-on-the-Lake, Ont. L0S 1J0 ⓒ **905/468-3263.** www.gatehouse-niagara.com. 10 units. C$145–C$245 (US$120–US$203) double. AE, MC, V. Free parking. **Amenities:** Restaurant; concierge. *In room:* A/C, TV, hair dryer.

Grand Victorian B&B 🕊️   This enormous mansion on the Niagara Parkway was built in the Victorian era in the Queen Anne Revival style as a rebellion against the boxy, crowded Victorian architectural fashion of the day. Evidence of Quaker influences can be seen throughout the property. A pretty sunroom/conservatory was added in 1899 and now serves as a breakfast nook for guests. The interior is beautifully presented, with a very open, airy feel, high ceilings, and an open floor plan allowing flow through the main-floor rooms. The property is popular for weddings; it's also a great place to stay for lovers of historical homes and antiques. The owner has acquired a considerable collection of antique furniture from Europe and North America over the years, in addition to a number of items from her grandmother's seaside homes in England, including draperies and china. The property is TV- and smoke-free. A "butler's basket" has been thoughtfully supplied for guests' use, which includes hair dryer, iron, and other accessories. Each room is individually decorated and appointed; all are charming.

15618 Niagara Pkwy., Niagara-on-the-Lake, Ont. L0S 1J0 ⓒ **905/468-0997.** Fax 905/468-1551. www.grandvictorian. com. 6 units. C$170–C$220 (US$141–US$183) room; C$225 (US$187) suite. MC, V. Free parking. **Amenities:** Outdoor tennis court; bike rental; business services; massage. *In room:* A/C, no phone.

Oban Inn 🕊️   Re-created after a devastating fire in 1992, this new Victorian home has all the charm of the original 1842 structure. The large veranda pours over the expansive garden and makes a great place to hold a romantic wedding ceremony. Roses from the garden fill the rooms with their sweet fragrance in the summertime. Four-poster beds, high-backed reading chairs, and dark exotic furniture contrast with light-colored decor, giving the inn an old charm and feel.

160 Front St. (at Gate St.), Niagara-on-the-Lake, Ont. L0S 1J0 ⓒ **866/359-6226** or 905/468-2165. www.obaninn.ca. 26 units. C$150–C$265 (US$125–US$220) double; suite from C$250 (US$207). Packages available. AE, DC, MC, V. Free parking. **Amenities:** Lounge; health club; spa; bike rental; babysitting. *In room:* A/C, TV, dataport, hair dryer, iron.

The Old Bank House 🕊️   This two-story Georgian home, built around 1817, has a gorgeous riverside location. It was originally the first branch of the Bank of Canada. In 1902, the Prince and Princess of Wales stayed here. Several of the units have private entrances, and the Garden Room has a private trellised deck. The comfortable sitting room features a cozy fireplace and a collection of eclectic antique pieces.

10 Front St., Niagara-on-the-Lake, Ont. L0S 1J0 ⓒ **877/468-7136** or 905/468-7136. www.oldbankhouse.com. 9 units. C$139–C$225 (US$115–US$189) double. Rates include breakfast. AE, MC, V. Free parking. **Amenities:** Jacuzzi. *In room:* A/C, no phone.

Just for Two

Looking for a romantic retreat? You'll find life is a bed of roses at the **Black Walnut Manor** (4255 Victoria Ave., Vineland, Ont.; ✆ **800/859-4786**), the **Gracewood Inn** (16052 Niagara Parkway, Niagara-on-the-Lake, Ont.; ✆ **905/ 468-9658**), the **Riverbend Inn** (16104 Niagara Parkway, Niagara-on-the-Lake, Ont.; ✆ **905/468-8866**), and the **Sheraton Fallsview Hotel & Conference Centre** (6755 Fallsview Blvd., Niagara Falls, Ont.; ✆ **905/374-1077**).

MODERATE

Moffat Inn *Value*   A great bang for your buck, this simply decorated inn feels like a country barn home. Flowered patterned sofas, brass frame beds, and homemade bedspreads—this is a home away from home. And to set the mood, each room has a teakettle and supplies. Fireplaces are in eight rooms. Grab a free coffee from the lobby and linger in the restaurant, Tetley's, for a cheese fondue, steak, or sushi. However, please be advised that most rooms are located on the second floor. If climbing stairs poses a problem, this isn't your place.

60 Picton St. (at Queen St.), Niagara-on-the-Lake, Ont. L0S 1J0 ✆ **905/468-4116**. www.moffatinn.com. 22 units. C$79–C$199 (US$66–US$165) double. AE, MC, V. Free parking. **Amenities:** Restaurant; bar. *In room:* A/C, TV, dataport, coffeemaker, hair dryer.

3 Wine Country

The choice of accommodations in wine country is as diverse as the wineries themselves. Each has a distinctive personality and ambience. The list below is a representative sample of the best of the region, although there are many more lovely properties nestled among the vines.

VERY EXPENSIVE

Inn on the Twenty *✿✿*   This upscale inn in Jordan features a variety of guest room and suite styles in a converted sugar warehouse and nearby buildings, including two small adjoining cottages and a historical home with three rustic suites. All the main-inn suites have gas fireplaces, comfortable seating areas, and Jacuzzi tubs. Some suites have private gardens. The room decor is an artistic blend of antiques and contemporary accessories. Bathrooms are spacious and luxuriously appointed. The Inn is located in the center of the compact, fashionable commercial area in Jordan Village, with gift shops, art galleries, designer clothing stores, and antiques retailers only a step away. Breakfast is served in the renowned On the Twenty Restaurant on the other side of the street from the guest accommodations. Please note that the reception desk is on the second floor of the main inn building. If you require assistance with your luggage, you'll need to climb the stairs to the lobby to alert the staff.

3845 Main St., Jordan, Ont. L0S 1J0 ✆ **800/701-8074** or 905/562-5336. Fax 905/562-0009. www.innonthetwenty.com. 29 units. C$169–C$256 (US$140–US$212) and up regular suite; C$235–C$325 (US$195–US$270) and up deluxe suites and cottage suites. Rates include breakfast. Children under 12 may share parent's room; C$35 (US$31) per rollaway bed per night. AE, DC, MC, V. Free parking. **Amenities:** Restaurant; bar; spa; bike rental; business services; shopping arcade; limited room service; massage; babysitting; same-day laundry service. *In room:* A/C, TV/VCR, hair dryer, iron. No smoking.

Niagara Region Accommodations

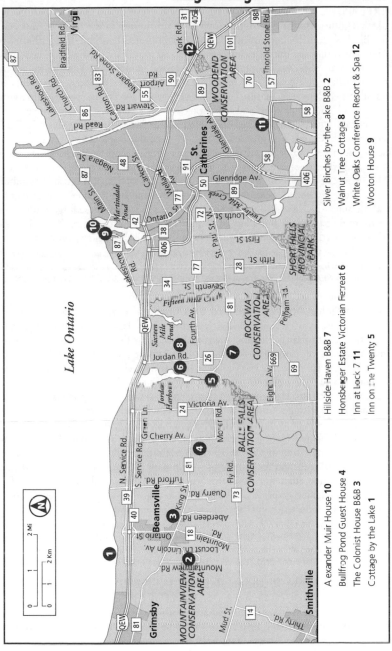

Silver Birches by-the-Lake B&B **2**

Walnut Tree Cottage **8**

White Oaks Conference Resort & Spa **12**

Wooton House **9**

Hillside Haven B&B **7**

Honsberger Estate Victorian Retreat **6**

Inn at Lock 7 **11**

Inn on the Twenty **5**

Alexander Muir House **10**

Bullfrog Pond Guest House **4**

The Colonist House B&B **3**

Cottage by the Lake **1**

EXPENSIVE

Black Walnut Manor ⚐   Billing itself as an urban oasis in the heart of wine country, Black Walnut Manor undeniably has a sophisticated boutique-hotel atmosphere.
The twist is that the three spacious en-suite guest rooms are decorated in cool, modern, ultra-chic style, yet the property is a historical homestead set in the rolling hills
near the village of Vineland. The rooms are named to evoke a feeling of tranquillity and
restfulness—"Retreat," "Return," and "Relax." Two of the rooms have private rooftop
terraces. The most luxurious and romantic room (and also the most expensive, natch)
is "Retreat," with its king-size bed draped in graceful sheers, an air-jet tub, and a shower
large enough for two. The proprietor's distinctive personality touches everything in the
house, from her trio of dogs (trained to stay at paw's length from the guests) to the
black-and-white photographs shot on a trip to Paris, to the eclectic dining-room decor,
with its mix of 1940s dining chairs, antique silver tea service, and brushed-aluminum
light fixture suspended above the table. Thoughtful touches to add to guests' comfort
include amenities bags filled with essential toiletries to replace those forgotten-at-home
items, fluffy bathrobes, and wineglasses and corkscrews in the rooms. There is a wine
fridge in the common room that guests can use to chill their winery purchases.

4255 Victoria Ave., Vineland, Ont. L0R 2E0 ✆ 800/859-4786 or 905/562-8675. www.blackwalnutmanor.com. 3
units. C$150–C$205 (US$124–US$170) double. Children in parent's room ages 3 and up C$25 (US$21) per night. AE,
MC, V. Free parking. **Amenities:** Bikes available for use free of charge. *In room:* A/C, TV/VCR, hair dryer, no phone. No
smoking.

Feast of Fields Organic Vineyard B&B Cottage ⚐ *Finds* *Kids* *Value*   A unique
experience awaits at Feast of Fields. As you drive up the laneway to this working farm,
you are likely to pass horses and cows in the adjacent fields. Curious peacocks may
form a welcoming committee—they roam free on the grounds. Around the back of
the restored farmhouse (ca. 1835), llamas hang their necks over a gated pen and seem
to smile at you. The farmhouse has been restored to a self-contained bed-and-breakfast cottage with full kitchen, sitting room, and two bedrooms upstairs. A queen-size
sofa bed in the sitting room can be used for sleeping, thereby providing accommodation for up to six guests in total. This is a tranquil countryside location, yet close to a
number of Niagara wineries—Rockway Glen and Trillium are two of the nearest. You
can join the Bruce Trail in a 10- to 15-minute leisurely walk from the cottage. Hikers'
packages are offered, and the proprietor will drop off and pick up hikers who are interested in exploring different parts of the Bruce Trail on different days. Wine made from
the farmer's organic grapes is available in limited quantities. The kitchen is stocked
with organic products for guests to prepare their own breakfast.

3403 11th St., Jordan, Ont. L2R 6P7 ✆ 905/562-0151. www.feast-of-fields.ca/bandb. 2-bed cottage with queen-size
sofa bed in sitting room. C$149–C$175 (US$124–US$145) 2 guests; C$25 (US$21) each additional guest to maximum
of 6 guests in the cottage. MC, V. Free parking. **Amenities:** Bicycles available free by prior arrangement; washer and
dryers. *In cottage:* A/C (bedrooms only), TV, dataport, kitchen, coffeemaker, hair dryer, iron, no phone. No smoking.

Honsberger Estate Victorian Retreat ⚐   This 6,000-square-foot Victorian
country house is one of the finest examples of its type in the Niagara region. The
Honsberger Estate is located on a 40-acre working farm, with orchards gracing the
fields leading up the sweeping drive to the home. The bedrooms are arranged in two
separate wings on the second floor, with four bedrooms in one wing and two bedrooms in the other. This arrangement is ideal for a multi-family or multi-generation
holiday, or for a wedding party. Booking the entire property is quite commonplace,

but bookings are also accepted for a minimum of eight guests (a full house is 12 guests). Breakfast is included with the rates, but for an extra cost the proprietor will arrange for a chef to prepare dinner, which is served in the elegant formal dining room. The grounds of the estate are peaceful and relaxing, with plenty of mature shade trees and even an old-fashioned wooden seated swing, suspended by ropes strung on a sturdy tree branch. If you've ever wanted to play the part of a country squire and his gentrified family, this is the place for you. This property is best suited to adults; older children accepted with prior arrangement.

4060 Jordan Rd., Jordan Station, Ont. L0S 1J0 © **905/562-6789.** Fax 905/227-4663. www.honsbergerestate.com. C$200 (US$166) double. *Please note a minimum of 8 guests must be booked; the maximum is 12.* **Amenities:** Massage. *In room:* A/C, dataport, iron, no phone. No smoking.

MODERATE

Cottage by the Lake   Directly facing the shore of Lake Ontario, the water laps almost literally under your window. The sound is soothing and a wonderful way to fall asleep after a hectic day. Nature lovers will savor the peace of early-morning sunrises and late-evening swims. The cottages appear tiny from the outside, but are cozy for a single or a couple to enjoy some quiet time—this is a good choice for those seeking solitude. Although without air-conditioning, the cottages are cooled in summer by the lake breeze and are situated in a shady area. A kitchenette is equipped with fridge, toaster oven, and coffeemaker. Kitchen utensils, dishes, and plenty of food for breakfast and snacks are provided. A unique experience awaits. Wineries of the Beamsville Bench are nearby.

5463 Blezard Dr., Beamsville, Ont. L0R 1B3 © **905/563-7434** or 905/708-7172. Fax 905/563-3284. www.cottage bythelake.com. 2 units. C$125–C$175 (US$104–US$145) double. AE, MC, V. Free parking. **Amenities:** Bikes available free of charge. *In room:* TV, kitchenette, fridge, coffeemaker, no phone.

Silver Birches by-the-Lake B&B   Silver Birches is much more than a B&B. Its level of comfort and amenities puts it more in the league of a country house or inn. With its large outdoor swimming pool, luxury indoor hot tub, tennis court, and three acres of park-like gardens, you will feel relaxed and pampered. You can extend the pleasure by pre-booking a four course gourmet dinner prepared by owners and hosts Paul and Leah Padfield (a minimum of four guests are required to book a dinner). Or take advantage of one of their many packages, put together in partnership with local wineries, restaurants, and theaters. Families can book the two-bedroom suite, which sleeps up to seven and has a private bathroom. Three other bedrooms, each with ensuite and individual decor, are located on the second floor. Gorgeous sunrises flood the sky above Lake Ontario and can be seen from the front porch—if you're awake early enough to enjoy them.

4902 Mountain View Rd., Beamsville, Ont. L0R 1B3 © **905/563-9479.** www.silverbirchesbythelake.com. 5 units. C$125–C$135 (US$104–US$112) double; suite from C$235 (US$195) based on 4 sharing. AE, MC, V. Free parking. Inquire about children. **Amenities:** Outdoor pool; outdoor tennis; indoor hot tub; bikes available free of charge; laundry service C$10 (US$8). *In room:* Dataport, hair dryer. No smoking.

Walnut Tree Cottage   Tucked away in the center of Jordan Village among the mature shade trees, Walnut Tree Cottage actually offers a choice of two accommodations: a tiny romantic guesthouse for two, or a suite in the main house next door where the proprietor lives. The cottage is a delightfully private retreat. Skylights in the cathedral ceiling flood the room with light—this is a former artist's studio. A pretty garden at the rear is available for guests' use. The cottage features a king-size bed, a fireplace, and a kitchenette with toaster, microwave, fridge, and small table with two chairs. Breakfast can be enjoyed in privacy if you wish—just let the proprietor know in advance, and she will leave a picnic basket on your front doorstep in the morning. The deck of the main house is so inviting, however, that guests staying in the cottage often choose to eat their breakfast there, where they may meet the occupants of the guest room in the main house.

3797 Main St., Jordan Village, Ont. L0R 1S0 ℭ 905/562-8144. www.bbcanada.com/walnuttreecottage.ca. 2 units (1 room, 1 cottage). Cottage C$125–C$140 (US$103–$US116) double; in-house suite C$90–C$110 (US$75–US$91). Free parking. **Amenities:** Bike rental available. *In room:* A/C, TV, no phone. No smoking.

INEXPENSIVE

Bullfrog Pond Guest House   If you like walking, whether it's a stroll to one of the nearby wineries or hiking the Bruce Trail, this is a good place to base yourself. The proprietors will cheerfully pack a picnic basket if you're heading out on an adventure by foot, on bicycles (there are several on-site for guests' use) or in your car. The guest accommodations are accessed at the rear of the house and are on ground level, so no steps to climb up and down. There is a common room with limited kitchen facilities and a cozy sitting area, and a hallway leading to two comfortable en-suite bedrooms, both with fireplaces. Guests are welcome to enjoy the one-acre sweep of lawns and flower gardens and the outdoor patio. You might luck out and arrive on a day when the proprietor has just baked a batch of her delicious chocolate chip cookies. Enjoy the full English breakfast.

3801 Cherry Ave., Vineland, Ont. L0R 2C0 ℭ 905/562-1232. www.bullfrogpond.com. 2 units. C$105–C$125 (US$87–US$104) double. C$15 (US$12) for extra person. MC, V. Free parking. **Amenities:** Bikes available at no charge. *In room:* A/C, TV/VCR, hair dryer, iron, no phone. No smoking.

The Colonist House B&B   Those with a passion for history or who are simply curious about the past will revel in The Colonist House. Not only is the 165-year-old property an exceptional example of an original two-story timber-framed, plank walled home built in the Colonial Georgian style, but also the owners, Lloyd and Jennifer Haines, are descendants of the original 1798 Mennonite settlers of the area. Jennifer's ancestors' family home is now on exhibit on the grounds of the Jordan Historical Museum of the Twenty. The Haineses are gentle, welcoming hosts who are pleased to discuss local history, whether it's Colonist House, their own family, or local events. The guest-rooms are accessed through the rear garden and have their own private hallway with windows overlooking the garden. A coffee bar for guests' use has thoughtfully been placed in the hall. No stairs to climb—unlike most B&Bs. An eclectic mix of antiques and contemporary furniture and accessories fill the modestly sized bedrooms, each with compact en-suite bathroom. A pretty deck at the rear has seating for warm summer days and evenings. Wireless Internet available.

4924 King St., Beamsville, Ont. L0R 1B0 ℭ 905/563-7838. www.colonisthouse.com. 2 units. C$110 (US$91) double. MC, V. Free parking. *In room:* A/C, TV, hair dryer, no phone. No smoking.

Hillside Haven B&B *Value*   Nestled among the rolling hillsides of Niagara's wine-country back roads, this secluded country property features a unique loft in an outbuilding separate from the owners' home. It's a perfect setting for a romantic weekend getaway. The comfortably furnished accommodations include a fully equipped kitchen for those who like to cook for themselves—with the wealth of fresh local produce available during the growing season, why wouldn't you? Rates include a thoughtfully stocked fridge and pantry so you can fix your own breakfast on a schedule that suits you and enjoy it in privacy. The large one-room apartment has a queen-size bed in an alcove and a comfortable couch for relaxing. Guests are invited to use the spacious deck and pool adjacent to the main house at any time. The Bruce Trail is on your doorstep, and there is plenty of opportunity to enjoy leisurely bike rides along the quiet country roads (bring your own bikes). The flower gardens are a rainbow of color in the summer, and fall is spectacular—the property lies in an area heavily populated with deciduous trees that blaze orange, yellow, and red. Winery dinner packages are available, which include a shuttle service to and from the restaurant.

3496 17th St., R.R. 1, St. Catharines, Ont. L2R 6P7 ☏ 905/562-7021. www.hillsidehaven.com. 1 unit (self-contained). C$100 (US$83) and up 1st night; C$85 (US$71) and up 2nd night. Rates include breakfast. MC, V. Free parking. **Amenities:** Outdoor pool. *In room:* A/C, TV/VCR, dataport, coffeemaker, hair dryer, iron, no phone. No smoking.

4 Welland Canal Corridor

The village of Port Dalhousie has a handful of bed-and-breakfast properties if you'd like to stay over and enjoy an evening at the community theater, or if you just want to stroll along the lakeshore and relax. For shipping enthusiasts, the Inn at Lock 7 is an ideal base—the ships pass right by the balconies of the building.

INEXPENSIVE

Alexander Muir House   On a quiet residential street just steps away from the shores of Lake Ontario and the boutiques, restaurants, and bars in the center of the village of Port Dalhousie, this B&B has considerable charm. A historical home of modest proportions, Alexander Muir House has been lovingly restored. If you're tall, don't forget to duck through the doorways—the ceilings are low compared with modern homes. Two en-suite rooms are available—one on the ground floor leading off the guests' sitting room/breakfast room, with a queen-size bed, and a larger one upstairs, with a king-size bed. The color palette for the walls and soft furnishings has been carefully selected to reflect the period in which the house was built. A lovely garden at the rear of the house is open for guests to enjoy. A hammock is provided in the summer, along with seating for relaxing. Experience a full European-style breakfast with local fruit in season, yogurt, a selection of breads, European cheeses (including Dutch Gouda and Edam), boiled eggs, and juices. Tea and coffee bar available for each room. Stroll the boardwalk near the property in the evening and watch the sun set while the pleasure boats drift in and out of the harbor. A quiet spot to spend a night or two.

43 Dalhousie Ave., St. Catharines, Ont. L2N 4W8 ☏ 905/935-3553. 2 units. C$110–C$125 (US$91–US$104) double. **Amenities:** Washers/dryers. *In room:* A/C, hair dryer, iron, no phone. No smoking.

Inn at Lock Seven   Watch international ocean freighters and tankers from your outdoor balcony. The Welland Canal water route—a link between the St. Lawrence and the Great Lakes—has seen more than two billion tonnes of cargo pass through since opening in 1959. Guests receive "The ABC's of the Seaway" and quickly become boat nerds, say owners Ed Kuiper and Patty Szoldra. Formerly the Lock Motel, this bed-and-breakfast is a mix of both styles: room walls are concrete and have simple matching bedspreads and curtains like a motel, while Patty and Ed have added their personal B&B touch—Patty sells her pottery wares in the gift shop, while Ed will take guests on motorcycle rides or a scuba dive. Only 15 minutes from the popular tourist destinations, this is a great jumping-off point to local wineries that won't break the bank. Set in a residential locale—enjoy some peace and quiet.

24 Chapel St. S., Thorold, Ont. L2V 2C6 ⓒ **877/INNLOCK7** (877-465-6257). www.innatlock7.com. 24 units. C$65–C$108 (US$54–US$90) double. Rates include breakfast. AE, DC. MC, V. Free parking. *In room:* A/C, TV, no phone.

Wooton House B&B   The pubs, lake marina, shops, and live theater of historical Port Dalhousie are all within walking distance of this charming home built in 1885. Watch world-class rowing on Lake Ontario from the lawn as you eat your Wooton House waffles with fresh fruit topping. The "View with a Room" room has a balcony overlooking Lake Ontario. Ideal for a long stay, this unit has its own kitchen and dining area, complete with microwave and en-suite bathroom with Jacuzzi. Discounts are available for longer stays. If you're the bookish type you'll appreciate the library room, with its skylight and built-in shelves full of classics. All rooms offer cable TV and are accessed through a private entrance. All beds are queen-size four-posters. Niagara-on-the-Lake and Niagara Falls are only a 15-minute drive away. The cozy corner room has an adjacent private bathroom.

2 Elgin St., St. Catharines, Ont. L2N 5G3 ⓒ **905/937-4696.** www.wootonhouse.com. 3 units. C$90–$150 (US$75–US$125) double. Rates include breakfast. Free parking. *In room:* TV, no phone.

6

Where to Dine

Dining out, whether on vacation or in your hometown, is one of life's greatest pleasures. Memorable meals are a synergistic blend of terrific food, fabulous ambience, and expert table service, and I'm delighted to be able to report that there are plenty of opportunities for great dining experiences in the Niagara region.

Dining in Niagara tends to fall into two categories—pricey but extremely good, or mundane and reliable. The former includes the excellent restaurants in Niagara's wine country and Niagara-on-the-Lake, with a sprinkling of places in other corners of the region. The latter encompasses the plethora of chains that have firmly established themselves in an area that sees 14 million tourists annually, many of whom just want fuel to keep their feet going as they are herded from attraction to attraction.

You can enjoy a leisurely lunch on a shady terrace with the lush vineyards spread out around you, dine by candlelight as you marvel at the rainbow colors of the illuminated Horseshoe and American Falls at night, or lounge around in a diner, chomping pancakes and bacon washed down with a bottomless mug of coffee. If you want to kick it up a notch, make a dinner reservation at a winery restaurant and order their tasting menu (a specially prepared set menu with matching wines for each course), or enjoy a traditional British-style afternoon tea in one of Niagara-on-the-Lake's gracious historical inns.

The following listings are by no means the only places to enjoy good food in the Niagara region, but they are representative of the better places to enjoy a meal. *Bon appétit!*

DINING NOTES Dining out in Niagara does not have to be an expensive venture, but be aware that taxes are high. Meals are subject to 8% provincial sales tax and 7% GST, so when you factor in an average tip, a whopping 30% is added to the bill. Tipping is usually left to the diner's discretion, although some establishments add 15% to the bill for parties of six or more.

Pay attention to the wine prices in restaurants—they can be quite high, even for the local Niagara wines. Don't be surprised to find your favorite vintage at double the price you'd pay at the liquor store or sometimes even at the winery. Savvy diners can take note of wine prices in the winery boutiques and compare them with those on the wine list in their chosen restaurant in order to better gauge how much markup has been applied. Note that a 10% liquor tax is added to alcoholic beverage purchases.

Hours vary quite markedly between summer and winter. The "high season," when opening hours are long, runs approximately from May to October for restaurants. Some restaurants close 1 or more days a week in the winter months. You should always call ahead if you have chosen a particular restaurant in order to avoid disappointment.

1 Restaurants by Cuisine

AMERICAN

Edgewater's Tap & Grill (Niagara Falls, Ontario, $$ p. 93)

Hard Rock Cafe *Kids* (Niagara Falls, Ontario, $$, p. 94)

Rainforest Café *Kids* (Niagara Falls, Ontario, $$, p. 94)

Red Coach Inn (Niagara Falls, New York, $$$$, p. 94)

The Secret Garden (Niagara Falls, Ontario, $$, p. 96)

Terrapin Grille (Niagara Falls, Ontario, $$$$, p. 90)

Zee's Patio & Grill (Niagara-on-the-Lake, $$$, p. 100)

BAKERY

Willow Cakes and Pastries (Niagara-on-the-Lake, $, p. 102)

CAFE/BISTRO

Cannery and Carriages Dining Room (Niagara-on-the-Lake, $$$$, p. 96)

Zooma Zooma Café (Wine Country, $$, p. 107)

CANADIAN

Queenston Heights Restaurant (Niagara Falls, Ontario, $$$$, p. 89)

Shaw Café and Wine Bar (Niagara-on-the-Lake, $$$, p. 99)

Wildflower (Welland Canal Corridor, $$$, p. 110)

Zest (Welland Canal Corridor, $$$$, p. 109)

CHINESE

Fan's Court (Niagara-on-the-Lake, $$, p. 102)

CONTEMPORARY

Charles Inn Restaurant (Niagara-on-the-Lake, Ontario, $$$$, p. 96)

Hillebrand Vineyard Café (Wine Country, $$$$, p. 103)

17 Noir (Niagara Falls, Ontario, $$$$, p. 90)

Wolfgang Puck Grand Café Niagara (Niagara Falls, Ontario, $$$, p. 92)

CONTINENTAL

The Buttery Theatre Restaurant (Niagara-on-the-Lake, Ontario, $$$, p. 99)

The Restaurant at Vineland Estates Winery (Wine Country, $$$$, p. 104)

DINER

Bob Evans Farms Restaurant (Niagara Falls, New York, $$, p. 93)

Falls Manor Motel and Restaurant (Niagara Falls, Ontario, $$, p. 94)

Little Red Rooster *Value* (Niagara-on-the-Lake, $$, p. 102)

ECLECTIC

Stone Road Grille *Finds* (Niagara-on-the-Lake, $$$, p. 100)

FRENCH

Peller Estates Winery Restaurant (Wine Country, $$$$, p. 103)

The Restaurant at Peninsula Ridge (Wine Country, $$$$, p. 104)

Terroir La Cachette (Wine Country, $$$, p. 106)

FUSION

Spice of Life Restaurant and Catering Services (Welland Canal Corridor, $$, p. 109)

Tiara Restaurant (Niagara-on-the-Lake, $$$$, p. 98)

Zooma Zooma Café (Wine Country, $$, p. 107)

INTERNATIONAL

The Epicurean Restaurant (Niagara-on-the-Lake, $$$, p. 99)

LIV Restaurant (Niagara-on-the-Lake, Ontario, $$$$, p. 98)

Key to Abbreviations: $$$$ = Very Expensive $$$ = Expensive $$ = Moderate $ = Inexpensive

The Watermark Restaurant 👁👁
(Niagara Falls, Ontario, $$$, p. 92)
Wellington Court 👁👁 (Welland
Canal Corridor, $$$, p. 107)

ITALIAN
Café Garibaldi (Welland Canal
Corridor, $$$, p. 107)
The Capri 👁 (Niagara Falls, Ontario,
$$$, p. 90)
Carpaccio Restaurant and Wine Bar
👁👁 (Niagara Falls, Ontario, $$$,
p. 91)
Ristorante Giardino (Niagara-on-the-
Lake, Ontario, $$$$, p. 98)

PIZZA
Boston Pizza 👁 (Niagara Falls,
Ontario, $$, p. 93)

REGIONAL CUISINE
The Niagara Culinary Institute Dining
Room 👁 Value (Wine Country, $$,
p. 106)
On the Twenty Restaurant 👁👁 (Wine
Country, $$$$, p. 103)
Peller Estates Winery Restaurant 👁👁👁
(Wine Country, $$$$, p. 103)

Queenston Heights Restaurant 👁
(Niagara Falls, Ontario, $$$$, p. 89)
The Restaurant at Peninsula Ridge
👁👁👁(Wine Country, $$$$, p. 104)
17 Noir 👁 (Niagara Falls, Ontario,
$$$$, p. 90)
Terroir La Cachette 👁👁👁 (Wine
Country, $$$, p. 106)
The Watermark Restaurant 👁👁
(Niagara Falls, Ontario, $$$, p. 92)
Wellington Court 👁👁 (Welland
Canal Corridor, $$$, p. 107)
The View Restaurant (EastDell
Estates Winery) 👁 (Wine Country,
$$$, p. 106)

STEAKHOUSE
The Keg 👁 (Niagara Falls, Ontario,
$$$, p. 92)

VEGETARIAN
Spice of Life (Welland Canal
Corridor, $$, p. 109)

VIETNAMESE
Mai Vi (Welland Canal Corridor, $$,
p. 107)

2 Niagara Falls, Ontario & New York

There certainly isn't a lack of places to eat in Niagara Falls, but there is somewhat of a dearth of good places to eat, unless you are a fan of roadhouse and fast-food fare. Those who are don't need a directory of where to find food—just scan the horizon for a familiar logo, pull your minivan into the parking lot, and get chomping. Below is a cross section of options for Falls-area dining; you will spot a chain or two among them, but only because they're inescapable.

Most of the tourist amenities, including restaurants, are concentrated on the Canadian side of the Falls, but in case you're in Niagara Falls, New York, for the day I've also included a few places to grab a bite to eat.

VERY EXPENSIVE
Queenston Heights Restaurant 👁 REGIONAL/CANADIAN   Perched above the Niagara River, the dining room of this restaurant in the heart of Queenston Heights Park offers a spectacular view. The view is at its most beautiful in the autumn, when the trees on both sides of the Niagara River blaze with warm fall colors. The menu features a variety of cuisines, with a number of Canadian-themed dishes, which may include local St. David's proscuitto on golden beet and arugula salad drizzled with apple cider vinaigrette, Ontario veal braised in tomato and garden herbs with Yukon mashed potatoes, and Canadian maple syrup mousse. Service is efficient, if a little distant. The children's menu is more imaginative than most—for instance, veal

scaloppini with capellini and vegetables in tomato sauce, or sirloin strips with spinach dumplings and seasonal vegetables. It's nice to see the kitchen making an effort for the kids as well as the grown-ups. In addition to lunch and dinner, the restaurant serves Sunday brunch seasonally and afternoon tea on weekends from May to October (daily in July and Aug). One more offering—Niagara Grand Dinner Theatre puts on shows here: matinee and evening performances along with a three-course menu. See chapter 10, "Niagara Region After Dark," for more information on the dinner theater.

14184 Niagara Pkwy., Queenston, Ont. ✆ 905/262-4274. Reservations recommended. Main courses C$20–C$33 (US$17–US$27). AE, DC, MC, V. Mar–Dec daily 11am–9pm.

17 Noir ✿ REGIONAL/CONTEMPORARY

It only makes sense that the Fallsview Casino has a restaurant that pays homage to gambling. Decorated in reds and blacks to mimic a roulette table, the chairs are fussy felt and the tables are round. The food is some of the best that your gambling money can buy, and it's worth the trip even if gambling isn't in your plans. Portions are large and the range is wide. A squash soup is a great blend of puréed squash with a creamy butter, which brings out the sweetness of the vegetable. And for fish lovers, I recommend an organic Irish salmon filet cooked to your liking, just like a steak. The salmon is perched on top of fingerling potatoes, double smoked bacon, and shallot veal reduction. Choose from other sumptuous treats like seared bison with celery-root purée, foie gras turnover, and seared sea scallops. Traditional Tahitian vanilla bean cheesecake is thick and bursting with worthy calories. Downstairs from the dining room, have a seat at the sushi and noodle bar, which is open late. Watch the Japanese master sushi chefs (two on staff) prepare delicacies right in front of your eyes.

6380 Fallsview Blvd. Niagara Falls, Ont. ✆ 888-WINFALL. Reservations recommended. Dining room: C$35–C$47 (US$29–US$39). AE, MC, V. Dining room daily 5–11pm; sushi and noodle bar daily 11am–4am.

Terrapin Grille ✿✿ AMERICAN

Named after Terrapin Point, a promontory that once extended beyond the brink of the American Falls allowing visitors a breathtaking view of the roaring water, this restaurant in the Marriott Niagara Falls Fallsview & Spa offers one of the best dining views of the Falls. With a wall of windows facing the panorama, every diner gets a piece of the action. Try to book a table in a prime position next to the glass, especially if you are celebrating a special occasion—which is quite likely, considering the price of the food. The cuisine is some of the city's best, fusing traditional Italian, French, and Asian cuisine. Their specialties, however, are succulent steak and terrific seafood, and they have won at least one local award for Best Fine Dining Restaurant in the city of Niagara Falls. The extensive wine list features Niagara wines. Other entrees include a penne pasta a la vodka, served in a tomato base with aged Parmesan, or try the rack of lamb served with Dijon mustard, rosemary, and crusted in a herb blend in red-wine reduction.

6740 Fallsview Blvd., Niagara Falls, Ont. ✆ 905/357-7300. Reservations recommended. Main courses C$28–C$85 (US$23–US$71). AE, DC, MC, V. Mon–Thurs 6:30–11am and 11:30am–11pm; Fri 6:30–11am and 12:30–11pm; Sat–Sun 6:30am–11pm.

EXPENSIVE

The Capri ✿ ITALIAN   This Niagara Falls landmark has been dishing up hearty portions of Italian fare for more than 40 years—the illuminated vertical restaurant sign, outlined in theater-style lightbulbs, gives away its age but no one seems to mind the time-warp feel—the place is usually quite busy, with locals and tourists alike. Their specialty is pasta, but you can also find a variety of veal and chicken dishes on the menu.

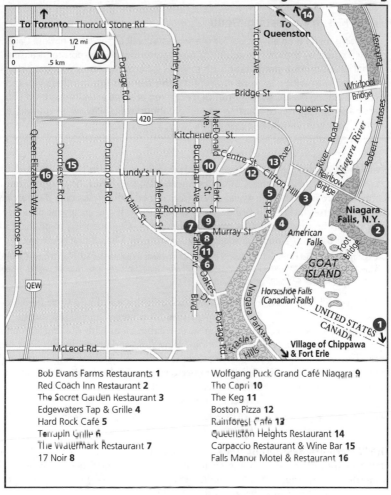

Niagara Falls Dining

To Toronto Thorold Stone Rd

To Queenston

Bridge St

Queen St.

420

Kitchener St.

Lundy's Ln.

Robinson St.

Murray St.

American Falls

GOAT ISLAND

Horseshoe Falls (Canadian Falls)

UNITED STATES / CANADA

Village of Chippawa & Fort Erie

McLeod Rd.

QEW

Niagara Falls, N.Y.

Whirlpool Bridge

Rainbow Bridge

Niagara River

Bob Evans Farms Restaurants **1**	Wolfgang Puck Grand Café Niagara **9**
Red Coach Inn Restaurant **2**	The Capri **10**
The Secret Garden Restaurant **3**	The Keg **11**
Edgewaters Tap & Grille **4**	Boston Pizza **12**
Hard Rock Café **5**	Rainforest Cafe **13**
Terrapin Grille **6**	Queenston Heights Restaurant **14**
The Watermark Restaurant **7**	Carpaccio Restaurant & Wine Bar **15**
17 Noir **8**	Falls Manor Motel & Restaurant **16**

Conventional lovebirds may like to try the "Honeymoon Special," featuring two New York striploin steaks served with sautéed mushrooms, tossed salad, choice of dessert, and tea or coffee for C$59 (US$49). You gotta come hungry—the serving sizes are generous.

5439 Ferry St., Niagara Falls, Ont. ℂ **905/354-7519**. Main courses C$12–C$37 (US$10–US$31). AE, DC, MC, V. Mon–Fri 11am–10pm; Sat–Sun 4–10pm.

Carpaccio Restaurant and Wine Bar ❋❋ ITALIAN This is one of the best places to dine in Niagara Falls. The rich, earthy tones of the décor, accented with mosaics and wrought iron, create a classy atmosphere that manages to stop just short of opulent, making the dining space welcoming and comfortable. The food is quite satisfying, a blend of traditional and contemporary Mediterranean Italian cuisine. The open kitchen is a great touch. The service is pleasant. There's not much to find fault with here at all, really. Try the mushroom risotto, which is expertly prepared and

---

Fun Fact **Try a Tasting Menu**

A tasting menu is an adventure for the senses as well as the imagination. Carefully created by the *chef de cuisine,* a tasting menu will incorporate local seasonal produce in a presentation of a series of small portion courses, often matched with wines. In some restaurants, the menu is set; in others you can choose among dishes. Advance notice is required at some establishments. If you are eager to experience a tasting menu, ask about availability when you call to make your reservation.

---

intensely flavorful. I highly recommend the thin-crust brick-oven pizzas, especially the *Quattro stagioni,* which features tomatoes, mozzarella, artichokes, black olives, mushrooms, and proscuitto. As you would expect from a good Italian restaurant, there are several main-course chicken and veal dishes to choose from. If you are a wine aficionado, hang out in the wine bar and let someone else drive—Carpaccio has more than 300 wines on its list, with 3-ounce tasting glasses available for a handful of selections.

6840 Lundy's Lane, Niagara Falls, Ont. ℂ **905/371-2063.** Reservations recommended Sat. Main courses C$16–$30 (US$13–US$25). AE, DC, MC, V. Summer Mon–Fri 11:30am–11pm, Sat–Sun 4pm–midnight; winter Mon–Fri 11:30am–10pm, Sat–Sun 4–11pm.

The Keg ℛ STEAKHOUSE   Dark ambience complemented by a stone fireplace— this chain restaurant will pleasantly surprise you. Steak comes cooked just the way you like it—it's their specialty. Choose from steak combinations with ribs and seafood or try the impeccable steak cuts such as sirloin, New York, and prime rib. But don't hold back. Try other mouthwatering items such as the baked garlic shrimp or the crab, Parmesan, and spinach dip. Baked goat cheese is warm and smooth, while steak and lobster—even though it's Atlantic frozen—is a real indulgence. Yes, it's a steakhouse, but you'll leave impressed—expect a little more.

5950 Victoria Ave., Niagara Falls, Ont. ℂ **905/353-4022.** Main courses C$17–$C43 (US$14–US$37). AE, DC, MC, V. Summer noon–1am daily ; winter Sun–Thurs noon–midnight, Fri–Sat noon–1am.

The Watermark Restaurant ℛℛ CONTINENTAL   On the 33rd and 34th floor of the Hilton, enjoy fallsview dining in the innovative atmosphere of Watermark, complete with aquariums, vaulted ceilings, and 5.5m-tall (18-ft.) windows to capture the panorama. The menu is heavy on the beef. Lighter fare includes a vegetarian fettuccine; roasted Atlantic salmon with golden vegetable caviar, red pepper cream, and watercress coulis; and grilled breast of chicken with a forest mushroom demi. Desserts are heavy—English-style bread pudding, chocolate fudge cake, and apple pie bundles with cinnamon ice cream.

6361 Fallsview Blvd., Niagara Falls, Ont. ℂ **905-353-7138.** Dinner reservations required. Main courses C$14–C$30 (US$12–US$25). AE, DC, MC, V. Summer daily 11:30am–3pm and 4:30–10:30pm; winter daily 11:30am–3pm and 4:30–9:30pm.

Wolfgang Puck Grand Café Niagara ℛℛ CONTEMPORARY   Difficult to believe that such high-quality, upscale food can be reproduced in a chain format, but be ready to be dazzled by the kitchen here at Wolfgang Puck's Niagara Falls home. Hats off to executive chef Jason Moss. His butternut squash soup with pesto cream is the best I've ever tasted, and there are a lot of versions of this recipe around these days with which to compare; it seems to have taken over from goat cheese and organic baby greens as a menu staple. The pumpkin ravioli with hazelnuts and brown butter sauce is also superb. Wolfgang's beer-batter crab cakes and chips with tartar sauce and malt vinegar are top-notch. The decor and staff are in tune with the food—smartly turned out, sleek, clean, and chic. If you have kids with you, come early for dinner (5:30pm-ish) and you'll feel more at ease. There's a kids' menu with the usual pizza, pasta, and burgers. Upstairs is Café TuTuTango, a funky, casual eatery decked out in bright Mediterranean colors. A good choice for a second lunch or dinner if you've already eaten at Wolfgang Puck's, it's an unexpected but entertaining combination of artist's studio, art gallery, and cafe.

6300 Fallsview Blvd., Unit A, Niagara Falls, Ont. © 905/354-5000. Weekend reservations recommended. Main courses C$14–C$38 (US$12–US$32). AE, MC, V. Summer Sun–Thurs noon–10pm, Fri–Sat noon–11pm; winter Sun–Mon noon–9pm, Tues–Thurs noon–10pm, Fri–Sat noon–11pm.

MODERATE

Bob Evans Farms Restaurant DINER   Yes, it is a chain, but it's a darn good, reliable one. As far as I can tell, it hasn't changed in the 15 years since I first sat down for breakfast at one of their restaurants a bit farther west in the state of Ohio, and personally I'm glad. Their all-day breakfast dishes range from C$4 (US$3.30) to C$10 (US$8). Main courses are generous in portion size and are likely to evoke happy but long-forgotten memories of hot gravy, mashed potatoes, and meatloaf in older folk. Service is fast and friendly. If you phone ahead, you can order entire home-style meals to go and whole pies.

6543 Niagara Falls Blvd., southeast corner of Hwy. 62 and Interstate 90, Niagara Falls, NY. © 716/283-2965. Main courses C$8–C$12 (US$7–US$10) . Daily 6am–9pm.

Boston Pizza (Kids) PIZZA   Convenient for the Clifton Hill mob, Boston Pizza has a menu that will overwhelm your eyeballs with more than 100 items. Best known for its pizza and pasta, Boston Pizza also serves up ribs, sandwiches, and salads. Arcade games and TV screens suck patrons' attention away from the food and the pace of the dining room seems to be stuck on fast forward, but no one would notice—the entire Clifton Hill district pulsates with neon energy from early morning to way past the witching hour every night. There is an outdoor patio for warm-weather dining. A great outing with lots of friends or the family—you'll find large portions, beer and wings, and a plethora of pizzas that are worth the trip. It's a watch-the-game or celebrate-a-birthday kind of place.

4950 Clifton Hill, Niagara Falls, Ont. © 905/371-1898. Main courses C$7–C$20 (US$6–US$17). Daily 11am–2am.

Edgewater's Tap & Grill AMERICAN   If you want to dine almost within reach of the Falls in the open air rather than sealed behind glass at the top of a multi-story tower, head to Edgewater's on a warm day and rest your weary bones on their huge second-floor patio. The balcony railings are bursting with flower-bedecked planters throughout the summer months, and breezes waft around the shaded deck. The menu features sturdy, reliable North American fare, such as half a barbecued chicken with french fries and baked beans, or grilled sirloin steak. Try the deep fried calamari—tender meat enveloped in a crisp batter. The spring rolls are tasty, too. During the busiest season, June until August, aim for an early lunch or dinner before the crowds arrive. You'll get your pick of the tables and by extension the best views. Downstairs on the main floor is the more casual Riverview Market Eatery.

6342 Niagara Pkwy, Niagara Falls, Ont. © 905/356-2217. Reservations recommended. Main courses C$10–C$20 (US$9–US$17). AE, DC, MC, V. May 5-Oct 29 11:30am–9pm daily Extended summer hours, call ahead

Falls Manor Motel and Restaurant ⭐ DINER   "Drive down Lundy's Lane until you see the big chicken," a local resident replied in response to an appeal for directions to Falls Manor. "You'll love the place," she added, and she was right. The Falls Manor Motel and Restaurant has been family-owned and -operated since 1953—that's a lot of roasted chicken. Falls Manor serves comfort food with a capital C and they really know how to deliver. Kettle-cooked barbecue ribs, pepper steak with mashed potatoes and gravy, toasted club sandwiches, hot corned beef, grilled cheese—this is food from the '50s and it is fab. A bottomless mug of coffee is just C$1.40 (US$1.15). The Hungry Jack breakfast is amazing value at C$7 (US$6)—two each of eggs, bacon, and sausage, plus a slice of Canadian peameal bacon, potatoes, and toast. The Belgian waffles are crisp, sweet, and filling. Seniors' portions are available for those over 60 years—you get a little less on your plate and a little less on your check. The front section of the restaurant is cozy, but if the tables are full there are plenty more in the back room, and even an outdoor terrace at the rear.

7104 Lundy's Lane, Niagara Falls, Ont. © **888/693-9357** or 905/358-3211. Main courses C$8–C$17 (US$7–US$14). AE, DC, MC, V. Summer Sun–Thurs 6am–9pm, Fri–Sat 6am–10pm; winter Sun–Thurs 6am–8pm, Fri–Sat 6am–9pm.

Hard Rock Cafe (Kids) AMERICAN   Situated at the main entrance to Casino Niagara, this upbeat, rockin' restaurant is full of music memorabilia and filling, tasty food. Start with Joe Perry of Aerosmith quesadilla, or try the Texas chili. Some mains include a classic French dip sandwich or a BLT. The menu is enormous and features barbecue favorites such as a hickory barbecue bacon burger and entrees such as New York strip steak or blackened chicken pasta. Top it all off with a good old-fashioned hot fudge sundae. If you're a night owl, stop in for a hearty fix of eats until 2am. The food is standard and tasty, but it takes a back seat to the wild scenery and high energy.

6705 Fallsview Ave., Niagara Falls, Ont. © **905/356-7625**. Main courses C$14–C$30 (US$12–US$25). AE, DC, MC, V. Daily 11am–2am. U.S. location: 33 Prospect St., Niagara Falls, NY. © **716/282-0007**. Sun–Thurs 11am–11pm; Fri–Sat 11am–midnight.

Rainforest Café ⭐ (Kids) AMERICAN   If you have kids in tow and they've never experienced a Rainforest Café, it's worthwhile having a bite to eat here—but be warned, once your children have entered the weird and wonderful world of the Rainforest, they will beg you to return again and again. It's rather fun, actually. Animatronic gorillas, snakes, and elephants entertain with their antics at regular intervals. The Niagara Falls Rainforest Café features a live shark exhibit (free) and promises daily encounters with live animals. The menu is family-friendly and lists plenty of familiar mealtime favorites—sandwiches, pastas, pizza, burgers, and salads.

Get your wallet ready for more than the check; the Rainforest Café shop has mountains of brightly colored Rainforest-themed merchandise, including an extensive line of private-label Rainforest Café clothing and more toys than Santa's sack.

5785 Falls Ave. Niagara Falls, Ont. © **905/374-2233**. Main courses C$10–C$26 (US$8–US$22). AE, DC, MC, V. Sun–Thurs 11am–10pm; Fri–Sat 11am–midnight.

Red Coach Inn Restaurant ⭐⭐ AMERICAN   The decor is all deep, dark wood and subdued tapestry, and the view toward the Niagara River rapids is a treat. Dine on the veranda in warm weather. Besides the choice of Frenched pork chops, black angus steak (several cuts), scallops, Australian lobster tail, and swordfish, the menu features an impressive list of sauces, a variety of breads, and a separate list of side dishes. Choose from dozens of toppers and sides, including fruit salsa, mushroom and Marsala wine sauce, smoked tomato coulis, chive cream cheese, or roasted red pepper.

Add au gratin sweet potatoes, french fried potatoes, pan-fried potatoes, or pasta with Romano cheese sauce and cucumber salad. The restaurant is exceedingly traditional and exudes a formal atmosphere.

2 Buffalo Ave., Niagara Falls, NY. © **800/282-1459** or 716/282-1459. www.redcoachinn.com. Reservations recommended. Main courses C$16–C$30 (US$13–US$25). AE, MC, V. Summer Mon–Thurs 11:30am–10pm, Fri 4–11pm, Sat 11:30am–11pm, Sun noon–10pm; winter Mon–Thurs 11:30am–2:30pm and 5–9pm, Fri–Sat 11:30am–10pm, Sun noon–9pm.

Tips Fallsview Dining

Although there is no question that one of the essential ingredients of a satisfying dining experience is a memorable setting, there is an important distinction to be made between the ambience of the surroundings and a view from a window or terrace. People seem to get caught up in a fantasy of eating a meal while romantically gazing at a beautiful panorama. In the case of the Falls, the tons of cascading water grab all the attention, leaving very little for your dinner, so it's best to treat the two as separate activities unless you have already had your fill of the spectacle and can restrain yourself to the occasional glance. One exception to this point of view is the romance angle as tackled by the **Sheraton Fallsview.** Book a room or loft suite with a glassed-in alcove overlooking the Falls, and ask the hotel to set you up a table for two in the alcove for one of their special in-room dinners.

There are several restaurants in town, of course, which have chosen to capitalize on one of the world's most famous scenic vistas. For those who like to view and chew, here's a taste of where to do it.

Edgewater's Tap & Grill (© **905/356-2217**) (p. 93) is one of the Niagara Parks Commission's restaurants. The second-floor dining room features indoor and outdoor dining. Farther upriver, overlooking the American Falls across the gorge, stands **The Secret Garden** (p. 96). Several hotels on Fallsview Boulevard at the top of the bluff overlooking the Falls have restaurants on their upper floors. Try **The Watermark Restaurant** on the 34th floor of the Hilton Hotel (p. 92) or **Terrapin Grille,** the Niagara Falls Marriott Fallsview's restaurant (p. 90). Finally, the two observation towers each have a fallsview dining room. The Konica Minolta Tower Centre (6732 Fallsview Blvd.; © **905/356-1501**), which hosts the Ramada Plaza Fallsview Hotel, has the **Pinnacle Restaurant.** You'll find this retro structure tucked in between recently constructed high-rise blocks, but don't be fooled—the views from the hotel rooms, observation deck, and restaurant are unobstructed. The distinctive **Skylon Tower** (5200 Robinson St.; © **905/356-2651**) has a revolving restaurant that completes each revolution in 1 hour, giving you a view of the Falls for approximately half that time.

Of these offerings, the better food is probably found at Watermark and Terrapin Grille, but expect to pay dearly for it. Reservations are recommended at all of these locations to avoid disappointment. Check the time of the illuminations before booking if you intend for one to be an integral part of your dinner.

The Secret Garden AMERICAN   Best visited during the summer so you can sit on the patio near the garden and take in the Falls—the view, and a beautifully manicured garden, are the Secret Garden's main draws. The food is basic fare including cheeseburgers, steaks, and pastas. They also offer a vegetarian selection including breaded eggplant with roasted red peppers on ciabatta bread. But beware: this stop is a favorite of tour groups and can be quite packed.

5827 River Rd., Niagara Falls, Ont. Ⓒ **905/358-4588.** Main courses C$11–C$30 (US$9–US$25). AE, DC, MC, V. Summer daily 8am–9pm; winter daily 8am–4pm.

3 Niagara-on-the-Lake

The town of Niagara-on-the-Lake, with its pastiche market of theater patrons, boutique shopping brigade, and lovers of historic homes, has an eclectic assortment of restaurants. Whether you are looking for an olde-English-style pub, an elegant Victorian dining room, a bright and breezy outdoor patio, or a small-town diner, you'll find it here. If you're torn between choices of where to eat, ask for opinions from your B&B host or hotel staff—they are knowledgeable about local restaurants and will be eager to share their recommendations with you. Some of the hotels and inns in town will provide a shuttle service to and from restaurants in the evening upon request, saving you hunting for an unfamiliar address and allowing you the indulgence of a glass or two of local wine.

VERY EXPENSIVE

Cannery and Carriages Dining Room Ⓕ BISTRO   The Pillar & Post Inn's restaurant serves sophisticated food in a down-to-earth manner. Blue crab cakes with pineapple salsa and chipotle aioli, poached pear and Cambazola bruschetta, and tiger shrimp marinated in garlic oil, julienned red peppers, and watercress seedlings are fantastic as appetizers. Match with a flight of white Niagara wines and you're all set. In the cooler months, ask for a table near the fireplace. The fireplace nook is dark, quiet, and romantic. At the heart of the dining room is a classic brick pizza oven, where thin-crust California-style pizza is baked. Executive chef Randy Dupuis was born and raised in Niagara; his approach to cuisine has been described as "food without attitude." A musttry is the fresh and flavorful *pasta con pollo affumicato:* a medley of smoked chicken, sun-dried tomatoes, and roasted garlic mixed in an extra-virgin olive oil.

48 John St., Niagara-on-the-Lake, Ont. Ⓒ **905/468-2123.** Reservations recommended. Main courses C$24–C$36. (US$20–US$31)AE, DC, MC, V. Summer Mon–Thurs 7–10am, noon–2pm, and 5:30–9pm; Fri–Sat 7–11:30am, noon–2pm, and 5–9:30pm; Sun 8–10am and 10:30am–2pm. Winter Mon–Thurs 8–11am, noon–2pm, and 6–9pm; Fri–Sat 7–11am, noon–2pm, and 5:30–9:30pm; Sun 8–10am and 10:30am–2pm. Lounge hours: summer daily 11–1am; winter Sun–Thurs noon–11pm, Fri–Sat 11:30–1am.

Charles Inn Restaurant ⒻⒻ CONTEMPORARY   "I believe a carrot should taste like a carrot," says *chef de cuisine* William Brunyansky. On his seasonal menu that uses only Canadian ingredients, each taste and flavor comes through without impeding the others. A simple starter soup combines baby bok choy, a cream potato and leek base, and pan-fried pickerel. Grilled tenderloin (AAA beef) sits on a roasted potato *galette,* surrounded by crisp green French beans, with fresh seasonal mushrooms: chanterelles from British Columbia and local honey mushrooms soak up the beef jus. Save room for farmhouse cheeses such as *fourme d'Ambert,* a French raw cow's milk, or 5-year-aged English white cheddar. It's a sumptuous menu that is worth the premium price. Just as the food is tantalizing your senses, the historic home soothes the soul—calm

Niagara-on-the-Lake Dining

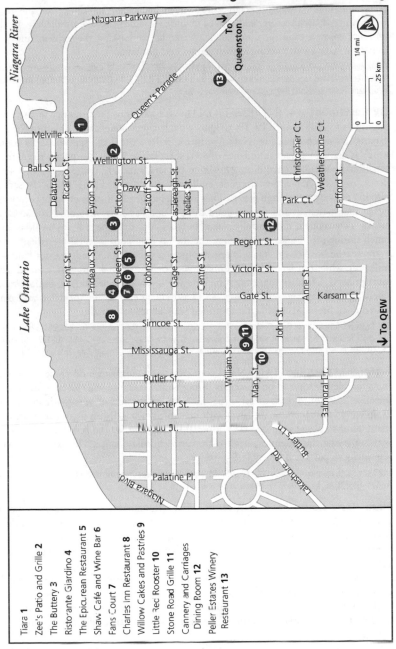

Tiara **1**
Zee's Patio and Grille **2**
The Buttery **3**
Ristorante Giardino **4**
The Epicurean Restaurant **5**
Shaw Café and Wine Bar **6**
Fans Court **7**
Charles Inn Restaurant **8**
Willow Cakes and Pastries **9**
Little Rec Rooster **10**
Stone Road Grille **11**
Cannery and Carriages
Dining Room **12**
Peller Estates Winery
Restaurant **13**

persimmon-colored walls, two large fireplaces, white crown molding from the 1832 Georgian style architecture, and replica chandeliers from the old apothecary. In the summer, enjoy a candlelit diner on the veranda overlooking the gardens and golf course, or have an afternoon tea with scones and preserves.

209 Queen St., Box 642, Niagara-on-the-Lake, Ont. ℂ **866-556-8883** or 905/468-4588. www.charlesinn.ca. Reservations recommended, especially for summer. Main courses C$25–C$35 (US$21–US$29). AE, DC, MC, V. Summer daily 7:30-10am, 11am–4pm, and 5–9pm; winter Wed–Sun 5–9pm.

LIV Restaurant ⭑⭑ INTERNATIONAL   It's hard not to surrender to the tranquillity and simplicity of LIV. Try to ignore the feeling, though, and sink into the role playing; it's much more fun. New Age music wafts around the spacious, airy room, which is draped with an abundance of soft, sheer white fabric. Simplicity rules, from the ultra-sleek upholstered dining chairs to the single stem of white freesia in a slender vase on the table. Servers glide endlessly around the dining tables, poised to respond to every signal from diners. They manage to invoke a sense of being pampered rather than pestered, and that's a good thing. Food at LIV is presented as a work of art, each component thoughtfully placed in relation to the others. From breakfast and lunch through to dinner and desserts, the menus emphasize natural ingredients. For example, the breakfast menu lists organic quinoa with dates, dried cherries, and soy milk; egg-white omelet with feta, tomato, and onion; toasted gluten-free bread; and local preserves. Dinner suggestions include the crushed grape tomato, buffalo mozzarella, grilled asparagus, red onion, and basil vinaigrette for an appetizer, and pan-seared duck breast, rack of lamb, or grilled sea scallops for a main.

253 Taylor Rd. (inside White Oaks Conference Resort & Spa), Niagara-on-the-Lake, Ont. ℂ **800/263-5766** or 905/ 688-2550. Reservations required in summer, recommended in winter. Main courses C$26–C$45 (US$22–US$37). AE, DC, MC, V. Summer daily 7am–2pm and 5–10pm; winter Sun–Thurs 7am–2pm, Fri–Sat 7am–2pm and 5–10pm.

Ristorante Giardino ITALIAN   A romantic restaurant with modern decor, featuring a marble bar top and brass accents throughout. Gaze into your lover's eyes over an appetizer of smoked duck breast carpaccio served with slices of port-marinated pears, or an entree of roasted loin of lamb with balsamic vinegar. If fish is your pleasure, the menu aims to please with deglazed imperial shrimp with a brandy sauce. Don't leave without trying the hazelnut parfait with warm chocolate sauce. The extensive menu also includes pasta and hearty Italian soups.

142 Main St., Niagara-on-the-Lake, Ont. ℂ **905/468-3263.** Reservations recommended. Main courses C$25–C$40 (US$21–US$33). AE, MC, V. Daily 11:30am–2:30pm and 5–10pm.

Tiara Restaurant ⭑⭑ CANADIAN   Tiara Restaurant, in the stately Queen's Landing Inn, is filled with natural light that floods in through a bank of windows overlooking the historic Niagara-on-the-Lake harbor. The formal dining room provides a memorable setting for the creations of executive chef Stephen Treadwell, who subscribes to the Niagara culinary theme of emphasizing local ingredients, organic when possible. A seven-course tasting menu can be experienced at a cost of C$85 (US$71) without wines, or C$135 (US$112) with paired wines. Entrees include grilled beef tenderloin with Dijon Yukon mashed potatoes and scorched onion jam, or my favorite—Atlantic salmon *tournedos* with chanterelle mushrooms and Charlevoix blue cheese.

155 Byron St., Niagara-on-the-lake, Ont. ℂ **888/669-5566.** Reservations recommended. Main courses C$32–C$45 (US$27–US$37). AE, MC, V. Daily 7–10:30am, 11am–2pm, and 5–9pm.

Tips

When dining out in the evening in **Niagara-on-the-Lake,** dinner reservations are recommended. If you have tickets to an evening performance at the Shaw Festival, reserve for 5:30pm or so. If you do not, then book a table for 7:30pm or later, and enjoy a leisurely meal after the theater crowd has left.

EXPENSIVE

The Buttery Theatre Restaurant CONTINENTAL/BRITISH   A good jousting never hurt anyone—so travel back in time to experience the food and revelry of the medieval times, Henry VIII style. Servers are dressed as wenches as "jongleurs" keep you smiling. And to relive the experience of the era, food is hearty and copious. During the 2½-hour feast, enjoy favorites such as the spiced chicken or wine and honey roast suckling pork. The family-operated restaurant has been putting on the show for more than 30 years. A regular tavern menu also includes salmon, scallops, and lighter fare such as salads.

19 Queen St., Niagara-on-the-Lake, Ont. ✆ **905/468-2564.** Reservations recommended during theater productions. Main courses C$22–C$28 (US$18–US$23). AE, MC, V. Summer Mon–Thurs 11am–11pm, Fri–Sat 11am–midnight; winter Sun–Thurs 11am–8pm, Fri–Sat 11am–10pm.

The Epicurean Restaurant INTERNATIONAL   This eatery has two faces—a laid-back, come-on-up counter at the front entrance, with sandwiches and daily specials chalked on a blackboard for daytime diners, and a casual fine-dining section at the rear that opens onto a gorgeous shaded patio for evening patrons. The rear section features an open kitchen, which always makes me happy. You can watch the chef and his team at work, absorb some of their energy, and maybe even pick up a few tips on food preparation. Terra-cotta tile flooring, Tuscan sunset wall coloring, and teal blue accents create an appealing backdrop to this delightful restaurant. Seafood is nicely prepared—you may find shrimp bisque, sea scallops with wilted leeks, garlic confit potatoes, and saffron cream sauce, or striped bass filet accompanied by tomatoes, olives, preserved lemons, and grilled fennel. French bistro fare includes steak and frites with peppercorn sauce and aioli on the side, and classic mussels steamed in a shallot, butter, white wine, and parsley broth. Warm chocolate cake with crème anglaise and butterscotch sauce is divine. The dinner menu includes suggestions for wine matched to each course.

84 Queen St., Niagara-on-the-Lake, Ont. ✆ **905/468-0288.** Reservations recommended. Main courses C$19–C$25 (US$16–US$21). MC, V. Summer daily 9am–9pm; winter Wed–Sun 9am–9pm.

The Shaw Café & Wine Bar CANADIAN   The Shaw Café is instantly recognizable by its unique architectural design, featuring a prominent circular dining area at one end of the building surrounded by an outdoor patio and laden with gorgeous flower boxes. A fountain statue adjacent to the restaurant's patio commemorates the cafe's namesake playwright. The menu is nicely balanced, with light lunch dishes for the midday crowd and cakes and pastries to savor with coffee or tea when it's time to take a break from shopping along Queen Street. Choose from a vegetable wrap with black-bean humus and roasted vegetables or a baby spinach salad with pear chips and Gorgonzola smothered in a creamy garlic dressing. Entrees include braised lamb shank or a delectable blackened catfish served with peppered cornbread, creamed spinach and tomato/corn salsa. Don't forget dessert: Grand Marnier cheesecake or a raspberry chocolate tart is just a sample.

92 Queen St., Niagara-on-the-Lake, Ont. © **888/669-5566** or 905/468-4772. Main courses C$15–C$22 (US$12–US$18). Summer 9am–midnight; winter Mon–Fri 10am–6pm, Sat–Sun 10am–9pm.

Stone Road Grille ☆☆☆ *Finds* REGIONAL/ECLECTIC   The Stone Road Grille, aka REST (the story of the birth of their alter ego is an amusing one; ask the server to relate it to you or read it on their website), has food so good you will find yourself alternately nodding with satisfaction at the imaginative dishes and sighing with delight at the depth of the chef's understanding of how to marry flavors and textures. Months after I ate there I could recall the taste of the food—restaurants like that are rare indeed. The proprietors work the front of house with style. They are proud to offer a 100% Niagara VQA wine list. At midday, order the vintner's lunch with a glass of wine. You'll receive a beautifully presented plate of house-made charcuterie, fresh artisanal breads, Canadian cheeses, fruit, and nuts. The menu is constructed with such talent that every dish is distinctive and appealing: a plate of tomato and eggplant gratin with a smoked tomato and lentil sauce, house-smoked salmon filled with salmon caviar and preserved lemon crème fraiche, a pair of mini bison burgers, one served with caramelized onion and blue cheese, the other with house smoked bacon and cheddar. Hungry yet? There's lots to tempt even the most jaded urban palate. And if you're wondering which dish still permeates my dreams at night, it's Stone Road Grille's iced plum soup, served with a generous mound of sour cream and lemon sorbet, garnished with a ginger crouton.

In the Garrison Plaza, corner of Mary St. and Mississauga St., Niagara-on-the-Lake, Ont. © **905/468-3474**. Main courses C$18–C$25 (US$15–US$21). MC, V. Summer Tues–Fri 11:30am–2pm and 5–10pm; Sat–Sun 5–10pm. Winter Tues–Fri 11:30am–2pm and 5–9pm; Fri–Sat 5–10pm; Sun 5–9pm.

Zee's Patio & Grill ☆☆☆ AMERICAN   One of the best dining experiences in the region, Zee's manages to be just casual enough in its atmosphere to entice diners to feel relaxed and just sophisticated enough in its service and food to instill a desire to become a regular patron. Purported to have the largest outdoor patio in Niagara-on-the-Lake, Zee's also has a cathedral-ceiling indoor dining room, heated with a blazing fireplace in winter. Startling sculptures of the human form are displayed on ledges far above the tables. The cavernous nature of the dining room creates somewhat of a challenge for conversation when there's a full house; if you're not heading for the theater, dine after the thespian-devoted crowds have departed (making a reservation for 7:30pm will ensure you've missed them).

Organic breads, baked on the premises, may include ancient grain, olive, or sourdough, served with unsalted butter dusted with coarse salt. The provision of a *l'amuse bouche* to signal the start of the meal is a nice touch. Service is crisp and enthusiastic without becoming overly chummy. Servers have a solid knowledge of local wines and are willing to guide you through tasting a flight if you so desire. Foodies will be delighted with the menu. Organic pork with maple roast apples and celery root on a ragout of Puy lentils, Ontario lamb shank slow-braised in a rich red-wine broth on soft garlic polenta with Taggliache olives and gremolata, and trio of Quebec duck are a sample of recent dinner mains. Lunch is also imaginative, with classic bouillabaisse, pasta stuffed with tomato, zucchini, and ricotta and served with a basil cream sauce, or grilled chicken seasoned with cumin, paprika, honey, and toasted almonds with braised local field greens. The selection of Canadian artisanal cheeses is superb. Enjoy a flight of red wines to accompany your cheese plate and settle in for an indulgent evening.

Cooking Up a Storm in Niagara

Would-be iron chefs and weekend kitchen wizards will be pleased to discover the culinary playgrounds of the Niagara region. Spurred by the growth of the wine industry, cooking classes for weekend kitchen warriors have sprung up across the area.

The Wine Country Cooking School (1339 Lakeshore Rd., Niagara-on-the-Lake, Ont.; (C) **905/468-8304**) is Canada's first winery cooking school. Based at Strewn Winery, the cooking school highlights the close relationship between food and wine in its teaching philosophy. Its bright, airy classroom, featuring an entire bank of windows along one wall, is a pleasure to work in. Cooking stations designed for pairs of cooks to work together are equipped with utensils and appliances that will make home cooks sigh with delight. A separate dining room is available for students to enjoy creations, matched with wines from Strewn's cellars. Strewn's winemaker and guest speakers often attend the dinners. Packages are available that include dinner at Terroir la Cachette, Strewn's winery restaurant, and overnight accommodations in nearby Niagara-on-the-Lake.

The Good Earth Cooking School (4556 Lincoln Ave., Beamsville, Ont.; (C) **905/563-7856**) is run by Nicolette Novak, a walking encyclopedia of the land and its fruits. "When people come down the rickety lane through the orchards, I want them to forget their stress and tune out for 3 hours." And that's just what you'll do—no more than 12 guests sit around the kitchen island and watch local chefs demonstrate how to make easy-to-replicate dishes. Don't be intimidated—Nicolette is a jeans and t-shirt kind of lady, and her open-cupboard kitchen is a gateway to good food no matter your experience. But do book ahead: spring classes are posted in February online, and nearly fill up within a month. In the summer, sit outside and enjoy the demonstration beside the stone hearth. Classes also include hands-on courses, 2-day team-building events, and kitchen parties.

Niagara Culinary Institute (Glendale Campus, 135 Taylor Rd., Niagara-on-the-Lake, Ont.; (C) **905/735-2211**) is part of the Hospitality and Tourism Division at Niagara College. They offer a variety of courses, ranging from half-day courses in desserts and other delights to full-day classes in soup making and a three-session bread making course. More extensive part time classes leading to certification in various aspects of the hospitality and tourism industry are also available, including sommelier training.

L'Escoffier (17 Lloyd St., St. Catharines, Ont.; (C) **905/685-7881**) is a retail kitchenware destination with a teaching kitchen on the premises. Local chefs teach evening classes in food preparation, presentation, and how to pair food and wine.

92 Picton St., Niagara-on-the-Lake, Ont. © 905/468-5715. www.zees.ca. Reservations recommended. AE, MC, V. Main courses C$19–$C29 (US$16–US$24). Summer Tues–Sat 7:30am–midnight, Sun–Mon 7:30am–9pm; winter Mon–Tues 5–9pm, Thurs–Sun noon–9pm.

MODERATE

Fans Court CHINESE   Expect more than deep-fried chicken rice at this Cantonese and Szechuan–style restaurant. Singapore beef, moo shu pork, and lemon chicken are fresh and tasty. The ambience is warm and light, with bamboo chairs and of course fans throughout the restaurant. In summer dine outside in the courtyard. Regulars come in from kilometers away to eat here—it serves up fresh, spicy selections sure to please any Szechuan or Cantonese connoisseur.

135 Queen St., Niagara-on-the-Lake, Ont. © 905/468-4511. Main courses C$13–C$20 (US$11–US$17). AE, MC, V. Mid-Feb to Dec Tues–Sun noon–9pm.

Little Red Rooster *Value* DINER   This spacious down-home diner is filled with comfy upholstered banquettes and booths. Popular with locals, it's a perfect spot to drop in and relax. If you're looking for cheap eats, you've found the place. Homey menu items include pork chop with apple sauce, liver and onions, toasted western sandwiches, and french fries with gravy. Home-baked pies, old-fashioned milkshakes, and ice-cream sundaes round out the sweet stuff. All-day breakfast with two eggs and bacon, ham, or sausage is only C$4 (US$3), and the kids' menu for 10 and under is just C$5 (US$4) for a main course, small drink, and ice-cream sundae.

271 Mary St. Niagara-on-the-Lake, Ont. © 905/468-3072. Main courses C$4–C$13 (US$3–US$11). MC, V. Daily 7am–8pm.

Olde Angel Inn Pub and Restaurant PUB   Everything you'd expect from a traditional pub—more than 16 draft beers, including favorites such as Creemore Springs lager and Toronto's own Steam Whistle Pilsner. Imported beers include Guinness Stout, Kilkenny Cream, and Stella Artois. Every Friday and Saturday tap your feet to local musicians. Choose from English menu staples such as shepherd's pie, fish and chips, and bangers and mash—this last offering is delicious rather than alarming. Bangers and mash is a dish featuring pork sausage and garlic mashed potatoes with Guinness gravy. The pub also has North American roadhouse munchies such as bruschetta and spring rolls. A great place to relax and unwind.

224 Regent St. in the Market Square, Niagara-on-the-Lake, Ont. © 905-468-3411. Main courses C$9–C$25 (US$7–US$21). AE, MC, V. Daily 11:30am–1am.

INEXPENSIVE

Willow Cakes and Pastries BAKERY   This is a delightful little place to duck in for a quick coffee and indulge in the guilty pleasure of a generous slice of chocolate cake or a buttery croissant. The pastries are a feast for the eyes. Quiche, *pain au choco- lat,* banana bread, *petits fours,* and more are on display in the brightly lit glass-fronted cabinets. The array of artisanal breads is quite intriguing. The shop has the feel of a chic French patisserie, but the distinctive charm of small-town Ontario shines through. A few small bistro tables are available to eat at, or you can grab takeout to enjoy outdoors.

242 Mary St., Niagara-on-the-Lake, Ont. © 905/468-2745. Most items under C$10 (US$8.50). AE, MC, V. Summer daily 8am–7:30pm; winter daily 8am–6pm.

4 Wine Country

The renaissance of the Niagara region's wine industry in the late 1980s and early 1990s attracted considerable interest from a handful of talented chefs. These chefs, with their innovative approach to cuisine and intimate understanding of the connection between the land and the cooking pot, nurtured the fledgling wine-country restaurant industry. Today, it is quite reasonable to expect good food on your travels through Niagara's vineyards. The bar is constantly being raised by the restaurateurs themselves, whose enthusiasm for food and wine continues to drive the industry to new heights. Relax, savor, enjoy.

VERY EXPENSIVE

Hillebrand Vineyard Café *AA* REGIONAL   Wine permeates this menu right from the start with cabernet whipped butter, brought with a selection of bread. Wine suggestions accompany the seasonal menu, which changes monthly to accommodate the seasonal vegetables available. A mushroom goat cheese salad comes alive with tangy beet vinaigrette dressing. Wild mushroom and thyme risotto is rich and salty with fresh Parmesan shavings on top. Try one of many fish or meat dishes such as filet of chestnut-dusted striped bass or a sampling of regionally inspired specialties. In between dinner and dessert, nibble on cheese as you finish your wine. Choose from selections such as Dragon's Breath from Nova Scotia, a soft creamy blue cheese with hints of mushrooms and almonds. The bland decor lacks a little ambience, but the expansive tasting menu and regional cuisine more than makes up for it. In the summer months, enjoy the outdoor cheese garden between 3pm and 5pm daily to bridge the hunger gap between lunch and dinner.

1249 Niagara Stone Rd., R.R. 2, Niagara-on-the-Lake, Ont. © **905/468-7123**. www.hillebrand.com. Reservations recommended. Main courses C$24–C$42 (US$20–US$35). AE, DC, MC, V. Summer daily 11:30am–3pm and 5–9pm; winter daily noon–2:30pm and 5:30–9pm.

On the Twenty Restaurant *AA* REGIONAL   As the pioneer of Niagara's estate winery restaurants, On the Twenty has a lot to live up to, and the restaurant has achieved consistency in the quality of its food over the years. Situated in quaint Jordan Village, the restaurant is associated with Inn on the Twenty across the street. Warm colors, soft lighting, and a pastoral view from the rear windows over Twenty Mile Creek combine to provide an intimate atmosphere. Service is professional and courteous. Dishes are distinctive: grilled veal sweetbreads on apricot bread pudding with walnut-scented lettuce hearts and fruit mustard, wild boar in phyllo with garlic and garbanzo, or lavender-honey roasted breast of chicken on bacon-fried greens. The wine list covers all the bases—Cave Spring Cellars' (also associated with the restaurant) own vintages, a good range of other Canadian wines, mostly Niagara, and choices from other wine regions of the world.

3836 Main St., Jordan Village, Ont. © **905-562-7313**. Reservations recommended. Main courses C$23–C$40. (US$20–US$34)AE, MC, V. Daily 11:30am–3pm and 5–9pm.

Peller Estates Winery Restaurant *AAA* FRENCH/REGIONAL   This unpretentious, inviting restaurant offers educated servers and impeccable food. Each server is trained in wine tasting, with mandatory continuing education. Pick their brains for wine to accompany any dish and feel free to inquire about basic wine knowledge.

The restaurant looks out over the vineyards, and its oak and cherrywood finishes and warm cream walls are soothing. An ever-changing menu, to keep up with the seasons, is fresh and creative. Blue crab and arugula salad is a nice start to whet the appetite. Try the coq au vin, tender fowl simmered in red wine and served with honey mushrooms and creamy whipped potatoes. Leave room for dessert: the cherry-soaked bread pudding oozes melted chocolate from the center, and will happily knock your diet into next week. But no matter, you will leave the place with a smile on your face. Enjoy the cheese garden on warmer days between 1 and 6pm.

290 John St. E., Niagara-on-the-Lake, Ont. © 888/673-5537. www.peller.com. Reservations recommended. Main courses C$24–C$42 (US$20–US$35). AE, MC, V. Summer daily noon–3pm and 5–9pm; winter daily noon–3pm and 5:30–8:30pm.

The Restaurant at Peninsula Ridge ⚜⚜⚜ FRENCH/REGIONAL   A splendid evening awaits those who choose to experience dinner at Peninsula Ridge. Chef Robert Berry's menu changes regularly to reflect the availability of seasonal produce. If pear and fennel soup appears on the menu, it's your lucky day—it is divine, particularly when accompanied by a glass of Niagara Viognier. I strongly recommend the five-course tasting menu, matched with wines (the total amount of wine served is two glasses—not excessive by any means). Whether you are a seasoned foodie or a newbie to wine-country dining, the tasting menu is a dream come true, because it allows the chef and his culinary team to take you on a gastronomic journey of dishes prepared with simplicity and using hand-foraged ingredients. At a cost of C$110 (US$96) per person including paired wines, this is well worth the investment. A prix-fixe lunch menu is good value at C$35 (US$29) for appetizer, main course, and cheese or dessert. Entrees are worth savoring: honey-and-pecan-glazed Cornish game hen or a seared breast of Hudson Valley duck served with green Dupuy lentils and duck confit. The restaurant is located in a superbly restored red-brick Victorian manor, originally built by local architect Frank Hill in Queen Anne style. A distinctive turret and cedar-shingled roof add to the character of the property. Ask for a table facing the lake which, depending on the time of year, will allow you to watch the sun set as you dine. Lunch on the patio is also a delight.

5600 King St. W., Beamsville, Ont. © 905/563-0900. Main courses C$25–C$40 (US$21–US$33). AE, DC, MC, V. Wed–Sun 11:30am–3pm and 5–9pm; Sun brunch 11am–3pm.

The Restaurant at Vineland Estates Winery ⚜⚜⚜ CONTINENTAL   One of the most consistently excellent restaurants in the Niagara region, Vineland Estates' restaurant is also arguably the prettiest of the winery restaurants. The menu changes seasonally and makes good use of local ingredients. A prix-fixe three-course lunch is excellent value at C$35 (US$29)—match with wines for another C$20 (US$17). Lunch a la carte may offer Ontario freshwater pickerel filet with mushroom ragout and mint gremolata or handmade spaghettini with oxtail morsels and roasted shallots. Seasonal ingredients are paired with complementary flavors: try rubbed Cumbrae ribeye in a smoked mushroom jus. In the fall, try the harvest squash and goat cheese ravioli. Highly recommended is the creative dinner, Vineland's version of a tasting menu. Five courses will cost you C$70 (US$58); add another C$30 (US$25) if you opt for paired wines. In the summer, reserve a table on the shaded patio if you can; you'll be treated to a view across the vineyards and toward Lake Ontario.

3620 Moyer Rd., Vineland, Ont. © 888/846-3526. Reservations required on summer weekends; recommended in winter. Main courses C$24–C$36 (US$20–US$30). AE, DC, MC, V. Summer daily 11:30am–2:30pm and 5–8:30pm; winter Wed–Sun noon–2pm and 5:30–8:30pm.

Niagara Region Dining

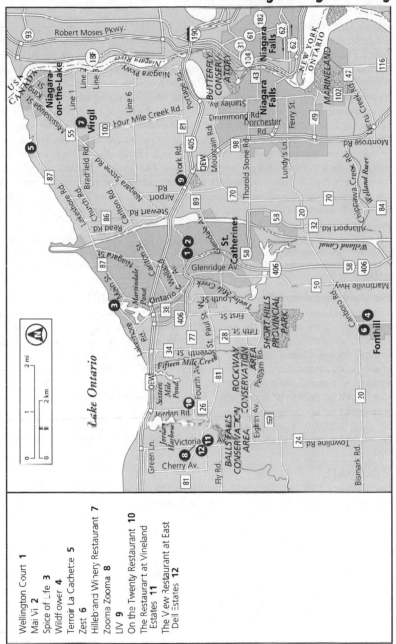

Wellington Court **1**
Mai Vi **2**
Spice of Life **3**
Wildflower **4**
Terroir La Cachette **5**
Zest **6**
Hillebrand Winery Restaurant **7**
Zooma Zooma **8**
LIV **9**
On the Twenty Restaurant **10**
The Restaurant at Vineland Estates **11**
The View Restaurant at East Dell Estates **12**

EXPENSIVE

Terroir La Cachette ✿✿✿ PROVENÇAL/REGIONAL　As its name implies, Terroir La Cachette focuses on regional wines and ingredients in its cuisine, although the French Provincial style of cooking that Quebecois chef Alain Levesque has perfected remains at the heart of the restaurant's dishes. The dining room and its pretty terrace overlook picturesque Four Mile Creek. The restaurant is located inside Strewn Winery, and although the ownership is independent, there is a strong relationship between the restaurant and the winery. A pleasing mixture of inventive and traditional dishes will satisfy adventurous and conventional dining patrons alike. When you visit you may discover skin-seared arctic char with shitake mushrooms, leeks, and lemon truffle vinaigrette; hazelnut gnocchi with fall squash ratatouille, chipotle cream, and chevre; or duck confit with sour cherries *bigarade.* The kitchen's version of traditional coq au vin is superb. House-made duck and green peppercorn terrine is another winner, especially when paired with a premium Strewn wine. Other Niagara wines are on the list; whites include Featherstone, Daniel Lenko, and Stoney Ridge, while reds are available from Creekside, Palatine Hills, and Malivoire.

1339 Lakeshore Rd., Niagara-on-the-Lake, Ont. (located inside Strewn Winery). © 905/468-1222. Reservations recommended. Main courses C$21–C$32. (US$18–US$27)AE, DC, MC, V. Summer Mon–Fri 11:30am–3:30pm and 5–9pm, Sat 11:30am–10pm, Sun 11:30am–9pm; winter Wed–Sat 11:30am–3:30pm and 5–9pm, Sun 11:30am–3:30pm and 5–8pm.

The View Restaurant (EastDell Estates Winery) ✿ REGIONAL　This restaurant, perched on high ground in the western reaches of Niagara's wine country, is decidedly country casual on the outside, but shows a little more refinement inside. There is, as you would expect, a view—in this case, it's of Lake Ontario and the Toronto skyline. Dinner entrees include grilled beef tenderloin rubbed with tandoor spices, pesto-crusted salmon, and three-cheese risotto. Lunches include Ontario beef wrapped in a tortilla shell, macaroni and cheese, and chicken liver pâté with artisanal bread. Service tends to be a little less polished than you would expect from a winery restaurant.

4041 Locust Lane, Beamsville, Ont. © 905/563-9463. www.eastdell.com. Reservations recommended, especially Sun brunch. Main courses C$17–C$26 (US$14–US$22). AE, MC, V. Summer daily 11am–9pm; winter Thurs–Sun 11am–9pm.

MODERATE

The Niagara Culinary Institute Dining Room ✿ *Value* REGIONAL　Take the opportunity to meet the next generation of innovative Niagara chefs and hospitality staff in the dining room of the Glendale Campus of Niagara College. Students enrolled in the Hospitality and Tourism Division assist in menu design, work in the kitchen, and perform front-of-house duties as part of their course requirement. Fresh herbs are supplied by the college's horticultural students, and the wine list features wines made by students at the Niagara College Teaching Winery, along with bottles from almost a dozen Niagara wineries. Most bottles are priced under the C$30 (US$25) mark. The food aims to be on a par with the better restaurants in the region, and with dishes such as maple-roasted pear and Benedictine blue cheese with spiced pecans on spinach and *frisee* salad, roasted butterfish filet with seafood cream sauce, and *tarte tatin* the students are hitting the mark. A three-course prix-fixe lunch is just C$20 (US$17), and a four-course prix-fixe dinner at C$35 (US$29) is great value for the dollar. The restaurant features panoramic windows and a casual atmosphere; student servers are charming and eager to please.

135 Taylor Rd., Niagara-on-the-Lake, Ont. 🕾 **905/641-2252.** Reservations recommended. Main courses C$17–C$19 (US$15–US$29). Tues 11:30am–2pm; Wed–Sat 11:30am–2pm and 5–8:30pm; Sun 11:30–2pm.

Zooma Zooma Café ☆ CAFE   More than just a cafe, Zooma Zooma is an escape into a mélange of retro decor and European cafe funk. Striking acidic tones of chartreuse, orange, and fuchsia wake up your senses before the first sip of espresso or cappuccino passes your lips. Great place for a light, casual lunch or midafternoon pick-me-up if you are touring wine country or hitting Jordan for its boutique shops, galleries, and antiques retailers. Their grilled vegetable sandwiches are a highlight. Packaged gourmet foods to go include brands such as Wildly Delicious, Ghirardelli, and Stonewall Kitchens. A selection of retro giftware is also on hand. Be cool, be there.

3839 Main St., Jordan, Ont. 🕾 **905/562-6280.** Reservations recommended. Main courses C$11–C$15 (US$9–US$12). AE, MC, V. Summer Sat–Thurs 10am–6pm, Fri 10am–10pm; winter Sun–Thurs 10am–5pm, Fri Sat 10am 9pm. Live music.

5 Welland Canal Corridor

The Welland Canal corridor takes in the communities of Old Port Dalhousie on the shores of Lake Ontario, the city of St. Catharines, and the town of Welland, among others. If you're exploring the area, or traversing it on the way to or from Niagara Falls, here are a few places you might like to stop for a bite to eat or a longer, more elaborate meal.

EXPENSIVE

Café Garibaldi ITALIAN   Locals like it, so there's an excellent chance you will, too. Dine on *di pesce* soup and veal scallopine. If you need a substantial feeding, a sumptuous serving of homemade lasagna will fill you up. Try local Niagara and imported Italian wines.

375 St. Paul St., St. Catharines, Ont. 🕾 **905/988-9033.** Reservations recommended. Main courses C$17–C$26 (US$14–C$22). AE, V. Mon–Sat 11:30am–2:30pm and 5–10pm.

Wellington Court ☆☆ REGIONAL   National magazines and newspapers herald this restaurant, and with good reason. Located in an Edwardian town house, local artists' paintings tastefully decorate the intimate rooms and photographs line the hallway. Appetizers include a creative blend of fried calamari with saffron yogurt, chile aioli and lemon candy and roasted garlic on Gorgonzola cream with grilled bread. Complement your dinner with a fine selection of regional wines. Expect to have your taste buds wakened with equally creative entrees: crab and ricotta manicotti in saffron tomato sauce with grilled shrimps and arugula, or pan-seared caribou on roasted cashew and rosemary bread pudding with white cheddar mornay and roasted garlic oil. Dishes are accented with herbs and light oils to coax out the true flavor of each ingredient. Menu items change with the seasons.

11 Wellington St., St. Catharines, Ont. 🕾 **905/682-5518.** www.vaxxine.com/wellington. Reservations recommended. Main courses C$20–C$30 (US$17 US$25). AE, DC, MC, V. Tues–Sat 11:30am–2:30pm and 5–9:30pm.

MODERATE

Mai Vi VIETNAMESE   Locals love this place, a classic telltale sign of a good restaurant. To be fair, it is off the beaten tourist track, being in downtown St. Catharines, but with the QEW cutting through the center of the city it's not much of an effort to find your way there—and if you're a fan of Asian food, Mai Vi is worth the trip. The

Tips Where to Stock Up for a Picnic—And Where to Enjoy It

With its lush green spaces, the Niagara region is ideal for a picnic. Here are a few places that will help you stock the perfect picnic hamper with delicious nosh.

Head down to **DeLuca's Cheesemarket and Deli** on Niagara Stone Road south of the Old Town (2017 Niagara Stone Rd., in the Forum Galleries Building, Niagara-on-the-Lake, Ont.; ℂ **905/468-2555**). Under the direction of one of Niagara's most renowned chefs, Tony DeLuca (former executive chef of Hillebrand Estates Winery), this friendly gourmet emporium has an exceptionally fine selection of cheeses. Picnic baskets, box lunches, and sandwiches are made to order to take out. Artisanal bread, charcuterie, and antipasti are all delicious.

Order a picnic from the **Shaw Festival Greenroom chefs** (Shaw Festival Box Office, 10 Queen's Parade, Niagara-on-the-Lake, Ont.; ℂ **800/511-7429**). Book when you order your theater tickets or up to 24 hours in advance of pickup time. If you're in the vicinity of Port Dalhousie, drop in to **Olson Foods and Bakery** (17 Lock St., Unit 112, Port Dalhousie, St. Catharines; ℂ **905/938-8490**). Well-known local pastry chef Anna Olson and her staff prepare yummy artisanal breads and divine desserts. Olson also stocks a first-rate variety of European and Canadian cheeses. Gourmet pantry items and upscale kitchen gifts are also available.

Wildflower restaurant (see review, below) is a little off the beaten tourist track, but with 24 hours' notice they will put together a gourmet picnic for you, with three set menus to choose from.

Just a few minutes south of Niagara-on-the-Lake on the Niagara Parkway, you'll find **Kurtz Orchards Gourmet Marketplace** (16006 Niagara Pkwy.; ℂ **905/466-2937**). This large food market and gourmet gift store has plenty of sampling stations, so you can try before you buy.

As you drive along the Niagara region's rural roads, you will find many **roadside fruit stands** during the harvest season. Some are more substantial than others and stock additional food and beverage items.

If you are touring the wineries, keep your eyes open when you browse the **winery boutiques**. Many of them keep on hand a few loaves of local artisanal bread, packets of gourmet crackers, and a limited selection of cheeses for purchase.

As for where to enjoy your picnic—turn to "Parks & Gardens" or "Hiking & Biking" in chapter 7, "What to See & Do in the Niagara Region," and choose an idyllic swath of green on which to spread your picnic cloth, recline gracefully, and while the afternoon away.

influences of Chinese, French, and Thai cuisine, classic characteristics of Vietnamese cuisine, are evident. Whether you go for stir-fry, curry, crispy roast duck, or traditional Vietnamese rice or noodle dishes, you'll not be disappointed. The menu has a separate listing for vegetarian dishes so you don't have to wade through the entire inventory of dishes if you are a meat-free diner. Equally convenient, lunch specials are grouped together for fast picks and quick munching. Portions are generous. Service is charming. A variety of healthful teas—green, ginger, or jasmine—are available.

55 St. Paul's, St. Catharines, Ont. (℗ **905/988-1426.** www.maivi.ca Reservations recommended. Main courses C$10–C$15 (US$8–US$12). AE, MC, V. Mon–Sat 11:30am–10pm; Sun 5–10pm.

Spice of Life Restaurant and Catering Services FUSION   Thank goodness for Spice of Life. Wine country aside, much of the Niagara region's cuisine is stuck in the mire of standard North American fare. Spice of Life dares to specialize in vegetarian, vegan, and gluten-free dishes but note that steak is on the menu for any carnivores who might be lurking in your dining party. The eclectic appetizers include chef Sue's award-winning samosas, a tasty concoction of spiced potatoes and green peas with fresh herbs wrapped in homemade pastry, served with a dollop of Niagara peach and pepper chutney. Hand-wrapped spring rolls come stuffed with Niagara potatoes and carrots, accented by South Asian spices and drizzled with raspberry coulis. Salads, pizza (available in vegetarian, vegan, and gluten-free forms), and pasta round out the menu. Niagara wines are available by the glass or bottle.

12 Lock St., Port Dalhousie, St. Catharines, Ont. (℗ **905/937-9027.** Reservations recommended. Main courses C$15–C$30 (US$12–US$25). AE, DC, MC, V. Summer 11:30am–3:30pm and 5–11pm daily; winter Wed–Sun 11:30am–2:30pm and 5–8:30pm.

6 Fonthill

The village of Fonthill is home to couple of restaurants whose reputation extends to the far reaches of the Niagara region.

VERY EXPENSIVE

Zest ℱ CANADIAN   The decor at Zest speaks big-city sophistication—distinctive teal blue walls, blond wood floors, and comfy leatherette upholstered chairs. But a look out of the front window will confirm small town—the view of the run-down buildings across the street is less than inviting. Thankfully, the food commands your attention. Daily specials are artfully described by the servers, their verbal delivery providing such detail as the cooking method and style of the dish and its accompaniments. Norwegian smoked salmon on a potato pancake with lemon, chives, crème fraiche, and delightful crisply fried onions makes a satisfying light lunch. Fresh herb sprouts are a surprisingly refreshing garnish. Steamed mussels in a lobster, tarragon, and champagne cream sauce is an equally pleasant alternative. Evening main courses are traditional bistro–based and well balanced. Think seared sea scallops on double smoked bacon and green lentils with black olive and tomato compote, or roasted Magret duck breast with rich game jus and honey-braised red cabbage. Or plump for the beef tenderloin, pheasant, partridge, or Quebec corn-fed chicken. The wine list is informative and a pleasure to read, with columns for the wine, vintage, origin, tasting notes, and price by the bottle and the glass. A glance from left to right sums up each wine in a flash. A good representation of Niagara grape varietals forms the backbone of the list, with *vitis vinifera* leading the way, although a French hybrid or two have bravely worked their way into the list.

1469 Pelham St., Fonthill, Ont. (℗ **905/892-6474.** www.zestfonthill.com. Reservations recommended. Main courses C$24–C$32 (US$20–$26). MC, V. Tues–Fri 11:30am–3pm and 5:30–9pm; Sat 5:30–9pm.

EXPENSIVE

Wildflower CANADIAN   Wildflower is the creation of chef/owner Wolfgang Sterr, a German-born chef who practiced his trade in Switzerland and western Canada before opening Wildflower in 1996. The eclectic midday menu, favored by ladies who lunch, features chicken, sun-dried tomato and feta quiche, croissants filled with soft-shell crab salad, and grilled veal cutlet with bread dumplings, light grain mustard, and herb cream sauce, a specialty from Sterr's hometown in Bavaria. Servings are generous—a special caution goes out to anyone considering the afternoon tea. The selection is heavily Canadian influenced, the plate groaning with thickly cut sandwiches, baked goods (scone, walnut cake, "squares," and chocolate layer cake), raspberry sorbet, fruit mousse, crème anglaise, and fresh fruit. Dinner entrees include salmon, rainbow trout, venison, and duck. There is a seasonal menu in addition to the regular menu, which showcases regional produce. The large dining room features a country look, with lots of wood.

More interesting to investigate is the Grass Roots Lounge & Bistro, a glass-enclosed wraparound veranda with comfy couches to sink into and big-city stylish high bar tables and chairs. Lunch, afternoon tea, and desserts are available during the day, but the real effort in Grass Roots is directed toward the 4-to-10pm crowd. Tapas, martinis, frozen tropical drinks, and live musical entertainment ranging from jazz guitarists to a harpist can be savored on Friday and Saturday evenings starting at 7pm.

219 Hwy. 20 E., Fonthill, Ont. (**©** **905/892-6167**. www.wildflowerrestaurant.com. Main courses C$18–C$35 (US$15–US$29). AE, DC, MC, V. Restaurant Wed–Sun 11am–9pm, lounge daily 11am–11pm.

7

What to See & Do
in the Niagara Region

The Niagara region has much to offer visitors. Naturally, first timers flock to the Falls, and quite rightly. Once you have had your fill of the Falls, there is an incredible array of activities and destinations to delight, educate, and entertain you. Many attractions are concentrated in the twin cities of Niagara Falls, Ontario, and Niagara Falls, New York, on either side of the border. The pretty town of Niagara-on-the-Lake, with its stately tree-lined streets and superbly restored and preserved historical homes, excellent live theater, and unique shopping, should be high on your list of priorities—it is one of my favorite places to visit in Canada. And no trip to Niagara is complete without a visit to the wine country to taste the award-winning VQA Ontario wines and sample the exceptional winery restaurant cuisine featuring local produce (an entire chapter is devoted to the wine region—see chapter 8, "The Wine-Country Experience").

As you delve into this chapter, you will get a good grasp of the top attractions in Niagara—a mosaic of museums, historical landmarks, galleries in which to while away an hour or two, and a smattering of the gaudy and the garish. I've also highlighted some activities that are ideal for families traveling with children. There are also many beautiful parks and gardens, which flourish in the unique microclimate of the Niagara Peninsula. Outdoor enthusiasts will find plenty of opportunities to enjoy hiking, cycling, and pastimes such as golf. Finally, I have listed some organized tours, and even provided a few self-guided ones.

Note that some advance planning may be required, since a few attractions eat up a fair bit of time, while others involve some driving. Call ahead to confirm admission hours, too—admission hours are very seasonal in the area, and can change up to 10 times during the course of the year.

1 The Top Attractions
ON THE CANADIAN SIDE
HORSESHOE FALLS ✿✿✿

There are two key factors that draw visitors in the millions to the Horseshoe Falls, or the Canadian Falls as they are also known. One is the sheer magnitude of the volume of water that flows along the Upper Niagara River and cascades over the U-shaped rock shelf into the Niagara Gorge below; the other is the fact that you can get so thrillingly close to this remarkable natural display. There are numerous vantage points, each which will give you a different experience, different emotions, and different souvenir snapshots to take home. To fully absorb the enormousness of this natural wonder, take in as many of these as you can. Top it off with the spectacle of the illuminations. If you are only in the area for a day trip, don't go home until you've seen the Falls by night.

Maid of the Mist ✶✶✶ *Kids*   A trip on the *Maid of the Mist* is a must for first-time visitors to the Falls. These small tour boats have been thrilling visitors to the Falls since 1846, when the first coal-fired steamboat equipped with two tall smoke stacks chugged daringly close to the thundering wall of water.

Before climbing aboard, you will be handed a large blue rain poncho (it's voluminous enough to cover even a backpack should you be sporting one). You can drop the poncho into the recycling bin on the way out after your trip, but you might be better off keeping it as a souvenir. You might even want to keep it on, as a protector against the mist that often drifts (or blows!) in from the Horseshoe Falls at Table Rock House, a few hundred yards upstream from the *Maid of the Mist* boat launch. Another piece of advice: resist the urge to bring out the electronics to record the event—you're better off with a waterproof disposable camera.

I must pass on a tip from a fellow passenger, who confided that he had studied the path of the boats the day before to discern the best place to stand, and kindly herded his family a little closer together so that my daughter and I could share his prime position on the upper deck of the starboard side of the boat (that's the right-hand side for you landlubbers). Most people crowd to the other side, eager to catch a close-up glimpse of the American Falls as soon as the boat leaves the dock. However, the Canadian *Maid* cautiously approaches the Horseshoe Falls with her starboard side closest to the waterfall, then veers left to return to the dock, thereby rewarding starboard passengers with a close-up of the Horseshoe Falls, followed by a panoramic sweep past the American Falls as it returns to the dock. The trip is short, so get your cameras snapping right away. Head for the upper deck for the best views and the wettest, most authentic experience. Stay below decks and you will miss the action. If you are visiting during July or August, schedule your boat ride for early- to midmorning (the first sailing is at 9am during peak season), before the lineups begin to form.

5920 River Rd., Niagara Falls, Ont. (near the foot of Clifton Hill). © **905/358-0311.** www.maidofthemist.com. Admission C$13 (US$11) adults, C$8 (US$6.60) children 6–12, free for children 5 and under. Daily Apr (opening date depends on ice conditions in the river) to late Oct. Sailing times vary by season: first trip of the day is at 9am in peak season, 9:45am in spring and fall. Last boat sails between 4:45 and 7:45pm.

Fun Fact **Niagara Trivia—Facts and Figures**

- The difference in elevation between Lake Erie and Lake Ontario is about 99m (326 ft.), with half of that height occurring at the Falls themselves.
- The Niagara River, which connects Lake Erie and Lake Ontario, is about 58km (36 miles) long.
- At Grand Island, the Niagara River divides into two channels—the Chippawa (Canadian) channel on the west, which carries approximately 60% of the total river flow, and the Tonawanda (American) channel on the east.
- The deepest section of the Niagara River is immediately below the Falls. The depth of the river here is equal to the height of the Falls—52m (170 ft.).
- There are some 500 other waterfalls in the world that have a greater elevation than Niagara Falls. However, many of them have relatively little water flow. The grandeur of Niagara Falls is attributed to a combination of its height, water volume, and picturesque setting.

Niagara Falls Attractions

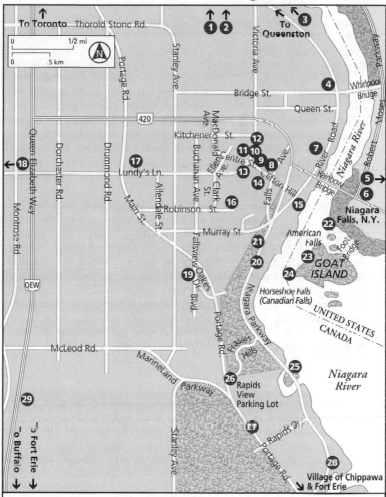

(Tips Best-Value Canadian Niagara Falls Experiences

Take advantage of the special package put together by the Niagara Parks Commission, experience the top attractions, save a bundle, and avoid line-ups all at the same time. The **Niagara Falls Great Gorge Adventure Pass,** available between May and October, grants you entry to the *Maid of the Mist,* **Journey Behind the Falls, White Water Walk,** and the **Butterfly Conservatory.** Included with the pass is all-day transportation on the **People Mover** bus and **Incline Railway** that connect the Fallsview area on top of the hill with the complex in front of the Horseshoe Falls at the bottom. The price of just C$41 (US$36) adults and C$26 (US$23) children 6 to 12 (free for kids 5 and under) is a fantastic bargain.

Between November and April, you can buy a **Winter Magic Pass,** which grants you entry to **Journey Behind the Falls, Niagara Parks Butterfly Conservatory, IMAX Theatre** *Legends and Daredevils* **Movie,** and the **Bird Kingdom** at the Niagara Falls Aviary. The Winter Magic Pass costs C$27 (US$22) adults and C$16 (US$13) children 6 to 12 (free for kids 5 and under). Coupons are included with the Winter Magic Pass that give you discounts on admission to the Skylon Tower and Niagara Helicopter Tours rides. In 2005, audio tours at the Journey Behind the Falls and the Butterfly Conservatory were added to the package at no extra cost. Another advantage is the ability to pre-book your entry time to the attractions at peak tourist periods. Rather than wasting time standing in line on busy days, use the People Mover to drop in to the attractions and book your visit for later in the day.

Konica Minolta Tower Centre *(Finds)*   Everyone wants a ride on the "yellow bug" that creeps up the outside of the Skylon Tower. But quietly standing to attention on Fallsview Boulevard, sandwiched in and overshadowed by the recent high-rise development on this stretch of the hotel district, the Konica Minolta Tower is an excellent place to view the Falls. Enter the minimalist, modestly sized lobby and purchase tickets to ride the elevator (alas, this one is enclosed by a mundane shaft) 160m (525 ft.) to the 25th floor, where you can view the Falls through a wall of outwardly angled glass, specially coated with a nonglare finish for better-quality photos. The room is carpeted, so there are no howling winds to contend with as you are likely to experience on the outdoor deck of the Skylon Tower, and if you go early in the morning you may have the entire viewing deck to yourself, since many of the hotel guests are still in the breakfast room and few other tourists are likely to be in the area at that time of day. Really early risers can watch the sunrise. Views of the illuminated Falls are also spectacular from this viewpoint. Hotel guest's have free access to the tower.

6732 Fallsview Blvd., Niagara Falls, Ont. (C) 866/325-5784 or 905/356-1501. www.niagaratower.com. Admission C$4.50 (US$3.30) adults, C$2.50 (US$2.10) children 6-12, free for children 6 and under. Purchase tickets at front reception desk of hotel. Tickets can also be purchased in advance. Year-round daily 7am–11pm.

Journey Behind the Falls   This self-guided tour takes you through tunnels bored into the rock behind the Canadian Falls, so if you suffer from claustrophobia, give this a miss—some people seem to find the idea of walking in a tunnel underneath the Falls quite unnerving, but my kids and I loved it. There are a couple of short offshoots from the main tunnel where you can peer through openings cut into the rock literally behind the Horseshoe Falls. There is not much to see except a wall of water, but it is nonetheless exhilarating to be on the "other side" of the mighty cascade.

The absolutely best part of the tour, though, is to venture outside onto the lower balcony at the northern edge of the base of the Falls. You will get wetter than wet (much more so than on the *Maid of the Mist*), but it is more than worth the inconvenience. Recyclable rain ponchos are provided (yellow, instead of the blue ones for the boat ride), but you're still likely to get drenched in spray or a rogue cascade of water depending on the wind direction and strength. Of all the ways and means you can access the Horseshoe Falls, this is the place where you will feel the power of the Falls at its mightiest. The roar of the water is thrilling beyond compare.

The Journey Behind the Falls is one of the attractions included in the Great Gorge Adventure Pass. During peak season, the attraction operates on a timed entry system with a maximum number of visitors allowed through at any one time. You can visit the ticket booth early in the day and pre-book your entry time, saving you the inconvenience and frustration of standing in line.

6650 Niagara River Pkwy., Niagara Falls, Ont., inside the Table Rock Complex. © 877/642-7275. www.niagaraparks. com/nfgg/behindthefalls.php. C$10 (US$8.30) adults, C$6 (US$5) children 6–12, free for children 5 and under. Year-round Sun–Fri 9am–7:30pm; Sat 9am–8:30pm. Last ticket sold 30 min. before closing.

Skylon Tower   One of the most distinctive structures on the skyline on the Canadian side of Niagara Falls is the 236m-high (775-ft.) Skylon Tower. Built in 1965, it dominated the landscape on the hill above the Falls for more than 30 years. In recent years increasingly taller hotels have been sprouting up in the district, but the Skylon still attracts attention—it's almost a vintage landmark. The brightly painted elevators that crawl up the outside of the tower are affectionately known as "yellow bugs," and most visitors don't feel like they've "done" the Falls until they've had a ride up to the observation deck. In addition to the indoor viewing area, there is an outdoor deck protected by a wire mesh screen. Be prepared for windy conditions outside, even if there is only a slight breeze at ground level. At the base of the tower there is a maze of shops selling trinkets and a cavernous arcade zone. Ticket prices are rather high—if you are planning to ascend the tower, I recommend dropping in to Niagara Falls Tourism (5515 Stanley Ave.; © **905/356-5567**) to find out whether discount coupons are available (often there are booklets that have coupons for many of the attractions not included in the Great Gorge Adventure Pass), or ask at your hotel.

5200 Robinson St., Niagara Falls, Ont. © **905/356-2651**. www.skylon.com. C$12 (US$9.50) adults, C$6 (US$5) children 12 and under. Summer daily 8am–midnight; winter daily 11am–9pm.

⌒Tips Catch the Rainbow

If you want to gaze upon the rainbow in the mist of the Horseshoe Falls, you need to view the Falls from the Canadian shore during the afternoon. Sunlight slants through the water droplets dancing in the air in mid- to late afternoon, depending on the time of year, creating the mystical band of color that is such a profound symbol of the wonder of nature.

BEYOND THE FALLS

Butterfly Conservatory   A visit to the Butterfly Conservatory can be combined with a leisurely stroll around the Niagara Parks Botanical Gardens, since the building is located right on the grounds. The Conservatory is a bright and airy rainforest-like environment that is carefully climate-controlled. A multi-level pathway (stroller and wheelchair accessible), winds its way through the lush foliage. There are an amazing 2,000 tropical butterflies representing 50 different species living freely in the Conservatory.

This is an absolutely delightful place to spend an hour or so. The trick is to walk slowly and pause often, since the most rewarding discoveries are usually found through quiet observation. Often the butterflies will land on visitors, but it is important not to touch them, because they are extremely delicate and easily injured. It can be quite comical to see butterflies hitching a ride on the hat or shoulder of the person in front of you, who may be wandering around completely unaware of their natural adornment. There is a butterfly "nursery" with an observation window looking onto several stages of metamorphosis, and the window is opened several times daily to allow newly emerged butterflies to enter their new home in the Conservatory.

There is an abundance of natural light, and since the butterflies do spend a considerable amount of time resting (you might almost believe they are posing for photos), it is a great place to bring your camera. The Conservatory doubles as the display greenhouse for the Niagara Parks Botanical Gardens. With more than 100 exotic plants in its tropical plant collection, the Conservatory also provides a rare opportunity to come into close contact with plants rarely seen in the Northern Hemisphere, and another reason for photographers to indulge in their passion.

The Conservatory is serviced by the People Mover bus and is one of the attractions included in the Great Gorge Adventure Pass. Due to space restrictions, the number of visitors allowed into the Conservatory at any one time is limited, and you may have to wait during peak season before entering.

2405 Niagara River Pkwy., Niagara Falls, Ont. (𝄐 877/642-7275. www.niagaraparks.com/nature/butterfly.php. Admission C$10 (US$8.30) adults, C$6 (US$5) children 6–12, free for children 5 and under. Year-round daily 9am–5pm. Closed Dec. 25. Last ticket sold 30 min. before closing.

Whirlpool Aero Car   Often called the Spanish Aero Car, since it was designed by Spanish engineer Leonardo Torres Quevedo and built in Bilboa, Spain, the Whirlpool Aero Car takes visitors on a hair-raising trip 75m (246 ft.) above the Niagara Gorge. Suspended between two points on the Canadian shore of the Niagara River, six sturdy cables support the uniquely crafted carriage, which holds 40 standing passengers. The car crawls along the cables on a 1km round-trip between Colt's Point and Thompson's Point, allowing tourists a bird's eye view of the natural phenomenon of the Niagara Whirlpool. Although the car remains in its original form when it began operating in 1916, the wheels, electric circuits, and track cable suspension system were modernized in the 1980s. The trip is only 10 minutes long, and you can see the whirlpool from the land, so if it's a busy day and the lineup is long, consider giving this attraction a miss. The winding stairwell that leads to the entrance to the aero car can be stifling on a hot day, too, despite the roof covering that gives some protection from the sun. And those who are afraid of heights should definitely stay on terra firma.

3850 Niagara River Pkwy., Niagara Falls, Ont. (𝄐 877/642-7275. www.niagaraparks.com/nfgg/aerocar.php. Admission C$10 (US$8.30) adults, C$6 (US$5) children 6–12, free for children 5 and under. Mon–Fri 9am–5pm; Sat–Sun 9am–6pm. Operation depends on wind and weather conditions. Last ticket sold 30 min. before closing.

(Fun Fact The Old Scow

If you look upriver from the Horseshoe Falls and scan the surface of the turbulent water, you will see an old scow that became stuck on the shoals way back in 1918. The scow, a flat-bottomed boat used for transporting cargo to and from ships, broke loose from its tugboat. Two men were stranded onboard as the scow made its way with increasing speed toward the Horseshoe Falls. In a desperate attempt to save themselves, the men opened the bottom doors of the scow and flooded it. Fortunately, the scow became wedged against a rocky ledge, but due to the complicated nature of the rescue operation it was 19 hours later when the men finally were brought on shore.

White Water Walk ⚸   Wow. The raw energy of nature pulsates through you as you make your way down the boardwalk that trails along the rocky, tree-lined shore at the base of the Niagara Gorge (an elevator takes you down to river level). Stand next to the Class V and VI Niagara River rapids, one of the world's wildest stretches of white water. The ever-changing spectacle of waves, swell, foam, and spray is mesmerizing. Fidgety folks will do the walk amiably enough, but then ask what's next on the agenda. Others, like myself, are drawn to the power of the water in motion and are quite content to stand and watch in fixed fascination, completely unaware of the passing of time.

Visit any time between April and November to see the rapids, but if you are in Niagara in the autumn you absolutely must take this walk, since the wooden walkway is constructed under a canopy of deciduous trees. Warm autumn sunlight, orange, red, and gold leaves, the raging torrents of the rapids . . . it's a spectacular sight. And photographers take note—there are great nature shots here.

4330 Niagara Pkwy., Niagara Falls, Ont. ℂ 877/642-7275. www.niagaraparks.com/nfgg/whitewater.php. Admission C$7.50 (US$6) adults, C$4.50 (US$3.75) children 6–12, free for children 5 and under. Mid-Apr to late Nov, Mon–Fri 9am–5pm, Sat–Sun 9am–6pm. Last ticket sold 30 min. before closing.

ON THE AMERICAN SIDE
AMERICAN FALLS ⚸

The crest line of the American Falls, also sometimes referred to as the Rainbow Falls, is approximately 290m wide (950 ft.); the depth of the water flowing over the crest line is only about half a meter (about 2 ft.). Just south of the main waterfall there is a smaller waterfall which is a mere 17m wide (56 ft.) at the crest line. This pretty waterfall resembles a bride's veil, hence the name Bridal Veil Falls, although it is also known as Luna Falls and Iris Falls. Bridal Veil Falls is separated from the American Falls by a thin strip of land called Luna Island. A massive amount of broken rock covers the base of the American and Bridal Veil Falls, contributing to their dramatic appearance. As the sun rises in the east, rainbows can often be seen as the light shines through the mist of the Falls. In order to feel the magnitude of the power of the churning water, you need to get up close and personal. Take the *Maid of the Mist* boat tour, which will take you past the American Falls and daringly close to the base of the Horseshoe Falls, walk along the pathway to the "Crow's Nest" at the base of the Observation Tower, or take the *Cave of the Winds* guided walking tour, which leads you along boardwalks down into the gorge—only 6m (20 ft.) away from the falling water at its closest point. Note, however, that the best views of the Falls are from the Canadian shore.

Cave of the Winds   This well-established attraction features a guided tour along wooden walkways at the base of the Bridal Veil Falls, and has recently been updated. Accessed from Goat Island, an elevator takes you 53m (175 ft.) down into the Niagara Gorge. Sporting a yellow recyclable waterproof poncho and snazzy Velcro-closure souvenir non-slip sandals, follow your tour guide along the boardwalks to the "Hurricane Deck," where you stand just 6m (20 ft.) from the thundering waters of Bridal Veil Falls. You are likely to get doused with a generous spray of water, so consider yourself warned. A second deck has been constructed 45m (150 ft.) away from the base of the Falls, designed especially for physically challenged visitors and adults carrying small children. For a really wild experience, descend after nightfall and enjoy the illuminations as you've never seen them before—surrounded by multi-colored cascading torrents of water.

Goat Island, Niagara Falls State Park, Niagara Falls, NY. ⓒ **716/278-1796.** www.niagarafallsstatepark.com. Admission C$9.60 (US$8) adults, C$8.40 (US$7) children 6–12 (must be at least 42 in. tall), free for children 5 and under; those under 42 in. tall must be accompanied by an adult and admission is restricted to certain areas of the walkway. Seasonal operation daily 9am–11pm.

Maid of the Mist   This is a must-do for visitors to the Falls—it might seem touristy, but it's well worth the trip. The *Maid of the Mist* operates on both sides of the Niagara Gorge, but each boat essentially provides the same experience, passing close to the base of the American Falls and into the horseshoe of the Canadian Falls. Boats on the American side dock at the base of the Observation Tower near Prospect Point in the Niagara Falls State Park. Recyclable blue rain ponchos are issued, which you can keep as a souvenir if you wish. Tickets include entry to the Observation Tower, since access to the boat dock is via the tower elevators. Admission included with the purchase of a *Passport to the Falls*. Tour lasts 30 minutes.

Inside Niagara Falls State Park, at the base of the Observation Tower, Niagara Falls, NY. ⓒ **716/284-8897.** Admission C$14 (US$12) adults, C$8 (US$6.75) children 6–12, free for children 5 and under. Apr–Oct daily 10am–8pm (depending on weather conditions).

Observation Tower   Included with the Niagara Falls State Park Passport to the Falls, this 85m-high (280-ft.) tower has an outside observation deck that extends past the Niagara Gorge cliff face to allow visitors a breathtaking view of the American Falls. Take the elevator to the top for the best views. The elevator also descends to the base of the gorge to provide tourists with access to the *Maid of the Mist* boat ride. At the base of the observation tower are a groomed pathway and stairs leading to the "Crow's Nest," an observation deck close to the huge boulders at the base of the American Falls—a unique perspective that is worth the journey.

Fun Fact **The Original Cave of the Winds**

The original Cave of the Winds was a true cavern, located behind the Bridal Veil Falls. It measured approximately 40m high (130 ft.), 30m wide (100 ft.), and 9m deep (30 ft.). Prior to the mid-1900s, tourists could enter the cave via a pathway. In 1954, a major rockfall occurred at Prospect Point, followed by several smaller rockfalls at Terrapin Point. Subsequently, an overhanging ledge of dolostone at the entrance to the cave was deemed to be in danger of collapse, and in 1955 the cave was demolished by a controlled dynamite blast.

Best-Value Niagara Falls American Experiences

Take advantage of the special package put together by the Niagara Falls State Park to experience the top attractions and save a bundle at the same time. The **Niagara Falls State Park Passport to the Falls** grants you entry to the *Maid of the Mist,* **Observation Tower, Festival Theater, Aquarium of Niagara,** and the **Niagara Gorge Discovery Center.** Included with the pass is all-day transportation on the **Niagara Scenic Trolley,** which takes you on a 4.8km (3-mile) guided tour of Niagara Falls State Park, with frequent stops to allow visitors to hop on and off at the major attractions and scenic vistas throughout the park. The price of just C$29 (US$25) adults and C$21 (US$18) children 6 to 12 (free for kids 5 and under) is a fantastic bargain. The Passport to the Falls also includes discounted admission to Artpark, Old Fort Niagara, and the Historical Wax Museum. Discounts at snack centers and gift shops are also included. You can purchase the Passport at the Niagara Falls State Park Visitor Center, the Niagara Gorge Discovery Center, and at American Automobile Association (AAA) offices in Buffalo, Rochester, and Syracuse, New York.

Inside Niagara Falls State Park, just north of the American Falls. © 716/278-1762. Admission C$1.20 (US$1) adults and children 6 and over, free for children 5 and under. Late Mar to Dec daily 9am–8pm.

BEYOND THE FALLS

Aquarium of Niagara   Experience marine life up close at the Aquarium of Niagara, just a short walk over the bridge from the Niagara Gorge Discovery Centre, one of the stops on the Niagara Scenic Trolley route. Several times daily, you can watch the penguin feeding, sea lion shows, and harbor seal sessions. Tidal pool and shark feedings are available for observation on alternate days. More than 40 exhibits contain a total of 1,500 aquatic animals from around the world. A great place to take the kids.

701 Whirlpool St., Niagara Falls, NY. © 800/500-4609 or 716/285-3575. www.aquariumofniagara.org. Admission C$9 (US$7.50) adults, C$6.60 (US$5.50) seniors, C$6.60 (US$5.50) children 4–12, free for children 3 and under. Late May to early Sept daily 9am–7pm; early Sept to late May daily 9am–5pm.

2 Museums & Historical Landmarks

From the War of 1812 to the American Revolution to the Underground Railroad of slavery, today's Niagara museums remain to tell the rich stories. The area boasts some of the best-reconstructed forts and historical sites in the country. Spanning from Niagara-on-the-Lake across to the Welland Canal, where thousands of ships come through every year, Niagara's museums present a broad range of artifacts and history that comes to life with educational interpreters and costumed guides at some of the larger venues. Follow the descriptions below, as some sites are more worthy of your time than others.

NIAGARA FALLS, ONTARIO AND NEW YORK

Chippawa Battlefield Park   On July 5, 1814, 200 Canadian, American, British, and Native warriors died in battle in the bloodiest and longest military operation during the War of 1812. About 2,000 British, Canadian, and Aboriginal forces fended off an invading American army of about 3,500 men. Many of these fallen soldiers are said to be buried on the site. Today, a cairn stands in memory of the battle and subsequent peace between Canada and the United States. On the grounds, visitors can take a self-guided tour outlined on storyboards. A memorial service is held annually on July 5.

9233 Niagara Pkwy. (beside Legends of the Niagara golf course), Niagara Falls, Ont. ℂ 905/371-0254.

Lundy's Lane Historical Museum   Find a collection of folklore and history pertaining to Niagara Falls inside this museum, situated in a limestone building dating back to 1874—there's everything from historical prints of the Falls to War of 1812 artifacts. (The Battle of Lundy's Lane was fought east of this soil—a significant battle of the War of 1812.) Later, the basement of the museum housed the Drummondville Fire Department; the building also served as the Stamford Town Hall until the township amalgamated with Niagara Falls. Outside the entrance, the Queen Victoria Memorial Fountain commemorates Victoria's reign of 64 years. Built in 1901 from 82 pieces of limestone, each stone represents a year of the queen's life. Museum artifacts—the uniforms of soldiers and firefighters—are housed in glass cases, which makes for a lackluster presentation. However, anyone who loves history can get lost in the eclectic mix of toys, uniforms, and soldier paraphernalia. A half-hour is enough to get a taste of this museum offering.

5810 Ferry St., Niagara Falls, Ont. ℂ **905/358-5082.** Fax 905-358-0920. www.lundyslanemuseum.com. Admission C$3 (US$2.50) adults, C$2.50 (US$2) students and seniors, C$2 (US$1) children 6–12, free for children under 6. Jan–May noon–4pm; May–Oct 31 10am–5pm daily; Nov–Dec Wed–Sun noon–4pm.

Old Fort Niagara ❀ 𝘒𝘪𝘥𝘴   Built as an outpost, it gradually became a fortress. Constructed in 1726 on the bluffs above Lake Ontario by the French, and strategically located at the mouth of the Niagara River, this fort held an important position helping to shape Canada. French maintained the first post here, but in 1759, during the French and Indian War, the British took over and retained control throughout the American Revolution. During the two world wars Fort Niagara served as a barracks and training station. Restoration was completed in the mid-1930s. Tour outside through the old buildings and enjoy the beautiful view of the lake. Educational tours are available. Inside, costumed interpreters provide tours three to four times a day in the summer, which typically last an hour (tours are included in admission price). Group tours are also available with advance notice only (between 1 and 2 hours). In the summer don't miss the musket firing demonstration.

Fort Niagara Historic Site, Youngstown, NY. ℂ **716/745-7611.** www.oldfortniagara.org. Admission C$10 (US$8.50) adults, C$6 (US$5) children 6–12, free for children under 6. Open daily 9am year-round; closing hours vary with seasons.

NIAGARA-ON-THE-LAKE AND QUEENSTON

Butler's Barracks   Originally a group of 19 buildings acting as the Indian Department British site, Butler's Barracks was named after Colonel John Butler, the deputy superintendent. The current two-story museum, built in 1817, was used primarily as a barracks storeroom until the mid 1960s. The site has also been a training camp for militia serving in World Wars I and II, the Boer War, the Korean War, and in peacekeeping efforts in the 20th century. Today in the 21st century, there's a handful of buildings left—the Korean War building, the gunshed, and the officers' quarters, to name a few. Take a tour through the outside area, guided by interpretive plaques. Worth a visit to get a history lesson.

Corner of John St. and King St., Niagara-on-the-Lake, Ont. ℂ **905/468-4257.** Free admission.

What to See & Do in Niagara-on-the-Lake

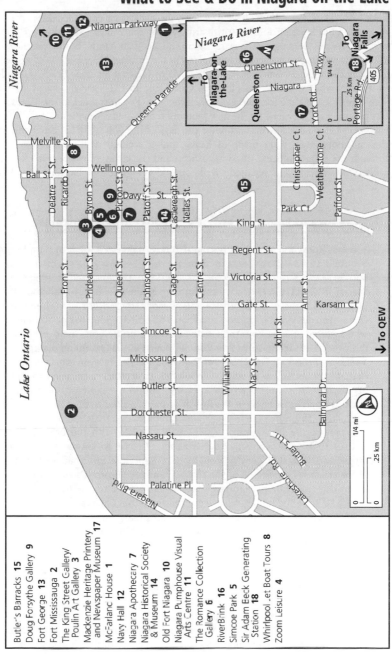

Bute's Barracks **15**
Doug Forsythe Gallery **9**
Fort George **13**
Fort Mississauga **2**
The King Street Gallery/
  Poulin Art Gallery **3**
Mackenzie Heritage Printery
  and Newspaper Museum **17**
McFarland House **1**
Navy Hall **12**
Niagara Apothecary **7**
Niagara Historical Society
  & Museum **14**
Old Fort Niagara **10**
Niagara Pumphouse Visual
  Arts Centre **11**
The Romance Collection
  Gallery **6**
RiverBrink **16**
Simcoe Park **5**
Sir Adam Beck Generating
  Station **18**
Whirlpool Jet Boat Tours **8**
Zoom Leisure **4**

Fort George ⊛ (Kids)   If you have time for only one fort on your trip, this is the one to see. As a headquarters for the British army during the War of 1812, this fort played a pivotal role in keeping the Niagara region in Canadian hands. Built from 1796 to 1799, this fort was constructed to complement the existing Navy Hall buildings safe-guarding the region. Commander-in-Chief Major-General Sir Isaac Brock was killed by a sniper when the Americans invaded Queenston in 1813 and destroyed the fort. The British re-took the fort and garrisoned the area. Reconstructed in the 1930s, the fort became a military base for the new Dominion of Canada Army until 1965. Today, visitors can step back in time and relive the days of the War of 1812. Enter through the enormous main gates made of heavy timber secured with iron spikes. Tour through the elegant officers' quarters, offices, and the artificers where war tools and artillery were made and repaired. Walk outside alongside the cannons facing the

The Story of Laura Secord: It's Not Just About Chocolate

You may know the brand of chocolate, but its namesake is a lady with her own tale. Laura Ingersoll Secord, wife of British Loyalist James Secord, was born in Massachusetts but residing in Queenston, Upper Canada during the War of 1812, as the Americans were fighting against the British (Canadians). In May 1813, three American soldiers invaded the Secord homestead in Queenston demanding lodging and food. As Secord tended to her husband, who suffered injuries from the Battle of Queenston Heights, she overheard the officers speaking: American Colonel Boerstler was planning a surprise attack on British Lt. Fitzgibbon at Beaverdams. The fate of the Canadian Niagara Peninsula was at stake. She told the soldiers she was going to visit her brother so as not to arouse suspicion, and in the morning began the 32km (19-mile) trek to warn the British of the invasion.

Walking through enemy lines and climbing the treacherous Niagara Escarpment, she finally met up with Natives allied with the British. The Natives took Secord directly to Fitzgibbon. Thanks to Laura Secord the attack was thwarted, leaving the Niagara Peninsula in Canadian hands. There are many renditions of the story—some say Secord walked barefoot along the way; others reported that she brought a cow with her as an excuse to leave the home. What is for certain is that Canada as we know it wouldn't be the same without her courageous feat.

Years later, at the age of 85, Secord finally received recognition: the Prince of Wales heard of her heroic act and gave her £100. In 1913, the centennial anniversary of Secord's journey, a small Toronto-based chocolatier named Frank P. O'Connor chose the name Laura Secord for his single Yonge Street location. O'Connor wanted his company to represent the same wholesome-ness, purity, domesticity, and cleanliness that Laura Secord espoused. Today, her silhouette still appears as the company logo. Visitors to the Niagara region can visit the old Secord homestead, complete with costumed tour guides and a monument dedicated to Laura Secord, located in the Queen-ston Heights Park (14184 Niagara Pkwy.). And while Canadians may view this intrepid lady as a heroine, Americans may not hold the same view.

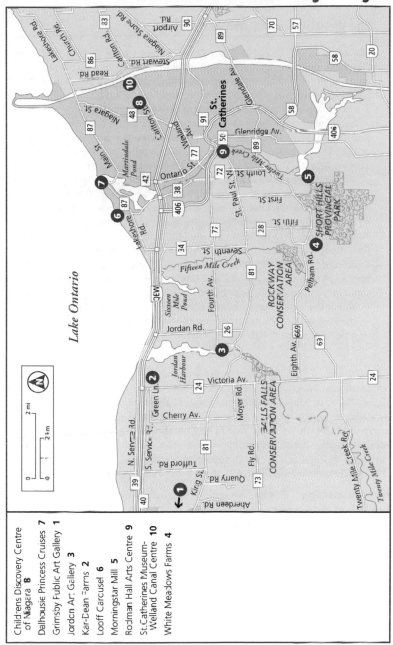

Children's Discovery Centre
  of Niagara **8**
Dalhousie Princess Cruises **7**
Grimsby Public Art Gallery **1**
Jordan Art Gallery **3**
Kar-Dean Farms **2**
Looff Carousel **6**
Morningstar Mill **5**
Rodman Hall Arts Centre **9**
St.Catherines Museum-
  Welland Canal Centre **10**
White Meadows Farms **4**

The Welland Canal Corridor

The 44km-long (27-mile) **Welland Canal** connects **Lake Ontario** with **Lake Erie** via a series of eight locks and roughly divides the Niagara region in half. The present canal, which is used primarily by bulk carriers transporting commodities such as grain and iron ore, was built in 1932. It is the fourth in a series of canals, the first of which was constructed in 1829.

At the head of the Canal sits the port city of **St. Catharines,** where you will find the **Welland Canal Centre** and **Lock 3 viewing platform** (see listing p. 127). The **St. Catharines Museum** is also located at this site. Moving south along the Canal, **Thorold,** with its **Lock 7 viewing area,** offers another great observation spot as well as a tourist information center with lots of information on the Canal and the ships that sail up and down the waterway, a wooden outdoor deck for viewing, and a small snack bar (50 Chapel St. S.; ✆ **905/680-9477**). The world-famous Twinned Flight Locks are also located in Thorold, although there isn't a convenient place to stop and view them in operation. These locks raise and lower ships up and down the Niagara Escarpment (43m/140 ft.). This is the only place on the canal where there is two-way vessel traffic. Thorold also boasts an inn where you can stay and view the ships passing by your balcony. Farther south is the city of **Welland.** Finally, at the connection with Lake Erie lies the marine city of **Port Colborne.**

The Welland Canal is open between March and December. Call ahead for ship viewing times ✆ **800/305-5134** or 905/984-8880.

American Fort Niagara and get a sense of how intense the fighting must have been almost 200 years ago. During the main season, there are regular re-enactments staged throughout the day, narrated by knowledgeable and highly entertaining costumed interpreters. See the "soldiers" prepare and fire the noon-hour cannon. Watch a musket drill or enjoy the military band.

26 Queen St., Niagara-on-the-Lake, Ont. ✆ 905/468-4257. www.pc.gc.ca. Admission C$10 (US$8.50) adults, C$8.50 (US$7) seniors, C$5 (US$4) children 6–12, free for children 5 and under. May to end of Nov daily 10am–5pm.

Fort Mississauga   This fort was built to help defend the British against subsequent attacks from the Americans after the War of 1812. After the Americans burned down the town of Newark (Niagara-on-the-Lake)—the first capital of Upper Canada—remaining stones and bricks were used to construct Fort Mississauga's central tower foundation. Today, the Niagara-on-the-Lake Golf Club resides here. Access the pedestrian trail on the corner of Simcoe and Front streets, which leads to the fort. There is no museum on this site, only exterior plaques and a fantastic view of Lake Ontario and the mouth of the Niagara River.

On the grounds of Niagara-on-the-Lake Golf Club at 143 Front St., Niagara-on-the-Lake, Ont.

Laura Secord Homestead   The former home of Laura Secord—a Canadian heroine of the War of 1812—is only a 10-minute drive along the Niagara Parkway from Niagara Falls. The home has been restored and includes Upper Canadian furniture from the era (1803–35) and artifacts recovered from an archaeological dig. Costumed staff add to the authenticity of the tours, which run every half-hour. Don't forget to stop by the small gift shop for refreshments and Canada's famous Laura Secord chocolates. A visit to the homestead will give you a good sense of Secord's heroic journey and the local history of the era.

29 Queenston St., Queenston, Ont. © **905/262-4851.** www.niagaraparks.com/heritage/laurasecord.php. Admission C$3.50 (US$3) adults, free for children 5 and under. Mid-May to mid-Sept Wed–Sun 11am–4pm.

McFarland House   Get a taste of living back—way back—in the 1800s in the old homestead of John McFarland. John and his sons constructed the house using bricks made in a kiln right on the property. The house later became a British military headquarters and then served as a makeshift hospital during the War of 1812 for both American and British soldiers. The home was badly damaged while McFarland was held prisoner during the war, and he was deeply saddened by its dilapidated state when he eventually returned from New York. Today the home, with re-created 19th-century herb garden, rooms, clothing displays, and teahouse, has been brought back to its glory days. Enjoy tea, home-baked goods, and light lunches while taking in the spectacle of flowers and greenery from the patio in the summer. Costumed interpreters educate visitors about the history of tea and the tumultuous history of the house and its era.

15927 Niagara Pkwy., Niagara-on-the-Lake, Ont. © **905/468-3322.** Admission C$3.50 (US$3) adults, free for children 5 and under. May 21–June 24 daily 11am–4pm; June 25–Sept 5 daily 11am–5pm.

Mackenzie Heritage Printery and Newspaper Museum (*Kids*)   See how far communication has come at Canada's largest working printing museum. Publisher William Lyon Mackenzie first printed *The Colonial Advocate* here in May 18, 1824. Mackenzie championed land rights, unfair court practices, and poor schools and roads from these very presses. See the Linotype in action as 5,000 moving parts work in conjunction to bring the news. Equally impressive is the 1760 "Louis Roy Press," known to be the oldest press in Canada and one of a very few wooden presses remaining in the world. The entire collection comprises 10 operating presses ranging from the mid-1800s to the 1900s. What's more, visitors can arrange their own type and print out pages using a hot metal typecaster. Stop the presses!

1 Queenston St., Queenston, Ont. © **905/262-5676.** www.mackenzieprintery.ca. Admission C$3.50 (US$3) adults, free for children 5 and under. Mid-May to mid-Sept Wed–Sun 11am–4pm.

How Does a Lock Work?

In simple terms, here's how a ship "climbs" up the river. (Just reverse the steps for going down.)

- The boat approaches the bottom gates of the lock, which has a water level the same as the river on the downstream side.
- The lock gates swing open on the downstream side and the ship enters the lock.
- The lock gates are closed behind the boat.
- Valves on the upstream side of the lock are opened to let water into the lock until the water level in the lock is the same as the water on the upstream side.
- The gates on the upstream side of the lock are opened and the ship leaves the lock.

Fun Fact **The Hermit of Niagara**

In 1829, a young man named Francis Abbott took up residence on Goat Island in an abandoned log cabin, despite a lack of permission from the landowners to live there. For the next 2 years he was the sole inhabitant of the island and often entertained tourists with his antics, such as balancing on the wooden pier leading to Terrapin Tower. He died by drowning in June 1831, while bathing in the Niagara River.

Navy Hall   British naval craftsmen from Fort Niagara built a barracks on the west bank of the Niagara River in 1765. A smattering of buildings over the years became known as Navy Hall. During the American Revolution, Lieutenant-Governor John Graves Simcoe made one of the buildings his home. It later served as a dining hall for Fort George officers. Navy Hall was destroyed during the War of 1812. The British rebuilt some of the buildings after the war—today, only one remains. The building is not open to the public, but the area is great for lounging and taking in the view of the Niagara Fort and the Niagara River.

26 Queen St., Niagara-on-the-Lake, Ont. ⓒ 905/468-4257.

Niagara Apothecary   This historical building on Niagara-on-the-Lake's best-known commercial street, Queen Street, is one of the oldest continually operating pharmacies in Canada—dispensing medicines from 1820 to 1964. Originally known as Field's Drug Store, the Niagara Apothecary has been restored by the Ontario College of Pharmacists with assistance from the federal government and the Ontario Heritage Foundation, which now owns the building. Many of the original containers, prescription books, and account books have been recovered and are on display. Stop in for a peek while shopping on Queen Street.

5 Queen St., Niagara-on-the-Lake, Ont. ⓒ 905/468-3845. Free admission. Mid-May to early Sept daily noon–6pm; early Sept to mid-Oct Sat–Sun 11am–6pm.

Niagara Historical Society & Museum   This museum serves as a repository for artifacts and treasures from Niagara-on-the-Lake's history. The Niagara Historical Society, formed in the mid-1890s by a local retired schoolteacher, began collecting local artifacts and documents at a time when most museums were focused upon acquisition and display of foreign objects of interest. The museum is a rich source of local knowledge, offering guided tours of the town, lectures, and special exhibitions. If you're a history fan, this place will take a good hour or two to visit. Prearranged tours are available.

43 Castlereagh St., Niagara-on-the-Lake, Ont. ⓒ 905/468-3912. www.niagara.com/~nhs. Admission C$5 (US$4) adults, C$3 (US$2.50) seniors, C$2 (US$1.65) students, C$1 (US85¢) children 5–12, free for children 5 and under. May–Oct daily 10am–5:30pm; Nov–Apr daily 1–5pm.

Sir Adam Beck Generating Station   The Niagara River is one of the world's most important sources of hydroelectric power, generating clean, low-cost, renewable, and reliable electricity. Sir Adam Beck Generating Station No. 2, one of Ontario's largest hydroelectric facilities, is built into the side of the Niagara Gorge, 10km (6 miles) downstream from Niagara Falls near Queenston. Water from the Niagara River is delivered to the power plant through two 9km (5½-mile) tunnels built under the city of Niagara Falls. Take a comprehensive, fully guided public tour of the power station. Learn about the history of the station and how it was constructed and soak up plenty of statistics (the guides are engineers). The tour lasts approximately 40 minutes and includes a short film presentation. If you've never been to a generating station, this is a great overview of how one works. Note that all bags, including purses, must be secured in lockers during the tour. Good for all ages.

14000 Niagara Pkwy., Queenston, Ont. ℂ 877/642-7275. www.opg.com. Admission C$7.50 (US$6) adults; C$4.50 (US$3.75) children 6–12, free for children 5 and under. Mid-Mar to early Dec daily 10am–4pm. Tours every 30 min, June–Aug, hourly remainder of the year.

ST CATHARINES

Morningstar Mill   This site is a unique example of early Ontario milling heritage and the mill and miller's house have been designated as buildings of historical and architectural interest and value under the Ontario Heritage Act. The Morningstar Mill Park, Interpretive Centre, and Museum are operated by volunteers. A number of buildings are on the site—the gristmill, a turbine shed, the miller's house, an icehouse, a barn, and a sawmill. The sawmill is a recently completed reconstruction, since the original building was abandoned during the 1930s and eventually completely dismantled. The volunteers who work to restore and maintain the site have been working on adding a blacksmith shop and carpentry shop. Bags of flour, bran, and cornmeal that have been ground on-site are on sale at the mill. Admission is free, although donations from visitors are always appreciated.

2710 Decew Rd., St. Catharines, Ont. Info@morningstarmill.ca. www.morningstarmill.ca. Free admission. Mid-May to mid-Oct Tues 9am–3pm, Thurs 9am–3pm, Sat–Sun noon–5pm; public holiday Mondays noon–5pm. Since the Mill is run by volunteers, these hours are not guaranteed.

Welland Canal Centre at Lock 3   Here, visitors can watch the ships pass by from a bird's eye view atop a gigantic raised platform. Inside, watch the 15-minute film *Welland Canals Past and Present* to learn about the history of one of the tallest water staircases in the world—100m high (327 ft.). This visit is worth at least a half-hour atop even if you're not a salty dog.

The **St. Catharines Museum,** housed in the same building, features an exhibit on the Underground Railroad as well as an impressive collection of maps, photographs, and more. Working models of the locks and bridges are on display. Don't leave without taking another half-hour to see this impressive museum.

1932 Welland Canals Pkwy., St. Catharines, Ont. ℂ 800/305-5134 or 905/984-8880. www.stcatharineslock3museum.ca. Admission C$4.25 (US$3.50) adults, C$4 (US$3) seniors, C$3.25 (US$2.70) students (over 14), C$2.50 (US$2) children 6–13, free for children 5 and under, family discount 15%. Summer daily 9am–5pm; winter Sat–Sun 10am–5pm.

FORT ERIE AND PORT COLBORNE

Fort Erie Historical & Ridgeway Battlefield Site   In June 1866, Irish-American veterans of the U.S. Civil War fought Canadian forces in hopes of gaining Ireland's independence from England. Today there is a commemorative cairn built on Highway 3, near Ridge Road, close to the old battlefield site; the site and cairn can be viewed at any time at the Ridgeway Battlefield Site. The Fort Erie Historical Museum tells a story dating back 10,000 years to the first aboriginal settlement—the outdated exhibits, viewed through glass cases, don't make it the most interesting visit but at least provide a thorough historical overview. The building, built in 1874, was once a jail turned town treasury, and still has the treasury vault. Ridgeway Battlefield Site is no longer a museum but instead an outside tour with interpretive plaques.

402 Ridge Rd., Ridgeway, Ont. (within Town of Fort Erie). ② **905/894-5322**. www.museum.forterie.ca. Admission C$1.50 (US$1.25) adults, C50¢ (US41¢) children. Sept–May Sun–Fri 9am–5pm; June–Aug daily 9am–5pm. **Ridgeway Battlefield Site**. Hwy. #3 (Garrison Rd.), Ridgeway.

Fort Erie Railroad *Kids*

At one time, Fort Erie was the third-largest rail yard in Canada. The jet-black steam engine #6218 ran from its debut in 1948 into the early 1960s. Inside the museum find artifacts such as tools and telegraphy equipment and exhibits featuring photos and train-related paraphernalia. The original Grand Trunk Railway Station in Ridgeway and CN B-1 at one time monitored traffic movement over the International Railway Bridge. Today this relocated station, with wooden waiting chairs and stoves, re-creates the feel of a good old-fashioned train station from back when steam billowed from the engines. Worth a visit even if you don't have a train collection at home.

400 Central Ave., Fort Erie, Ont. ② **905/871-1412**. Late May to Aug daily 9am–6pm; Sept to mid-Oct Sat–Sun 9am–6pm.

Mildred Mahoney Dollhouse Gallery *Kids*

This historical home has more than 140 dollhouses from around the world—England, Europe, Japan, the U.S., and Canada. Peek at rare miniature homes dating back to 1780. Inside each home you'll find antique miniature furniture and crocheted pieces—some even made by Mrs. Mahoney herself. Mrs. Mahoney kept all the dollhouses (37 years' worth) in her home until 1983, at which point they were moved to Bertie Hall—a historical landmark. The doll collection is a unique, charming, and homey tribute to a woman's childhood dream come true. Bertie Hall also served as a stopping point for black slaves seeking freedom in Canada during the time of the Underground Railroad. Little girls will adore this place.

657 Niagara Blvd., Fort Erie, Ont. ② **905/871-5833**. Admission C$6 (US$5) adults, C$5 (US$4) seniors, C$4 (US$3) students up to 16 years, free for children 5 and under. May–Dec daily 9:30am–3pm.

Old Fort Erie *Kids*

Built in 1764, this structure was the first British defense fort in the area. The original building, built below the current structure, was a supply depot and port for ships along the Upper Great Lakes. Seeing battle during the American Revolution as a supply base for British troops, Loyalist Rangers, and Iroquois warriors, the tiny fort sustained much damage and another was built. During the War of 1812 the Americans occupied the fort, eventually destroying it when they vacated the premises. After the end of the war, the fort continued to play an important role—most notably as a stop for American slaves seeking freedom in Canada during the mid-1800s. Today, visit impressively restored buildings such as the guardroom, soldiers' barracks, or the kitchen—where a fierce battle took place as the British tried to capture the fort from the Americans. The Curtain Wall that connected the two barracks together, with its 3m-thick (10 ft.) walls and wooden spikes, stands as an ominous reminder of a tumultuous era. Worth a visit if you have the time. Regular 1-hour tours available with interpreters dressed in period costume.

350 Lakeshore Rd., Fort Erie, Ont. ② **877/NIA-PARK** or 905-371-0254. Admission C$8.50 (US$7) adults, C$4.50 (US$3.70) children 6–12, free for children 5 and under. May–June daily 10am–5pm; July to early Sept daily 10am–6pm; early Sept to Oct daily 10am–4pm.

Port Colborne Historical and Marine Museum *Kids*

Inside the museum is a re-creation of the history of Port Colborne. The Heritage Village is complete with a network of paths and buildings including the log schoolhouse, the Sherk-Troup log home, the FW Woods Marine Blacksmith shop, the Graf Loom, and the Carriage House gift shop. Artifacts inside the museum include photos, textiles, glassware, marine artifacts, housewares, and community archives related to Port Colborne and the Welland Canal. You'll also find Canada's Century Car, the Neff Steam Buggy. Made in 1901, this car is one of the oldest automobiles in Ontario and was built in Port Colborne. More exhibits within the museum cater to the sea buff—check out the Wheelhouse from the Yvon

Niagara Freedom Trail (Underground Railroad)

The trail is a tribute to the estimated 40,000 black American slaves who came to Canada seeking freedom in the 19th century when Canada passed the Slavery Abolition Act, making their way through Fort Erie and Niagara Falls and into St. Catharines. The Freedom Trail as it stands today isn't so much a trail as it is a series of markers, historical sites, and plaques. The trail is marked with a Running Man symbol.

Fort Erie has a significant plaque—**The Crossing**—which marks the spot where many slaves crossed over into Canada from Buffalo. Also in Fort Erie is **Bertie Hall**—today the Mildred M. Mahoney Doll House Gallery (p. 128). This home was a site for refugees seeking shelter and has a secret tunnel entrance that led from the house to the riverbank. Fort Erie is also home to "Little Africa." In the late 1700s the population grew from 80 to 200 black American slaves who made a living supplying lumber to the ferry and railway services. Here, Little Africa thrived—residents enjoyed working and farming walnut and hickory farms.

In Niagara Falls, the **Norval Johnson Heritage Library** houses more than 2,000 books by, about, and from black settlers on the subject of black heritage (5674 Peer St.; ✆ **905/358-9957**). Next door is the **Nathaniel Dett Chapel**, built in 1836 and named after the church organist, a musician in his own right.

St. Catharines is home to the **Salem Chapel**, a British Methodist Episcopal church that served as a refugee safe haven (92 Geneva St.; ✆ **905/682-0993**). Harriet Tubman, a former slave living in St. Catharines, helped an estimated 300 slaves to freedom and also attended the Salem Chapel. **The Anthony Burns Gravesite and Victorian Lawn Cemetery** honors Reverend Burns—the last man tried under the Fugitive Slave Act, which sent him back to slavery (Queenston St., west of Homer Bridge). He eventually moved to St. Catharines. The **Richard Pierpoint plaque** in Centennial Park commemorates an African-born slave who came to America and was sold to a British officer. Pierpoint later joined the Colored Corps, an all-black military company, and was awarded land for his service.

If you can't tour the entire trail, the **St. Catharines Museum** at the Welland Canal Centre has a comprehensive gathering of facts and memorabilia, giving an impressive historical overview. The African Canadian Heritage Tour, the Central Ontario Network for Black History, and the Ontario Government have collaborated to produce a booklet outlining all 29 trail sites within the province. Visit the website for a downloadable (pdf) brochure and complete list of trail markers and descriptions: www.africanhertour.org.

Dupre Jr. Tug Boat, the anchor from the *Raleigh*, and a real lifeboat from the SS *Hochelaga*. The museum also hosts many events: in the spring enjoy the Pie Social, the History Fair, and the Antique Road Show; in the summer, participate in Canal Days; in December savor the special Christmas pudding in Arabella's Tea Room—the original 1915 Edwardian-style homestead of Arabella Williams that serves steaming hot biscuits and homemade preserves. A great interactive village and educational museum to spend half a day with the kids. Tours offered on request with knowledgeable locals.

The Museum, Heritage Village, and Gift Shop. 280 King St., Port Colborne, Ont. ✆ 905/834-7604. Free admission. May–Dec daily noon–5pm, including holidays. **Arabella's Tea Room.** June–Sept daily 2–4pm, including holidays.

3 Galleries

From landscape to contemporary, Niagara galleries host a small array of unique pieces. A few galleries also feature a creative mix of media and styles from artists in the region and across the country.

NIAGARA FALLS

Niagara Falls Art Gallery   The permanent collection includes the William Kurelek Art Collection and the John Burtniak Niagara Collection of historical Niagara Falls artwork dating from the 18th century to the mid–20th century.

8058 Oakwood Dr., Niagara Falls, Ont. ✆ 905/356-1514. www.niagarafallsartgallery.ca. Admission by voluntary donation. Summer Mon–Fri 11am–5pm, Sat–Sun 1–5pm; winter daily 1–5pm.

NIAGARA-ON-THE-LAKE

Doug Forsythe Gallery   Doug Forsythe is an established Canadian artist. Many of his collections feature landscapes, seascapes, marine themes, and figure studies. He works in computer graphics, watercolor, oil, and acrylics, and is skilled in etching, engraving, dry point, collagraphs, woodcuts, serigraphs, and woodcarving. Local scenes include Niagara-on-the-Lake, Niagara Falls, and Niagara vineyards. Forsythe also creates intricate guitars and fine scale-model ships.

92 Picton St., Niagara-on-the-Lake, Ont. ✆ 905/468-3659. www.dougforsythegallery.com. Apr–June 10am–5:30pm; July–Sept 10am–6pm; Oct 10am–5:30pm; Nov–Dec 10am–5pm; Jan–Mar Fri–Sun 10am–5pm, Mon–Thurs by chance or call.

The King Street Gallery/Poulin Art Gallery   This gallery in a historical home in Niagara-on-the-Lake features works by Canadian artist Chantal Poulin, who has twice won the award for Canadian artist of the year. Poulin's works range from portraits of children to landscapes, still life, and contemporary art. A number of vineyard landscapes are available. The gallery also displays other artists' work, including a number from Quebec.

153 King St., Niagara-on-the-Lake, Ont. ✆ 905/468-8923. Tues–Sun 10am–5pm.

Niagara Pumphouse Visual Arts Centre   The work of local artists is displayed in the salon. Exhibitions range from raku pottery and relief sculptures to etching, photography, and paintings. Lectures and programming for children and adults are offered throughout the year.

247 Ricardo St., Niagara-on-the-Lake, Ont. ✆ 905/468-5455. www.niagarapumphouse.ca. Free admission. June–Aug daily 1–4pm; Sept–May Fri–Sun 1–4pm.

RiverBrink ✪ *Finds*   Home of the Samuel E. Weir Collection, this gallery features a fascinating collection of Canadian and international historical fine art and decorative

> **Fun Fact** **Hold the Foam**
>
> The brown foam you can see floating on the water below the Falls is not caused by pollution. It is simply a suspension of clay particles and decayed vegetative matter, originating mostly from the shallow eastern basin of Lake Erie. The foam is a natural consequence of the tons of water that plummet over the crestline of the Falls.

art, plus many antiques and an impressive 5,000-volume reference library. Of particular interest are the works by Tom Thomson and the Group of Seven, who were the first artists to capture the power and spirit of Northern Canada. You'll also find many Quebec landscapes, Georgian portraiture, and War of 1812 pieces, plus a number of paintings of Niagara Falls. Works of art include paintings, drawings, prints, sculpture, decorative arts, and books. Weir lived and worked as a lawyer in London, Ontario, and began collecting art in his twenties. RiverBrink was built to display his extensive collection and to serve as his retirement residence. Following Weir's death in 1981, the collection has been managed by The Weir Foundation, which ensures its continuing accessibility to the public.

116 Queenston St., Niagara-on-the-Lake, Ont. © **905/262-4510.** www.riverbrink.org. Admission C$5 (US$4) adults, C$4 (US$3.30) seniors, free for children under 12 when accompanied by parent. Mid-May to mid Oct Wed–Sun 10am–5pm.

The Romance Collection Gallery   The Romance Collection Gallery's home is quite appropriately in one of Niagara-on-the-Lake's 19th-century historical houses. The artist featured in the gallery is Trisha Romance, whose gentle, whimsical pastel portraits of hearth and home are collected with fervor around the world. Her most sought-after pieces are her limited-edition reproductions, which have sold out as quickly as they have been released over the past 25 years. The gallery is open for public viewing. Trisha, a New York State native, now makes her home in Niagara-on-the-Lake. Pieces for sale range between C$195 (US$162) and C$1,180 (US$979) for limited editions (more for the artists' proof collection).

177 King St., Niagara-on-the-Lake, Ont. © **800/667-8525** or 905/468-4431. www.romancecollection.com. Tues–Sat 10am–5pm; Sun 1–5pm.

ST CATHARINES
Rodman Hall Arts Centre   See one of the Niagara region's finest visual arts collections, featuring a permanent display of more than 850 works including Canadian and international artists. Gaze at contemporary and historical pieces including paintings, drawings, prints, sculptures, and outdoor installations. Established in 1960, Rodman Hall recently became part of Brock University's School of Fine and Performing Arts.

109 St. Paul Cres., St. Catharines, Ont. © **905/684-2925.** Sept–June Mon–Thurs noon–9pm, Fri–Sun noon–5pm.

JORDAN VILLAGE
Jordan Art Gallery ☞   This gallery is owned by a group of local artists who also staff the store, so there is always a knowledgeable and enthusiastic steward on hand to chat about the art on display. In addition to the showcased work of the gallery owners, other selected artists' works are exhibited. The styles and media of these artists are quite remarkable. This gallery should be marked as a must-see if you are in the Twenty Valley area.

3845 Main St., Jordan Village, Ont. © **905/562-6680.** Summer Mon–Sun 10am–6pm; winter Wed–Sun 10am–5pm.

GRIMSBY

Grimsby Public Art Gallery Monthly exhibitions, tours, and programs are featured. Recent exhibitions include a tribute sculpture to Canadian ski legend Herman Smith-Johannsen and locally made folk-art boats.

18 Carnegie Lane, Grimsby, Ont. ✆ **905/945-3246.** Free admission. Mon 10am–5pm; Tues–Thurs 10am–8pm; Fri 10am–5pm; Sat–Sun 1–5pm.

4 Niagara Falls for Thrill Seekers

AMUSEMENTS

CLIFTON HILL Clifton Hill is a compact entertainment district wedged between Victoria Avenue at the top of the hill and Falls Avenue at the bottom. The lights, noise, and nonstop mayhem spill over its edges and seep along the side streets, but The Hill is without a doubt the center of the maelstrom. The contrast between the garish kitsch of the Clifton Hill district and the breathtaking natural beauty of the Falls could hardly be more extreme. The area is sensory overload both day and night. You'll either hate it or love it.

Just be sure to bring plenty of cash—admission prices for the novelty tourist attractions are steep—for example, **House of Frankenstein** (4967 Clifton Hill; ✆ **905/357-9660**) charges C$9 (US$7.50) for adults and C$7 (US$6) for children, and **Ripley's Believe It or Not! Museum** (4960 Clifton Hill; ✆ **905/356-2238**) will set you back C$15 (US$13) for adults and C$7 (US$6) for children. Often you'll find promotional brochures that contain discount coupons for some of the novelty attractions at hotels, some restaurants, and tourist information centers, so if you're planning to head to The Hill it's worth your while to hunt down one of these booklets before you step into the madness. If you plan to stay long enough to eat a meal or snack in the area, it also helps if you're a fast-food fanatic.

But beware: while some of the facades of these attractions may look enticing, new, and flashy, what's inside can be a huge disappointment. **The Louis Tussaud's Waxworks,** which feels like it hasn't changed inside since opening in 1949, does have well-constructed celebrity clones, if that's your style (5907 Victoria Ave.; ✆ **905/356-2238**). Ripley's Believe It or Not has interesting, albeit odd, sights—visitors can engage in interactive exhibits such as making wax molds of their hands, or see two-headed cats and shrinking heads. And the **Haunted House** (4943 Clifton Hill; ✆ **905/357-2200**), with its trap doors and hidden ghouls, can be a good scream for the younger kids.

THEME PARKS Niagara Falls has many theme parks to keep the kids running around and the parents trying to catch up. The most popular is **Marineland,** where whales are the main attraction (7657 Portage Rd., Niagara Falls, Ont.; ✆ **905/356-9565;** www.marinelandcanada.com). Walkways allow visitors to view the marine mammals above and below water. Live performances featuring trained dolphins, walruses, and sea lions are scheduled several times daily. Fish, deer, black bears, and elk can also be seen. Marineland has an amusement park with a dozen or so rides, including roller coasters, a Ferris wheel, and a carousel. Season's pass available for an additional C$5 (US$4) when purchasing a regular-price day admission to the park, subject to availability. Younger kids can easily spend a full day here—but be sure to bring a lunch, as cafeteria prices are expensive and the food isn't especially healthy.

The Brave and the Foolhardy—Niagara's Daredevils

Barrel, tightrope, rubber tube, Jet Ski, kayak, or only the clothes on their backs—thrill seekers worldwide have used every conceivable contraption to go over, under, or through the Niagara Falls. Some made it—some didn't.

Captain Joel Robinson set out onboard the *Maid of the Mist II* to conquer the gorge rapids and whirlpool. During the ordeal the smokestack snapped, but all crew and Robinson survived the journey in one piece. Their reward was a mere $500; Robinson retired soon after. **The Great Blondin,** aka Jean François Gravelot from France, balanced over the Falls on a precarious 335m-long (1,100-ft.) tightrope. On June 30, 1859, Blondin walked from Prospect Park in New York to Oakes Garden in Niagara Falls. Subsequent walks included carrying his manager on his back and pushing a wheelbarrow across. On one occasion, Blondin cooked omelets on a small stove and lowered them on a cord to passengers on the *Maid of the Mist.* On her 63rd birthday on October 24, 1901, New York native **Annie Taylor** was the first human to go over the Falls in a barrel. Without any prior experience, the widow emerged from the barrel saying: "No one ought ever to do that again."

But many more daredevil stunts followed, including those by **William "Red" Hill, Sr.,** who rode through the Great Gorge rapids and whirlpool in a steel barrel contraption. The 290-kilogram (640-lb.) red barrel had to be rescued from the whirlpool vortex. But ever-determined, Red continued on to Queenston. Wishing to carry on his father's legacy, **William "Red" Hill, Jr.,** went over the Falls in a tower of inner tubes tied together precariously with fish net and canvas. "The Thing," as it was called, sank down into the bubbling water. Moments later, detached inner tubes surfaced—but no Red in sight. His body was recovered the next day.

In the "not intending to seek fame" category, on July 9, 1960, **Roger Woodward**, a 9-year-old American boy, was boating on the Niagara River with his sister and a family friend when the engine of their boat cut out and the force of the rapids propelled the boat toward the Falls. The 40-year-old family friend didn't make it, but Woodward, in what is dubbed "the miracle of the Falls," survived a trip over the Horseshoe Falls wearing only a lifejacket and bathing suit. His sister was rescued by horrified bystanders just seconds before she would have been swept over the brink.

Please note: It is illegal to perform any kind of stunt pertaining to the Niagara Falls under the Regulations of the Niagara Parks Act. In addition to legal prosecution, individuals performing stunts can be fined up to $10,000.

However, older kids may find the rides tiresome, lacking the thrill factor in comparison to facilities that specialize in rides.

Martin's Fantasy Island (2400 Grand Island Blvd., Grand Island, NY; © 716/773-7591; www.martinsfantasyisland.com) is a seasonal amusement park with wet and dry rides, water slides, a wave pool, and live shows. Many of the attractions, such as Kiddie Land and a petting zoo, are geared toward the younger kids. The Silver Comet roller coaster is tame in comparison to other parks. One admission price covers all shows, rides, and attractions, including a petting zoo, canoes, and the water park. Parking is free. **Fallsville Splash Water Park** (701 Falls St. at the corner of John B. Daly and Rainbow Boulevards, Niagara Falls, NY; (© **716/285-8963**) isn't worth crossing the border to visit, but if you're already on that side and need to keep the kids cool, stop in. Its slides and water tubes will keep them busy, but it's not the best water park in the area. **Americana Conference Resort and Spa** (8444 Lundy's Lane, Niagara Falls, Ont.; (© **800/263-3508;** www.americananiagara.com) is a 25,000-square-foot indoor water park with beach-entry wave pool, tube slides, body slides, kiddy pool interactive play structure, and whirlpools. There's an arcade and lounge area, but this facility isn't as large or fun as the outdoor counterparts. Young kids will appreciate half a day to get wet.

Prices range between C$13 (US$11) for Fallsville Splash Park and C$25 (US$21; child and adult same price) for a weekend trip to Americana. Hours vary but generally open late morning (11:30am) and close just before dark, while Marineland is open until 10pm.

THRILL RIDES

National Helicopters   Take a 20-minute ride over the Falls panorama, choosing from wine-tour flights, wedding flights, or the Niagara Grand Tour—more than 60km (35 miles) over the Niagara wine country to the Horseshoe Falls and back. Cameras are encouraged to record all the sights. For an additional C$20 (US$17) per person, a newlywed couple can have a Grand Tour all to themselves!

Niagara District Airport, 468 Niagara Stone Rd., Niagara-on-the-Lake, Ont. (© 800/491-3117 or 905/641-2222. From C$139 (US$115) adults, C$115 (US$95) seniors, C$80 (US$66) children 2–12. 4–6 per group, call in advance for discount group rates.

Niagara Helicopters Limited   A 9-minute ride covers 27km: over the hydroelectric waterways system and Niagara Parks Botanical Gardens, along the Niagara River and Gorge to the American and Horseshoe falls, past Queen Victoria Park, and returning to base. Complimentary headsets with commentary on the flight.

3731 Victoria Ave., Niagara Falls, Ont. (© 800/281-8034 or 905/357-5672. www.niagarahelicopters.com. C$105 (US$87) adults (C$200/US$166 for 2), C$60 (US$50) children 2–12, free for children under 2. Family and group rates, call first. Daily flights 9am–sunset weather permitting.

Whirlpool Jet Boat Tours   Those who experience the jet boat tours find the experience a real thrill. You have a choice of two boats—a "Wet Jet" boat, which is open to the elements (by which they mean water, of course), or a "Jet Dome" boat, which is enclosed. Life jackets, splash suits, and wet boots are provided, but a complete change of clothing is recommended for riders of the Wet Jet, since guests do get soaked despite the protective gear. The trip, about 1 hour on the water if you climb aboard at Niagara-on-the-Lake and about 45 minutes if you board at Lewiston, takes you upriver through the Niagara Gorge, the white water of Devil's Hole, and the famous Whirlpool. A photography team takes digital photos of the jet boat (offered on the wet jet and the jet dome) that are electronically transferred back to the dock for passengers to view upon their return, with an option to purchase. The Jet Dome has undergone a redesign to allow easier and safer loading and seating on the boat. The original dome glass has been replaced in order to improve visibility for passengers. Book online for either experience and you may get a discount of up to C$10 (US$8.30) per person.

61 Melville St., Niagara-on-the-Lake, Ont. (© 888/438-4444 or 905/468-4800. www.whirlpooljet.com. Access also available on the U.S. side (the dock is at the end of Center St. in Lewiston, New York). Admission C$54 (US$46) adults,

C$44 (US$39) children 6–13 years and minimum height of 44 inches required for Wet Jet boat ride, children 4–13 years and minimum 40 inches tall for Jet Dome ride. Passengers under 16 years of age must be accompanied by a parent or guardian. Children under 6 are not permitted to ride on the Wet Jet boats and under 4 are not permitted on the Jet Dome boats. Reservations recommended.

5 Especially for Kids

Here's a lineup of the best things for kids to see and do in the Niagara region. It's a good mix of entertainment that will have kids either squealing with joy careening down a water slide or ooh-ing and ahh-ing walking through a historical fort. There is a plethora of places to go with kids—it seems Niagara Falls was built with them in mind. But be wary of where you go—some are not worth a second glance. Here's our top picks that will make them want to return:

- *Maid of the Mist* (p. 112): You can't get much closer to the Falls than this. Kids will love the intense mist and thunderous sound of the Falls. They'll also appreciate the disposable poncho that matches the one you get.
- **Mackenzie Heritage Printery and Newspaper Museum** (p. 125): Kids can learn how to make a newspaper page the old-fashioned way. This museum is full of interactive and unique pieces that will have them busy for hours.
- **Marineland** (p. 132): Younger kids won't want to leave the rides and the magnificent animals here. It's one of the main draws for children in the area.
- **Fort George** (p. 122): Little soldiers will love the musket firing, cannons, and giant wooden wall fortifications. Come on a July weekend, when kids can see reenactments of War of 1812 drills.
- **Ripley's Believe It or Not! Museum** (p. 132): Imagine seeing a two-headed cat (stuffed), or a Statue of Liberty made from more than 100,000 match sticks. Also, catch a 4-D movie that flops you around like a fish—feel like you're actually *in* the movie!
- **White Meadows Farms** (p. 142): While in Rome, er, Canada, kids should experience the true Canadian experience of "sugaring off"—eating maple syrup poured on crisp white snow during February and March.

Childrens Discovery Centre of Niagara   Open year-round, this is an entertaining educational experience for children of all ages and their families. The emphasis is on hands-on, interactive exhibits and galleries. A Wetland Park was installed in 2005. Key features include a dinosaur gallery, water conservation exhibit, recycling and environmental gallery, hydro gallery, and agricultural gallery.

Tips Keeping the Kids Entertained

When you're traveling with children, if you can put their needs first when planning your itinerary and include activities that all ages will enjoy then everyone will have a more pleasant vacation. Be sure to schedule plenty of time for relaxation (and naps, if your children are very young). The best advice you can follow is not to over-schedule. Don't expect your kids to act like adults—young children have short attention spans. When they start to wiggle and fidget let them have a half-hour to blow off steam in a playground, sit with them on a park bench and lick ice-cream cones, or take them to a movie.

The Mystery of the Whirlpool—Solved!

The Whirlpool is a natural phenomenon in the Niagara River, occurring at the point where the river makes a sharp right-angled turn. The Whirlpool is a huge basin 518m (1,700 ft.) long by 365m (1,200 ft.) wide and 38m (125 ft.) deep at its deepest point.

When the Niagara River is at full flow, the water travels along the 1.6km (1-mile) stretch known as the Whirlpool Rapids at speeds up to 9m per second (30 ft./sec.). The water enters the basin, then travels counterclockwise around the pool and past the natural outlet.

As the water tries to cut across itself to reach the outlet, pressure builds up and forces the water under the incoming stream. This creates the whirlpool effect. The water then continues on its way to Lake Ontario.

360 Niagara St., St. Catharines, Ont. (℃ **905/646-4365**. www.childrensdiscoverycentre.org. Admission C$6 (US$5) adults, free for children under 2. Tues–Fri 10am–4pm; Sat 10am–5pm; Sun 11am–5pm.

HorsePlay Niagara   Trail rides are available year-round. Take a 1- or 2-hour ride through the woods and past the ponds and abandoned quarries of adjacent Wainfleet Conservation Area. Themed activities include sunset rides and half-day adventures including a cowboy cookout. Children's play area includes a hay maze, playground, and petting zoo.

Hwy. 3, west of Port Colborne, Ont. (℃ **800/871-1141** or 905/834-2380. www.horseplayniagara.com. Daily year-round 10am–5pm.

Looff Carousel   One of the largest and best-preserved examples of a Looff menagerie carousel, the carousel at Lakeside Park on Lake Ontario in Old Port Dalhousie is a fantastic sight. There are 69 carousel animals arranged in four rings. And the cost is only a nickel a ride! This beautifully preserved carousel celebrated its 100th birthday in 2005 and is one of only nine historic carousels in Canada. A recently constructed children's playground is situated between the carousel and the harbor walkway, in Lakeside Park.

Lakeside Park, accessed from Lakeport Rd., Old Port Dalhousie, St. Catharines. Admission C$5 (US$4). Mid-May to early Sept daily 10am–9pm.

Niagara Falls Aviary—Birds of the Lost Kingdom   This is a handy place to take the kids for some diversion, since it's within easy walking distance of the Falls as you travel upriver on River Road alongside the Niagara Gorge. Tropical plants, a waterfall, and moss-covered carvings combine to re-create a rainforest experience, complete with exotic species of birds from Australia, South America, and Africa. More than 300 tropical birds are housed in the aviary—some free flying and some contained in observational exhibits.

5651 River Rd., Niagara Falls, Ont. (℃ **888/994-0090** or 905/356-8888. www.naigarafallsaviary.com. Admission C$15 (US$12) adults, C$14 (US$12) seniors, C$10 (US$8) children 5–12, free for children under 5. Mid-June to early Sept daily 9am–9pm; early Sept to mid-June daily 9am–6pm. Last admission is 1 hr. prior to closing.

Simcoe Park   This beautiful park has a gently rolling landscape, colorful flower beds, plenty of mature shade trees, and lush green lawns. There is a children's playground and a wading pool. Located in pretty Niagara-on-the-Lake.

Bordered by Picton St., King St., and Byron St. in Niagara-on-the-Lake.

Zooz Kids love animals, and Zooz features more than 400 of them, both exotic and domestic, and all housed in natural habitats. Lots to keep young ones busy for hours on end—splash pad, Gator Express tram rides, catch-and-release fishing in a stocked pond, paddle boats, kite flying, petting area, and children's play zone. Live interactive animal presentations and guided educational tours.

2821 Stevensville Rd., Stevensville, Ont. ℂ **866/367-9669** or 905/382-9669. www.zooz.ca. Seasonal operation: hours may change, so call ahead. Daily May 14–June 30 10am–5pm; July 1–Sept 5 9am–6pm; Sept 6–Sept 18 10am–4pm; Sept 19–Oct 10 10am–4pm.

6 Parks & Gardens

NIAGARA PARKS COMMISSION

Dufferin Islands Situated just upriver from the Falls on the Niagara Parkway, this oasis of land is a 10-acre area formed by glacier drift. Today, a labyrinth of trails and several bridges make this a great place to picnic and explore for the day. In an effort to encourage further naturalization of the area fish have been introduced and bird feeding stations and birdboxes have been installed. Indigenous vegetation has also been planted. All eight islands—each island is only a couple hundred feet—are connected via bridges. It takes about 15 minutes to walk the perimeter of the islands. If you prefer, you can bring your bike and scoot around. During the Winter Festival of Lights between mid-November and January several animated light displays are placed around the perimeter of the islands.

7400 Portage Rd., Niagara Parks Commission, Niagara Falls, Ont. ℂ 877/642-7275.

Floral Clock This unusual horticultural display draws hordes of tour buses. The clock is definitely worth a look, but a quick photo op and then back on the road seems to suit most folk. The design is changed twice a year, with violas providing color in spring, followed in late May by a labor-intensive operation to install 16,000 carpet bedding plants to form the 12.2m-diameter (40-ft.) clock face. The clock was originally built in 1950 by Ontario Hydro, inspired by the famous floral clock in Princes St. Gardens in Edinburgh, Scotland. Curving around the front of the clock is a 3m (10-ft.) pool. A tower at the head of the clock houses Westminster chimes, which mark each quarter-hour and strike on the hour.

If you are lucky enough to visit in late May or early June you will be able to enjoy the adjacent lilac garden in full bloom (and full fragrance!). There are 1,200 mature lilacs planted on 4 hectares (10 acres), representing an amazing 225 varieties.

14004 Niagara River Pkwy., Niagara Falls, Ont. Free admission. Clock display is at its peak between Apr and late Sept.

Kings Bridge Park This park, located just south of the Falls near the village of Chippawa, is a great place to access the Niagara River Recreation Trail. Facilities

---

〔Tips 〕 Peek Inside the Clock

If you walk *behind* the Floral Clock (most people are much too occupied taking pictures of their family and friends standing in front of the clock to ever do this), you may be able to peek inside; the door is often open to allow visitors to see the drive mechanism of the clock. There is also a collection of photos of the clock in past years so you can compare the wildly different designs and colors as they change from year to year.

include a picnic pavilion, picnic tables, washrooms, and a playground and splash pad for children. On summer weekends and holidays there is a parking fee of C$10 (US$8).
7870 Niagara River Pkwy. ⓒ 877-NIA-PARK.

Niagara Parks Botanical Gardens   This is one of the most endearing places to me in the Niagara region, particularly in the spring when the bulbs are in full bloom. The beds and borders have provided much inspiration over the years for my own gardening projects. The formal herb garden, planted in a symmetrical design, has benches tucked into niches in the clipped hedges that surround the display. On a warm summer's day, you can sit in contented solitude for a while, taking in the beauty of the plants or just dreaming about the future transformation of your own garden at home. There are numerous vegetable beds in an area adjacent to the herb garden and a rock garden. The plants in the perennial garden are handily labeled for reference, so bring a notebook and pen if you are a really keen green-thumber. The arboretum holds one of Canada's finest collections of ornamental trees and shrubs.

The Botanical Gardens were originally established in 1936 to provide a teaching facility for the School of Apprentice Gardeners. The site received its declaration as a Botanical Garden in 1990, as a result of the expansion of the variety and quality of the plant collections living in its extensive grounds. The Botanical Gardens continue to serve as a training ground for students of the School of Horticulture. The students gain practical experience through the maintenance and development of the gardens, although they also attend classroom lectures in horticultural theory.

The gardens are a short drive north of the Falls along the Niagara Parkway, about 9km (6 miles) north of the Horseshoe Falls. The site is serviced by the People Mover bus.
2565 Niagara Pkwy., Niagara Falls, Ont. ⓒ 877-NIA-PARK. www.niagaraparks.com/nature/botanical.php. Free admission. Daily dawn–dusk year-round.

Oakes Garden Theatre   Located on the west side of the Niagara River Parkway, just south of the Rainbow Bridge at the base of Clifton Hill, Oakes Garden Theatre marks the entrance to Queen Victoria Park, which extends south along the Niagara Parkway to the Horseshoe Falls. This is a fine example of a formal public garden, with extensive application of local Queenston limestone, a curved pergola, rock gardens, and lily ponds among the various features. It's a popular site for weddings, especially for photographs, since the American Falls can be captured in the background. Many open-air concerts are held here throughout the summer season. There is a splendid shaded promenade, reminiscent of the fine formal gardens so favored in France, overlooking the Niagara River and the American Falls.
Located at the entrance to Queen Victoria Park.

Navy Island   This island has been preserved in its natural state. Situated 7km (4¼ miles) south of the Falls in the Niagara River, Navy Island is accessible only by boat. There are strict regulations for visitors' conduct (see www.niagaraparks.com/nature/navyisland.php for more details). Overnight camping requires a permit, which can be obtained from the Niagara Parks Commission at the Niagara Parks Police Office, 6075 Niagara Pkwy., Niagara Falls, Ont. This wilderness island has a rich history, going back 10,000 years to Native inhabitants, who used the island for fishing and canoe building. During the 1700s the French and later the British used Navy Island for shipbuilding and as a naval base. On the island you will find an abundance of deer. Vegetation includes

Please Don't Feed the Geese

A breed of non-migratory Canada Geese has made a comfortable year-round home throughout southern Ontario, thanks to the unwitting generosity of folk who feed them grain and bread. These geese have no natural predators and their numbers are growing unchecked, causing city parks and walkways to be overrun with geese in some areas. Goose droppings, ripped-up sod, and damaged grass are just a few of the problems that have resulted. Park authorities are pleading with the public *not* to feed Canada Geese, in order to encourage them to fly south in the winter and keep the population in check.

wild raspberries, grapes, pawpaw, hickory, oak, and blue beech. Beware the poison ivy that covers much of the island.

℘ 905/356-1338. Camping fees C$8 (US$6.65) adults, C$4 (US$3.30) children 13–17, free for children 12 and under.

Niagara Parks Greenhouse   Gardening enthusiasts simply must pay a visit to this 11,000-square-foot greenhouse and surrounding gardens, located just a short distance south of the Horseshoe Falls on the Niagara Parkway. Owned and operated by the Niagara Parks Commission, the greenhouse produces all of the beautiful spring and summer bedding plants that you will encounter as you enjoy the various other parks in the area managed by the Niagara Parks Commission, including Queen Victoria Park, Kings Bridge Park, and Queenston Heights Park, among others. Horticultural shows are staged throughout the year, each centering on specific themes including hydrangeas, geraniums, begonias, and chrysanthemums. The outdoor gardens, which feature an abundance of roses complemented by statues and a fountain, are popular as a venue for weddings.

7145 Niagara Pkwy., Niagara Falls, Ont. www.niagaraparks.com/nature/greenhouse.php. Free admission. Late May to early Sept daily 9:30am–8pm; early Sept to end Nov 9:30am–5pm. Opening hours vary during winter and early spring.

Queen Victoria Park   This beautiful park is enjoyed by millions of visitors each year, since it is in the heart of Niagara Falls. Its borders are the Niagara Escarpment, Niagara Gorge, and the Niagara River. Features include a hybrid tea rose garden, carpet bedding displays, and a rock garden. In the early spring, half a million daffodils light up the park with their cheerful, nodding yellow blooms. Later in the spring, magnolias, tulips, and colorful blossoms bring beauty to the landscape. With the summer comes a profusion of formal bedding displays. There are vast expanses of lush green lawns and plenty of park benches to entice visitors to linger.

Situated along the Niagara Gorge and River (starting from the brink of the Horseshoe Falls and extending to Oakes Gardens Theatre). Parking available at the Falls parking lot across from Table Rock House. Open year-round.

Queenston Heights Park   Only a few minutes' drive north of the Butterfly Conservatory and the Niagara Parks Botanical Gardens, this popular summertime destination is particularly good for families, history buffs, and those who enjoy hiking and cycling. Facilities at the park include two picnic pavilions, washrooms, and a bandshell. During the summer a small snack bar is in operation. On hot summer days, let your kids wade in the shallow water of the splash pad or burn off their energy in the children's playground. There are plenty of mature shade trees and open grassy areas for ballgames and family fun. For those who like to hike and bike, you'll be pleased to learn that Queenston Heights Park is the southern terminus of the Bruce Trail, Canada's oldest and longest continuous footpath. The trail runs along the Niagara Escarpment, spanning a distance of 850km (528 miles); the northern terminus is at Tobermory in southwestern Ontario. See "Hiking & Biking," in the section titled "Outdoor Pursuits" later in this chapter for more details.

A walking tour of the Battleground of the Battle of Queenston Heights is clearly marked throughout the park, and takes about 45 minutes to 1 hour to complete if you're walking at a leisurely pace. There are five plaques stationed along the way, which explain various stages of the battle and their consequences. See the section on tours later in this chapter for a more detailed description of the walking tour. Brock's Monument, a tribute to Major-General Sir Isaac Brock, the brilliant military leader who planned the defense of Upper Canada and was killed during the Battle of Queenston Heights, towers above Queenston Heights Park. The 56m-high (185-ft.) structure is the second one to be built on the site. The original monument, completed in 1824 and including a tomb holding the remains of Brock and his aide-de-camp, John Macdonell, who also died in the battle, was destroyed by a bomb in 1840. During the 1850s, the current monument was built. Note that the monument was closed for repairs in 2005, and a reopening date had not yet been scheduled. When the monument does reopen, though, you will be able to ascend the 235-step winding staircase inside the column and enjoy the view from the small windows at the top. You should be in good physical condition to do the climb. Be prepared to be herded to the narrow sides of the pie-shaped stairs from time to time as you meet other visitors going in the opposite direction. To the right of **Queenston Heights Restaurant,** you will find a monument dedicated to **Laura Ingersoll Secord,** who risked her life by taking a grueling 32km (19-mile) trek through trackless frontier forest to reach Lieutenant Fitzgibbon's headquarters and warn him of an impending attack on his forces by American soldiers.

Queenston Heights Restaurant provides an elegant setting with a spectacular view of the Niagara River, looking north toward Lake Ontario. The restaurant is perched on the edge of the Niagara Escarpment. For more detailed information on the restaurant, see the listing in chapter 6, "Where to Dine." Free parking is available on the left as you enter the park.

14184 Niagara Pkwy., Queenston, Ont. ⓒ **905/262-4274.** Free admission to park.

NIAGARA FALLS, NEW YORK
Niagara Falls State Park   This is the oldest state park in the United States. The park hugs the eastern shoreline of the Niagara River in the city of Niagara Falls, New York, beginning just west of John Daly Boulevard and ending just north of the Aquarium of Niagara near Pine Avenue. All of the major falls attractions are contained within the park. Admission to the park grounds is free, although a parking fee is charged to vehicles during the main tourist season. Attractions vary in their admission price; the best deal is to obtain a **Passport to the Falls** (see "Tips: Best-Value Niagara Falls Experiences" above). Drop into the visitor center at Prospect Park to obtain information, buy a park passport, enjoy a snack, or watch a short film on the history of the Falls (nominal admission fee charged to view the film).

Eastern shore of Niagara River in downtown Niagara Falls, NY. ⓒ **716/278-1796.** www.niagarafallsstatepark.com. Free admission to grounds; vehicle parking charge in main tourist season; attraction admission prices vary. Summer daily 8am–10pm; winter daily 8am–6pm.

Niagara Gorge Discovery Center   If you want to learn more about the natural and local history of Niagara Falls and the Niagara Gorge, this is the place. Fossils, minerals, and ancient layers of rock are on display. A multi-screen theater gives you a 180-degree perspective on how the Niagara Gorge was formed as the Niagara River eroded rock and soil over a time span of 12,000 years. The **Niagara Gorge Trailhead Building** is next to the **Discovery Center.** From this point, you can access hiking, walking, and cycling trails. Guided hikes are on offer during the summer months, ranging from an easy 1-hour hike to a difficult 3-hour hike. Note that steep stairs are involved and there are rocks to climb over and around during the hikes. Call ✆ **716/278-1780** for more information. Also on the site is a 9m-high (30-ft.) outdoor climbing wall with three degrees of difficulty. The climbing wall is open seasonally, subject to weather conditions; ✆ **716/278-0337.**

Robert Moses Parkway, inside Niagara Falls State Park, Niagara Falls, NY. ✆ **716/278-1070.** Admission to Discovery Center C$6 (US$5) adults, C$3.60 (US$3) children 6–12, free for children 5 and under. Small fee to join guided hikes, or access the trails without a guide free of charge. Apr–Dec.

ST. CATHARINES

The city of **St. Catharines** has earned the title of Ontario's Garden City. More than 1,000 acres of gardens, parks, and trails are within the city limits, all open for the public to enjoy. One of St. Catharines' jewels is **Burgoyne Woods,** accessed from Edgedale Road, off Glendale Avenue. Families will find this particularly appealing, since there are swimming and wading pools, a playground, and plenty of picnic areas and nature trails. Paved trails are wheelchair accessible. **Ontario Jaycee Gardens** is one of Niagara's prettiest garden displays and St. Catharines' largest single planting of annual and perennial flowering plants. The northern perimeter of the park overlooks Old Port Dalhousie, including Martindale Pond and the Royal Canadian Henley Rowing Course. The land was originally part of the third Welland Canal. The Gardens are located on Ontario Street, north of the QEW and south of Lakeport Road. On the edge of the downtown core, **Montebello Park** is designated under the Ontario Heritage Act. Noteworthy features in the park include a magnificent rose garden with more than 1,300 rose bushes, and a bandshell and pavilion dating from 1888. Mature shade trees cast their majestic branches over walking paths, picnic tables, and a children's playground. The park is located at the corner of Lake Street and Ontario Street in downtown St. Catharines. Avid gardeners will enjoy the **Stokes Seeds Flower Trial Gardens,** one of the official sites of All-American Trial Gardens. July and August are the peak months for viewing the flowers, which are spread over several acres of farmland. Located off Lakeshore Road between Seventh Street and Fifth Street.

Kids A PLAYGROUND FOR ALL

Along the Niagara Street frontage of Lester B. Pearson Park in St. Catharines, there is a special place. The Infinity Playplace, funded by the St. Catharines Kiwanis Club, is designed to offer play opportunities that can be enjoyed by all children, regardless of ability. A looped ramp system provides wheelchair access, visual orientation strips are placed at openings, and wide decks are featured. The entire surface is made of rubber to allow full accessibility.

Farm Living Is the Thing for Me

Experience the fruits of the earth up close—Niagara soil nurtures juicy fruit orchards, world-class vineyards, and expansive lush farms. As you drive around the Niagara region, stop by one of the many roadside stands for fresh produce, just hours from the vine or branch to the basket. Or spend a happy hour or two picking your own strawberries in June, sour cherries in mid-July, or pumpkins in October at farms such as **Kar-Dean Fruit Farms** (3320 First Ave., Vineland Station, Ont.; ✆ 905/562-4394), **Sommers' Family Farm** (290 Main St. W., Grimsby, Ont.; ✆ 905/945-4448), or **Mathias Farms** (1909 Effingham St., Fonthill, Ont.; ✆ 905/892-6166).

If you're interested in touring a working farm, try one of the many agritourism farms, such as **Puddicombe Estate Farms & Winery** (1468 Hwy.#8, Winona, Ont.; ✆ 905/643-1015; www.puddicombefarms.com). This 208-year-old family farm has lots to do. Learn about wine grapes on a wagon-ride tour, or taste estate wine while munching on some cheese and crackers on a wine tour on the farm starting at C$10 (US$8). Pick your own in-season fruits or buy already-picked cherries, pears, or apples. Enjoy a hearty lunch at the bakery cafe and bring home some goodies from the general store.

For specialty food items visit the huge gourmet marketplace at **Kurtz Orchards,** located at 16006 Niagara Pkwy., Niagara-on-the-Lake, Ont. (✆ 905/468-2937; www.kurtzorchards.com). In the marketplace, sample homemade mustards, specialty teas, maple syrup, Ontario honey, oils and vinegars, and chunky cookies. Watch how they're made at demonstrations, or try a workshop—visit the website for event times. Tour the 100-acre farm on a tractor-pulled tram led by Mr. Kurtz himself, starting at C$20 (US$17), which includes a farm lunch.

White Meadows Farms (2519 Effingham St., Pelham, Ont.; ✆ 905/682-0642) is a maple syrup farm where visitors can get their fill of all things maple. They also grow grapes and raise dairy cows. White Meadows offers a year-round sweet shop, with maple sweets and syrup. Spring (Feb to mid-Apr) includes pancake weekends complete with preserves. When the sap starts to flow—February and March—join events revolving around "sugaring off," where visitors can make and taste fine Canadian maple syrup.

For something less sweet but also a good bet for the taste buds, visit the **Niagara Herb Farm** (1177 York Rd., Niagara-on-the-Lake, Ont.; ✆ 905/262-5690; www.niagaraherbfarm.com). Stroll through gardens with more than 350 varieties of culinary, medicinal, fragrant, and native herbs (book tours during summer months only). There is also a retail barn open March through December. Spend a summer Sunday afternoon at an herbal or craft workshop. Events include the Annual Open House, National Herb Week, and the Lavender Festival. Take home a satchel of lavender or jar of herbal jelly at the gift barn, open year-round.

7 Outdoor Pursuits

BIRDING

The **Niagara River Corridor** has been designated as a "Globally Significant Important Bird Area" by major conservation groups in Canada and the United States. The river is a significant wintering feeding zone for migrating birds, since the swiftly moving water keeps the river free of ice at a time of year when many other waterways are frozen over. Gulls, in particular, use the Niagara River as a major stopping-off point on their migratory flights. Almost half of the world's 43 species of gull have been identified by birders along the Niagara River. Species that have been noted include Bonaparte's gull, Franklin's and Sabine's gull, and rarely seen species such as the California, Slaty-backed, and Ross's gulls. The best time of year to view gulls is from mid-November to mid-January.

The **Niagara Gorge** is a prime spot for birders; not only because small fish are abundant in the river, but also because large fish are sucked into the hydro turbines and chopped into pieces, which in turn attracts gulls to the area. Overlooking the gorge at the site of the Sir Adam Beck power station, located on the Niagara Parkway north of the Butterfly Conservatory, many birds can be seen. The **Hydro Reservoir** is home to many gulls, ducks, geese, and herons. A footpath circles the reservoir and can be accessed from behind 2058 Stanley Ave. in north Niagara Falls, Ontario. Just upriver from the Horseshoe Falls on the Canadian side, opposite the Niagara Parks Greenhouse, a variety of birds may be seen, including purple sandpiper, harlequin duck, and red-necked and red phalarope. Other spots include the Niagara Glen Nature Reserve, the Niagara Parks Botanical Gardens, and the Whirlpool Rapids Overlook (by the Whirlpool Aero Car). **The Beamer Memorial Conservation Area** (mentioned below) is also a wonderful forest for exploring and watching wildlife—experience views of Forty-mile Creek Valley, Lake Ontario's shoreline, and the escarpment ridge.

BOATING

Opportunities for boating are plentiful in the Niagara Region, including the major waterways of **Lake Ontario, Lake Erie,** the **Niagara River,** and the **Welland Canal.** Numerous smaller waterways are suitable for canoes and kayaks. Docking and boat-launching facilities are of good quality and are situated along the Niagara River, Lake Ontario, and Lake Erie shores. For detailed information and contact addresses on all aspects of recreational boating in Niagara, obtain a copy of the annual *Ontario Marina Directory* by contacting the **Ontario Marine Operators Association** (OMOA) (Suite 49, 2 Poyntz St., Village Square Mall, Penetanguishene, ON, L9M 1M2; ℂ **888/547-6662;** omoa@omoa.com).

WELLAND CANAL   If you wish to navigate a leisure craft through the Welland Canal between Lake Erie and Lake Ontario, contact the St. Lawrence Seaway Management Corporation at ℂ **905/641-1939** for information, regulations, and fees involved in traveling via the canal.

ST. CATHARINES   Canoeists, kayakers, and yachtsmen and -women are fond of the Lake Ontario shoreline and its connecting tributaries. Call ℂ **800/305-5134** for more information or visit www.stcatharines.ca. In 1999 St. Catharines was host to the World Rowing Championships, and since 1903 has been a major rowing attraction.

PORT DALHOUSIE   You'll find **Martindale Pond** located between the Henley Bridge on the QEW and Port Dalhousie harbor. The **Henley Rowing Course** is home of the annual **Royal Canadian Henley Regatta** (www.henleyregatta.ca).

NIAGARA RIVER   If you are looking for a public marina on the River, the only one on the Canadian side is the **Niagara Parks Marina** at 2400 Niagara Pkwy., Fort Erie, Ont. There are 135 seasonal docks, boat launch ramp, gas pump, showers, and washroom facilities.

PORT COLBORNE   Port Colborne is a popular center for sailing and power boat enthusiasts; the town hosts a number of sailing regattas and dockside events during the summer months. Port Colborne has three marinas, the largest of which is **Sugarloaf Harbour Marina,** featuring 350 seasonal berths, 150 guest docks, showers, washrooms, restaurant, four-lane boat launch ramp, and more (3 Marina Rd.; ✆ **905/835-6644**).

CROSS-COUNTRY SKIING

The Niagara region has a multitude of trails, which can be accessed in the winter for cross-country skiing. The most easily accessible for visitors is the **Niagara River Recreational Trail,** which runs alongside the Niagara River Parkway between Fort Erie in the south and Niagara-on-the-Lake in the north. The trail is ungroomed, but it is popular with skiers and you are likely to find tracks to follow. Just park your vehicle in any designated parking area along the east side of the Niagara Parkway, step into your skis, and off you go.

FISHING

Some of the best sport fishing in North America is found in Niagara, home to more freshwater species than anywhere on the continent. Game fish found in the waters of the Niagara region include coho salmon, rainbow trout, lake trout, walleye, yellow perch, smallmouth bass, northern pike, and muskellunge. Chinook salmon can be found in Lake Ontario between April and September; from September to November you can try your luck in the Niagara River. Some species have open and closed seasons; contact the Ontario Ministry of Natural Resources (see below) for more information. For information on dock fishing, boat launching, and annual fishing derbies, call the Game & Fish Association at ✆ **905/937-6335.**

To fish in Ontario, those aged 18 and over must obtain a valid fishing permit, as stipulated by the Ministry of Natural Resources. Ontario residents, other Canadian residents, and nonresidents all need different licenses. More information is available by calling ✆ **800/387-7011** or visiting online at www.mnr.gov.on.ca/MNR/fishing. Fishing is permitted on the Welland Canal, along the Niagara River, and on Lake Ontario and Lake Erie. Note there is a "catch and release" program in the Dufferin Islands, located just a short way upriver from the Falls on the Canadian side.

GOLF

The Niagara region is becoming a hot golf destination. Its varied topography and gentle climate are ideal attributes for hosting golf courses, and Niagara is teeming with them—more than 40 courses are contained within the Niagara Peninsula. The diverse landscape provides beginner and experienced golfers with a range of challenges on Niagara's well-designed and professionally maintained public and semi-private golf courses.

The **golf season** in Niagara runs for 7 months, from April to October. Temperatures range from an average of 59°F (15°C) in April, to 82°F (28°C) in mid-summer, and a comfortable 67°F (19°C) average monthly temperature in October. Greens fees vary widely, dependent upon the season, day of the week, time of day, whether it is an advance reservation or walk-in, and other factors. Expect to pay around C$100 (US$83) and up for a round including cart.

The newest course to open, in the summer of 2005, is **Thundering Waters Golf Club** (6000 Marineland Pkwy., Niagara Falls, Ont.; ☏ **905/357-6000** or 877/833-DALY; www.thunderingwaters.com), located just south of the Falls and the Fallsview accommodations and entertainment district in Niagara Falls, Ont. Course designer John Daly attempted to hit a golf ball from Table Rock next to the Horseshoe Falls in Canada to Goat Island in the U.S., the island that lies between the Canadian and American Falls. He failed but the publicity was positive, and Daly proved to be a great ambassador for Niagara Falls and the new golf course. **Legends on the Niagara** (9561 Niagara Pkwy., Niagara Falls, Ont.; ☏ **866/GOLF-NIA;** www.niagaraparksgolf.com/legends), another relatively new course, with 45 holes along the Niagara River, has earned a distinguished Platinum rating (based upon KPMG's scoring criteria). **The River Course at Grand Niagara Resort** (8547 Grassy Brook Rd., Niagara Falls, Ont.; ☏ **905/384-GOLF**) was designed by Rees Jones, one of the top golf course architects in the world. **Royal Niagara Golf Club** (1 Niagara-on-the-Green Blvd., Niagara-on-the-Lake, Ont.; ☏ **905/685-9501;** www.royalniagara.com) is situated alongside the Niagara Escarpment and is one of Niagara's most scenic courses. The **Whirlpool Public Golf Course** (3351 Niagara Pkwy., Box 150, Niagara Falls, Ont.; ☏ **866/GOLF-NIA;** www.niagaragolftrail.com), on the Niagara Parkway north of the Falls, is consistently ranked as one of the top public courses in Canada.

For more information on Niagara's golf courses, contact these online resources: the Niagara Parks Commission at www.niagaraparks.com and www.niagaragolftrail.com, the Golf Association of Ontario at www.gao.ca, or Ontario's Online Golf Course Guide at www.ontgolf.ca.

HIKING & BIKING

No matter what your speed—whether you like to take a leisurely bike ride stopping at every historical site, or if you love mud flying in your face whipping down a "bum over the saddle" hill, Niagara's varied topography caters to all. If you're a hiker, spend a day in one of the more than 35 conservation areas that vary from wetlands to waterfalls to lush forests full of rare and exotic wildlife. Most parks and conservation areas touch into the infamous Niagara Escarpment and can make for challenging climbs on bike or on foot. The Niagara Escarpment is a UNESCO World Heritage Site (there are only 12 in Canada), hits heights up to 510m (1,675 ft.), and is home to more than 300 bird species, 53 mammals, 36 reptiles and amphibians, and 90 fish and flora including 37 types of wild orchids. The sedimentary rock here formed more than 450 million years ago. What remains today is an outdoors enthusiast's playground. The escarpment rises near Rochester, New York, and runs west through the Niagara Peninsula, south of Lake Ontario and then to Hamilton, where it takes a turn north straight up to the end of the Bruce Peninsula; see www.escarpment.org. Bring maps, water, and a friend if venturing out.

The Niagara community has also made huge strides in organizing well-maintained, paved, multi-use paths that pass by various historical sites and waterways of the region. And if you're so inclined, put a basket on the front of a rented bike, visit some wineries, and take home some goodies.

BIKE RENTALS

If you want to pick a path and go it alone, rent a bike from **Steve's Place Bicycle & Repair** (181 Niagara Blvd., Fort Erie, Ont.; ☏ **888/649-BIKE**). Steve rents hybrid bikes (cross between a road and a mountain bike) for C$25 (US$21) a day or C$125

(US$121) for a full week. Rentals include a lock but you must provide your own helmet. The store is just off the Niagara River Trail—great location. Another spot to pick up a bike is **Zoom Leisure** (42 Market St., Niagara-on-the-Lake, Ont.; ℂ **866/ 811-6993**). Choose from Trek hybrid bikes, tandems, kids', or mountain bikes for off-road riding. Every bike comes with map, helmet, and bike lock. Prices around C$12 (US$10) per hour; C$20 (US$17) half-day up to 3 hours; C$30 (US$25) for full day until dark. Finally, you can also rent bikes from **Leisure Trails Bicycle Rentals** (4362 Leader Lane, Niagara Falls, Ont.; ℂ **888/264-4490** or 905/371-9888). Geared toward families, Leisure Trails rents tag-along bikes, trailers, and trail bikes, which are in between street and mountain bikes. They charge C$5 (US$4) per hour, and for a full day adults pay C$20 (US$17) adults and kids C$15 (US$12)—helmet and lock included in price.

THE BRUCE TRAIL

The **Bruce Trail** is a meandering path that begins at Queenston Heights and ends almost 850km (528 miles) later in Tobermory, on the northern tip of the Bruce Peninsula. Hikers experience fantastic views overlooking waterfalls, opening up through lush fauna and flora and a kaleidoscope of colors (biking is not permitted on the trails). Opened in 1967, it is proudly the oldest and longest trail of its kind in Canada. For more information including maps, visit the Bruce Trail Association website: www. brucetrail.org. The **Niagara Bruce Trail section** runs between **Beamsville** and **Queenston,** overlooks the Niagara River and passes through countless orchards and wineries, yet feels secluded and wild. Within this area there are six recommended hiking routes. The trails are marked, but always carry a detailed map.

The first and most popular is the Brock's Monument to **Woodend Conservation Area.** The 18km hike (11 miles), east to west, has parking on either side. Starting at the east end of Queenston Heights Park from the cairn you'll first come across the Queenston Quarry (Queenston Trails) 2km (1 mile) into the hike, which deviates onto its own set of trails that highlight more of the Niagara Escarpment. Within the Queenston trails, a must-see sight is St. David's—an expansive view of fields and orchards below the escarpment. Farther north are remnants of a workers' village built in 1897 for those working in the quarry. A detour off the main path leads to a network of limestone caverns and the massive quarry pit. **Woodend Conservation Area** is dominated by hardwood species such as sugar maple, beech, red oak, shagbark hickory, and rock elm. This 45-hectare section that sits atop the Niagara Escarpment includes a view of the United Empire Loyalist homestead and limestone kiln. This section is perfect for picnics, hiking, and even cross-country skiing for a day trip.

The Decew Falls and Morningstar Mill is the next section north—the mill and waterfall make it a popular destination. It is located west of the intersection with Merritville Highway in the southern part of St. Catharines. This trail is a great jumping-off point for bike trips moving south to Short Hills Provincial Park, St. John's, and Effingham. The Decew Falls—22m (72 ft.) in height—is a quiet spot. Follow along the trail a few hundred meters eastbound and look for a place to go down into the gorge, which offers a great view—and a little water spray to boot!

West from the Mill, start descending the escarpment and you'll be in the **Short Hills Provincial Park** in Pelham—a multi-use trail system that with more than 10km of singletrack trails is a mecca for fat-tire mountain bikers (call Ontario Parks ℂ **800-667-1940** or Short Hills Provincial Park direct ℂ 905/774-6642 in summer, or 905/827-6911 in winter). Visit www.friendsofshorthillspark.ca for a downloadable trail map. The expansive 735-hectare day-use park includes six trails and the Bruce Trail and has a distinctly different landscape from the rest of Niagara. Short Hills is a series of small but steep hills formed during the last ice age. Whether you hike, mountain bike, or ride a horse, the Swayze Falls and Black Walnut trails are open for enjoyment. Please be mindful of all users. The tour is wheelchair accessible, or can be enjoyed from a car or on a bike—the trail is about 10km long. Also note that the Scarlet Tanager, Hemlock Valley, Terrace Creek, and Paleozoic Trails are for hikers only. There are two waterfalls within the park. A great jumping-off point is the St. John's Education Centre.

A more secluded location, nestled within Short Hills Provincial Park, is **St. John's Conservation Area** in Pelham. Fish, walk, and enjoy nature at its most serene along the Sassafras Stroll—a self-guided walk named after the sassafras trees that grow wild in the area. The entire stroll takes only about 20 minutes and is wheelchair and stroller accessible. Since the area has never been farmed, keep your eyes open for rare species and trees well over 200 years old. At the northern end of the Conservation Area lies a large pond teaming with trout. The man-made pond was built in 1964 to regulate the water flow into Twelve Mile Creek, where in 1792 a sawmill attracted an entire community with foundry, stores, and jobs. For a detailed topographic map visit www.info niagara.com.

West from the Decew Falls, you'll find **Louth Conservation Area** in Lincoln County. With moss-covered rocks, two magnificent waterfalls, and a cornucopia of flowers, this trail is a secluded place to spend the day—don't be surprised if you don't see anyone. A busy spot, and the most touristy but worth the stop, is **Ball's Falls Conservation Area** off the QEW at Vineland. This area offers a glimpse into a 19th-century hamlet—a barn, pavilion, church, and two waterfalls spread across 80 hectares (200 acres) of magnificent land, woven with even more trails spotted with hundreds of plant species including wild sarsaparilla and green and white trilliums (Ontario's official flower). The falls themselves are two-thirds the height of Niagara Falls, although the volume of water is considerably less. Within Ball's Falls hike the Cataract Trail, which starts at the west side of the Twenty Mile Creek bridge. Walk alongside the creek on the way up, and inland on the way back. Depending on what time of year you go, the falls can be gentle or a raging force of water. Camping is also available.

The final leg of the journey is the **Cave Springs.** Please note that access to the caves is by appointment only, by calling (C) **905/563-6353.** Margaret Reed tends the land, which is now owned by the Niagara Peninsula Conservation Authority. The area is said to contain secret caves and includes much folklore about the former village of the Neutral Indians who are said to have lived here. The magnesium sulfate–rich spring—similar to the soothing properties of Epsom salts—is a natural draw. Also, don't leave without seeing the ice cave that holds ice year-round.

OTHER TRAILS

GREATER NIAGARA CIRCLE ROUTE   Closer to civilization is the Greater Niagara Circle Route ((C) **905/680-9477** or contact via e-mail: campaignoffice@bellnet.ca), which is a 150km (90-mile), mostly paved path for cyclists, in-line skaters, and walkers—the 3m-wide (10-ft.) trail spans from Lake Erie to Lake Ontario. The trails are wheelchair accessible save for a few railway crossings. The trail includes four sections:

- **The Friendship Trail,** part of the Trans-Canada Link Trail, extends from Port Colborne to Fort Erie along Lake Erie—about 14km (9 miles). The route can be accessed in Fort Erie near the Ridgeway Battlefield site (1km north on Ridge Rd.), and along Lake Erie on Windmill Point Road and Stone Mill Road. The trail follows the abandoned C.N. Rail line, passing through some quiet residential streets, and is great for a short ride or walking and jogging.

- **The Niagara River Recreation Trail,** which spans all the way from Fort Erie to the tip of Niagara-on-the-Lake, is the longest stretch in the circle, approximately 60km (35 miles), and is also part of the Trans-Canada Link Trail—access points include the north entrance from Fort George in Niagara-on-the-Lake. This is my favorite section as it's a winding trail, and most of the trail has a great view overlooking the gorge and the U.S. neighbors. The trail is divided into four sections, each taking about an hour or two to complete on a bike: Niagara-on-the-Lake to Queenston; Queenston to the Whirlpool Aero Car; Chippawa to Black Creek; and Black Creek to Fort Erie. While strolling or riding, take in the hundred or so historical plaques that tell of soldiers defending the frontier and of significant Upper Canadian historical sites such as Fort George, McFarland House, and early battle sites. Seasonal washrooms and free parking are available throughout. Coming up the grueling 1km hill into the Height of Queenston, think of Sir Isaac Brock riding to his death. Today the large column, Brock's Monument, marks his final resting place. Bring a backpack and spend a day biking along this route.

- **The Waterfront Trail** picks up from the Recreation Trail and meanders along the shore of Lake Ontario—all the way to Brockville (outside of the Niagara Circle). The trail passes through more than 31 communities, including several farmlands and wineries. In total, it spans 450km (280 miles). Access points include one near Fort George and another near Port Weller in Niagara-on-the-Lake, and Ansell Park in St. Catharines. Sections of the trail are not completed. For a detailed downloadable map visit www.waterfronttrail.org. This trail is mostly flat—great for an easy ride, depending on how far you go!

- **The Welland Canal Recreation Trail** spans all the way from Lake Ontario to Lake Erie, passing through St. Catharines, Thorold, and Welland and finishing at Port Colborne. Access this section north of Lock 3 in St. Catharines or at the southern end of Seaway Park in Port Colborne. This trail is a bit busier, as it passes through towns and the sometimes-busy ports of the Welland Canal.

NIAGARA CONSERVATION AREAS ⟨ꝑ⟩ There are 35 separate conservation areas in the Niagara Region, operated by the Niagara Peninsula Conservation Authority (© **905/788-3135;** www.conservation-niagara.on.ca). Visit the website for a complete list—and remember, these trails are open for hiking only! The forested areas have less formal trail systems and are great for watching the birds, but can offer a hard hike depending on which trail you choose. Trails on the escarpment tend to be for seasoned hikers.

Tour a 19th-century village at **Ball's Falls Heritage Conservation Area** (Victoria Ave., R.R. 1, Jordan), which offers several hiking trails and access to the Bruce and Cataract trails. Or be alone with the hawks flying overhead at **Beamer Memorial Conservation Area,** Ridge Road, Grimsby, where examples of Carolinian forest abound with sassafras, tulip, and wild crab trees. Also, look for birds such as the least bittern and yellow-breasted chat. Be prepared to climb to find spectacular views of the escarpment and Lake Ontario on well-marked trails. There are also four lookout points—a great vantage point for bird-watching. Take the Lookout Trail to see the 23m (75 ft.) falls. Three wheelchair platforms lead to observation areas.

The conservation areas also include wetlands—bring boots. **Wainfleet Wetlands,** Quarry Road, Wainfleet has informal trails where hikers can see fossils—but please,

---

⌜Tips⌟ Scenic Drives Along the Niagara Gorge and Niagara River

On both sides of the border, you can take a leisurely drive alongside the Niagara River and Niagara Gorge. On the Canadian side (western shore), you can follow the Niagara Parkway all the way from Fort Erie at the southern end of the Niagara River to Niagara-on-the-Lake at the northern end where it empties into Lake Ontario. On the U.S. side (eastern shore) start farther upriver, where the Robert Moses Parkway begins, first heading west at the junction with Interstate 90 and following it as it turns north with the natural bend in the river. You will pass through Niagara Falls State Park (or head through downtown Niagara Falls, although it is a less picturesque route), then through several other state parks, including Whirlpool, Earl W. Brydges Artpark, and Joseph Davis, ending at the northern end of the Niagara River in Fort Niagara State Park.

---

don't take them home. **Wainfleet Bog,** Erie Peat Road, Wainfleet, near Port Colborne has more than 800 hectares of land and informal trails—be sure to bring a compass. Trails are short and lead to quarry sites where bass fish are abundant. **Humberstone,** Neff Road, Port Colborne, has challenging informal trails; beware of hunting activity. **Mud Lake** is a series of short trails leading to an observation area and is located at Regional Road 80 (Elm St.) in Port Colborne.

Large forested conservation areas, with less formal hiking trails but great wildlife sightseeing, are available at **Ruigrok,** Caistorville Road (Regional Rd. 2, Dunnville), and **Hedley,** Townline Road E., Dunnville.

For phenomenal rock formations and cliffs (wear proper hiking shoes), visit areas on the Niagara Escarpment. **St. John's,** Barren Road, Pelham, offers some wheelchair accessibility. It also has well-marked trails where hikers can get sweaty climbing the escarpment's gradual hills. Some favorites include the Tulip Tree Trail, Sassafras Trail, Horseshoe Trail, or the St. John's Ridge Trail—watch for endangered species and a small coldwater trout pond. **Cave Springs,** Cave Springs Road, Vineland (by appointment only via Margaret Reed at ⌓ **905/563-6353**) is great for a leisurely nature walk and talk. **Louth,** Staff Road, Lincoln County, has trails and access to the Bruce Trail. Louth also has two waterfalls and touches upon the escarpment. **Woolverton,** Woolverton Road, Grimsby, has informal trails for bird and wildlife watching, accessible through the Bruce Trail.

Niagara Glen Nature Reserve 𝒜𝒜   The Niagara Glen Nature Reserve is located alongside the Niagara Gorge between the Whirlpool and the Niagara Parks Botanical Gardens. This flat area of land was once part of the riverbed of the Niagara River. As you enter the Glen, you will descend a staircase into the gorge. A series of seven different pathways link through this nature reserve, ranging in length from .4km (¼ mile) to 3.3km (2 miles). The various paths take you past unique and fascinating natural landscape formations. Along the **Eddy Path** you will see the Wilson Terrace Passages, which are narrow passageways between huge boulders that toppled from Wintergreen Cliff many thousands of years ago. Along the **River Path** you will see Devil's Hole, which is the narrowest point of the Niagara River. A natural spring flows from the sandstone cliff. Note that all of the paths, or the access to them, are steep in places (River Path is the flattest path, but you need to descend the cliff to reach it).

The Niagara Parks Commission produces an excellent small field guide (C$10/US$8) in a miniature hard-backed binder with a history and description of the Glen and listings of the trees, vines, flowers, insects, and birds to be found in this unique habitat, complete with beautiful color photos to aid identification of species as you explore the Glen. The staff in the Niagara Glen shop are Niagara Parks Commission employees and are knowledgeable about the Glen. The reserve has a parking lot, gift shop, small cafe and washrooms located at the side of the Niagara Parkway on a table of land known as Wintergreen Flats (1km/½ mile) north from Whirlpool Golf Course on Niagara Parkway, Niagara Falls, Ont. (© **877/NIA-PARK;** www.niagara parks.com/nature/rectrailarea.php).

8 Organized Tours

BY BUS

Grayline Niagara   The oldest and largest of the bus tour companies, Grayline is accessible from selected hotel lobby desks or by pre-arranged pickup. Tours are also available through Expedia, Travelocity, and other Web engines. The Canadian Rainbow Tour is a 4- to 5-hour tour, stopping at Horseshoe Falls, Table Rock House, Queen Victoria Park, Sir Harry Oaks Gardens, Upper Canadian Rapids, Lower Niagara River and Gorge, and the mighty whirlpool in the Niagara Gorge. Tour includes admission to the Skylon Tower Observation Deck, the IMAX presentation *Miracles, Myths, and Magic,* and seasonal *Maid of the Mist* cruise. A full-day tour, lasting 7 to 8 hours, includes similar sights and more, with dinner and boxed luncheon. Accepts advance reservations or same day. Discounts for groups of 10 or more.

3466 Niagara Falls Blvd. N., Tonawanda, NY. © 800-695-1603. www.grayline.com. Half-day from C$80 (US$66) adults, C$60 (US$50) children; full day C$230 (US$191) adults and children. Tours vary as do availability times.

Niagara Airbus   This company offers bus tours to wineries, sightseeing tours, and packages that include lunch. The Niagara Falls tour, for example, includes lunch and a ride on the *Maid of the Mist* (or a journey behind the Falls in winter). See the Floral Clock, Botanical Gardens, Queenston Heights, and Spanish Aero Car Observation Area, then stop in Niagara-on-the-Lake for free time to stroll the pretty streets and do some shopping. Buses will pick up guests at any hotel or bed-and-breakfast in the region.

8626 Lundy's Lane, Niagara Falls, Ont. © 905/374-8111. www.niagaraairbus.com. Tours start from C$60 (US$50). Book online and receive 10% discount.

BY BIKE

Steve Bauer Bike Tours   What's the best way to see Niagara? Using your own two feet and a couple of wheels. And who better to organize your tour than former silver medal road racing Olympian Steve Bauer. Bauer's company offers customized or guided tours for groups of 10 or more people. Guided tours include a support vehicle to carry water, snacks, spare tires (and riders, if they get tired). Call at least 2 weeks in advance to be sure of booking a space. Customers range from hard-core bike enthusiasts who want to cycle 140km a day to those who just want to take in the sights while enjoying the fresh air. Wine-tour rides are available—choose from about three different tours.

P.O. Box 342, Beamsville, Ont. © 905/563-8687. Fax 905/563-9697. Prices depend on customization. Full day (10:30am–4pm) with gourmet picnic C$111 (US$92).

Zoom Leisure   Providing more than 100 bikes to choose from, this company caters to family cyclists and those who want to tour the area on their own or with a guided group. Zoom Leisure provides child-friendly bike accessories such as trailers and child seats that mount on the bike. Other amenities include handlebar bags, bells, H2O cages, and kickstands. If you want to tour with a group, choose from tours that visit three wineries, sampling the wine as you go, or choose an extended package (with optional lunch), which includes four wineries. Each bike has an optional basket in the front to bring home goodies from your voyage. Group and custom tours—where you can choose different routes, lunch, and wineries—are also available. Reserve tours in advance (48–72 hr. ahead for most).

2 Market St., Niagara-on-the-Lake, Ont. ℭ **866/811-6993** or 905/468-2366. www.zoomleisure.com. Tours starting at C$60 (US$50) to C$115 (US$96).

BY BOAT
Dalhousie Princess Cruises   Between May and October, enjoy historic Port Dalhousie harbor from a grand boat with open deck. View the Welland Canal, wine country, and the southern shore of Lake Ontario. Have lunch or dinner or try a themed cruise such as Who's Your Daddy (featuring a local funk band), fireworks dinner, retro '80s cruise, or Venice dinner cruise (C$50/US$42). Book in advance—reservations for themed cruises must be booked a minimum of 48 hours prior to the cruise.

9 Lock St., St. Catharines, Ont. ℭ **905/937-BOAT**. www.dalhousieprincess.com. C$45 (US$37) family pass, C$19 (US$16) adults, C$17 (US$14) seniors and students with ID, C$13 (US$11) children 6–12, free for children 5 and under.

9 City Strolls

Niagara-on-the-Lake is a picturesque town, so I've provided two tours, one for those equipped with a bike and the other for people wearing comfortable walking shoes, with plenty of chances to stop and shop. I also added a tour of St. Catharines, which is inland and has a different feel, for another tour of a historical area.

CYCLING TOUR   HISTORICAL NIAGARA-ON-THE-LAKE

Start:	Fort George parking lot, link onto Greater Niagara Circle
Finish:	Fort George
Time:	Plan to spend 1 to 2 hours, with time for stopping.
Best Time:	Take this tour in the morning as shops begin to open and the town is at its most peaceful.

This tour will take cyclists through some of the most historical areas of the town and Lake Ontario views.

❶ Cross Queen's Parade to the recreational pathway. This path is the Otter Trail. Near the small bridge stands the Indian Council House (ca. 1796), headquarters of the British Indian Department.

During the War of 1812, British and Natives met here to discuss politics.

❷ The **Butler's Barracks** were constructed to replace Fort George after the War of 1812. It was here that soldiers trained to fight in the Boer War, World War I and World War II, and the Korean War. Turn right, crossing King Street, and continue on Mary Street.

❸ At the corner of King Street and Mary Street stands **Brockamour Manor** (433 King St.). Here Sophia Shaw is said to have become engaged to General Sir Isaac Brock. Brock never returned home, coming to an untimely death at the Battle of Queenston Heights. The ghost of Sophia is said to walk the halls sobbing. Follow Mary Street to Simcoe Street and turn right.

❹ First occupied as a private home, then becoming a residential school, **Green House** (20 Simcoe St.) has been substantially altered and changed during its existence. Continue straight on Simcoe Street.

❺ One of the first homes built after the War of 1812, **Storrington House** (289 Simcoe St.) was residence to Adam Lockhart, the secretary for the Niagara Harbour and Dock Company. Servants' quarters were built for the hired help.

❻ Continue on Simcoe and cross Queen Street, passing by **Keily House** (ca. 1832). Built for lawyer Charles Richardson, this house is built on the soil of **Fort Mississauga.** The sweeping veranda around the house was built in the late 19th century. In the cellar there is a long vaulted chamber—a tunnel that connects to Fort Mississauga. Behind the house, now operating at the Charles Inn, is the Niagara-on-the-Lake golf club.

❼ This is the oldest golf course in Canada. Back in the day golfers started here for 9 holes then moved on to Fort George to finish the game. Behind the Niagara-on-the-Lake golf course sits Fort Mississauga.

❽ Built at the end of the War of 1812, **Fort Mississauga** was built to replace Fort George. A few parts of the tower were built from limestone from Ontario's first lighthouse, which was burned here by enemy forces in 1813.

❾ Follow on to the end of Simcoe onto Front Street. Front Street is renamed Ricardo Street beyond King. To the left is the dock area used in the early 1780s. Many large steamboats were built in the yards of **Niagara Harbour and Dock Company.** Continue along until the end of the street.

❿ At one time, the engine that pumped water into the town was housed at what is now the **Pumphouse Art Gallery.** Go straight along the Niagara Parkway.

⓫ Lieutenant-Governor John Graves Simcoe lived and worked for the Executive Council of Upper Canada on this site in 1792. American cannons destroyed the original buildings in 1813; they were rebuilt in 1815. To the right are ramparts of Fort George. At **Navy Hall,** Ricardo Street becomes the Niagara River Parkway, which leads all the way to Niagara Falls. Continue here to Queen's Parade, and cross the street to link up with John Street, where the path continues. Continue along the path then take a right to link up with the **Otter Trail** once again.

⓬ From 1796 until its capture by the American army in 1813, **Fort George** was the British military headquarters. Unfortunately, the Americans destroyed the original fort and after the war it was completely abandoned by the British. In 1930 it was reconstructed. Stop by for a tour complete with costumed guides and a history lesson or two.

Cycling and Walking Tours

CYCLING TOUR

1 Indian Council House
2 Butler's Barracks
3 Brockamour Manor
4 Green House
5 Storrington House
6 Kelly House
7 Golf Course
8 Fort Mississauga
9 Dock
10 Pumphouse Art Gallery
11 Navy Hall
12 Fort George

WALKING TOUR

1 Sylvia's Antiques
2 The Nutty Chocolatier
3 Angel Inn
4 Dee Building
5 Greaves Jams
6 Niagara Home Bakery
7 McLelland's West End Store
8 Candy Safari
9 Oban Inn
10 Bank of Upper Canada
11 Doug Forsythe Gallery
12 Courthouse

WALKING TOUR 1	NIAGARA-ON-THE-LAKE SHOPPING DISTRICT

Start: Sylvia's Antiques on the corner of St. Mary's and Nassau sts.

Finish: The Courthouse

Time: A slow 1-hour walk

Best Time: Mid-afternoon, when the lunch crowd has gone—stop for tea and browse the stores

Niagara-on-the-Lake offers some one-of-a-kind stores filled with unique gifts and tasty delights. Stroll and enjoy.

❶ Stop in to **Sylvia's Antiques** (376 Mary St.) to browse through an eclectic mix of furniture and accessories. Work up a little sweat walking along Mary Street, where giant trees stand beside grand manors and meticulously gentrified homes. Turn left onto King Street.

❷ Just past Platoff Street find **The Nutty Chocolatier** (233 King St., Niagara-on-the-Lake)—a great place to fill up on homemade fudge, truffles, and creamy Belgian chocolate. On Loonie Tuesday stop in for a C$1 ice-cream cone.

❸ Proceed along Market Street and turn left onto to Regent Street. Pass by the **Angel Inn** (224 Regent St.; ca. 1825)—a fine place for a pint of ale or glass of Niagara wine. But beware—they say this house is haunted by a solider from the War of 1812. Turn left onto Queen Street.

❹ The **Dee Building** (54–58 Queen St.; ca. 1843), a two-story limestone building, has housed everything from a clothing store to grocers. Take note of the original shop front facing Regent Street.

❺ For a homemade souvenir, stop off at **Greaves Jams** (55 Queen St.; ca. 1845). Take note of the architectural features of this building—deep boxed cornices on the hip roof.

❻ And for something to put under the jam, pick up a bag of goodies from **Niagara Home Bakery** (66 Queen St.; ca.

1875). Enter the store through a double leafed door and enjoy the sunlight steaming in through the glassed transom over the doorway.

❼ Past Victoria Street is **McLelland's West End Store** (106 Queen St.; ca. 1835). To accommodate the boom in population during the 1830s, locals could pick up groceries, and their fix of wines and spirits. The large "T" sign is a sign of a provisioner—the store that sold everything! The store expanded into 108 Queen Street.

❽ The **Candy Safari** (135 Queen St.; ca. 1835) is a Gothic Revival house, originally built as a residence and shop for shoemaker and leatherworker John Burns. Today, it satisfies the sweet-tooth cravings of shoppers.

❾ Turn right onto Gate Street and on the corner of Front and Gate take a peek at the **Oban Inn.** The original inn was built in 1822, and became a hotel in 1895. A fire destroyed the building in 1992. But as with all good things, it came back and remains true to its original form.

❿ Turn right onto Front Street and walk a little toward 10 Front St.—the Bank of Upper Canada. With a stucco front and rough cast side treatment, this old bank was rebuilt after the War of 1812. It still has the original steel vaults and is the location of a grand bed-and-breakfast now. Walk until Queen becomes Ricardo Street, then turn left onto Wellington Street and right onto Picton Street.

⓫ Stop in to browse the fascinating **Doug Forsythe Gallery** (92 Picton St.). Find unique etchings and paintings using fascinating print-making techniques.

⓬ Turn right on King Street, then right onto Queen Street to view the **Courthouse** (26 Queen St.; ca. 1847). This national historical site changed its function from a courthouse and jail cells to the town hall. The Shaw Festival was founded here and still performs the Court House Theatre of the Shaw. From jail to theater—if only the walls could talk.

| **WALKING TOUR 2** | **HISTORIC DOWNTOWN ST. CATHARINES** |

Start:	Old Courthouse
Finish:	Same location
Time:	2 hours
Best Time:	Take a midafternoon stroll through the area just after lunch.

Known as the garden city, St. Catharines' city streets are busting with color against the backdrop of well-maintained historical homes.

❶ Start at the **Old Courthouse,** constructed in 1849. Note the beautifully ornate stained glass transom and curving balustrades. On the St. James side notice the steer's head and wheat sheaf in recognition of the nearby market. The water fountain is a gift from Mayor Lucius Oille.

❷ Northeast on Church Street, you will find **St. Catharine of Alexandria Cathedral.** Built in 1845 for Irish Catholic immigrant workers, many working on the canal, today the facade is a wonderful example of English neo-Gothic.

❸ This lovely home at **134 Church St.** was a wedding gift from farmer Stephen Parnell to his daughter and son-in-law, local merchant James Wood, who would later become a prosperous merchant.

❹ Turn on to **King Street** and look for nos. **173–175.** This stream of row houses is typical of its era in 1860. Notice the red brick, popular frieze, and brackets at the roofline. Now, follow Academy Street East.

❺ Turn right onto St. Paul Street and note nos. **224–226.** This Italianate facade, with bulging exterior, reveals unique window shapes and large openings for windows, unique by 19th-century standards. It also resembles a palace on the Grand Canal in Venice, Italy.

❻ At **88 St. Paul St.,** built in 1869, marvel at the ornate decoration of the windows and the roofline with cast-iron markers on the facade.

❼ Turn onto **Ontario Street,** where nos. **37 and 39** are the former Masonic temple buildings of 1873. Notice the cast-iron columns and window frames—a new material replacing brick and stone during its era.

❽ Returning back to St. Paul Street, overlooking Twelve Mile Creek to the south is the **statue of William Hamilton Merritt.** Merritt was a prominent businessman of the 19th century. He also conceived a water channel from Lake Erie to Lake Ontario, which became the Welland Canal. Cross to Yates Street and enter into the **Yates Street heritage district.**

❾ **24 Yates St.** was the home of miller John Woodward. This home is representative of an elegant 19th-century style in contrast to the Italian style mentioned above.

❿ Turn right onto Norris Place. At **7 Norris Place** a carriage maker built this home with sidelights and transom above the doorway—typical of its day.

⓫ Turn left off Norris; on a diagonal you will see **105 Ontario St.** where there's another example of row houses from 1860 built for Josiah Holmes and his partner W. W. Greenwood.

⓬ **83 Ontario St.** is the former home of J. F. Mittleberger, another prosperous businessman of his day. Take a look at the unique faces on the door.

⓭ Across the street is the **Welland Canal House Hotel,** built in the 1850s. Today it is a student residence. Walk 2 blocks farther to Queen Street and turn left.

⓮ The last house on the tour is **64 Queen St.,** former home of Chauncey Yale, an American manufacturer. Notice the familiar style of home and fence, which represents a traditional home (ca. 1851).

8

The Wine-Country Experience

Wine regions are characterized by delicious cuisine and picturesque countryside, and infused with the infectious enthusiasm of the women and men who are driven to create the best wine, agricultural produce, and cuisine they possibly can. Since its transformation over the past quarter of a century into a world-class wine-producing area, Niagara can step forward to stand proudly alongside venerable Old World and other New World wine regions. There are still improvements to be made and plans to execute, but the vision shared by the growers, producers, and merchants is strong and clear. Niagara's wine region is a rising star.

1 Introducing the Niagara Wine Region

HISTORY OF THE NIAGARA WINE REGION

Niagara's vibrant wine industry had humble beginnings, with the first European settlers making use of the native Labrusca grapes, which were ideal for juice, preserves, and desserts but unfortunately did not produce the light, dry, sophisticated style of table wines that dominates the world's markets today. During the 1900s, Niagara vintners achieved modest success with Canadian hybrids.

During the 1960s and 1970s, a number of enterprising growers began planting *Vitis vinifera* vines, the so-called "noble grape" varietals that produce many of the world's finest wines, such as chardonnay, cabernet, gamay, and Riesling. Fertile, rich soils and a unique microclimate make Niagara a prime grape-growing region, and—contrary to the expectations of most—the vinifera vines thrived.

The biggest contributor to the transformation of Ontario's wine industry was the introduction of international trade agreements in 1988. The loss of tariff and retail price protection put the retail price of Ontario wines on a par with imports from the world's most respected and well-established wine regions. The industry had to reinvent itself as a worthy contender. Growers, wineries, and the provincial government decided to revitalize the wine industry, and together they rose to the challenge.

Between 1989 and 1991, growers removed almost half of Ontario's Labrusca and hybrid vines and replaced them, over time, with traditional European varieties, as part of a government-initiated program to move toward increased production of higher-quality table wines. The focus was firmly and permanently shifted to *Vitis vinifera* production.

Today, Niagara has approximately 16,000 acres under vine, in an area stretching from Niagara-on-the-Lake in the east to Grimsby in the west. More than 60 wineries now make their home in Niagara, many with fine restaurants and boutiques on-site.

A large number offer wine tasting and tours to the public. Niagara wines consistently bring home medals and awards from many of the world's most prestigious wine competitions.

World attention has turned to the Niagara wine industry not least because of the superb quality of its icewine, a dessert wine produced from grapes that have been left on the vine after the fall harvest to freeze naturally. The frozen grapes are handpicked and immediately pressed to capture the thick, yellow-gold liquid, high in natural sugars and acidity.

THE HEART OF A WINE REGION'S SUCCESS—TERROIR

Winegrowing, or viticulture, is more or less restricted to two temperate bands around the world—where the summers are warm enough to consistently ripen the grapes and the winters are cold enough to allow the vines a period of dormancy.

Although the macroclimate of a district is the major factor determining whether grapes can be grown at all, it is the microclimate, soil, and topography, and the effects that each of these characteristics have on each other, that influence the type of wine that can be produced in a particular area. The French have coined a term for this combination of climate, soil, and topography as it relates to the world of winemaking: *terroir.*

The Niagara wine region is situated in one of the world's most northerly grape-growing regions. Despite Niagara's emergence onto the world wine stage over the last quarter-century, many people are still surprised to learn that the Niagara Peninsula is an ideal zone for the production of high-quality grapes. In fact, the growing season in Niagara enjoys a similar climate to that of Burgundy, France.

The area is designated a "cool climate viticulture region." However, although many vine growers in cool climates have to contend with summers that are not warm enough to fully ripen the grapes, the unique climate of the Niagara peninsula provides a more conducive environment. The moderating influence of Lake Ontario and Lake Erie protects the region from extreme temperature fluctuations. The presence of the escarpment further moderates the climate.

Finally, the soil in the Niagara Peninsula is composed of deposits of clay, loam, sand, and gravel, which vary by district. The soil is also rich in essential minerals and trace elements originating from the variety of bedrock present in the region, providing important nutrients to the vines and contributing to the complexity of the wines produced.

 Tips

When you purchase a Niagara wine in a restaurant, wine boutique, or retail store, check the label for the designation **VQA (Vintners Quality Alliance).** Wine-producing regions around the world establish governing bodies to dictate the conditions under which that region's wine is produced. The VQA in Ontario requires that wines with this designation have been made exclusively with grapes grown in one of the three recognized Ontario viticultural areas— Niagara Peninsula, Lake Erie North Shore, and Pelee Island. In addition, the wine must be made entirely in Ontario from officially approved grape varieties. These specifications ensure the consumer will receive a quality product and serve to protect the wine industry's reputation.

---

2 Essentials

THE WINE REGION IN BRIEF

The Wine Council of Ontario has divided the Niagara Peninsula Wine Region into three districts: Grimsby & Beamsville, Jordan & Vineland, and Niagara-on-the-Lake. For ease of discussion, these districts have been used here, although the wine region extends seamlessly from Fifty Road in the west to the shores of the Niagara River in the east, bordered on the north by Lake Ontario and the south by the Niagara Escarpment. The entire area stretches about 55km (34 miles) from Fifty Road to the Niagara River, so if you were really keen to sample wines from right across the region it could be done in a day. However, it is much more relaxing to home in on a small section of the map and meander up and down the country roads at a leisurely pace.

GRIMSBY & BEAMSVILLE The highest point of this part of the Niagara Escarpment sits behind Grimsby. There are a few wineries in the extreme west of this area, but most are concentrated south of Beamsville, in an area bordered by Thirty Road on the west and Cherry Avenue on the east. The country roads winding up and down the Escarpment are flanked by deciduous trees (not forgetting the vineyards!) and are particularly picturesque in the summer and fall.

JORDAN & VINELAND This winegrowing area extends roughly from Cherry Avenue in the west to the east side of the Welland Canal and the city of St. Catharines. The **Twenty Valley Creek** tumbles down the side of the escarpment, eventually flowing into Jordan Harbour and then Lake Ontario. With more than two dozen wineries, historical Jordan Village, and numerous sites of natural beauty, this area is a great place to base yourself for an overnight stay or weekend of wine-country pleasure.

NIAGARA-ON-THE-LAKE This wine area is bordered by the Welland Canal, Lake Ontario, the Niagara River, and the Niagara Escarpment. The wineries here are primarily in two clusters: one in the lee of the escarpment, the other in the northeast of the region, mostly on flat land surrounding Niagara-on-the-Lake. Many are located either right on the Niagara Parkway, along Niagara Stone Road (Highway 55), or on Lakeshore Road. The town of Niagara-on-the-Lake has a huge choice of accommodations; historical inns and heritage bed-and-breakfast properties are in abundance. Despite the large number of rooms in the town, it can be difficult if not almost impossible to secure a room at short notice, so book well ahead if you plan to stay in the town.

VISITOR INFORMATION

The **Wine Council of Ontario (WCO),** a nonprofit trade organization, produces an excellent map of Niagara's wine country with the official *Wine Route* clearly marked. As you drive along the highways and byways of the Niagara Peninsula, you will see these distinctive road signs, which feature the symbol of a bunch of white grapes against a deep blue background, often with names of vineyards, distances, and arrows added to aid your navigation. The map is available as a pocket fold-out and also appears as a pull-out centerfold in the annual *Official Guide to the Wineries of Ontario.* The guide and pocket map are widely available throughout the Niagara region—at tourism offices, wineries, and retail stores that carry wine. Visit their website at **http://winesofontario.org** for a wealth of information, including an events calendar, advice on matching wine and food, trip planning advice, maps, a list of winemaker members and their wineries, an explanation of the various grape varietals, and a history of Niagara's wine region—and much, much more.

Note: Not all wineries are members of the WCO. A number of establishments, either because they are smaller in size or brand-new, are not listed in the guide, although you will see signposts directing you to their properties as you tour around. Many of them produce award-winning wines and they all have their unique stories to tell. I urge you to venture into these wineries to enrich your experience of Niagara's wine country.

You can also check out **www.cheersniagara.com**, which is the online home of the syndicated "Cheers to Wine and Food" radio show, broadcast in the Niagara region on 91.7 Giant FM at 7:25pm daily.

Each individual district of the wine region offers its own tourist resources. If you are touring in the Grimsby & Beamsville district in the western end of the wine country, your best bet for tourist information is **Tourism Niagara at the Gateway Information Centre,** 424 South Service Rd. (exit 74 off the QEW), Grimsby, Ont. (© **800/263-2988** or 905/945-5444; www.tourismniagara.com). For Jordan & Vineland, Twenty Valley Tourism Association produces an excellent guidebook to the area called *Discover Twenty Valley,* which lists accommodations, dining, events, and more. Find out more at www.20valley.ca. For information on wineries in Niagara-on-the-Lake (and loads of other tourist information on the immediate area), visit **Niagara-on-the-Lake Visitor & Convention Bureau,** 26 Queen St., Courthouse Building, Lower Level, Niagara-on-the-Lake, Ont. (© **905/468-1950;** www.niagara onthelake.com). This facility also operates an accommodations service, whereby you can give them your accommodations requirements and preferences and they will find a property for you (a small fee applies for this service).

GETTING AROUND

Driving a car is probably the best way to see the wineries, as they are spread out over the entire Niagara region. Keep in mind that a tour of four to six wineries a day is more than enough. If you want to bike your way through your tour, choose a section and pick a couple of wineries. For example, the Greater Niagara Circle route (see chapter 7, "What to See & Do in the Niagara Region," for bike path info) hits many wineries en route. Another great option is to cycle the quiet country roads—they're wide open and there are not many road hazards. If you opt for the bus, note that public transit does not visit individual wineries. Instead, check out the bus tour options below that cater to the wine-hopping crowd.

WINE-TASTING TOURS

Crush on Niagara   More than just transportation to the wineries, Crush prides itself on offering the extras such as meeting with winemakers, or tasting wine straight from the barrel. The owner is a sommelier, so bring your notepad and learn about some of Canada's finest winemakers on each tour. Tours depart in the morning or afternoon—4 hours through the Niagara Escarpment or the wineries of Niagara-on-the-Lake. Choose from a three-winery tour with the Sip and Savour with lunch from C$99 (US$82). Custom tours (with groups of six or more) are C$65 (US$54); Sniff and Swirl include four wineries for C$69 (US$57). All day (11am–4pm) is C$125 (US$104) with a three-course luncheon. Call ahead to reserve a ticket; Saturdays fill up fast. Crush will pick up guests at their hotel (within the wine region) or select a meeting place. Tours run twice daily, 7 days a week.

4101 King St., Beamsville, Ont. (administration office only) © **866/408-WINE** or 905/562-3373. www.crushtours. com. Summer and winter Mon–Fri 9:30am–5pm; Sat 9:30am–2:30pm.

Niagara Wineries in the U.S.

Nestled between the escarpment and Lake Ontario, in an area northeast of Niagara Falls, New York, lay a handful of wineries. A brochure, entitled *Niagara Wine Trail USA,* with descriptions of the wineries and a map showing their locations, can be obtained from tourist information centers in Niagara Falls, New York, and at tourist information centers inside Niagara Falls State Park, or you can visit **www.niagarawinetrail.org**. Opening hours vary quite markedly among vineyards; some are limited to weekends in the colder months, so call ahead to avoid disappointment.

Eveningside Vineyards (4794 Lower Mountain Rd., Cambria, NY; ✆ **716/867-2415**; www.eveningside.com) is a boutique winery. Family owned and operated; production of their European-style wines is limited. **Niagara Landing Wine Cellars** (4434 Van Dusen Rd., Lockport, NY; ✆ **716/433-8405**; www.niagaralanding.com) has vineyards dating back to the 1800s. They produce wine from native Labrusca grapes and European viniferas. **Vizcarra Vineyards at Becker Farms** (3760 Quaker Rd., Gasport, NY; ✆ **716/772-7815**; www.beckerfarms.com) is a family destination, with pick-your-own produce, a playground, and a store filled with pies, jams, and other treats in addition to their winery. **Warm Lake Estate Vineyard and Winery** (3868 Lower Mountain Rd., Lockport, NY; ✆ **716/731-5900**; www.warmlakeestate.com) is located on the south shore of Lake Ontario. The winery offers a picnic area, winery tours and tasting, and numerous summer events.

Niagara-on-the-Lake Trolley Wine Country Tours   Sit back and relax onboard a vintage trolley, while your tour guide narrates the way through Niagara's wineries. Tours are approximately 2¼ to 3 hours long, inclusive of pickup and drop-off and wine tastings at the wineries.

48 John St., Niagara-on-the-Lake, Ont. ✆ **888-669-5566** or 905/468-2195. C$55 (US$46). May–Oct daily. 2 tours each day.

Niagara World Wine Tours   This multipurpose company offers bicycle, van, or coach excursions through the Niagara wine region. From spring through fall, enjoy a bike tour as you meander at a leisurely pace through wine country. Areas covered include the Niagara Escarpment, the Niagara Peninsula, Jordan, and Beamsville. Stop for wine tasting—and don't forget to take a break for lunch. Prices range from C$65 to C$120 (US$54–US$100). If you prefer, tour the area in a luxury SUV, van, or minicoach stopping at wineries, then tasting fine cuisine at restaurants such as Terroir La Cachette. Packages available.

92 Picton St., Niagara-on-the-Lake, Ont. ✆ **800/680-7006**. www.niagaraworldwinetours.com.

Steve Bauer Bike Tours   The best way to see Niagara—using your own two feet and a couple of wheels. Bike to a few wineries, stop for a picnic, then return to your hotel. (Or skip the wineries and bike all day—Steve Bauer tours offer customized or guided tours for groups of 10 or more people: see chapter 7, "What to See & Do in the Niagara Region.") Call at least 2 weeks in advance to be sure of booking a space. Customers range from hard-core bike enthusiasts who want to cycle 140km a day to

---

Tips **Never Drink & Drive**

There are no exceptions—do not drink and drive. Period. There are lots of options to explore to ensure everyone gets to enjoy their visit to the wine country.

- Designate a driver. If you are staying more than a day, rotate the responsibility.
- Contact a tour company and allow them to transport you. You'll have the added bonus of a knowledgeable guide.
- If you are touring wineries in the Niagara-on-the-Lake region, there is a step-on/step-off bus service. Several wineries in the area provide shuttle buses, too.
- Become adept at tasting like a professional. Discipline yourself to expectorate the wine you taste and discard the remaining wine. There are vessels for just this purpose at every tasting bar.

And don't think you're okay as long as you're wobbling along on a bicycle—if you are under the influence of alcohol, you are a potential danger to yourself and other road or trail users.

---

those who just want to take in the sights while enjoying the fresh air. For wine tours, choose from a half-day tour (1-4:30pm), which covers 20km and offers samplings at Inniskillen and Reif wineries. A full-day, 30km tour (10am–4:15pm) includes a 3-course lunch at Peller Estates and a tasting at Marynissen Winery.

P.O. Box 342, Beamsville, Ont. ✆ **905/563-8687.** Prices depend on customization. Full day with lunch C$139 (US$115); half-day C$75 (US$62).

Zoom Leisure   With more than 100 bikes to choose from and a list of wine tours, this is a great place to start touring the region. Tour three wineries, sampling the wine as you go, or choose an extended package (with optional lunch), which includes four wineries. Each bike has an optional basket in the front to bring home goodies from your voyage. Group and custom tours, where you can choose different routes; lunch and wineries are also available. Reserve tours in advance—48 to 72 hours ahead for most tours.

2 Market St., Niagara-on-the-Lake, Ont. ✆ **866/811-6993** or 905/468-2366. www.zoomleisure.com. Tours starting at C$60–C$115 (US$50–US$95).

STRATEGIES FOR TOURING NIAGARA'S WINE REGION

It would be impossible to visit Niagara's 70-plus wineries in one trip, unless you happen to have a couple of free weeks on hand and devote yourself to the task full time. And touring the wine country is an activity that you must savor, not rush! My advice is to put together an itinerary before you arrive, but be flexible: be ready to pull into an enticing property that is not on your list, or to change your route to accommodate wineries with award-winning icewines, for instance, if that becomes your newfound passion during your visit.

   Tour smarter, not harder are the words of advice to keep close to your heart as you leaf through this chapter in the process of planning your Niagara wine-country trip.

First decide whether you would like to tour in your own vehicle, travel by bicycle, or join an organized tour. Bicycle rental companies are listed in chapter 7, "What to See & Do in the Niagara Region," and I look at a few tour options earlier in this chapter.

Begin with a guided tour of one of the larger wineries to get a good grounding in how wine is made. Next, I recommend taking part in a **tutored tasting.** Even if you are a seasoned wine aficionado, a refresher may well rekindle your passion for the noble grape. **Hillebrand Estates Winery** (p. 174) offers several educational seminars daily. I highly recommend the **Essence Seminar,** an hour of absolutely fascinating instruction on the art of wine tasting—which, by the way, is all about smell and only a little about tasting—but more of that in "The Art of Wine Tasting" later in this chapter.

As you draw up your shortlist of the wineries you will call upon, **aim for a balance** among the big guns and the mom-and-pop operations, the sophisticated estates and the modest weathered barnboard tasting rooms. And at least one meal in a **winery restaurant** is compulsory (in my opinion, at least).

Take it slowly—**aim to visit between three and six wineries** for a day's outing. You'll give yourself the opportunity to get to really know not only the wines but also the story behind each winery: its history, the types of wines it makes and where the grapes are grown, and the passionate people behind the scenes who make it all happen. Only by visiting the Niagara wine region will you gain a deep appreciation of the effort and experience that goes into every bottle produced. The winery staff are quite approachable and knowledgeable; it's not unusual to spend a half-hour chatting about the intricacies of a good bottle of Baco Noir with a winemaker. You are likely to enjoy getting to know the winemakers just as much as the wines.

If you are looking for the undivided attention of the tasting room staff, **tour in the morning.** Most wineries open at 10am. Later in the day, when the winery parking lots are filling up with vehicles, you'll be enjoying an after-lunch espresso or *digestif* on the terrace of a winery restaurant nestled among the vines, or shaking the crumbs from your picnic blanket and contemplating an afternoon nap.

Beyond that, since the length of time you'll have to spend in the wine region and your level of wine knowledge are variables known only to you, it's impossible for me to provide you with a personalized touring strategy—you must devise your own itinerary that will best suit your intentions and wishes.

3 Niagara Region's Wineries

I would love nothing more than to be able to include a personal review of every Niagara winery, but that would necessitate an entire book dedicated only to the wineries, not to mention the fact that there are so many new ones springing up it would be impossible to stay up-to-date. As a result, this section of the chapter contains recommended wineries, but please, please remember that the selection is limited only by space and that there are dozens more waiting to be discovered.

GRIMSBY & BEAMSVILLE

Angels Gate Winery   The setting for this winery is quite idyllic. The recently constructed mission style building sits on land once owned by the Congregation of Missionary Sisters of Christian Charity in Ontario. The winery is built into the hillside—the underground facility allows the earth to keep the cellars cool and minimize temperature variation. Wine production, including receiving, crushing, and fermentation, also occurs underground. Grapes are grown on the property, adjacent to the winery and in two other Beamsville Bench locations. As you walk up to the winery door you pass by a tranquil garden complete with seating, which is nestled into the hillside. A waterfall lends a peaceful element to the open-air garden room. Facing a fabulous view of Lake Ontario is a generous-sized terrace used for warm-weather dining, a new offering that was very popular in 2005. Angels Gate expects to offer light fare from late morning through late afternoon again next year; call ahead for opening dates and times. Tours include a guided tour of the vineyards, cellar, and barrel rooms, followed by a tasting and cheese platter. Tours by appointment are C$5 (US$4), refunded if you purchase a bottle of wine. Sampling of four wines is free, while icewine samples are C$2 (US$1.65). Expect to pay between C$12 (US$10) and C$40 (US$33) for individual bottles of wine. Seminars are held on the hows and whys of decanting, how to build and stock a home wine cellar, and other wine-related topics. Winemaker Natalie Spytkowsky is usually on-site to speak with visitors.

4260 Mountainview Rd., Beamsville, Ont. ✆ 877/264-4283 or 905/563-3942. www.angelsgatewinery.com. June–Oct Mon–Sat 10am–5:30pm, Sun 11am–5:30pm; Nov–Dec Mon–Fri 11am–5pm, Sat 10am–5pm, Sun 11am–5pm; Jan–May Mon–Fri 11am–5pm, Sat 10am–5pm, Sun 11am–5pm.

De Sousa   This family-owned and -run winery is distinctly southern European in design, a feeling that is extended into the old-world styling of the boutique and tasting room. The estate boasts a formal white villa with a red roof, manicured gardens with clipped shrubs, a terrace with a pond, and groves of trees surrounding the property. Traditional Portuguese wines and VQA wines are produced here. Mother De Sousa hosts wine tastings daily in the tasting room—ask for your tasting of red wine in the old-fashioned Portuguese tradition of serving wine in a clay cup. Samplings are free and available Saturday and Sunday only in the winter; tours from April to the end of October are also free. On weekends in July and August, partake of the vineyard barbecue fare. Wine prices range from C$9 (US$7) to C$50 (US$41).

3753 Quarry Rd., Beamsville, Ont. ✆ **905/563-7269.** www.desousawines.com. May–Oct daily 10:30am–5:30pm; Nov–Apr Sat–Sun 10:30am–5pm. Daily tours May–Oct.

EastDell Estates   A very pretty country lane leads to EastDell Estates, an 85-acre property with spectacular views over the countryside as it rolls down toward Lake Ontario—hence the restaurant's name, The View. The tasting room and restaurant are housed in a rustic building built entirely of wood and stone sourced from the property. Daily wine tours are offered twice a day in the summer, and less often in the winter depending on the demand. Tours cost around C$5 (US$4), depending on the wine for tasting. Sampling is available free, and wine prices vary between C$8 (US$6) and C$25 (US$21). There are more than 5km (3 miles) of hiking and cross-country ski trails accessible to visitors. Tours include a 45-minute hike through the vineyards, with commentary on the unique topography and geology of the region and how it contributes to the Bench's location as a prime grape-growing area. You can educate your palate with one of several tasting seminars. Fees apply and schedules vary, so call ahead. Between May and November you can rent a cute cottage (big enough for only two) that perches right on the edge of a pond on the estate, surrounded by woodland and vineyards.

4041 Locust Lane, Beamsville, Ont. ✆ **905/563-9463.** www.eastdell.com. Daily 11am–8pm; winter hours may vary.

Malivoire Wine Company ✯   The distinctive label of this limited-production winery features a ladybug, which was chosen as the winery's symbol as a representation of balance between the importance of the vineyards and the responsibility to

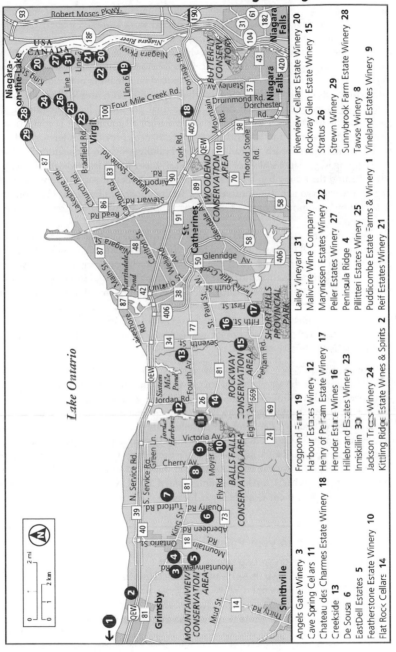

Niagara Region Wineries

Angels Gate Winery **3**
Cave Spring Cellars **11**
Chateau des Charmes Estate Winery **18**
Creekside **13**
De Sousa **6**
EastDell Estates **5**
Featherstone Estate Winery **10**
Flat Rock Cellars **14**

Frogpond Farm **19**
Harbour Estates Winery **12**
Henry of Pelham Estate Winery **17**
Hernder Estate Wines **16**
Hillebrand Estates Winery **23**
Inniskillin **30**
Jackson Triggs Winery **24**
Kittling Ridge Estate Wines & Spirits **2**

Lailey Vineyard **31**
Malivoire Wine Company **7**
Marynissen Estates Winery **22**
Peller Estates Winery **27**
Peninsula Ridge **4**
Pillitteri Estates Winery **25**
Puddicombe Estate Farms & Winery **1**
Reif Estates Winery **21**

Riverview Cellars Estate Winery **20**
Rockway Glen Estate Winery **15**
Stratus **26**
Strewn Winery **29**
Sunnybrook Farm Estate Winery **28**
Tawse Winery **8**
Vineland Estates Winery **9**

steward the land in an environmentally protective manner. The application of insecticides and herbicides is avoided, and the vineyard work is done by hand. The vineyards are managed using sustainable viticulture methods.

The winery itself is definitely worth a visit due to its unique location and architectural design. A large ravine at the center of the northern limits of the property drops 30 ft., providing an ideal location for a gravity-feed winemaking operation. The multilevel production process allows gentler handling of the wine, and Malivoire reaps the rewards of superior balance and finesse in the final product. The inspiration for the design of the unusual convex-shaped roof came from a Quonset hut (a prefabricated building with a semicylindrical corrugated roof) that the previous landowner had used as a parking shelter for his tractor. Inside the building—which feels almost as if you are stepping into a large-scale Hobbit hole—everything is spotlessly clean, all steel and glass. Behind the tasting bar, with its nifty modern chandelier, you can view the workings of the winery in all its multilevel glory. Tastings are complimentary, and tours are available by appointment only—a charge may apply depending on how many are in the group.

Some quite noteworthy wines are produced here, including the French hybrid Marechal Foch "Old Vines," harvested from vines planted on Malivoire's 10-acre Jordan vineyard more than 30 years ago. A block of vineyard has been reserved for Malivoire's Courtney Gamay. Intensive canopy management and pruning is employed in this block to improve fruit quality. The result is a more complex, fuller, round-in-the-mouth red that is quite intriguing—not typical gamay characteristics by any stretch, but very quaffable. Wines range from C$15 (US$13) to C$54 (US$45).

4260 King St., Beamsville, Ont. (🕿) 905/563-9253. www.malivoirewinecom.com. Mar–Dec Mon–Fri 10am–5pm, Sat–Sun 11am–5pm; Jan–Feb by appointment.

Peninsula Ridge 🍷🍷 An exquisitely restored and renovated Queen Anne–revival Victorian home is the showpiece of this winery, standing sentinel at the end of the long sweeping drive into the estate. The Restaurant at Peninsula Ridge is ensconced within the heritage building, and is highly recommended for lunch or dinner (see chapter 6, "Where to Dine," for listing information). The Winery Retail Shop is located in a meticulously restored 1885 post-and-beam barn. The atmosphere manages to be sophisticated and casual at the same time, making the space an inviting one in which to linger. Allow the staff to guide you through a tasting of VQA wines. Tastings are C$2 (US$1.65) for four samples, and C$2 (US$1.65) for one sample of icewine. No appointment is necessary if fewer than 10 people. Tours of the winery

---

(Tips **Be Kind to your Palate**

If you're planning on visiting several wineries in a day, and therefore potentially tasting one or two dozen wines (law dictates that each winery may serve up to four 1-ounce samples of wine), try narrowing your tasting choices in order to make the most of your olfactory and taste experience. The simplest plan is to stick to red or white. Beyond that, you could choose a vintage known to be a particularly good year locally, or a single varietal, or only light or full-bodied wines. Have fun with it—taste whites in the morning and reds in the afternoon, or stick to icewines and fruit wines. It's your choice!

production facilities and the traditional underground cellar are available for free at 11:30am and 3pm daily. Keep an eye out for their Viognier—smooth, dry, and fruity. Icewine here is made with my number-one choice of grape for this delectable nectar—Cab Franc. The strawberry aroma and flavor are intensely desirable and unforgettable. Wine prices vary between C$10 (US$8) and C$55 (US$46).

5600 King St., Beamsville, Ont. ℭ **905/563-0900**. www.peninsularidge.com. May–Oct daily 10am–6pm; Nov–Apr Mon–Fri 11am–5:30pm, Sat–Sun 10am–5:30pm. Tours daily at 11:30am and 3pm.

Puddicombe Estate Farms & Winery *Kids*   This 300-acre working farm was established more than 200 years ago by the Puddicombe family, who still own and operate the business today. Along with its family-based activities (including a petting zoo and agricultural train ride, "What to See & Do in the Niagara Region," for more details), the Puddicombes offer a wine shop that's worth a visit—prices range between C$9 (US$7) and C$28 (US$23). Award-winning wines are available to sample at the tasting bar at C$1 (US83¢) for four samples. Try the sauvignon blanc or raspberry fruit wine. Grapes grown in their vineyards include Colombard, Viognier, and Muscats. Hikers take note—the farm property backs onto the Bruce Trail. Light fare is available in the licensed Harvest Café and Tea Room. Pick your own apples, pears, peaches, berries, grapes, and vegetables in season. Tours for 10 or more are available by appointment only and vary from regular winery tours and tastings for C$3 (US$2.50) per person to C$11 (US$9) for a wagon ride tour and more.

1468 Hwy. 48, Winona, Ont. ℭ **905/643-1015** or 905/643-6882. www.puddicombefarm.com. Jan–Apr Mon–Fri 9am–5pm, Sat–Sun 10am–4pm; May–Dec daily 9am–5pm. Tours June–Oct daily 11am and 1pm; Nov–May by appointment.

JORDAN & VINELAND

Cave Spring Cellars *&*   Cave Spring Cellars' tasting room, wine shop, and cellars are located in a historical building (1871) on the main street in the village of Jordan (which is worth a visit in its own right—see the dining and shopping chapters for more detailed information). Cave Spring Cellars has been producing wine from *Vitis vinifera* grapes for 20 years, on land first scouted by plane and chosen for its hillside location, heavy clay soils, and proximity to the moderating influences of Lake Ontario. Tutored tastings are held on weekends at 3pm Friday through Sunday in the winter, and noon and 3pm in the summer. The lineup for 2005/2006 included vertical tastings (comparing a single grape varietal from several vintages), the story behind the trend toward unoaked chardonnay, the many faces of Niagara Riesling, and the benefits of aerating wine. For tastings, expect to pay C50¢ (US41¢) per tasting and C$4 (US$3) for icewine. A late-harvest wine sample is C$2 (US$1.65). Packages are available in partnership with the adjacent Inn on the Twenty (see chapter 5, "Where to Stay," for listing information) and its prestigious fine-dining restaurant, which include overnight accommodations, a winemaker's dinner, and a private tutored tasting. Bottles of wine cost C$13 (US$11) to C$30 (US$25) for table wines and up to C$60 (US$50) for icewines.

3638 Main St., Jordan, Ont. ℭ **905/562-3581**. www.cavespringcellars.com. June–Oct Mon–Thurs 10am–6pm, Fri–Sat 10am–7:30pm, Sun 11am–6pm; Nov–May Mon–Thurs 10am–5pm, Fri–Sat 10am–6pm, Sun 11am–5pm. Tours June–Sept daily noon and 3pm; Oct–May Fri–Sun 3pm.

Creekside   The inviting visitors' building brings you into an intimate tasting bar with its adjacent covered deck for summertime dining and sipping. You are welcome

Tips Serve Your Wine at Its Ideal Temperature

You may not be aware, but as you wander in and out of tasting rooms and winery bars the wine you taste will (hopefully) have been carefully stored and served at the optimum temperature for its particular characteristics.

Pay heed to the following practical advice, if for no other reason than that the wines you taste while touring and then lug home by the caseload will simply not taste the same at home unless you serve them at their intended temperature.

Some simple principles to remember are:

• The cooler the wine, the less bouquet it will have, and conversely, the warmer the wine, the more bouquet will be detectable.

• Acidity and tannins are accentuated at lower temperatures and diminished at higher temperatures.

Here are some simple guidelines for serving temperatures. Light, sweet white wines and sparkling wine may be refrigerated for 4 or more hours. Most other white wines and light reds may be chilled for 1½ to 2 hours in the fridge. Full, dry white wines may be served slightly warmer—1 hour in the fridge will do. Medium and full, rich red wines should be served slightly below room temperature, and certainly no more than 18°C (64°F). If you do not have a temperature-controlled wine fridge (and not many of us do), then you will have to get creative as to how you cool your red wines for serving. In the Rhone Valley in France, for instance, you will see bottles of wine sitting outside the door of many a home in the early evening. This is not an offering to St. Vincent, the patron saint of French *vignerons,* but a practical method of coaxing the wine to the correct serving temperature in time for the evening meal, which is served much later in the evening in France than in North America.

And finally, don't mistreat the wine you have just purchased by letting it cook in your car on a hot summer's day. Bring a cooler and a few ice packs with you to protect your wine from deteriorating due to exposure to high temperatures.

to bring your own food, or enjoy the light fare on weekends from noon to 4pm. Menu items include suggestions for wine pairing. A variety of wines are produced here, using different production methods and grapes sourced from their own on-site vineyards, vineyards along the St. David's Bench in Niagara-on-the-Lake, and several local growers. Their wines have a variety of price points, a mix of single varietals and blends, and are categorized into estate and reserve labels. Prices start at C$8 (US$6.65) for an Estate Wine Rose to C$35 (US$29) for a 2001 Grand Meritage Reserve Wine. Icewines top at C$40 (US$33) a bottle. Reserve wines are quite limited in quantity but worth investigating. If you're interested in acquiring wines for cellaring, ask the tasting-bar staff for recommendations. Sample prices are C50¢ (US40¢). Tours of the Estate are C$3 (US$2.50) and C$5 (US$4) for reserve tours that include the barrel cellars and production facilities.

2170 Fourth Ave., Jordan Station, Ont. © 877/262 9463 or 905/562 0035. www.creeksidewine.com. May–Oct daily 10am–6pm; Nov–Apr daily 11am–5pm.

Featherstone Estate Winery   Located on the fertile Beamsville Bench, Featherstone is a small but earnest winery with high standards of land and crop management, resulting in wines of high quality, although limited quantity. The estate is a modest 23 acres, but its size makes it amenable to the personal care and attention lavished upon it. The vineyards are insecticide-free. Beneficial insects including ladybugs and lacewings are released to control aphids, and pheromone traps are used to control the grape berry moth population. Woodchips have been placed under the vines in an experimental effort to reduce weed growth, and therefore allow decreased use of herbicides. Control of birds, which can do extensive damage to grapes (as well as eating them!), is managed using several methods. Grapes designated for icewine are covered by netting, which is a standard practice in the region. "Bird bangers," propane-powered noisemakers that simulate a gun blast, are employed in the late summer and fall. But the most intriguing method used at Featherstone is a trained hawk, owned and flown by the winery's co-owner. The owners also provide tours, lasting about 40 minutes, for groups of eight or more people by appointment only. The C$5 (US$4) tour includes three samples. Three to four tasting samples, without the tour, are complimentary.

A surprisingly wide choice of wines are available, but some wines are limited in production to as few as 40 cases, so buy a case or two right there and then if there's a wine that really speaks to you. Individual bottles cost about C$12 (US$10) to C$30 (US$25). Featherstone serves light lunches on the covered wraparound veranda of the 1830s farmhouse, which also hosts the small retail store and tasting bar. Food is served between 11am and 4pm Fridays to Mondays from late May to early September.

3678 Victoria Ave., Vineland, Ont. © 905/562-1949. www.featherstonewinery.ca. Apr–Dec Fri–Mon 10am–6pm; Jan–Mar by appointment or chance.

Flat Rock Cellars ☞   This young winery, opened to the public in spring 2005, has stunning architecture, surpassed only by the view from the generous floor-to-ceiling windows over the vineyards and across Lake Ontario. The feeling when you walk into the light-filled tasting bar is as if you've entered an eagle's nest, albeit one with some very tasty wine on hand. From the tasting bar, a short walk across a bridge takes you to the production facility. Tours are available for free and by appointment only and

---

(Fun Fact) Strange Sights and Sounds

As the grapes head toward their peak of ripeness in September and October, you will hear frequent bursts of a booming sound in the vineyards, the noise rolling and echoing as it spreads across the fields. No, the farmers aren't shooting the birds that flock to eat the ripening grapes—but you would be correct in thinking the noise is designed to scare the feathered creatures away. The boom is created by the firing of carbide guns, known as **"bird bangers."** You may also see **wind machines** in the vineyards. With the recent unusually harsh winters in the Niagara region, these are being installed in increasing numbers. When these machines are in operation, they help to break up layers of warmer and cooler air, moderating temperatures. Wind machines are quite effective at reducing winter damage to the vines.

are highly recommended, since the production area is tour-friendly (a catwalk around the perimeter of the production area allows you to clearly see the various stages of production from an elevated position). The grapes, which have been deliberately restricted to simply Riesling, chardonnay, pinot noir, and Vidal, are handpicked and entirely sourced from Flat Rock's own vineyards. The entire process from vine to bottle is handled as gently as possible—the juice for red wines is even hand-stirred while skins are in contact rather than using a mechanically operated stirring device. The 2003 pinot noir was drinking exceptionally well in 2005—ask tasting-bar staff for a recommendation for a similar wine. Tastings are C$3 (US$2.50) for four wine samples. Note that Flat Rock's entire production utilizes screw caps. Many members of the wine industry are very supportive of screw caps from a practical point of view, but consumers still show some resistance. I urge you to get over your sentimental idea of popping a cork and judge the wine, not the method used to seal the bottle. I found the wines here at Flat Rock quite enjoyable and of very high quality. To bring a bottle home, pay between C$15 (US$12) and C$30 (US$25) for table wine and up to C$40 (US$33) for icewine.

2727 Seventh Ave., Jordan, Ont. ⓒ 905/562-8994. www.flatrockcellars.com. May–Oct daily 10am–6pm; Nov–Apr Sat–Sun 10am–6pm or by appointment. Tours available upon request.

Harbour Estates Winery   These vineyards and winery are situated on land that was originally a fruit farm. The property was gradually converted to vines over a number of years, and now Harbour Estates has established itself as a producer of fine Niagara wines. The off-dry Riesling has a refreshing acidity that nicely balances the detectable sweetness of fruit. One of their most popular reds is a cabernet sauvignon/Cabernet Franc/merlot blend that is best described as "easy drinking." Their vineyards produce enough grapes to meet their annual target of 10,000 cases, but the owners and winemaker prefer to do some trading with other wineries in order to have access to a greater selection of grape varieties for the production of their wines.

Tips **The Ins and Outs of Shipping Wine Home**

Most of the wines you will encounter in the Niagara wine region are available only at the winery. A number of the larger producers do sell some of their series in Ontario retail stores across the province, and a few export selected wines to the United States. For the most part, however, the best way to get your case (or cases!) home is to arrange for the winery to handle shipment. Each winery has its own policy for delivery of wine—many deliver only in Ontario, some deliver across Canada and to selected U.S. states, still others are willing to send product overseas, while a few sell their wines only on the premises.

If you are a resident of Ontario, you can order Niagara VQA wines online from **www.winecountryathome.com**. Wine Country at Home was established in response to customer demand for wines that are not usually available for purchase at places other than the wineries themselves. It's also worth visiting the websites of individual wineries for information on ordering and shipping their wines.

The estate itself includes 549m (1800 ft.) of frontage onto Jordan Harbour with dinghy access, so that visitors are welcome to arrive by boat if they are out for a sail or cruise in the harbor or on the lake. There is even room for a helicopter landing. Visitors are also welcome to walk through the Carolinian forest on the property, along the Harbourside Trail and backwood paths; a self-guided tour of the winery is available free of charge. Guided walking tours of the estate are offered but must be booked in advance; cost is C$15 (US$12) per person. The retail shop and tasting bar has a down-to-earth country look; samples are free. Wines are modestly priced, with most bottles falling into the C$10 to C$15 (US$8–$12) range. The owners eagerly share their knowledge of wines, vines, and the ins and outs of making an agricultural living on the Niagara Peninsula. A variety of events are held throughout the year, including concerts, art exhibits, and, yes, grape-stomping.

4362 Jordan Rd., Jordan Station, Ont. © 905/562-6279. www.harbourestateswinery.com. June–Oct daily 10am–6pm; Nov–May daily noon–5pm. Tours available.

Henry of Pelham Family Estate Winery

If you have an interest in heritage buildings, this winery is a must-see on your tour. There are two historical buildings, currently housing the tasting bar and retail store; the oldest dates from 1842. The property was originally a tavern and bustling coaching inn—apparently it was not unusual to see as many as 22 teams of horses tied to the hitching posts at any one time. The winery is owned and operated by the Speck family; the land was deeded to their great-great-great-grandfather in 1794. A nicely balanced offering of wines include unoaked chardonnay, dry and off-dry Rieslings, sauvignon blanc, gamay, baco noir, cabernet/merlot blends, and more. Try their award winning Cuvee Catherine sparkling wine.

If you are touring this area of the wine region between June and October, plan to have lunch in the Coach House Café. Light dishes are available between 11:30am and 5pm Wednesday to Monday. Wine by the flight or the glass can be sipped on the patio. Picnic baskets for two can be ordered, or you can choose from a mouthwatering selection of Canadian artisanal cheeses at the walk-up counter. Winery events include the annual raw oyster weekend (with matching wines, of course), held in July. Tours are offered year-round for a nominal fee; they run daily at 1:30pm between May and October, but must be booked ahead during the winter months. Wines start at around C$11 (US$9) and rise to around C$50 (US$42) for reserve wines. A small fee of C$2 (US$1.60) will get you four samples; the money is donated to a local college.

1469 Pelham Rd., St. Catharines, Ont. © 877/735-4267 or 905/684-8423. www.henryofpelham.com. May–Oct daily 10am–6pm; Nov–Apr 10am–5pm daily. Free tour May–Oct daily 1:30pm; Nov–Apr by request.

Hernder Estate Wines

The landscape at this large vineyard (almost 500 acres are under vine), which includes a picturesque wooden covered bridge, a restored 1867 barn (which houses the tasting room), and a pond, all set among gently rolling hills, attracts weddings, bus tours, and lots of cameras. The winery has a long-standing reputation for top-quality aromatic white wines, including their Rieslings and Gewürztraminers. Ontario fruit wines are also produced here. Live entertainment is offered on the licensed patio on summer weekends. One of their hallmarks is that the estate produces only vintage-dated varietals; a tasting here would make a nice comparison exercise with a winery that focuses on blends. Tours run year-round on weekends at 1:30 and 3:30pm; there is no charge. Samples are also free. Wines range between C$8 (US$7) and C$20 (US$17) a bottle.

1607 Eighth Ave., St. Catharines, Ont. ℂ **905/684-3300**. www.hernder.com. Daily 10am–5pm. Tours Sat–Sun 1:30pm and 3:30pm.

Rockway Glen Estate Winery   This winery is somewhat unusual since it shares space with Rockway Glen Golf Course, an 18-hole championship course with full amenities, including a clubhouse restaurant (on the same premises as the tasting bar, wine boutique, and wine museum), driving range, and putting and chipping greens. The *musée du vin* is worth a visit, particularly if you opt for a guided rather than self-guided tour, since you will get a much more in-depth explanation of the artifacts on display and will have an opportunity to ask questions to further your knowledge of the history of the winemaking process. The museum's collection features a variety of antique implements and accouterments sourced from French vineyards, and depicts the journey of the noble grape from the vine to the bottle. The *musée du vin* is open 11am to 4pm daily. Guided tours must be pre-booked. Admission fee is C$5 (US$4) per person, whether guided or self-guided. Three wine samples are complimentary.

Rockway Glen's special reserve wines are pricier than their regular estate and VQA wines, but very commendable. Try the cabernet sauvignon special reserve 2002 or the VQA Niagara Peninsula merlot special reserve 2002. Wine prices range between C$10 (US$8) and C$30 (US$24) for a special reserve merlot and C$40 (US$33) for icewines.

3290 Ninth St., St. Catharines, Ont. ℂ **877/762-5929** or 905/641-1030. www.rockwayglen.com. May–Oct Mon–Sat 11am–7pm Sun 11am–5pm. Nov–Apr Mon–Fri 11am–4pm Sat–Sun noon–4pm.

Tawse Winery ⭑   One of the youngest wineries in the Niagara region, Tawse opened in the spring of 2005. The modern architecture of the winery building features clean, simple lines, making its presence in the landscape unobtrusive. A large pond is situated in front of the winery, providing the building with geothermal energy for heating and cooling. Due to its geographical position on the Vineland "Double Bench," the winery is able to use the hillside terrain to its advantage, and uses a multilevel gravity-feed system for its winemaking process. The winery plans to focus on traditional Burgundy-style wines, and its chardonnays are certainly stirring the hearts of local wine critics. Small amounts of Cabernet Franc, pinot noir, and Riesling wines are also produced here. Many of the grapes used for Tawse wines are sourced from old-growth, low-yield vines, which have a tendency to yield greater depth of character when vinified. This winery seems to be one to keep your eye on as it evolves over the coming years, and a good bet to add to your tour list. Tours of the innovative production facilities, which include sampling in the winery store and in the barrel cellar, cost C$20 (US$17) per person and must be booked in advance. In the tasting room, you can get two 2-ounce samples for C$5 (US$4). Wines hover around the C$30 to C$40 (US$25–US$33) mark.

3955 Cherry Ave., Vineland, Ont. ℂ **905/562-9500**. www.tawsewinery.com. Wed–Sun 10am–5pm or by appointment. Call ahead to confirm opening hours.

Vineland Estates Winery ⭑⭑⭑   This is a storybook winery, pretty as a picture. Vineland's stone-clad coach house and adjacent buildings create an ambience of romance and sophistication that has led the property to become one of the most popular for weddings. Vineland Estates is one of the largest wineries in Niagara, and is an excellent ambassador of the region. You will find Vineland wines in the U.S., U.K., Japan, and many other countries around the world. In their stylish wine boutique, there are wines on offer in every price range, from C$10 (US$8) to C$125 (US$104).

> **Fun Fact Tasting a Flight**
>
> A *flight* is an array of wines, with each showing different characteristics rang-
> ing from the origin of the grapes used and production methods to the year the
> wine was produced and the producer itself. Tasting a flight allows you to get a
> sense of how influences such as age, production, origins, year of harvest, and
> winemaker styles can affect the bouquet and flavor. It's a great way to become
> more familiar with a particular **varietal**. You can also experience a **vertical tast-
> ing,** which is several vintages of the same wine, or a **horizontal tasting,** which
> is several producers tasted from the same vintage.

The cabernet sauvignon 2002 is an excellent example of this fine varietal. Try several
vintages—the large tasting bar has a good selection of wines and the staff are eager to
share their knowledge and personal points of view on the various wines available for
tasting. Summer lunch on the shaded terrace of the restaurant, which serves among
the very best of Niagara cuisine, will give visitors a taste of the tranquil and intimate
atmosphere that is Vineland's specialty. (See chapter 6 for more information about the
winery's restaurant.)

Organized tours and tastings are available, ranging from a basic tour of the vineyards, production area, and cellars to tour and tasting combinations that include wine
and cheese, or specialized icewine tours and tastings. Tours, which cost C$6 (US$5),
run twice daily between May and October, at 11am and 3pm, weekends only at 3pm
in the fall and spring. No tours are available between January and March. Lower-
priced wines can be sampled free of charge; a nominal fee applies for premium wines.
Bottles range from C$10 (US$8) to around C$40 (US$33).

3620 Moyer Rd., Vineland, Ont. ② **888/846-3526** or 905/562-7088. www.vineland.com. May–Dec daily 10am–6pm;
Jan–Apr daily 10am–5pm; tours late May to Oct daily 11am and 3pm; Nov to mid-May Sat–Sun 3pm.

NIAGARA-ON-THE-LAKE

Frogpond Farm ✿   This small country winery produces the only certified organic
wine in Ontario. The proprietors are on hand to enthusiastically discuss their organic
farming methods and offer free tastings of their organic Riesling and cabernet merlot.
Try the oak-aged Riesling, which has been aged in huge 2,500-liter (660 gal.) oak
casks, an unusual treatment for a Riesling (it is much more common to find oak-aged
chardonnay). The barrels are old, so they allow air to reach the wine but do not impart
the typical vanilla, toast, or caramel notes you would find from a young oak barrel.
Rather, the flavor is richer and more complex than an unoaked Riesling. Prices are reasonable, ranging from C$12 to C$16 (US$10–US$13).

Grapes are handpicked, and natural pest control methods used include companion
plants to attract predators of pesky leaf hoppers and kites to scare the birds away from
the ripening fruit.

If you are in a position to transport them home, when you drop in ask if there are
any eggs for sale that day. They are quite simply the best-tasting eggs I've ever had. You
will even see the chickens they came from, running around the farmyard.

1385 Larkin Rd., Niagara-on-the-Lake, Ont. ② **905/468-1079**. www.frogpondfarm.ca. Tues–Sat 1–5pm. Free guided
tours on Sat afternoons or by appointment.

Hillebrand Estates Winery ⑅⑅   This winery is a great starting point for a tour of the wine country because of its extensive facilities. Established in 1979, Hillebrand has an impressive tour and seminar program, offered daily to the public. A complimentary vineyard and winery tour follows the trail of the winemaking process, and is especially recommended for the first-time visitor.

If you want to unveil the mysteries of how a wine interacts with your senses of sight, smell, and taste (and of course you do, or you would not be visiting wineries), then you must find the time to attend one of the daily Essence Seminars (C$10/US$8 per person). The seminar is suitable for wine novices, but experienced oenophiles may find this to be a welcome refresher course. Led by Hillebrand's knowledgeable and charismatic resident wine consultants, the essence seminar is a lesson in the assessment, understanding, and appreciation of wine tasting. You will learn the visual clues as to a wine's age, alcohol content, and grape composition. Your nose will receive a tutorial in aroma identification with the aid of several pure essences, including cedar, raspberry, vanilla, and green apple. Finally, the mouth is addressed, with an explanation of where in the mouth and on the tongue various tastes are perceived, and the importance of aerating a mouthful of wine in order to fully assess its qualities. Three wines are studied during the seminar, usually a white, a red, and an icewine. Other seminars include specialized sparkling wine and icewine sessions and an explanation of cellaring, with tips for identifying wines that will benefit from aging.

While at the winery, visit the boutique and tasting bar or enjoy a glass of wine on the summer terrace or in the Wine Garden. The tasting bar offers a flight of three pre-selected wines for C$5 to C$10 (US$4–US$8), or you can select your own wine to sample. Table wine prices run from C$10 to C$80 (US$8–US$66). Hillebrand Estates Winery Restaurant is one of the top Niagara wine-country dining destinations, open for lunch and dinner. *Toronto Life*, an urban lifestyle magazine whose restaurant reviews are almost slavishly followed by the Toronto dining-out set, recently awarded the restaurant four stars. See the listing in chapter 6, "Where to Dine."

1249 Niagara Stone Rd., Niagara-on-the-Lake, Ont. ⓒ **800/582-8412** or 905/468-7123. Daily 10am–6pm; varies slightly by season.

Inniskillin ⑅   The history of Inniskillin's modern winemaking activities goes back to 1975, when Inniskillin Wines Incorporated was granted the first winery license in Ontario since 1929. The present winery, on the Braeburn Estate, is located two kilometers from its original site. The buildings are picturesque, white-washed timber-framed structures juxtaposed with a 1920s barn. If you are looking for a free self-guided tour, Inniskillin is a great place to go. The tour path is clearly marked and numbered, and each "station" has a large panel with text and illustrations. The first few panels on the tour chronicle the history of the winery and give visitors an in-depth perspective on Niagara's unique topography and resultant microclimate, which is so conducive to growing cool-climate grapes. As you follow the tour, you will pass within inches of the vines. Vidal grapes, used to make Inniskillin's award-winning icewines, grow next to the winery buildings. Free guided tours are offered daily between May and November (weekends only Dec–Apr), and include two tasting samples of table wines. Samples are otherwise offered at C$1 (US80¢) for table wines—more for icewines. Bottles range from C$11 to C$30 (US$9–US$25).

Inniskillin, being one of the largest Niagara wineries, has a well-stocked wine boutique housed in the barn with gifts and accessories, including linens displaying the

Niagara's Jewel—Icewine

Icewine is a truly sensational experience for the palate. Its key characteristic is a perfect balance of sweetness and refreshing acidity. Icewine delivers delicious aromas, ranging from lychee, apricot, pear, and vanilla in a Vidal icewine to strawberries and raspberries in a Cabernet Franc. Complex fruit flavors explode in the mouth with each and every sip. Officially classed as a dessert wine, icewine also may be served as an aperitif with pâté or foie gras or on its own.

The grapes used to produce icewine are left untouched on the vines and covered with a layer of protective netting once the fruit has reached full ripeness in October. Close attention is paid to the falling temperatures as winter envelops wine country. When the temperature drops below 17°F (−8°C) (although most vintners prefer to operate at temperatures a few degrees colder) and the grapes are frozen solid, there is a sudden flurry of activity in the vineyards. Dozens of volunteers arrive, usually at midnight or later, when there is the least danger of the temperature rising.

The grapes are handpicked and quickly transported to the winery to be de-stemmed and crushed, then immediately pressed while still frozen. The water in the grape juice remains frozen, and a relatively minute amount of sweet juice is extracted, so concentrated that its consistency is like honey.

After the sediment has been cleared, the juice undergoes a slow fermentation process, which takes several months, and is then aged. Both fermentation and aging take place in stainless-steel containers at cool temperatures in order to maximize fruit concentration.

Icewine was first discovered in Germany in the late 1700s by farmers trying to rescue their semifrozen grape crop after a sudden cold snap. However, German winters are not consistently cold enough to freeze the grapes—it happens only once or twice every 10 years or so. Moving forward to Niagara in the mid 1980s, insightful and enterprising winemakers realized that Ontario's cold winters would provide just the right conditions for producing an annual icewine vintage.

Hillebrand Estates was the pioneer of icewine production in Niagara, beginning in 1983. A year later, Inniskillin made its first vintage of icewine. By the early 1990s, Niagara's icewine entered the world stage when it began attracting favorable attention at international wine competitions, including the prestigious Vinexpo in Bordeaux, France.

Niagara icewine is always produced as a varietal, with the majority being made from Vidal and Riesling. Other varieties include Gewürztraminer, Cabernet Franc, merlot, pinot gris, chardonnay, muscat ottonel, and gamay. Winemakers vary slightly in their recommendations for serving. Chill the bottle for 1½ to 3 hours in the fridge, which will bring the serving temperature down to between 5°C and 10°C (41°F–50°F). Serve one to two ounces per person in a small tulip-shaped glass, which will encourage the wine to flow over the tip of the tongue (where most of the sweetness-detecting taste buds are concentrated) as you taste. A small white wineglass is an acceptable alternative.

Tips   Affordable Icewine?

There's no denying the fact that icewine is expensive. The cost is justified by several hard facts. The grapes are at the mercy of nature in every vintage, and vintners cannot predict or control how much fruit will be left on the vines when the time for harvest eventually arrives, or what condition the grapes will be in. The process is labor-intensive, since the grapes are hand-picked within a brief timeframe. Labor costs are high, since trained workers (depending on the winery) must be enticed to go into the vineyards at short notice, in the middle of the night in extreme cold to pick the frozen grapes. Yields are small—it takes 3 to 3.5 kilograms (6.6–7.7 lb.) of grapes to make one 375mL (12.7-oz.) bottle of icewine. The same amount of grapes would make three 750mL (25.4-oz.) bottles of table wine.

Having said all of that, if your wallet will not stretch to icewine's price tag, seek out one of the new, smaller 200mL (6.7-oz.) bottles. Watch out for sales of older vintage icewines in the winery boutiques.

For exceptional value, try a select late-harvest dessert wine. This is made from the second pressing of the grapes, after they have thawed for several hours. The resulting wine retains much of icewine's delectable aromas, but approximately one-third of the sugar content—and one-third of the price.

attractive Inniskillin logo and a selection of glassware in addition to a wide variety of wines. In addition to their tasting bar, there is a designated icewine tasting bar. Upstairs in the barn loft you'll find a gallery displaying the work of local artists.

Visit during the harvest in September and October and you will be rewarded with the heady, blissful aroma of fresh juice as the grapes are gathered and processed right alongside the main visitor entrance

S.R. 66, R.R. 1 Niagara Pkwy., Niagara-on-the-Lake, Ont. ✆ **888/466-4754** or 905/468-2187. www.inniskillin.com. May–Oct daily 10am–6pm; Nov–Apr daily 10am–5pm.

Jackson-Triggs Niagara Estate Winery   If you have a keen interest in technology, you will be intrigued by the tour at Jackson-Triggs. Their state-of-the-art, gravity-flow-assisted winery is one of the most technologically advanced in Canada. The main winery building is contemporary in design, with a clean glass, steel, and concrete facade. Enter the cavernous foyer and sign up for a public tour at the concierge desk on your right. Hour-long tours are available for C$5 (US$4) (refunded with purchase of wine) and include three tastings. Individual bottles of Jackson-Triggs wine range between C$9 (US$7.50) and C$30 (US$25) for table wine and between C$45 (US$37) and C$75 (US$62) for icewine. Although there isn't a restaurant on-site, the winery holds special food and wine events throughout the year—including their popular "Savour the Sights," a unique dining experience with several courses, each served at different locations within the winery. Tucked away beyond the rear of the winery lies a charming open-air amphitheater, with rows of curved stone seating built into the grassy hillside. Seasonal entertainment is on offer between July and September—call ahead for details of who is performing and when. There are two tasting rooms—a complimentary tasting bar within the boutique, and a premium tasting room with an outdoor terrace, where each sample has a price tag of C$3 to C$4 (US$2.50–US$3). Cheese platters can be purchased to accompany wines by the glass. Keep your eyes open for the half-dozen or so sample rows of different grape varietals growing in front of the winery. It's a great opportunity to see the vines and their fruit at close quarters.

2145 Niagara Stone Rd., Niagara-on-the-Lake, Ont. (C) 905/468-4637, ext. 3, concierge desk. www.jacksontriggs winery.com. Summer daily 10:30am–6:30pm; winter daily 10:30am–5:30pm.

Lailey Vineyard   Lailey's tasting room is a delight because of its simplicity in design and function. Stand at the spotlessly clean counter, learn a little about the wines on offer from the approachable, knowledgeable staff, and enjoy an interesting variety of wines. Samples may include an unoaked chardonnay (with an extremely pleasant green apple note), dry Riesling, cabernet/merlot blend, or their icewine. Lailey Vineyard and its winemaker Derek Barnett were the first commercial vintners to release wines fermented in Canadian oak barrels—their 2001 chardonnay. Four additional varietals have now been added to the Canadian oak method. The family has been making their exclusively estate-grown *Vitis vinifera* wines for more than 35 years, but the tasting room is a relatively recent venture where most samples are free. Wines start at C$10 (US$8) and reach $45 (US$37). Since the winery is small, tours are available by prior appointment only. Introductory tours start at C$5 (US$4) and include four samples, while tours including a cheese platter, four samples, and two icewines cost C$15 (US$12).

15940 Niagara Pkwy., Niagara-on-the-Lake, Ont. (C) 905/468-0503. www.laileyvineyard.com. May–Oct daily 10am–6pm; Nov–Apr daily 10am–5pm.

Marynissen Estates Winery   Trundle along the pretty Concession 1 side road and pull into the cozy, welcoming weathered wood–clad tasting room and wine store. This small estate vineyard is family-owned and -run—you are likely to meet family members across the tasting-bar counter. From 10am to 5pm daily come in for a taste for C50¢ (US41¢)—no charge with purchase of wine. Some of the oldest vines in Canada thrive in the vineyards here. Winemaker John Marynissen was the first grower to successfully cultivate cabernet sauvignon grapes in Canada, at a time when the belief was firm that the Ontario climate was too harsh to support vinifera grapes. John's daughter Sandra is now the head winemaker. The resident cat may greet you upon arrival. Because the winery is small, there are no formal tours available. Varietals include sauvignon blanc, pinot gris (pinot grigio), gamay, merlot, and their prestigious cabernet sauvignon, ranging from C$9 (US$7.50) to C$24 (US$20).

R.R. 6, 1208 Concession 1, Niagara-on-the-Lake, Ont. (C) 905/468-7270. www.marynissen.com. May–Oct daily 10am–6pm; Nov–Apr daily 10am–5pm.

(Tips) Dining Out Wisely

Dining at a winery restaurant can be quite a hedonistic experience, not least due to the many courses you will undoubtedly be tempted to order and the variety of wines available to sample. It's best to plan to have one extended, leisurely meal (lunch and dinner both have their unique charms), and picnic or snack the rest of the day. A few delectable cheeses served with fresh bread make a perfect light meal or snack to have on hand while touring the wine country.

Niagara College Teaching (NCT) Winery   Members of the public are welcome to visit the Glendale Campus of Niagara College and see the students in action at the Niagara College Teaching Winery. There is a vineyard and winery on the campus, where students practice what they learn in the classroom. Their award-winning VQA wines are available for purchase at the wine boutique located near the entrance to Niagara College's Culinary Institute Dining Room (see chapter 6, "Where to Dine," for more information on the restaurant). Expect to spend between C$10 (US$8) and $50 (US$41) for a bottle and between C$1 and C$2 (US$.85–US$2) for samples. While at the college, enjoy the beautiful multilevel display gardens designed to mimic the Niagara Escarpment, which forms a backdrop to the college. The Bruce Trail can be accessed nearby, and there are walking and biking trails on campus. The campus greenhouse is open to the public as well. Locals flock here to buy a wide variety of plants for home and garden, particularly in the spring bedding plant season and in the weeks leading up to Christmas, when the greenhouse is filled with brightly colored poinsettias. There is even somewhere to rest your weary bones for the night after a hard day touring the wineries—the student residence offers overnight accommodations in the summer months. For groups of eight or more, book a tour—choose from a half-hour guided walk with three samples for C$3 (US$2.50), an hour educational tour for C$16 (US$13) (minimum 15 people), or choose a wine and cheese tour (minimum 20 people) cost by quote only.

Niagara College, Glendale Campus, 135 Taylor Rd., Niagara-on-the-Lake, Ont. ✆ **905/641-2252**. www.nctwinery.ca. Winery and retail store open Mon–Sat 10am–5pm; Sun 11am–5pm.

Peller Estates Winery 🎭🎭🎭   One of Canada's largest producers of wine, Peller Estates is a grand property that echoes the distinguished château estates of the Old World. The interior of the main entrance immediately evokes a feeling of stepping into a splendid hotel lobby. Sweeping staircases, comfortable upholstered seating, a feature fireplace, wood paneling, warm caramel walls, and spacious public spaces all contribute to the luxurious setting. The reserve wines are reliably first-rate. If you are a sauvignon blanc devotee, make sure you taste one or more here. Wine prices start at C$10 (US$8) and top at C$40 (US$33) for table wine selections. Icewines can hit C$95 (US$79). Excellent seminars are on offer, and they are carefully coordinated with nearby Hillebrand Estates seminars so that the seminars complement each other rather than repeat content between the two wineries. At Peller, past seminars have included culinary demonstrations, a study of stemware, and tutorials on pairing wine and food. Winery tours are offered year-round for C$5 (US$4) and include two VQA tastings. Tours start at 10:30am in the summer, running on the half-hour every hour until typically 7:30pm. In the winter, tours start at 11:30am and run until 5:30pm. Individual samples range from C$1 to C$5 (US$.85–US$4) for icewine selections. Peller Estates Winery Restaurant, led by chef Jason Parsons, is quite simply one of the best in Niagara's wine country. Menus feature local ingredients, and tasting menus are available. See chapter 6, "Where to Dine," for more detailed information. A shuttle service is available between Niagara-on-the-Lake's old town district and the winery—call the winery for details. Packages that include lunch or dinner at the winery restaurant, tickets for the Shaw Festival, and overnight accommodations are available.

290 John St. E., Niagara-on-the-Lake, Ont. ✆ **905/468-4578** (winery) or 888/673-5537 for information on events in and around the vineyard. www.peller.com. Daily 10am–6pm; extended hours in summer.

Reif Estates Winery   Just a few minutes south of the town of Niagara-on-the-Lake, Reif Estates features a tasting room and winery boutique located in a restored coach house, reminiscent of a European country cottage. Reif Estates wines are produced using only grapes from their own vineyards. In addition to their selection of red, white, and dessert wines, a premium line of cabernet sauvignon, merlot, and pinot noir, with "Premier Cru" designation, have been created. These wines must adhere to strict guidelines, including minimum age of vines, maximum yields per acre, and a minimum of 26 months fermenting and aging in oak barrels. The first tasting sample is free, and it's C$1 (US83¢) for subsequent tastings—icewine is C$3 (US$2.50) per sample. Reif is well known for its Late Harvest Vidal, and its Riesling, Vidal, and Cabernet Franc icewines (high-end varieties cost C$55/US$46) per bottle). Consequently, there are lots of choices when it comes to purchasing these wines—there are varying bottle sizes, right down to single-serving miniatures and gift packs combined with truffles. Wine prices vary between C$9 (US$7) and C$50 (US$41) (for premium first-growth reds).

The wine boutique has gifts as well as locally made jams, jellies, and fudge. There is a limited selection of Canadian cheese and crackers available for takeout if you decide on an impromptu picnic. Facing the car park are sample rows of the types of grapes grown at Reif, so you can get a close-up view of the vines and fruit. Winter tours are not available, but summer offers two daily tours for C$4 (US$3): 11:30am and 1:30pm. The price includes three tastings, one of which is an icewine. No appointment is required. There are plans for expansion that include a new retail building, landscaped gardens with vine-covered walls, a fountain feature, and seating areas. This project is slated for completion in 2006.

15608 Niagara Pkwy., Niagara-on-the-Lake, Ont. ✆ **905/468-7738.** www.reifwinery.com. Apr–Oct daily 10am–6pm; Nov–Mar daily 10am–5pm. Tours May–Sept daily 11:30am and 1:30pm; Oct–Apr by appointment only.

Riverview Cellars Estate Winery   This is a small, family-owned and -operated winery. A small tasting bar is located inside the country fruit market on the edge of the scenic Niagara Parkway. A larger tasting room overlooking the vineyards is situated at the rear of the building ask for free samples of table wine; select harvest samples cost C$2 (US$1.65) and icewines C$3 (US$2.50), refunded with purchase of wine. Fresh local fruit is available in season, plus you'll find wine-related gifts and local baked goods. The atmosphere is down-to-earth, country-style hospitality—definitely no pretensions here. Premium VQA wines and icewines are available. Riverview's most popular wine is a blend comprised of cabernet sauvignon, merlot, and baco noir, crafted and styled to please a palate that prefers sweeter wines—an unusual trait for a red wine. Table wine selections cost between C$15 (US$12) and C$27 (US$22). Icewines can reach up to C$50 (US$41).

15376 Niagara Pkwy., Niagara-on-the-Lake, Ont. ✆ **905/262-0636.** www.riverviewcellars.com. Apr–May daily 10am–6pm; June–Sept daily 10am–7pm; Oct–Nov daily 10am–6pm; Dec–Mar daily 10am–5pm.

Stratus 🍷🍷   A flurry of media attention hovered around Stratus Vineyards when it opened in 2005. Much of that has been focused on the winery's attention to sustainable production. When the winery opened to the public, it became the first Leadership in Energy and Environmental design (LEED) building in Canada, and apparently the only LEED-certified winery in the world. In addition to such features as geothermal heating and cooling technology and a system for composting organic waste, the winery is four stories high to allow a gravity-feed production system to

Dine Among the Vines

A number of wineries have restaurants or cafes on their premises. As you would expect in a wine region, the cuisine is exceptional. Opening days and times vary considerably depending on the property and the season, so call ahead. Reservations are recommended, although not required. For reviews and full descriptions of the following dining destinations, see chapter 6, "Where to Dine."

The region's longest established estate winery restaurant is **Inn on the Twenty Restaurant and Wine Bar,** located in the center of pretty Jordan Village, across the street from Cave Spring Cellars (3836 Main St., Jordan Village, Ont.; ✆ **905/562-7313**). **The Restaurant at Peninsula Ridge** can be found in a historical Queen Anne–revival Victorian home on the grounds of Peninsula Ridge Estates Winery (5600 King St. W., Beamsville, Ont.; ✆ **905/563-0900**). There are picnic and patio facilities at **Henry of Pelham Family Estate Winery** (1469 Pelham Rd., St. Catharines, Ont.; ✆ **877/735-4267** or 905/684-8423); their **Coach House Café** offers casual light fare, cheese platters, and picnic baskets. **Hillebrand Winery Restaurant,** long in the talented hands of renowned chef Tony de Luca, is open for lunch and dinner (1249 Niagara Stone Rd., Niagara-on-the-Lake, Ont.; ✆ **800/582-8412** or ✆ 905/468-7123). For great value, sample the fare and service of the students of Niagara College at the **Niagara Culinary Institute Dining Room** (135 Taylor Rd., Niagara-on-the-Lake, Ont.; ✆ **905/641-2252**, ext. 4619). Enjoy the creations of Marc Picone and his culinary team in a picturesque setting at **Vineland Estate Winery Restaurant** (3620 Moyer Rd., Vineland, Ont.; ✆ **888/846-3526**, ext. 33 or 905/562-7088, ext. 33). At the western end of Niagara's wine region, along the Beamsville Bench on the Niagara Escarpment, lies **EastDell Estates' The View Restaurant,** named for its panoramic view of the surrounding vineyards and Lake Ontario (4041 Locust Lane, Beamsville, Ont.; ✆ **905/563-9463**). Wine-country cuisine awaits at **Peller Estates Winery Restaurant** (290 John St. E., Niagara-on-the-Lake, Ont.; ✆ **888/673-5537** or 905/468-4678). **Terroir La Cachette Restaurant & Wine Bar** features Provençal-style cuisine and is located within Strewn Winery (1339 Lakeshore Rd., Niagara-on-the-Lake, Ont.; ✆ **905/468-1222**).

function, a necessity on the relatively flat landscape of the Niagara-on-the-Lake region and in stark contrast to other gravity-feed wineries in the area that have taken advantage of topography and built into the natural slopes of the escarpment. But some of the media attention has been centered on the wines, too, and local critics have been singing their praises. Premium prices have been set for the narrow range of wines on offer. The French-born winemaker has chosen to create two signature blends, Stratus White and Stratus Red, with a small number of single varietals including chardonnay and merlot. It's urban, it's high-end, it's sleek. But it's well worth the experience. Just be sure to wear black. Tastings are offered from Wednesday to Sunday and no reservation is needed. Sample three wines for C$10 (US$7). Tours are by appointment only and cost C$15

(US$12) per person. Table wines typically run between C$30 and C$40 (US$25–US$33), and C$55 (US$46) for the highest.

2059 Niagara Stone Rd., Niagara-on-the-Lake, Ont. © **905/468-1806.** www.stratuswines.com. Daily 11am–5pm. Seminars held weekly; call for times and to reserve a space.

Strewn Winery ☞ On Lakeshore Road, close to Niagara-on-the-Lake and just west of Sunnybrook Farm, which produces excellent fruit wines (see below), lies Strewn Winery. Your first impression as you pull into the parking lot at Strewn may leave you feeling a little puzzled, since the industrial nature of the site is in stark contrast to many of the wineries in the district. You'd be right in thinking industrial, since the concrete-block winery buildings are, in fact, located in what was once an abandoned cannery. Step inside, however, and you will find a wood-clad wine boutique on your left, a state-of-the-art cooking school on your right, and to the rear of the building, a tasting bar and restaurant serving Provençal-inspired cuisine and backing onto the picturesque woodland bordering Four Mile Creek. Public tours of the vineyard, barrel cellar, and production facilities are daily at 1pm for groups of 10 or more—call to make an appointment first.

Special events are held throughout the year; check the website for up-to-date information. Past events have included invitations to take part in pruning the vines in early spring, a fall participation event that includes grape picking, assisting with the grape crushing and a sample of grape juice to take home, and an interactive seminar on identification of the characteristics of wines made from different grape varieties. *Terroir la Cachette* is Strewn's winery restaurant, featuring the French Provincial cooking expertise of chef Alain Levesque, with an emphasis on local ingredients. The Wine Country Cooking School offers a variety of classes that feature food and wine. One-day classes, 2-day culinary weekends, and 5-day culinary vacations are available. (See chapter 6, "Where to Dine," for more detailed information on the restaurant and the cooking school.) For those who truly love to indulge in fine food and wine, particularly hands-on, Strewn is the place to be. To walk in and sample a wine, tastings range between C50¢ (US40¢) to C$2 (US$1.65) for icewine varieties. To take a wine home, expect to pay between C$11 (C$9) and C$34 (US$28) per bottle.

1339 Lakeshore Rd., Niagara on the Lake, Ont. © 905/468 1339 (winery), 905/468 1222 (restaurant), or 905/468 8304 (cooking school). www.strewnwinery.com; www.winecountrycookingschool.com. Daily 10am–6pm. Free tour daily 1pm.

Sunnybrook Farm Estate Winery   Sunnybrook Farm, a short drive west of Niagara-on-the-Lake along the southern shore of Lake Ontario, is unique among the Niagara wineries since it produces exclusively fruit wines, many of which are sourced from their own orchards. This small family-owned and -operated fruit winery is proud of the many awards its wines have accumulated over the years. When you visit the cozy tasting room, you will see the bottles displayed on the shelves with their medals hanging around their necks. No formal tours are available, but staff are ready to pour samples 7 days a week—it's C$2 (US$1.65) for four tastings. Notable wines include blackcurrant, spiced apple, and black raspberry. Peach, pear, and other fruit wines, many of them dry or off-dry, are a nice refreshing change to grape wines. Their Ironwood Hard Cider has received critical praise. All of Sunnybrook's wines are Quality Certified (QC), which is the fruit wine equivalent of VQA for Ontario grape wines. Prices to pick up a bottle range from C$13 (US$11) to C$25 (US$21).

1425 Lakeshore Rd., Niagara-on-the-Lake, Ont. © **905/468-1122.** www.sunnybrookfarmwinery.com. May–Oct daily 10am–6pm; Nov–Dec daily 10am–5pm; Jan–Feb Thurs–Mon 10am–5pm; Mar–Apr daily 10am–5pm.

OTHER WINERIES

A few other notable wineries scattered along the Wine Route include **Chateau des Charmes Estate Winery,** a large winery located at 1025 York Rd., Niagara-on-the-Lake, Ont. (© **905/262-4219**); **Kittling Ridge Estate Wines & Spirits,** 297 South Service Rd., Grimsby, Ont. (© **905/945-9225**); **Pillitteri Estates Winery,** 1686 Niagara Stone Rd., Niagara-on-the-Lake, Ont. (© **905/468-3147**); and **Royal DeMaria Wines,** 4551 Cherry Ave., Beamsville, Ont. (© **888/562-6775** or 905/562-6767), whose entire operation is devoted to icewine.

9

Shopping

While there are pockets of great shopping for those who just love to spend their leisure time swiping plastic and signing credit card receipts, Niagara has other charms that are frankly much more attractive ways to while away vacation time. But consumerism is firmly engrained in North American culture, and in deference to the shop-til-you-drop brigade here are a few guideposts to the best of the shopping scene. I've also provided some suggestions in the "Shopping A to Z" section below, where the better retailers have been ferreted out and listed for your shopping pleasure.

1 The Shopping Scene

From a shopping standpoint, the Niagara region serves both the huge influx of tourists and its diverse regional population base. As a result, there tends to be extremes in the shopping landscape. The area immediately surrounding Niagara Falls on the Canadian side of the border is awash in souvenir shops, with a cluster of upscale stores attached to the recently opened Fallsview Casino. The economically depressed Niagara Falls, New York, has little to offer in the way of shopping with the exception of The Outlets at Niagara Falls USA, a mall that features Manhattan-style shopping destinations with everyday discounts of up to 60%. Niagara Falls, Ontario, also has an outlet complex, on Lundy's Lane.

Heading to the more sophisticated tourism areas, you will find boutique-style shopping with unique products. Niagara-on-the-Lake is the shopping jewel of the entire Niagara region. Jordan Village, although much smaller in scale, also offers an upmarket shopping experience. Old Port Dalhousie on the Lake Ontario shoreline has a few gems tucked away in its town center. Antiques lovers will find irresistible hunting around the Twenty Valley district and in the vicinity of the town of Virgil, just south of Niagara-on-the-Lake.

The malls and shopping centers in the Niagara region tend toward the practical and predictable—valuable attributes for serving their resident population, to be sure, but not top of the list for tourists when it comes to seeking out shopping destinations.

2 Great Shopping Areas

ANTIQUING

There are many fine antiques dealers and a host of collectibles shops in the Niagara region, but if you want to hit a few places in a single neighborhood then head for Virgil, a village just a few kilometers south of Niagara-on-the-Lake on Niagara Stone Road. Another good hunting ground is the Twenty Valley—its antique retailers are located mainly around Jordan and Vineland. If you're a country-drive kind of person who likes to pull over now and then when an antiques market catches your eye, cruise along Victoria Avenue between the QEW and Fly Road (if you turn onto the North Service Rd. first you can catch Prudhomme's 25-vendor market before heading south on Victoria toward Vineland), or Niagara Stone Road (Hwy. 55) between the QEW and Niagara-on-the-Lake.

Take note that opening hours for antiques retailers differ from typical shopping hours. Many are closed on Mondays (except holiday Mon) and some also close Tuesday and Wednesday, although most are open 7 days a week in July and August. As always, if there is a particular vendor you wish to visit call ahead to avoid disappointment.

JORDAN VILLAGE

Jordan Village is a delightful rural community that is compact enough to explore on foot. Two large, century-old warehouses have been converted into an eclectic assortment of retailers, punctuated by a luxurious inn, an award-winning fine-dining restaurant, and a well-established Niagara winery. In addition, there are numerous retailers scattered along Main Street and Nineteenth Street, bounded on the south by Highway 81 (King St.) and on the north by Wismer Street. Shopping is higher-end in focus, with a mix of art galleries, designer fashions, giftware, antiques, home and garden accessories—and even a shop catering to dogs.

NIAGARA FALLS

If you are a souvenir hound, you don't need a guidebook to give you suggestions for where to buy souvenirs. You will see souvenirs at every turn of your head as you stroll around the tourist areas by the Falls. If you like themed souvenirs, then you will find them by the ton at the exit of most of the major tourist attractions. If you want upscale shops, visit the Galleria inside the Niagara Fallsview Casino Resort. For duty-free shopping, see section 3 below.

NIAGARA-ON-THE-LAKE ☞☞

Niagara-on-the-Lake wins best in show for its shopping. Centered along one stretch of road through the middle of town, cheerily spilling over onto a few of the cross streets, "Canada's prettiest town" also boasts Canada's prettiest shopping. Storefronts are tasteful and quaint. You will find fudge, a Christmas store, Brit imports, kitchen gadgets, wine, upscale men's and women's fashions, giftware . . . every store is a delight. You'll need oodles of self-control if you can't spare the time to step across the threshold of each and every merchant. There are benches thoughtfully placed at regular intervals along the flower-bedecked sidewalks, and some shady spots for hot summer days. Refreshments are easy to come by, whether your idea of a pick-me-up is a cup of tea, a mug of joe, or a double-scoop ice-cream cone. The town sparkles in the winter too, so shopping can be slotted into the agenda no matter what the weather.

Tips **Visitor Tax Rebate**

Visitors to Canada (nonresidents) can apply for a tax refund. The federal (7%) sales taxes on non-disposable items that will be exported for use can be recovered. Keep all your receipts. For details, see "Taxes" under "Fast Facts: Niagara Region" in chapter 4. Duty-free allowances for citizens of Canada, the U.S., and the U.K. can be found in chapter 2.

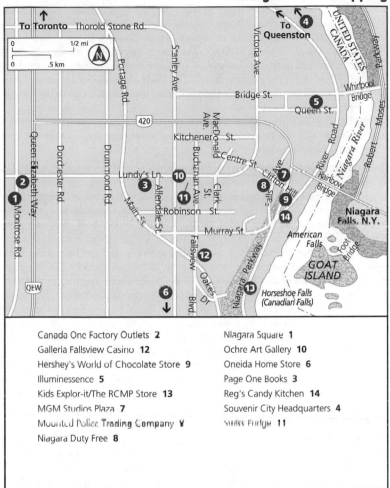

Canada One Factory Outlets **2**
Galleria Fallsview Casino **12**
Hershey's World of Chocolate Store **9**
Illuminessence **5**
Kids Explor-it/The RCMP Store **13**
MGM Studios Plaza **7**
Mounted Police Trading Company **¥**
Niagara Duty Free **8**

Niagara Square **1**
Ochre Art Gallery **10**
Oneida Home Store **6**
Page One Books **3**
Reg's Candy Kitchen **14**
Souvenir City Headquarters **4**
Swiss Fudge **11**

PORT DALHOUSIE

This waterfront village, nestled on the south shore of Lake Ontario, has attracted some interesting boutiques and specialty stores. It's small enough that you can park the car in one spot and walk around the village center. There are restaurants and bars in addition to gift stores, women's fashions, and a candy emporium.

3 Malls & Shopping Centers

NIAGARA FALLS, ONTARIO AND NEW YORK

Canada One Factory Outlets High-profile brands are the order of the day at this outlet store complex. The 40 or so stores are arranged in a U-shape with the parking lot in the middle. Each store has an outside entrance, but there is a covered walkway to help shield shoppers from adverse weather. Savings are advertised to be as high as 75% on regular retail prices. Stores include Roots, The Body Shop Depot, Club Monaco Outlet Store, Samsonite Company Stores, Tootsies Factory Shoe Market, Time Factory Watch Outlet, and Mexx. The number of retailers is only a fraction of the huge outlet mall in Niagara Falls, New York, but if you're looking for Canadian or European-based stores (for example Roots, The Body Shop, Rocky Mountain Chocolate Factory, or Mexx), then Canada One will serve you better. Or go to both if you're a shopaholic and want to give your credit cards a meltdown. Call ahead or visit the website before your trip for an up-to-date listing of retailers. 7500 Lundy's Lane (at QEW), Niagara Falls, Ont. ✆ **905/356-8989.** www.canadaoneoutlets.com. Mon–Fri 10am–9pm, Sat 10am–6pm; Jan–Apr 10am–9pm; May–Dec Sun 10am–6pm.

Galleria Fallsview Casino   The architecture, decor, and construction materials are all sumptuous and luxurious, in keeping with the upscale money, money, money atmosphere of the casino. Whether you're a shopper or not, it's worth a wander around the Galleria. Stroll up past the shooting fountains and waterfalls with their everchanging multi-colored lights and enter by the main doors. You'll come face to face with Hydro-Teslatron, a monstrosity of a "living" sculpture that must be seen to be believed. At regular intervals, H-T comes alive with a sound and light show, leaving some bystanders bemused, although many seem to be fascinated by this imaginative structure. At the rear of the Galleria is a huge rotunda under a magnificent multi-story glass domed ceiling. Escalators lead down to an eclectic food court that features Johnny Rocket's, a 24-hour retro-style diner (not cheap, but the best chocolate milkshakes my family has ever had). Other eateries offer pasta, pizza, sandwiches, and ice cream. Casual and fine-dining restaurants are also on-site. Retailers lean toward the high-end, including Swarovski Austrian crystal, Linda Lundstrom designer women's fashions, Cherchez la Femme European women's fashions, and Philippe Artois imported Italian menswear. For souvenirs check out Canada's Finest, the official supplier of souvenir RCMP clothing and accessories, or First Hand Canadian Craft & Design, which stocks arts and crafts by Canadian artists. 6380 Fallsview Blvd., Niagara Falls, Ont. ✆ **905/371-3268.** www.fallsviewgalleria.com. Sun–Thurs 10am–11pm; Fri–Sat 10am–midnight.

Niagara Square   This regional shopping center is anchored by The Bay and Sportchek. A separate Cineplex Odeon movie theater complex is on-site. A small food court serves shoppers. Several mall stalwarts cover the women's fashion scene, including Cotton Ginny, Suzy Shier, Tabi, La Senza, and TanJay, but men's and youth fashions are not as well represented. Bargain stores include Payless Shoesource and Dollarama. 7555 Montrose Rd. (corner of McLeod Road and the QEW) in Niagara Falls, Ont. ✆ **905/357-1110.** www.niagarasquare.com. Mon–Fri 10am–9pm; Sat 9:30am–5:30pm; Sun noon–5pm.

The Outlets at Niagara Falls USA   This huge outlet mall is crazily busy, and you may find yourself cruising the parking lot for a while, especially on a weekend, to find a parking space. It's worth it, though. Many Canadians make the trek across the border to this clean and well-designed mall. The closest bridge is the Rainbow Bridge, but you can zip up Highway I-90 from Fort Erie or down from the Lewiston–Queenston Bridge. Around 150 brand-name stores offer everyday discounts on their stock, up to as high as 60% off the regular retail prices. The directory of stores reads like a New York shopping street. If it's famous, it's here. Polo Ralph Lauren, Guess, Gap, Calvin Klein, Burberry, Liz Claiborne, Rockport, and Jones New York are just a handful of the women's fashion retailers. Housewares include Mikasa, Pfalzgraff, and Corningware Corelle Revere. Kid's clothing can be found at OshKosh B'Gosh, The Children's

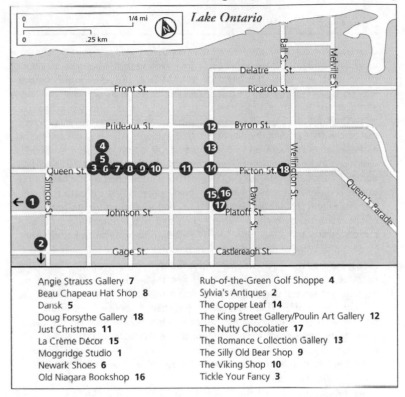

Angie Strauss Gallery **7**
Beau Chapeau Hat Shop **8**
Dansk **5**
Doug Forsythe Gallery **18**
Just Christmas **11**
La Crème Décor **15**
Moggridge Studio **1**
Newark Shoes **6**
Old Niagara Bookshop **16**

Rub-of-the-Green Golf Shoppe **4**
Sylvia's Antiques **2**
The Copper Leaf **14**
The King Street Gallery/Poulin Art Gallery **12**
The Nutty Chocolatier **17**
The Romance Collection Gallery **13**
The Silly Old Bear Shop **9**
The Viking Shop **10**
Tickle Your Fancy **3**

Place, Nautica, and more. Luggage, accessories, shoes, and menswear are well repre-sented throughout. Specialty stores include a Christmas Store, Fragrance Outlet, KB Toy Outlet, and OFF 5TH Saks Fifth Avenue Outlet. You'll sigh with delight at every corner. 1900 Military Rd., Niagara Falls, NY (take Hwy. I-90 to exit 22 to Factory Outlet Blvd.). ℂ **716/297-2022**. www.theoutlets.us. Mon–Sat 10am–9pm; Sun 11am–6pm.

ST. CATHARINES
Fairview Mall This mall serves local residents and features around 60 stores and services. Anchors are Zellers, Chapters, Mark's Work Wearhouse, Future Shop, and Zehrs. There is a Cineplex Odeon nine-screen movie theater complex on-site. 285 Geneva St. (near the QEW—take the Lake St. exit), St. Catharines, Ont. ℂ **905/646-3165**. Mon–Fri 10am–9pm; Sat 9:30am–5:30pm; Sun noon–5pm.

The Pen Centre This large indoor mall has approximately 180 stores and is the largest mall in the Niagara region. Anchor stores include The Bay, Gap, Pier 1, Sears, Zehrs, Zellers, HomeSense, SportChek, Winners, and Old Navy. There are a half-dozen full-service restaurants, a food court, and numerous snack retailers. If you want a break from shopping, there is a Famous Players Silver City on-site with eight movie theaters, and a glow-in-the-dark minigolf course. Dozens of women's and unisex fashion stores; less in the way of children's and men's fashions. Customer service is comprehensive, as

Duty-Free Shopping

Check for the current duty-free allowances before making your purchases. Canadian residents please note: if you are traveling to the U.S. you may purchase goods you wish to bring back to Canada at duty-free stores before leaving Canada. If you will be out of Canada for 48 hours or more, you may also purchase duty-free alcohol and tobacco. U.S. residents may purchase up to $200 of duty-free goods (excluding alcohol and tobacco) for trips across the border that are less than 48 hours. U.S. residents who stay in Canada for 48 hours or longer can bring back up to $800 worth of duty-free goods, which can include one liter of liquor and one carton of cigarettes. Nonresidents of Canada, please see the "Visitor Tax Rebate" box at the beginning of this chapter that explains the tax rebate process. Please note that customs rules and regulations are subject to change, and visitors to both sides of the border should check current rules and regulations before making out-of-country purchases they intend to bring home with them, whether those goods were purchased duty-free or not.

Niagara Duty Free   An array of duty-free goods are available, including perfume, cosmetics, jewelry, Swiss watches, china, crystal, chocolate, wine (including Niagara wines and icewines), and liquor. Instant visitor tax refunds are on offer. There is a currency-exchange service. Save up to 50% on regular retail prices. Located beside the Rainbow Bridge on the Canadian shore—the closest duty-free store to the Falls. The Rainbow Bridge is the shortest route to Interstate 90 from Niagara Falls, Ontario, and is a truck-free route. 5726 Falls Ave. (beside the Rainbow Bridge), Niagara Falls, Ont. © 905/374-3700. www.niagaradutyfree.com.

Peace Bridge Duty Free   Billed as North America's largest duty-free shopping complex, the Peace Bridge Duty Free has a wide variety of items. In addition, there is a handy Travel Services Center, which offers currency exchange, tax rebates, customized maps, tourist information, and business services. Other amenities include a food court with branded fast-food outlets, bathrooms, an ATM, and phones. Duty-free goods include Canadian souvenirs, leather goods, imported chocolate and gourmet foods, perfumes, china and crystal, wine, icewine, beer, liquor, and tobacco. 1 Peace Bridge Plaza (beside the Peace Bridge), Fort Erie, Ont. © 800/361-1302. www.dutyfree.ca.

Peninsula Duty Free   This duty-free shop is next to the Queenston–Lewiston Bridge, the most northerly of the three public border crossings in the Niagara region (the Whirlpool Bridge is reserved for frequent travelers). Beside the Queenston–Lewiston Bridge, Queenston, Ont. © 905/262-5363.

you would expect from a major mall. Strollers and wheelchairs are on hand, lockers are available for coats and parcels, and helpful staff will wrap your gifts, give your car a battery boost, or even help you find your car if you've forgotten where you've parked it. More than 1 million square feet of shopping. Hwy. 406 and Glendale Ave., St. Catharines, Ont. © 800/582-8202 or 905/687-6622. www.thepencentre.com. Mon–Fri 10am–9pm; Sat 9am–6pm; Sun 11am–6pm.

WELLAND
Seaway Mall   Serving Welland and district, Seaway Mall has a cinema complex and is anchored by Sears, Wal-Mart, and Zellers. Customer services include coat check, strollers, wheelchairs, and an infant change station. A good selection of mall chain sportswear, shoes, unisex fashions, and women's fashion retailers can be found here. There are also banks, a post office, and a food court. 800 Niagara St., Welland, Ont. ℃ 905/735-0694. www.seawaymall.com. Mon–Fri 10am–9pm; Sat 9:30am–5:30pm; Sun noon–5pm.

4 Shopping A to Z
ANTIQUES & COLLECTIBLES
Bartlett House of Antiques   Those with an interest in military history would be wise to pay a call at this antiques store, which also specializes in china, jewelry, and fine furniture. 1490 Niagara Stone Rd., Niagara-on-the-Lake, Ont. ℃ 905/468-1880.

Blue Barn Antiques & Collectibles   Collectors are invited to browse at the Blue Barn in the Twenty Valley antiques district. Two floors of antiques and collectible treasures. 4107 Cherry Ave., Vineland, Ont. ℃ 905/562-4606. www.bluebarnantiques.ca.

Forum Galleries Antiques & Collectibles   A variety of dealers showcase their wares at this large 8,000-sq.-ft. (743.2-sq.-m) antiques market. Furniture from Canada and Europe is available, with many different eras represented—from Victorian and country to Art Nouveau, Art Deco, '50s and '60s, and much more. You name it, they've probably got it—jewelry, glass, books, lamps, art, silver, china, toys, fine antiques, Canadiana . . . lose yourself for an hour or so as you wander the aisles. 2017 Niagara Stone Rd. (Hwy. 55), Niagara-on-the-Lake, Ont. ℃ 905/468-2777, www.forumgalleries.com.

Granny's Boot Antiques and Country Pine   Hand-crafted country pine pieces are a specialty at Granny's Boot. You'll also find a great selection of folk art, unique antiques, rustic furniture, and primitives. 3389 King St., Vineland, Ont. ℃ 877/211-0735 or 905/562-7055.

Harp & Swan Gallery   Located "on the bend" of Main Street inside the Jordan Village Guest Manor, this location specializes in Group of Seven reprints, quilts, antique European furniture, and reproductions. Collectibles are also featured. Hours vary, so call ahead. 3864 Main St., Jordan Village, Ont. ℃ 905/562-8269.

Jordan Antiques Centre   This village marketplace carries inventory from 25 antiques dealers and features a permanent show year-round. Specialized items include antique toys, Christmas decorations, jewelry, and silver. The Centre has a sound local reputation as a gift resource and showcase for large pieces of antique furniture. 3836 Main St., Jordan Village, Ont. ℃ 905/562-7723. www.jordanantiques.com.

Nothing New Antiques   This is the place for Canadiana, country furniture, and accessories. 1823 Niagara Stone Rd., Niagara-on-the-Lake, Ont. ℃ 905/468-7016.

Parkwood Galleries   This store specializes in fine furniture, decorative arts, and collectibles. On display you will find dining-room suites, bedroom suites, occasional furniture, china and glass, estate jewelry, prints, paintings, and lighting. Pianos are one of their specialties. Walnut and mahogany wood furniture pieces are featured. Ceramic pieces and smallware are on display. If you are searching for a particular item, ask a staff member—not all of their wares are on the floor all the time. 3845 Main St., Jordan Village, Ont. ℃ 877/337-4577 or 905/562-5415. www.parkwoodgalleries.com. www.parkwoodpianos.com.

Prudhomme's Antique Market   On the shores of Lake Ontario stands a restored turn-of-the-20th-century farmhouse that is home to a wide selection of antiques and collectibles, representing 25 vendors. 3319 North Service Rd., Vineland, Ont. ✆ 905/562-5187.

RJ's Antiques & Things   Two floors of antiques, collectibles, and nostalgia side by side in a 19th-century converted barn. 3831 Victoria Ave. S., Vineland, Ont. ✆ 905/562-3933.

Rovers Antiques & Collectibles   A variety of interesting objects from the past, including garden accents, jewelry, vintage clothing and accessories, and items to create the "shabby chic" look in your home. 3799 Main St., Jordan, Ont. ✆ 905/562-9036.

Vineland Antiques   Housed in the original general store in the village of Vineland, this antiques market is a multi-dealer enterprise. 4227 Victoria Ave., Vineland, Ont. ✆ 905/562-9145. www.vinelandantiques.com.

MORE ANTIQUES STORES   Here are a couple more antiques and collectibles destinations to check out: **Sylvia's Antiques,** 376 Mary St., Niagara-on-the-Lake, Ont. (✆ 905/468-5271) and **Europa Antiques,** The Old Red Brick Church, 1523 Niagara Stone Rd., Niagara-on-the-Lake, Ont. (✆ 905/468-3130).

If you're looking for a market-type place with multiple dealers, head for **Lakeshore Antiques & Treasures,** 855 Lakeshore Rd., Niagara-on-the-Lake, Ont. (✆ 905/646-1965), **Antiques of Niagara-on-the-Lake,** 1561 Niagara Stone Rd., Niagara-on-the-Lake, Ont. (✆ 905/468-8527), or **Antiques at the Creamery** (they serve ice cream in the summer), 758 Niagara Stone Rd., Niagara-on-the-Lake, Ont. (✆ 905/688-9649). And just a short drive down Four Mile Creek Road from Virgil, in the village of St. David's, you'll find two places that specialize in china and glass, linens, lighting, and furniture: **Anna's Antiques & Collectibles,** 253 Four Mile Creek Rd. (✆ 905/262-5524), and **S&B Antiques & Collectibles,** 246 Four Mile Creek Rd. (✆ 905/262-7007).

ART GALLERIES

Angie Strauss Gallery   Renowned local artist Angie Strauss creates oil and water-color paintings and has a line of women's fashions (see below). In the recently expanded gallery, one of the largest private galleries in the Niagara region, you will find limited editions, prints, and originals. Strauss paints popular local scenes and landmarks, florals, landscapes, and country collages. 129 Queen St., Niagara-on-the-Lake, Ont. ✆ 888/510-0939 or 905/468-2255. www.angiestrauss.com.

Doug Forsythe Gallery   Doug Forsythe is an established Canadian artist. Many of his collections feature landscapes, seascapes, marine themes, and figure studies. He works in computer graphics, watercolor, oil, and acrylics, and is skilled in etching, engraving, dry point, collagraphs, woodcuts, serigraphs, and woodcarving. Local scenes include Niagara-on-the-Lake, Niagara Falls, and Niagara vineyards. Forsythe also creates intricate guitars and fine scale-model ships. 92 Picton St., Niagara-on-the-Lake, Ont. ✆ 905/468-3659. ww.dougforsythegallery.com.

First Hand   This store features Canadian-designed and handcrafted arts. Categories include Inuit sculpture, art glass, ceramics, jewelry, and folk art. Galleria, Niagara Fallsview Casino & Resort, Niagara Falls, Ont. ✆ 905/354-2006.

Jordan Art Gallery ๛   This gallery is owned by a group of local artists who also staff the store, so there is always a knowledgeable and enthusiastic steward on hand to chat about the art on display. In addition to showcasing the work of the gallery owners, other selected artists' works are exhibited. The styles and media of these artists are

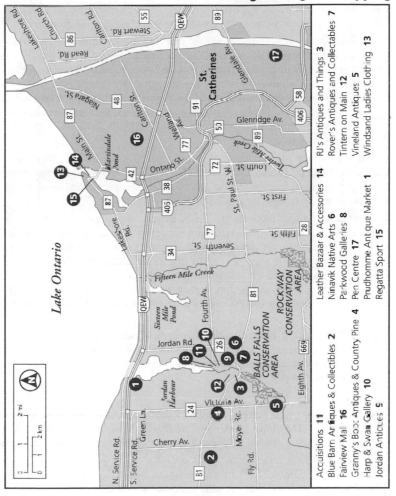

Accusitions **11**
Blue Barn Antiques & Collectibles **2**
Fairview Mall **16**
Granny's Book Antiques & Country Pine **4**
Harp & Swan Gallery **10**
Jordan Articles **9**

Leather Bazaar & Accessories **14**
Ninavik Native Arts **6**
Parkwood Galleries **8**
Pen Centre **17**
Prudhomme Antique Market **1**
Regatta Sport **15**

RJ's Antiques and Things **3**
Rover's Antiques and Collectables **7**
Tintern on Main **12**
Vineland Antiques **5**
Windsand Ladies Clothing **13**

quite remarkable. This gallery should be marked as a must-see if you are in the Twenty Valley area. Main St., Jordan Village, Ont. ✆ 905/562-6680.

The King Street Gallery/Poulin Art Gallery   This gallery in a historic home in Niagara-on-the-Lake features works by Canadian artist Chantal Poulin, who has twice won the award for Canadian artist of the year. Poulin's works range from portraits of children to landscapes, still life, and contemporary art. A number of vineyard landscapes are available. The gallery also displays other artists' work, including sculptures from Quebecois collaborative artists Yann Normand and Nancy Ferland, and Olivier Henley. 153 King St., Niagara-on-the-Lake, Ont. ✆ 905/468-8923.

Moggridge Studio   In a quiet residential area with a view of Lake Ontario, this gallery and framing studio handles a huge variety of categories. In addition, the work of distinguished Canadian wildlife artist Robert Bateman is available here. Other

Canadian artists whose work you'll find here include Bev Doolittle and Trisha Romance. 285 Niagara Blvd., Niagara-on-the-Lake, Ont. © 800/265-4889 or 905/468-2009. www.artlineetc.com.

Ninavik Native Arts ✦   This beautiful store features an impressive collection of Native art and sculpture. Initially the focus was purely on Inuit works, but the owners have expanded their product line to include Iroquois artists. Stunning pieces by established Native sculptors run as high as five figures. Works from younger, up-and-coming indigenous artists are also featured. Soapstone, ivory, bone, and antler are used to create the works of art. Fabrics, prints, pottery, paintings, and masks are also on display. Pieces may be purchased in person or online. 3845 Main St., Jordan, Ont. © 800/646-2848 or 905/562-8888. www.ninavik.com.

Ochre Art Gallery   Original paintings by Canadian artists are available for sale in this gallery within the Doubletree Resort in Niagara Falls. Paintings have been selected to reflect the beauty of nature and the great Canadian outdoors. 6039 Fallsview Blvd. (inside the Doubletree Resort Spa Fallsview), Niagara Falls, Ont. © 800/730-8609.

The Romance Collection Gallery   Trisha Romance's gentle, whimsical pastel portraits of home and hearth are collected with fervor around the world. Her most sought-after pieces are her limited-edition reproductions, which have sold out as quickly as they have been released over the past 25 years. Fans of Trisha can now purchase biographies, limited-edition figures, and collectable plates in addition to her beloved paintings. Trisha, a New York State native, now makes her home in Niagara-on-the-Lake. 177 King St., Niagara-on-the-Lake, Ont. © 800/667-8525 or 905/468-4431. www.romance collection.com.

Wyland Galleries   Canadian marine life artist Wyland creates bronze sculptures and paintings in a variety of media. Wyland's own work is featured along with other internationally recognized artists. Galleria, Niagara Fallsview Casino Resort, 6380 Fallsview Blvd., Niagara Falls, Ont. © 905/354-7474.

BOOKS

Chapters   Chapters has become a familiar name and favored destination for Canadian book lovers. They offer an extensive selection of books and magazines; larger stores carry CDs and a growing selection of giftware. Fairview Mall, 285 Geneva St., St. Catharines, Ont. © 905/934-3494.

Coles   Under the umbrella of Chapters Indigo, Coles is a mainstream general bookseller that favors mall locations. A wide selection of new and established titles and authors, book-related accessories, and gifts. Niagara Square Shopping Centre, 7555 Montrose Rd., Niagara Falls, Ont. © 905/357-1422; The Pen Centre, Hwy. 406 and Glendale Ave., St. Catharines, Ont. © 905/685/4961; Seaway Mall, 800 Niagara St. N., Welland, Ont. © 905/735-6146.

Old Niagara Bookshop   This independent bookstore carries literary works, specializing in Canadiana and children's books. Most titles are new. They carry some out-of-print and collectors' items, but not secondhand books. 233 King St., Niagara-on-the-Lake, Ont. © 905/468-2602.

Page One Books   Most of the books in stock here are used rather than new. Since they serve a relatively small community, the subject areas are wide-ranging—they try to carry a little bit of everything. Fun for a browse. 5984 Main St., Niagara Falls, Ont. © 905/354-9761.

CDS, MOVIES & MUSIC

Larger shopping malls have at least one store specializing in CDs and DVDs, although they tend to limit their selection to mainstream bestsellers and charge full price. Three of the most popular chain stores in the Niagara region are **HMV Canada, Music World,** and **Sunrise Records.**

MGM Studios Plaza   If you're a film buff, you will enjoy the MGM store. Besides a wide selection of DVDs and CDs, there is a range of interesting movie memorabilia and licensed movie-themed gifts and clothing. Great collection of James Bond, Pink Panther, and Rocky stuff. 4915 Clifton Hill Niagara Falls, Ont. ℂ **905/374-2663.**

CHOCOLATES & SWEETS

Hershey's World of Chocolate Store *Kids*   As you stroll along Falls Avenue at the foot of Clifton Hill, keep your eyes open for the gigantic silver-colored Hershey's Kiss that marks the location of this sweet treat emporium. If you have a sweet tooth, you'll be delighted with the free samples of Hershey products—milkshakes, fudge, truffles, Kisses, and more. The 7,000-sq.-ft (650.3-sq.-m). store's shelves are loaded with calories. Fudge-making demonstrations on-site. Parking is available in a parking garage immediately adjacent to the store. 5685 Falls Ave., Niagara Falls, Ont. ℂ **905/374-4444.**

Laura Secord   Named after a local heroine of the War of 1812, Laura Secord is Canada's largest and best-known chocolatier. If you are looking for chocolate-themed gifts, Laura Secord is a winner. Every major holiday in the calendar has a theme at Laura Secord. They stock gift-wrapped boxes of chocolates, and their gift baskets are second to none. Their French Crisp ice cream just has to be experienced. Niagara Square, 7555 Montrose Rd. (corner of McLeod Rd. and the QEW) in Niagara Falls, Ont. ℂ **905/357-1110.** www.niagarasquare.com; The Pen Centre, Hwy. 406 and Glendale Ave., St. Catharines, Ont. ℂ **800/582-8202** or 905/687-6622. www.thepencentre.com.

The Nutty Chocolatier   Fashioned after a Victorian candy store, this shop has antique candy bins and mahogany cases. Imported chocolate, candies, and fudge. 233 King St., Niagara-on-the-Lake, Ont. ℂ **905/468-0788.**

Reg's Candy Kitchen   Reg Wall has been making fudge at this location for more than 36 years. You can watch him at work in his candy kitchen. Delicious flavors include chocolate mint, butterscotch, maple walnut, and vanilla. The shop is just one block from the *Maid of the Mist* along River Road, right under the Rainbow Bridge. Rainbow Bridge Plaza, Niagara Falls, Ont. ℂ **905/356-4229.**

Swiss Fudge   High-quality chocolate and candy from around the world is featured in the scrumptious Swiss Fudge shop in the Galleria shopping complex inside Niagara Fallsview Casino Resort. Try a sample or buy a slab of their famous fudge—Swiss Fudge has been making fudge in Niagara Falls since 1966. The divinely delectable Godiva brand of fine chocolate products is stocked here. Whether your sweet tooth craves English, American, Italian, Canadian, or French candies, it will be satisfied here. Plenty of prettily packaged, sweet gifts on display. 6380 Fallsview Blvd., Niagara Falls, Ont. ℂ **905/356-5691.**

Toute Sweet Ice Cream & Chocolate   I always say you can never have too much ice cream, and if you are touring around the Twenty Valley, this cute little ice-cream parlor (with a natty outdoor patio for summer pleasure) in Jordan Village is just what you need. You can customize your ice cream by choosing fresh fruit, brownies, cookies, chocolate, or nuts, and they will blend it with their premium ice cream on a frozen granite stone while you wait. Chocoholics should stop by, too, for hand-molded Belgian chocolates. Icewine truffles on the premises. Yum. 3771 Nineteenth St., Jordan, Ont. ℃ 905/562-9666.

CHRISTMAS STORES

Just Christmas ℛ You might think a store that sells only Christmas decorations wouldn't do much trade outside of the Christmas season, but you'd be wrong. People don't just browse out of season here, they buy. And the store is like Doctor Who's Tardis (deceptively small outside, very large inside). Every Christmas decorating theme you could imagine is covered here, for you to discover as you make your way from room to room, following the crowds of shoppers.

34 Queen St., Niagara-on-the-Lake, Ont. ℃ 905/468-4500.

DEPARTMENT STORES

The Bay Established in the Canadian North more than 300 years ago as a fur-trading post known as The Hudson's Bay Company, The Bay carries standard department-store collections of fashions and housewares. Sales and promotions are frequent, and merchandise is good quality. The Bay occupies an anchor spot at two Niagara-region malls—the Pen Centre in St. Catharines, and Niagara Square in Niagara Falls, Ont. The Pen Centre, 221 Glendale Ave., St. Catharines, Ont. ℃ 905/688-4441; Niagara Square Mall, Niagara Falls, Ont. 7555 Montrose Rd. ℃ 905/357-5442.

Sears Offering a comprehensive range of consumer goods, Sears anchors the Pen Centre in St. Catharines and Seaway Mall in Welland. Like The Bay, sales and promotions are offered on an ongoing basis. The Pen Centre, 221 Glendale Ave., St. Catharines, Ont. ℃ 905/682-6481; Seaway Mall, 800 Niagara St., Welland, Ont. ℃ 905-732-6100.

FASHION, MEN'S & WOMEN'S

Roots Although Roots has been a well-known Canadian label for many years, their sponsorship of the Nagano Winter Olympic games several years ago catapulted their coats, sweaters, and caps into the world spotlight. Demand has grown for their clothing line since that time, particularly in the United States. This casual clothing, in infant to adult sizes, washes and wears well. Only selected stores carry kids' merchandise. Roots has expanded their product line to include fragrances, jewelry, leather goods, and shoes. In the Table Rock Complex, Queen Victoria Park, Niagara Falls, Ont. ℃ 877/642-7275. Also at Canada One Outlet Mall, 7500 Lundy's Lane, Niagara Falls, Ont. ℃ 905/371-2322.

FASHION, MEN'S

Phillip Artois Exclusively Italian-made, high-end menswear, specializing in smart casual clothing including shirts, slacks, sportswear, and sweaters. Leather shoes, accessories, better suits, dress shirts, and sports jackets round out the selection. Galleria, Niagara Fallsview Casino Resort, 6380 Fallsview Blvd., Niagara Falls, Ont. ℃ 905/356-7400.

FASHION, WOMEN'S

Angie Strauss Fashions Featuring the creations of fashion designer and local artist Angie Strauss, this boutique stocks clothing, hats, jewelry, and accessories. Styles are aimed at more mature women; plus sizes are available. Mix and match separates. Some items feature Strauss's watercolor paintings. Accessories and gifts include gift cards, desk clocks, tote bags, silk scarves, aprons, and paper tole kits. 129 Queen St., Niagara-on-the-Lake, Ont. ℃ 888/510-0939 or 905/468-2255. www.angiestrauss.com.

La Crème Décor Elegant, fashionable, chic. And all in shades of ivory, white, taupe, and caramel, with gold and silver accents. Within the store is an "Essentially BLACK" department, color themed in black, charcoal, and chocolate brown. Mostly designer and private-label fashions, plus jewelry, shoes, sandals, purses, hats, scarves, and shawls. Specializes in special-occasion formalwear that provides an alternative to the traditional look. Really sweet formalwear for little girls. 233 King St., Niagara-on-the-Lake, Ont. ℂ 866/868-0652 or 905/468-0652. www.lacremedecor.com.

Nantucket Casual and high-fashion clothing and home and garden accessories. Fashion advisor Jennifer Thrasher fills the store with imports from Europe and hand-crafted items from the south to create an eclectic assortment of merchandise. 3836 Main St., Jordan, Ont. ℂ 905/562-9281.

Tintern on Main This mecca for head-in-the-clouds fashionistas features the collections of designer and boutique owner Jacqueline Del Col, under the label of Tintern Road. Del Col's work utilizes higher-end fabrics and fine detailing, yet strives to combine style with practicality. A number of other fine designer labels, selected by Del Col, are also available and include Franco Mirabelli, Misura, Teenflo, and Virani. 3836 Main St., Jordan Village, Ont. ℂ 905/562-5547. www.tinternonmain.ca.

Windsand Ladies Clothing Ladieswear for casual living, with an emphasis on quality, comfort, and function. A boutique with clothing from small to extra-large. 26 Lakeport Rd., Port Dalhousie, St. Catharines, Ont. ℂ 905/646-3322.

GARDENING

The Copper Leaf Gardeners will happily browse here for ages, wandering among the statuary, garden tools, furniture, garden decor items, and a small selection of live plants. Gardeners are dreamers and visionaries, and they will find plenty of fuel for their creativity at The Copper Leaf. Founders of the business are two brothers who hold diplomas from the Niagara Parks Commission School of Horticulture. Two locations in the Niagara region to catch all the upscale green-thumb shoppers out there. 3845 Main St., Jordan, Ont. ℂ 905/562-0244; 10 Queen St., Niagara-on-the-Lake, Ont. ℂ 905/468-5323. www.thecopperleaf.com.

GIFT & SOUVENIR SHOPS

The Canada Store One of Jordan's most recent Main Street retailers, The Canada Store has plenty of souvenirs and Canadian-made crafts. 3636 Main St., Jordan, Ont. ℂ 905/562-9714.

Heritage Gift Shop Proceeds from sales at this shop support the Jordan Historical Museum of the Twenty, which is just 2 minutes down the road on the valley side of Main Street. The museum has several old restored buildings and artifacts, a cemetery where a number of pioneers are buried, and access to the Twenty Valley hiking trails. In the shop, which is fully staffed by volunteers, you will find an assortment of gift items and pieces for the home, many of them with a Victorian flavor. Choose from china, pottery, glassware, candles, linens, and decorative seasonal florals. At the back of the store there is a fudge counter with slices of freshly made sweet, creamy fudge. 3836 Main St., Jordan, Ont. ℂ 905/562-4849.

Illuminessence Specializing in handcrafted pure beeswax candles made by chandler Will Beaudoin, this shop stocks all kinds of candles, from simple tapers and tealights to angels and Easter Island statues. Local artists show their work—you'll find dreamcatchers, canvas, and watercolor paintings for sale. Indoor water fountains and crystals are also available. 4349 Queen St., Niagara Falls, Ont. ✆ **905/356-5756**. www.illuminessence.ca.

Mounted Police Trading Post　Royal Canadian Mounted Police collectibles and souvenirs abound in this small shop. Bears, figurines, hats, shirts, and much more. 5685 Falls Ave., Niagara Falls, Ont. ✆ **800/372-0472**. www.mountedpolicetradepost.com.

The RCMP Store　This is one of four specialty boutiques within the Table Rock Complex located on the Niagara Parkway, near the lip of the Horseshoe Falls. Merchandise is themed around the Royal Canadian Mounted Police. Shops of Table Rock, Queen Victoria Park, Niagara Falls, Ont. ✆ **877/642-7275**.

The Silly Old Bear Shop　This adorable shop is dedicated entirely to Winnie-the-Pooh gift items. Music boxes, bookends, dinnerware, sun catchers, stuffed animals, and more. Tiny but lots of fun. 80 Queen St., Niagara-on-the-Lake, Ont. ✆ **905/468-5411**.

Souvenir City Headquarters　This is a volume tourist souvenir stop. Groups and buses welcome; browse 15,000 square feet of stuff to cart home to remind you of your trip to Niagara Falls. There is a First Nations crafts section with totem poles, hand-carved buffalo horns, raccoon hats, and Native dolls. The Chocolate Factory serves up fast food and, of course, chocolate. 4199 River Rd., Niagara Falls, Ont. ✆ **905/357-1133**.

Swarovski　World-famous fine Austrian lead crystal. This shop is an absolute delight to browse in. The displays are skillfully illuminated to reflect and refract the light. Galleria, Niagara Fallsview Casino Resort, Niagara Falls, Ont. ✆ **905/354-0118**. www.swarovski.com.

Tickle Your Fancy　For Canadian-made sweets, gifts, cards, jewelry, and original art, head for this store. Their specialties include gourmet chocolate, fudge, and yummy maple-flavored indulgences. 106 Queen St., Niagara-on-the-Lake, Ont. ✆ **905/468-9939**.

The Viking Shop　If you're an avid collector of ornaments, head here. The Viking Shop carries Hummel, Royal Doulton, Precious Moments, Lilliput Lane, Peter Rabbit, Willow Tree Angels, Wedgwood, Waterford Crystal, Boyd's Bear, Cherished Teddies—the list goes on. 76 Queen St., Niagara-on-the-Lake, Ont. ✆ **905/468-2264**.

HATS

Beau Chapeau Hat Shop 🕊　They declare that there is no such thing as a bad hair day, just a good hat day. There are literally thousands of hats in the store. Say fedora, homburg, bowler, or safari. They're all here. And that sexy number Harrison Ford sports in those Indiana Jones movies—yep, officially licensed Indiana Jones wool felt and genuine fur hats are available. Women's hats range from inexpensive knitted beanies to handmade cloches, with berets, upturns, buckets, and wide brims filling out the selection. Check out their website for hat etiquette, hat care, and hat tips. 126 Queen St., Niagara-on-the-Lake, Ont. ✆ **905/468-8011**. www.beauchapeau.com.

HOME DECOR

Acquisitions　For those who love to decorate their homes, room by room, with dedication to detail, look no further than Acquisitions, a retail store that also offers a professional interior design service. Fabrics, wallcoverings, decorative accents, custom furnishings, lighting, mirrors, and artwork can all be found here. 3836 Main St., Jordan, Ont. ✆ **905/562-1220**.

L'Esprit Provence/Tableclothsetc.com　This store originally exclusively sold products imported from the South of France. They recently re-launched the business as Tableclothsetc.com to focus on tablecloths, napkins, and coordinating products for dressing the dining table. The product line has been expanded to include products from Italy, Spain, and South Africa. Fabric by the yard is available for most of the patterns they carry. They will send fabric swatches by post, and they do custom orders if required. If you can't get to Europe, stop in here. Besides a wide range of tablecloths, placemats, runners, and so on, they carry lamps, wireware, bath products (including the marvelous Marseille soaps), books and magazines, music, and kitchen knives. 106C Queen St., Niagara-on-the-Lake, Ont. (℃ **905/468-1817**. www.tableclothsetc.com.

Santa Fe Trading Co.   Home decor items and furniture abound here, but you will also find casual clothing, hand-blown glass, and jewelry. The theme is American Southwest, and there is a mix of authentic and reproduction pieces. K. John Mason, a third-generation blacksmith and sculptor (whose ironworks studio is close by and may be toured by prior appointment) exhibits his work here. Custom ironwork is also available. Niagara area craftsmen display their custom pine cabinetry. 3836 Main St., Jordan, Ont. (℃ **905/562-3078**.

KITCHENWARE
Dansk   The distinctive bright colors and simple lines of Dansk tableware and linens are displayed with flair in this lovely shop. Drinkware, cookware, gifts, home accessories, dinnerware—it's all here for the cook and those who love to entertain at home. 91 Queen St., Niagara-on-the-Lake, Ont. (℃ **905/468-2614**.

Oneida Home Store   This outlet store features Oneida-brand holloware, stainless-steel flatware, and silverplate flatware. Savings can be substantial, but some merchandise is imperfect and some patterns are ones that have been discontinued. 8699 Stanley Ave. S., Niagara Falls, Ont. (℃ **905/356-9691**. www.oneida.com/home/ONDAforyourhome.asp.

LEATHER
The Leather Bazaar & Accessories   If you're in Port Dalhousie, drop in to the Leather Bazaar on Lakeport Road for leather goods of all kinds, from belts, pouches, and gloves to handbags, shoes, and clothing. 50 Lakeport Rd., Port Dalhousie, St. Catharines, Ont. (℃ 905/930-5010.

PERFUME
The Perfume Factory   If you plan to cross the border as part of your trip, you can purchase perfume products at duty-free shops. Or you can head to the Perfume Factory on York Road near the Niagara-on-the-Lake exit of the QEW. Brand-name fragrances (more than 1,000 to choose from) are offered at discounted prices, with the store claiming most prices to be lower than duty-free. Tax rebate forms are available at the store for nonresidents. Sterling silver jewelry and men's and women's watches are also available. 393 York Rd., Niagara-on-the-Lake, Ont. (close to the Niagara-on-the-Lake exit from the QEW, not in the town). (℃ **800/463-0012** or 905/685-6666. www.perfumefactory.ca.

PETS
Sirius the Dog Store   If a dear little pooch or kitty is the center of your universe, you will coo over the dozens of gifts you can buy to pamper your pet. Everything you could imagine for darling dogs and cool cats. Food, dishes, bedding, accessories, toys, and (gulp) clothes. 3775-B 19th St. ("The Shops on 19th"), Jordan Village, Ont. (℃ **905/562-0863**. www.siriusthedogstore.com.

SHOES

Arezzo Shoes   Boutique styles in footwear, plus accessories and lingerie. Exclusively for women, this is a "girls' day out" kind of shop, where you can ooh and ahh together to your heart's delight. 3836 Main St., Jordan, Ont. ℂ 905/682-9419.

Newark Shoes   This upscale casual shoe store features shoes by Clarks, Birkenstock, Josef Seibel, and more. Leather handbags, gloves, wallets, and other accessories also available. 122 Queen St., Niagara-on-the-Lake, Ont. ℂ 905/468-7637.

SPORTS EQUIPMENT & CLOTHING

Regatta Sport   Whether you're a recreational athlete or national champion, you will find this specialist clothing and equipment store quite fascinating. Training and racing gear for rowers, dragonboaters, cyclists, runners, and athletes. 50 Lakeport Rd., Port Dalhousie, St. Catharines, Ont. ℂ 905/937-7858. www.regattasport.com.

Rub-of-the-Green Golf Shoppe   Dedicated to serve those who love the game of golf, this store specializes not only in golf apparel and accessories, but also in golf art, collectibles, and memorabilia. And if there is something you hanker after but can't find in the store, the owners may be able to source it for you. Authentic framed photos, game balls, flags, club heads, and more. And if you're looking for some insider advice on where to golf in Niagara, the owners can dispense that, too. 106 Queen St., Niagara-on-the-Lake, Ont. ℂ 905/468-8584.

TOYS

Kids Explor-it. *Kids*   Inside the Table Rock Complex located on the Niagara Parkway, near the lip of the Horseshoe Falls there is a shop just for children, designed to be an interactive store and play center. Shops at Table Rock, Queen Victoria Park, Niagara Falls, Ont. ℂ 877/642-7275.

Turtle Pond Toys *Kids*   Play areas are set up around the store to encourage kids to try out the merchandise. Higher-quality toys, games, and puzzles for children of all ages. Galleria at Niagara Fallsview Casino Resort, 6380 Fallsview Blvd., Niagara Falls, Ont. ℂ 905/357-7710.

WINE & SPIRITS

Most of Ontario's wine, some beer, and all spirits are purchased through the provincial government-owned **Liquor Control Board of Ontario** retail stores. There are locations throughout the Niagara region. Look for the vintages section for the best selection of wines from around the world. Individual winery boutiques are also licensed to sell wine, but you can't buy alcoholic beverages in a grocery or convenience store in Ontario. Beer is also available at The Beer Store, a provincially owned and operated business with plenty of locations in the region.

10

Niagara Region After Dark

When night falls in Niagara Falls, by far the best entertainment is the spectacular view of the illuminated cascading waters of the American and Horseshoe Falls. The light show happens nightly all year around. Beginning at dusk and ending at midnight, an ever-changing rainbow of color floods the Falls. During the main tourist season, the lights are accompanied by a brilliant fireworks display on Friday and Saturday evenings.

There are other forms of entertainment for those who like to venture out after dark, although for the most part it's a bit of a sedate area after nightfall. Niagara-on-the-Lake offers world-class theater with the Shaw Festival, internationally renowned for its productions of plays by George Bernard Shaw and his contemporaries—from Oscar Wilde and Noel Coward to Chekhov, Ibsen, and Brecht. You'll find stylish places in Niagara-on-the-Lake's compact town center where you can relax with a glass of wine or a cocktail before or after the show.

If you're looking for live music or somewhere to dance the night away, the listings in this chapter will give you a taste of Niagara's nightlife, which is primarily clustered around the Falls—on Victoria Avenue, Fallsview Avenue, Clifton Hill, and Lundy's Lane.

Tip: Keep an eye out for *Niagara Hot Spots,* the free entertainment guide to what's happening around Niagara, or visit www.niagarahotspots.ca.

1 The Performing Arts

Since the lion's share of visitors to Niagara Falls come in the warmer months, the region has a thriving summer theater presence. The biggest draw for theatergoers is the fabulous **Shaw Festival.** Throughout the year, concerts, plays, and dance recitals are held in the **Centre for the Arts at Brock University** (500 Glenridge Ave., St. Catharines, Ont.; © **905/688-5550**). Other events in the performing arts arena take place as part of various festivals held in Niagara's many towns and villages (see "Calendar of Events," chapter 2).

THEATER

Shaw Festival 🎭🎭🎭   The **Shaw Festival** is unique, exclusively producing plays by **George Bernard Shaw** and his contemporaries and plays about the period of Shaw's lifetime (1856–1950). Shaw's long life provides the festival with a nearly bottomless source of material to present each year, and their eclectic offerings range from intimate dramas to rollicking musicals. During the 2005 season, the Festival presented 10 full productions on its three stages, including Shaw's *You Never Can Tell* and *Major Barbara,* Somerset Maugham's *The Constant Wife,* and the Weill and Brecht musical *Happy End.*

The Festival, whose season runs from April to November, has three venues in Niagara-on-the-Lake. The largest is the flagship **Festival Theatre,** which features a cafe and shop. The **Court House Theatre,** where the Festival began in 1962, is located on the site of Upper Canada's first Parliament. The **Royal George Theatre,** at 85 Queen St., was originally built as a vaudeville house in 1915 for the purpose of entertaining troops stationed on the Commons in the town during World War I.

To enrich your Shaw experience, plan to attend one of the many theatrical events that take place throughout the season. **Backstage tours** are held Saturday mornings from June to October. Between May and August, informal **pre-show chats** give an introduction to the evening's play prior to most performances. On most Tuesday evenings post-performance, the audience is invited to remain in the theater for an informal **Q&A session.** The public can **engage in discussions with members of the theater company** on selected Saturdays during July and August prior to the matinee performance. **Free concerts** are held on selected Sundays throughout the season in the lobby of the Festival Theatre at 11am. The festival also offers staged readings and workshops throughout the season; check their website for more information.

The Shaw announces its festival program in mid-January. Tickets are difficult to obtain on short notice, so book in advance. Contact the box office at the Festival Theatre for tickets for all three venues. 10 Queen's Parade, P.O. Box 774, Niagara-on-the-Lake, Ont. L0S 1J0. ℭ **800/511-SHAW (511-7429)** or 905/468-2172. www.shawfest.com.

REPERTORY & DINNER THEATER

Firehall Theatre   The Niagara Falls Music Theatre Society is a community theater performing a selection of musicals, drama, and comedies. They stage a three-play season through the fall and winter months. 4990 Walnut St., Niagara Falls, Ont. ℭ **905/356-4953.**

Greg Frewin Theatre   This 700-seat dinner theater presents a Las Vegas–style magic show, complete with large cats, showgirls, and astounding illusions by Greg Frewin, the award-winning International Grand Champion of Magic. Show starts at 8pm all year around; optional pre-show dinner is served at 6:30pm. Suitable for the whole family. 5781 Ellen Ave., Niagara Falls, Ont. ℭ **866/779-8778** or 905/356-0777. www.gregfrewintheatre.com.

Gypsy Theatre, Fort Erie   Primarily a summer theater company, the Gypsy Theatre has a permanent professional acting company that is increasingly gaining recognition throughout the Niagara region and upper New York State. Offerings include musicals, drama, monologues, mysteries, and more. 465 Central Ave., Fort Erie. ℭ **877/990-7529** or 905/871-4407. www.gypsytheatre.com.

Niagara Grand Dinner Theatre   Located in the picturesque Queenston Heights Restaurant, with views of the Niagara River, the Niagara Grand offers lunch and dinner shows. Meals are served at the table and include soup of the day, a choice of three entrees (recent dishes included salmon filet with lemon-grass cream and roast prime rib of beef), dessert, and coffee or tea. Plays are selected for their suitability for all ages; recent shows included the homespun humor of *Weekend Comedy* and a rollicking Christmas season play, *Wrong Chimney.* Season runs from March to December. Queenston Heights Restaurant, Queenston Heights Park, 14184 Niagara Pkwy., Niagara Falls, Ont. ℭ **866/845-7469** or 905/357-7818.

Oh Canada Eh! Dinner Show   An evening of Canadian comfort food and squeaky clean musical entertainment awaits. During the main tourist season, the Oh Canada Eh! Show plays daily. Dinner is served at 6:30pm and the shows ends at 9pm. Matinees are scheduled on some days beginning at 3pm. In the late fall and winter, a variety of

Moments The Falls by Night

The spectacle of the **Falls illuminations** must not be missed. It is a truly breath-taking sight best that's viewed from above, so take a trip up the **Konica Minolta Tower** or **Skylon Tower**. If you're lucky enough to have a **fallsview hotel room**, crack open a bottle of bubbly and watch the ever-changing pattern of rainbow colors from the comfort of your home away from home.

Twenty-one xenon lights illuminate the Falls, each with a 76-centimeter diameter (30 in.). Eighteen lights are located at the Illumination Tower beside Queen Victoria Place, and three are located below street level in the Niagara Gorge opposite the American Falls.

The show starts between 5pm and 6:30pm in winter, between 7pm and 8:30pm in spring and fall, and at 9pm in summer, and runs until at least 10pm from January through April and until midnight the rest of the year. All times are approximate and subject to change according to light conditions, so feel free to call ahead if you're on a tight schedule but don't want to miss the show—and you *don't* want to miss it, believe me (© **800/563-2557** or 905/356-6061).

The Falls were first illuminated in 1860 in celebration of a visit by the Prince of Wales, using calcium, volcanic, and torpedo lights and an assortment of fireworks. Electric-powered lights were first used in 1879, and the lights have operated almost continuously since 1925—when the Niagara Falls Illumination Board, a joint venture between Canada and the U.S., was established to finance and operate the light show.

In addition, enjoy a **free fireworks display** over the Falls **every Friday and Sunday evening at 10pm from late May to early September** (weather permitting). During the major Canadian and U.S. holiday weekends, they kick it up a notch.

dinner shows are scheduled. Family entertainment. Since the show debuted in 1994, it has been voted "Attraction of the Year" six times and has played to almost half a million guests. Meet Mounties, hockey players, lumberjacks, Anne of Green Gables, and more. 8585 Lundy's Lane, Niagara Falls, Ont. © 800/467-2071 or 905/374-1995.

Port Mansion Dinner Theatre, Port Dalhousie   Separate dining and theater facilities are offered here. Fine dining is available at **Tremolo** in one of two dining rooms overlooking Port Dalhousie harbor. The adjacent 85-seat cabaret-style **Theatre in Port** theater provides an intimate theater experience all year around, performing musicals, comedies, and dramas. Lively nightlife hops nonstop at **PM.** In the summer, PM stages theme nights including Friday after-work martini parties, Bandstand Mondays, and DJs from local radio station Wild 101 spinning tunes on Wednesdays. 12 Lakeport Rd., Port Dalhousie, Ont. © 866/452-7678 or 905/934-0575; www.portmansion.com.

Showboat Festival Theatre, Port Colborne   A variety of comedy, drama, mystery, and musical performances are produced during the spring and summer season by the Showboat Festival Theatre. The intimate 220-seat theater-in-the-round is located in the historical setting of the Roselawn Centre for the Living Arts, a facility that incorporates Roselawn, a stone-and-brick 1860 Victorian building. 296 Fielden Ave., Port Colborne, Ont. ✆ 888/870-8181 or 905/834-0833.

Twenty Valley Playhouse   This community theater in the heart of Vineland village offers a variety of plays, ranging from musicals to comedies, murder mysteries, and thrillers. Packages are available that include local restaurants and accommodations. 3994 Victoria Ave., Vineland, Ont. ✆ 905/562-9719. www.twentyvalleyplayhouse.com.

MUSIC

Although the Niagara region offers great live theater, its options for a night of music are a little more limited. Pop performers with a decidedly retro bent often perform for baby boomers at the **Avalon Ballroom** in the Niagara Fallsview Casino Resort (6380 Fallsview Blvd., Niagara Falls, Ont.; ✆ **888/836-8118**). More diverse fare from folk to rock to classical can be found during July and August at the 500-seat open-air **amphitheater at Jackson-Triggs Winery** (2145 Niagara Stone Rd., Niagara-on-the-Lake, Ont.; ✆ **866/589-4637**). For lovers of symphonic and choral music, **Chorus Niagara** and the **Niagara Symphony** perform at the Centre for the Arts, Brock University (500 Glenridge Ave., St. Catharines, Ont.; ✆ **905/688-5550**). Chorus Niagara's repertoire includes a diverse range of choral programs, from full orchestra accompaniment to a cappella, and from ancient music to premiere performances. The Niagara Symphony Orchestra plays both classical and pop concerts.

2 The Club, Live Music & Bar Scene

Downtown Niagara Falls, Ontario, pulses with noise and crowds, particularly along Falls Avenue and Clifton Hill. Niagara-on-the-Lake is much quieter, offering cozy and elegant hotel bars and a pub or two. St. Catharines caters to the student crowd. Outside of these places, the region is rather sedate.

Dance clubs, bars, and live entertainment venues are by nature constantly evolving, as they try to keep up with or keep ahead of their patrons' latest passions in terms of music and drinks. By the time you visit some of the venues listed here they may have changed the type of music they offer, the decor, the beer, or even their name. Amble on out for the evening and take a gamble—you never know what you might stumble upon.

COMEDY CLUBS

House of Comedy   Stand-up comedians entertain adults of all ages in the House of Comedy's resident venue at the Americana Conference Resort and Spa. Entertainers from both sides of the border will make you chuckle. Stand-up comics and impressionists deliver fast-paced jokes with high energy and plenty of style. Shows are Friday and Saturday nights. Dinner and show packages available. Bar snacks served during the show. Occasional open-mic nights. At the Americana Conference Resort and Spa, 8444 Lundy's Lane, Niagara Falls, Ont. ✆ 905/357-7469 for show tickets.

DANCE CLUBS & LOUNGES

365 Club   Located just steps away from the action on the vast gaming floor of the Niagara Fallsview Casino Resort, this intimate lounge and bar has no cover charge. Sip cocktails while being entertained by a variety of cabarets, lounge singers, and other live stage acts, ranging from Jam Night to Comedy Night. The action usually starts around

Shooting the Falls

If you're a film buff, check out *Niagara (1953)* and *Superman II (1980)*. *Niagara,* starring Marilyn Monroe, is a movie in the "film noir" genre, advertised in its day with the slogan *"Niagara and Marilyn Monroe: The two most electrifying sights in the world!".* The film reveals the Falls in its mid-20th-century glory, before much of the commercial building got underway. *Superman II,* starring Christopher Reeve and Margot Kidder, gives moviegoers a peek into hokey honeymoon heaven, complete with a heart-shaped bathtub and vibrating bed. And, naturally, a couple of dramatic Superman rescue scenes—first, a young boy who falls into the water, closely followed by a foolhardy Lois Lane who flings herself into the rapids in what turns out to be an unsuccessful attempt to prove that Clark Kent is Superman.

7:30pm and runs until just after 1:30am. Inside the Niagara Fallsview Casino Resort, 6380 Fallsview Blvd., Niagara Falls, Ont. ✆ 888/FALLSVUE (325-57883).

Club Rialto   One of the few places catering to the over-30 crowd, with music that's a little less hip-hop and a little more Billy Joel. DJs and karaoke rule. You'll find it tucked away at the back of the Casa d'Oro Restaurant. 5875 Victoria Ave., in Casa d'Oro Restaurant, Niagara Falls, Ont. ✆ 905/356-5646.

Hard Rock Club   Can't decide what you want to do tonight? The Hard Rock Club has a dance floor with doors that open to the street, so you can see the Falls while you boogie. Not in the mood for dancing? Relax in the retro lounge, accented with red plush velvet, or check out the martini bar. The outdoor patio is popular in the summer—sip a drink while you take in the view. Check out the huge electronic disco ball. Local trendy 20- and 30-somethings like to hang here. 5701 Falls Ave., Niagara Falls, Ont. ✆ 905/356-7625.

Pumps Nite Club & Patio   Aimed squarely at the younger (read: much younger) age, this club plays top 40 dance music. Featuring a large outdoor patio and karaoke. Prices in U.S. and Canadian dollars. 5815 Victoria Ave., Niagara Falls, Ont. ✆ 905/371-8646.

Rumours Night Club   If you've got the energy to dance, dance, dance, then head to Rumours, smack in the middle of the carnival atmosphere of the "Street of Fun" at the top of Clifton Hill. This perennially popular club regularly sees lines out the door. Huge video screens, blasting sound, and laser show. Music ranges from retro '80s and '90s to top-40 tunes, with an all-request mix on Sunday nights. Dress to impress. Cover charge is five bucks, in either Canadian or U.S. currency. 4960 Clifton Hill, Niagara Falls, Ont. ✆ 905/358-6152.

Splash Bar   On the gaming floor of the Niagara Fallsview Casino Resort, this bar features live music every night of the week from around 6:30pm to 2am on a stage situated directly behind the bar. Inside the Niagara Fallsview Casino Resort, 6380 Fallsview Blvd., Niagara Falls, Ont. ✆ 888/FALLSVUE (325-57883).

ECLECTIC

After Hours   This restaurant and lounge is frequented by an easygoing 30-plus crowd, dropping in for appetizers, dinner, or Niagara wines and willing to take in whatever music is on offer. Entertainers include vocalists, quartets, and bands, singing and playing everything from Celtic tunes, acoustic guitar, and rock to jazz and blues. 5460 Victoria Ave., Niagara Falls, Ont. ℂ **905/357-2503.**

The Moose & Goose   Student hangout with some great live bands. Past performers include Billy Talent, Finger 11, Kim Mitchell, The Tea Party, and The Trews. 54 Front St., Thorold, Ont. ℂ **905/227-6969.**

JAZZ & BLUES

Bumpin Uglies   With a name like that, how could a place be anything but great? "Matinees" held on Saturdays and Sundays midafternoon to early evening. House band and guests. Call ahead for schedule. 249 Paul St., St. Catharines, Ont. ℂ **905/988-3900.**

Café Etc.   With a curvy polished-wood bar whose architectural lines are echoed in the ceiling recess, this cafe-cum-jazz-bar swings with live music on Friday and Saturday nights. 462 Third St., Niagara Falls, NY. ℂ **716/285-0801.**

3 Film

IMAX

Imax Theatre   IMAX technology is a Canadian invention. The screen is more than six stories high, which is almost overwhelming in terms of visual stimulation. Add 12,000 watts of digital surround sound, and you've got the whole picture. The film *Niagara: Miracles, Myths, and Magic* has been the star of the theater for many, many years and has become a little dated, but it nevertheless gives tourists who are unfamiliar with the Falls and all its history a broad appreciation of the seventh forgotten wonder of the natural world. The re-creation of such spectacles as the Great Blondin's tightrope antics over the gorge, Annie Taylor's foolhardy yet brave plunge over the Falls in a barrel, and the daring folks who have shot the rapids makes for interesting viewing.

There is an impressive collection of original daredevil barrels and other historical artifacts in the **Niagara Falls Daredevil Gallery,** which is free whether you have movie tickets or not. The containers are open for viewing and visitors are invited to touch, unlike most museums. Also on-site is a **National Geographic** gift shop. 6170 Fallsview Blvd., Niagara Falls, Ont. ℂ **905/374-IMAX (374-4629).**

REPERTORY CINEMA

If you're a fan of independent, foreign, and second-run films, check out events at **Brock University,** 500 Glenridge Ave., St. Catharines, Ont.; ℂ **905/688-5550.** Brock University Film Society screens films on Sunday evenings in the David S. Howes Theatre

 Tips   Save on IMAX Tickets

Discounts on IMAX tickets are plentiful—if you know where to look. Most hotels offer discounted tickets—just ask at the reception desk. You can also purchase tickets online at a lower price than the box office. Another way to save (if you are planning a trip up the nearby Skylon Tower) is to buy a Sky-Max combo ticket.

on campus. Visit www.brocku.ca/cpcf/bufs/BUFSmain.html for schedules, pricing, and parking details.

The **Niagara Indie Filmfest** is held annually in June in the David S. Howes Theatre. The festival showcases Canadian short film and video works. For more details visit www.niagaraindiefilmfest.org or call the Festival Hotline ((𝒞) **905/688-5550**, ext. 3998).

4 Gaming

Casino Niagara   Niagara's original casino, this casino features more than 2,400 slot and video poker machines on two gaming levels. Table games include blackjack, roulette, craps, Sic-Bo, Pai-Gow, baccarat, mini-baccarat, three-card poker, and Let it Ride. Lower-limit tables and an exclusive high-limit gaming area on-site. Beginners can play the slots with ease; there are plenty of machines to go around even on a busy night. The atmosphere tends to be less smoky and boozy than U.S. casinos. Getaway packages in conjunction with local hotels are available—call 𝒞 **888/918-2888** for details. A choice of valet parking or Park'n'Ride shuttle service from a nearby parking lot. Dining choices include the Grand Café overlooking the gaming area and popular chains Planet Hollywood and the Hard Rock Cafe. The Casino is open 24 hours a day, every day of the year. 5705 Falls Ave., Niagara Falls, Ont. 𝒞 **888/WIN-FALL (946-3255)**.

Fort Erie Racetrack & Slots   The Fort Erie Racetrack, more than 100 years old, features live thoroughbred racing in a season that stretches from late April to early November. In addition, simulcast racing is on offer. The Racetrack hosts one of the Canadian horse-racing season's most prestigious events, the Prince of Wales Crown, which is the second leg of Canada's Triple Crown. Those who like to gamble on the slots will find 1,200 slot machines to keep them occupied. Dining ranges from all-you-can-eat buffets to roadhouse-style menus. Bertie St., Fort Erie, Ont. 𝒞 **800/295-3770**. www.forterieracin.com.

Niagara Fallsview Casino Resort   The luxurious Niagara Fallsview Casino Resort, opened in 2004, features a 200,000-square foot (18,580-sq.-m)casino that operates 24 hours a day, every day of the year. There are 150 gaming tables and more than 3,000 slot machines in the vast gaming area. If you want to take a break from the gambling, you can take in a show at the Avalon Ballroom or watch some live entertainment while having a drink at the 365 Club. There is a 368–guest room **hotel,** a full-service hotel **spa,** and a luxury **shopping galleria.** A unique hydroelectric water sculpture dominates the main entrance to the resort. In front of the complex, a series of waterfalls provides an ever-changing display, complete with colored lighting after

 Tips Gambling Should Be Fun, Not Obsessive

Many people enjoy playing games of chance for entertainment. But for a minority of people, gambling becomes a real problem and they find themselves unable to control the amount of money they spend. Information on dealing with a gambling problem can be obtained by calling the Ontario Problem Gambling Helpline at 𝒞 **888/230-3505**

dark. A total of 10 dining options ensure there is an offering to suit every pocketbook and palate. 6380 Fallsview Blvd., Niagara Falls, Ont. © **888/FALLSVUE**. www.fallsviewcasinoresort.com.

Seneca Niagara Casino & Hotel   There are 3,200 reel-spinning and video slot machines at this Niagara Falls casino in the United States. Almost 100 gaming tables are on-site, including blackjack, craps, roulette, and more. A separate poker room is available for play. Parking is free, as are all beverages. Patrons must be 21 years of age or over and must have photo ID available. Hungry gamblers can choose steak, buffet, or sports pub–style food. 310 Fourth St., Niagara Falls, NY © **877/873-6322** or 716/299-1100. www.senecaniagaracasino.com.

Appendix A:
The Niagara Region in Depth

The Niagara region's rich history spans an extensive period of several thousand years, although its modern-day existence as one of the world's best-known tourist destinations began less than 2 centuries ago. The fascinating story of this landscape of remarkable beauty, encompassing Niagara Falls, the Niagara River and Gorge, the environmentally significant Niagara Escarpment, and the burgeoning wine country, has been condensed in the next few pages.

1 History 101

FROM HUNTING GROUND TO BATTLEFIELD

The history of the Niagara Region stretches back 10,000 years, to the time when the glaciers of the last ice age retreated north. Vast herds of game roamed the boreal forests surrounding Lake Ontario and its environs, bringing tribes of hunters to the area. For several millennia, the first peoples of Niagara survived as hunters, fishers, gatherers, and eventually agriculturalists.

The first Europeans arrived in the mid-1600s, driven by the desire to expand the fur trade and led by French explorers and missionaries. Although several white men visited the Falls prior to Father Louis Hennepin, he was the first to record a description of the mighty wonder of nature following his visit in 1678. His account of the Falls was a dramatic exaggeration, leading to the production of a hand-tinted engraving that depicted the Falls much higher and narrower than in reality, with mountains rising in the distance. This misrepresentation became the standard pictorial representation for many decades to follow.

For the next hundred years or so, the Niagara area remained populated by various Native groups, although their numbers were increasingly depleted by European-borne diseases and clashes with warring tribes.

Dateline

- **1678** Father Louis Hennepin is the first person to record a description of The Falls.
- **1721** A trading post is established by the French at Lewiston to protect the fur trade.
- **1726** The French build a sturdy stone fort on the east bank of the Niagara River at the point where it flows into Lake Ontario, called Fort Niagara.
- **1759** Fort Niagara is attacked by the British. Nineteen days later, the French surrender and withdraw from the Niagara Peninsula.
- **1764** Fort Erie is constructed by the British.
- **1792** John Graves Simcoe is appointed Governor of Upper Canada and the town of Newark (now known as Niagara-on-the-Lake) is established as the capital.
- **1793** The first Parliament of Upper Canada passes a bill that prevents further slavery in Upper Canada.
- **1812** The War of 1812 commences when the fledgling country America declares war on Britain, sending U.S. forces north into Canada. Because of its proximity to the border, Niagara becomes the focus of a major offensive.
- **1813** The first wave of freedom-seeking black slaves

French and British troops fought for control of the continent during the first half of the 18th century. During this period, Fort Niagara was built by the French on the east bank of the Niagara River at the point where it flows into Lake Ontario. At the end of the Seven Years War in 1763, all of New France was ceded to Great Britain, and the British established control of the Niagara River. Fort Erie was built in 1764 on the west side of the mouth of the Niagara River and Lake Erie.

The next wave of newcomers to the district were the United Empire Loyalists, who fled to Upper Canada seeking sanctuary from the fierce fighting of the American Revolution of 1775 to 1783. When the war ended, remaining Loyalists were expelled from American territory and many of them settled along the western shore of the Niagara River.

At the end of the American Revolution, Fort Niagara, on the eastern side of the Niagara River, was in the hands of the United States. To protect their interests in Upper Canada, the British constructed a fort on the opposite side of the river. In 1802, Fort George was completed and became the headquarters for the British army, local militia, and the Indian Department.

The War of 1812 was the last military confrontation between Canada and the U.S. Eager to expand the nation, the United States declared war on Britain in June 1812. By attacking on four fronts, one of which was Niagara, the Americans hoped to achieve a swift victory. Several bloody battles ensued over the next 2 years, but the eventual outcome was a stalemate. The Treaty of Ghent, signed on Christmas Eve 1814, brought the hostilities to a close and the Niagara River was re-established as the border between Upper Canada and the U.S. Throughout the region, historic forts, monuments, and memorials stand as reminders of the war.

Upper Canada became the first place in the British Empire to abolish slavery, when Governor General John Graves Simcoe introduced legislation in 1793. In the years that followed, the country became a haven for black men and women escaping from slavery in the American South. To enable the freedom seekers to reach safety, supporters of the abolition of slavery throughout America and Canada provided secret "safe houses" where escaping slaves were given food, shelter, and directions north. The routes that passed by the safe houses became known as the Underground Railroad. Niagara was one of the main termini for the freedom seekers. Fugitive men, women, and children were transported

arrives in the region via the Underground Railroad.

- **1814** The War of 1812 comes to an end upon the signing of the Treaty of Ghent. The Niagara River is re-established as the border between Upper Canada and the United States.
- **1820** The Falls becomes a sightseeing attraction, visited by the burgeoning tourist class.
- **1827** The establishment of a strip of hotels between

Robinson Street and Table Rock marks the beginning of uncontrolled commercial development.

- **1829** The first Welland Canal is completed, opening a shipping lane between Lake Ontario and Lake Erie.
- **1845** The second Welland Canal opens.
- **1846** The first *Maid of the Mist*, a steamboat carrying passengers daringly close to

the American and Horseshoe Falls, is launched.

- **1848** As unbelievable as it sounds, the Niagara River ceases its flow and The Falls stop for 30 long, silent hours when millions of tons of ice at the source of the river block the channel.
- **1855** With the completion of the first railway suspension bridge across the gorge, and arrival of the steam train in the town of Clifton, Niagara

across the Niagara River at Fort Erie. Niagara Falls, Niagara-on-the-Lake, and St. Catharines became important settlement areas for refugee slaves. From the early to the mid-1800s, thousands of fugitive slaves made their way into Canada through Fort Erie.

THE BIRTH OF TOURISM AT THE FALLS

Tourists first began to visit the Falls in the 1820s. Official guides were available to take sightseers on a tour of the major points of interest in the area. By the time the first *Maid of the Mist* steamboat was launched on the American side of the Falls in 1846, with its accompanying water-powered Inclined Railway to take passengers down the face of the gorge to the boat dock, the Falls were welcoming 50,000 summer visitors a year. A mere decade later, following the completion of the world's first railway suspension bridge, which included a plank roadway for foot passengers and horse-drawn carriages on its underside, Niagara Falls became the best-known tourist destination in North America.

One of the main attractions in those early days of tourism was Table Rock, a large platform of dolostone at the edge of the Horseshoe Falls. Although the overhang dramatically collapsed in 1850, the landmass remains the most beloved vantage point on the Canadian side. Just over a century later, most of Prospect Point, the prime location to view the Falls on the American side, collapsed and 185,000 tons of rock crashed into the gorge below.

As the crowds grew, a rowdy strip of concession stands, hotels, and carnival booths sprung up, all eager to grab a piece of the tourist dollar. Despite the popularity of these attractions, many members of the public were concerned at the desecration of such a wonder of nature. Accordingly, in 1878, Lord Dufferin, then Governor General of Canada, proposed that a strategy be developed to preserve the natural beauty of Niagara Falls. Seven years later, the Niagara Parks Commission was founded. Its mandate was to preserve and enhance the natural beauty of the Falls and the Niagara River corridor. On the U.S. side of the border, the New York State Reservation at Niagara Falls was established in the same year. But the kitsch could not be suppressed, and to this day Niagara audaciously exhibits both extremes of the tourist experience—the majesty and grandeur of the Falls, surrounded by beautifully groomed parks and pristine gardens, and the noise and clutter of the Clifton Hill district and Lundy's Lane, with its neon lights, fast food, carnival atmosphere, and motel strip.

Falls becomes the best-known tourist destination in North America.

- **1859** Frenchman Jean Francois Gravelet, known as "The Great Blondin," is the first of many tightrope walkers to cross the gorge of the Niagara River.
- **1860** Funambulist Bill Hunt, from Port Hope, Ontario, billed as "Signor Farini," challenges Blondin's position as the champion of Niagara.
- **1878** The area beside the Horseshoe Falls becomes such a magnet for undesirables that Lord Dufferin proposes a strategy to preserve the natural beauty of the district.
- **1881** The third Welland Canal is constructed. Part of the route is altered, and contrary to the previous two canals, the banks are kept free of mills by government policy.
- **1885** The Niagara Parks Commission is founded. Its mandate is to preserve and enhance the natural beauty of the Falls and the Niagara River corridor.
- **1888** The Niagara Parks Commission opens Queen Victoria Park, a 154-acre park adjacent to the Horseshoe Falls.
- **1895** The first large-scale hydroelectric station in the world begins operation in the Niagara Gorge, using alternating-current generators.

NIAGARA'S OTHER INDUSTRIES: SHIPPING AND AGRICULTURE

The commercial growth at the Falls was not restricted to the tourist industry. Engineers and scientists of the 19th century eagerly contemplated the potential of the powerful rapids and waterfalls. Since the 1700s mills had made use of the water to drive their machinery, but the full potential of Niagara to produce hydroelectric power could not be realized until the invention of the alternating current system, the basis of the long-distance transmission of electricity. In 1891, Nikola Tesla, who had invented alternating current dynamos, transformers, and motors, sold his patents to George Westinghouse. Together, they designed generators for the first large-scale hydroelectric plant in the world, the Adams Station. Since then, a number of power stations have been constructed in Canada and the U.S., and in total, the Niagara River now generates approximately 4,400 megawatts of electricity. In order to protect the thunder of the Falls as a major tourist attraction, only half of the river's flow is available for power, mostly at night. But only the most perceptive of tourists can distinguish the difference in flow.

The other major endeavor that boosted the area's economy was the construction of a shipping canal between Lake Erie and Lake Ontario. The St. Lawrence River and the Great Lakes form the largest inland waterway in the world, extending 3,700km (2,300 miles) from the Atlantic Ocean to the heart of North America, and a canal was needed to bypass the Niagara River corridor and establish a mighty commercial shipping route.

The first canal was completed in 1829. Consisting of 40 wooden locks, the canal served its purpose for only a few years before deterioration of the wood and the increasing size of ships required a second canal to be built. The Second Welland Canal had 27 cut stone locks and went into operation in 1845. In 1881, a third canal was built, following the same route as previous canals in the southern part of the region, but taking a new line in the north. The banks of the Third Welland Canal were kept free of industry by government decree. The fourth canal, known as the Welland Ship Canal, was completed in 1932. The number of locks was drastically reduced to eight and the canal adopted a direct north-south route over the escarpment.

Agricultural development of the region was aggressively pursued due to the unique combination of climate, physical geography, soil, and location. More than

- **1900** Irish-American Fenian sympathizers target Lock 24 of the Welland Canal in an unsuccessful bombing attack.
- **1901** Schoolteacher Annie Taylor is the first person to conquer the Falls, when she plunges over the Horseshoe Falls in a barrel.
- **1912** Three tourists lose their lives on the "ice bridge" when it suddenly breaks up, and from this point people are prohibited from crossing the frozen Niagara River during the winter.
- **1922** The Clock Tower, now a well-known landmark on Queen Street in Niagara-on-the-Lake, is erected as a memorial to the Niagara men who died in World War I.
- **1925** The first illumination of the Falls, a nightly event that has continued uninterrupted since that time, much to the delight of millions of visitors.
- **1930s** The government takes on a series of projects aimed at boosting tourism to Niagara, including the construction of the roadway now known as the Queen Elizabeth Way and the reconstruction of Fort George, which had been destroyed in the War of 1812 with the exception of the 1796 powder magazine.
- **1932** The fourth Welland Canal, consisting of eight concrete locks in a direct

50% of the Niagara land base is farmed, although increasing pressure for urban expansion and urban-type land use is a threat. Fruit trees dominate the agricultural landscape, although greenhouses and agri-food processing industries (including wineries) generate the most revenue in the agricultural sector of Niagara's economy.

The thriving Niagara wine industry had humble beginnings, with the first European settlers making use of the native labrusca grapes, which unfortunately did not produce palatable table wines. Modest success was achieved with Canadian hybrids, and the grape industry became established in Niagara during the early 1900s. By mid-century, six million vines were growing in the province, with the bulk of them in Niagara. French hybrids were becoming more popular, as consumer taste shifted toward dryer, lower-alcohol table wines and away from sweeter table and dessert wines.

By the 1970s, several enterprising growers had already begun planting *Vitis vinifera* vines, the so-called "noble grape" varietals that produce many of the world's finest wines, such as chardonnay, cabernet, gamay, and Riesling. Fertile, rich soils and a unique microclimate make Niagara a prime grape-growing region, and contrary to popular public opinion of the proposed outcome, the vinifera vines thrived.

The biggest contributor to the transformation of Ontario's wine industry was the introduction of international trade agreements in 1988. The loss of tariff and retail price protection put Ontario wines on a par with imports from the world's most respected and well-established wine regions, and the industry was faced with surrendering its market share or reinventing itself as a worthy contender. Growers, wineries, and the provincial government decided to revitalize the wine industry, and together they rose to the challenge.

Today, Niagara has approximately 16,000 acres under vine, in an area stretching from Niagara-on-the-Lake in the east to Grimsby in the west. More than 60 wineries now make their home in Niagara, many with fine restaurants and boutiques on-site. A large number offer wine-tasting and tours to the public. Niagara wines consistently bring home medals and awards from many of the world's most prestigious wine competitions. World attention has turned to the Niagara wine industry not least because of the superb quality of its icewine, a dessert wine produced from grapes that have been left on the vine after the fall harvest to freeze naturally. The frozen

north-south route over the Niagara Escarpment, opens.

- **1940s** Hybrid grape varieties are introduced to Ontario and a fledgling wine industry is born.
- **1950** The Floral Clock, consisting of 15,000 plants, is constructed along the Niagara Parkway north of the Botanical Gardens.
- **1953** Niagara Falls becomes the backdrop for the Marilyn Monroe film *Niagara*.

- **1954** Prospect Point, the most famous viewing point for the Falls on the American side, collapses into the gorge below.
- **1960** A 7-year-old boy is swept over the Horseshoe Falls following a boating accident in the upper Niagara River, wearing only a lifejacket. He survives and is rescued by the *Maid of the Mist* tourist boat.
- **1962** The Shaw Festival stages its first two productions

in the old courthouse in Niagara-on-the-Lake, presenting *Candida* and *Don Juan in Hell* from *Man and Superman* to appreciative audiences.

- **1969** The flow over the American Falls is stopped completely for several months while the feasibility of removing much of the loose rock from the base of the waterfall is investigated. It is decided that the expense grapes are handpicked and immediately pressed to capture the thick, yellow-gold liquid, high in natural sugars and acidity.

NIAGARA TODAY

The Niagara Region today has a population of more than 400,000 living in 12 municipalities, ranging from large urban, industrial, and service centers to rural locations. The area is very well placed for accessibility to major markets in North America and around the world. Niagara is within a 1-day drive of approximately half of the population of Canada and the United States. Its major industrial sectors include tourism, manufacturing, telecommunications, agriculture and greenhouse production, and service industries. Locals and visitors alike enjoy a wealth of golf courses, wineries, parks, and marinas under a sun that shines more than 2000 hours annually.

Niagara as a region has great potential for prosperity. The word "Niagara" has global brand recognition and its diverse economic base ensures a degree of stability. Recent investments have been huge, from the multitude of new wineries and hotels to the $1-billion Niagara Fallsview Casino Resort. Niagara's outstanding natural beauty, crowned by the Falls and its proximity to the border, are exceptional attributes.

Despite Niagara's strengths, the region on both sides of the border tends to perform below its economic potential. A 5-year economic growth strategy, projected to the year 2010, has been crafted by business, government, and community stakeholders and is already underway, helping to steer the region toward a more prosperous future.

---

would be prohibitive, and the Falls flow again.

- **1970s** Local grape growers begin planting viniferas, the so-called "noble grape" varietals that produce many of the world's finest wines—cabernet, chardonnay, gamay, and Riesling.
- **1973** The purpose-built Shaw Festival Theatre opens in Niagara-on-the-Lake.
- **1975** Niagara-based Inniskillin Wines is granted

the first new winery license in Ontario since 1929.

- **1979** Niagara Falls finds Hollywood fame once again when scenes from *Superman II,* starring Christopher Reeve and Margot Kidder, are filmed there.
- **1988** The introduction of international trade agreements induces the Niagara wine region to reinvent itself as a worthy world competitor in order to survive.

- **1989** The Vintners' Quality Alliance appellation system is introduced to ensure standards of excellence in Ontario winemaking.
- **1996** The 150th anniversary of the launch of the first *Maid of the Mist* is celebrated.
- **2004** The $1-billion Niagara Fallsview Casino Resort opens.
- **2006** An astounding 14 million visitors a year pour into the Niagara region.

Appendix B:
Wine 101

By John Thoreen and Louise Dearden

For those who wish to enrich their experience of Niagara's wine country, here is a taste of everything you wanted to know about wine but were afraid to ask. As you venture into Niagara's wineries, though, don't be shy. Niagara's winemakers are enthusiastic and genuinely hospitable folk, eager to lend a helping hand as you discover the world of wine.

1 Introduction to Winemaking

Transforming grapes into a rudimentary wine is a relatively simple process. Ripe grapes contain sugar, which, in the presence of certain yeast organisms, is converted into alcohol and carbon dioxide. For thousands of years, this process was carried out in a fairly crude manner, with early vintners making passable—but certainly not great—wines.

The science called *oenology*, which revolutionized winemaking, was developed after Louis Pasteur's work with fermentation and bacteriology around 150 years ago. Only in the past few generations have winemakers acquired intensive technical training and earned PhDs in viticulture (the science of grape growing) in a concentrated effort to deepen their understanding of wine and winemaking. In Niagara, both Brock University in St. Catharines and Niagara College Teaching Winery at the Glendale Campus of Niagara College in Niagara-on-the-Lake offer a variety of programs related to the grape growing and wine industry.

GROWING GRAPES

The re-birth of Niagara's wine industry occurred a quarter of a century ago; the majority of the vineyards are fewer than 15 years old. Many of the vines are planted in a north-south orientation in order to take full advantage of the sun and reap the maximum benefits of the moderating air currents that flow from above Lake Ontario toward the Niagara Escarpment. The fertility of the grape variety and soil type determines how the growers train the vine canopy, in a perpetual search for the perfect balance between quality and volume of yield. Growers also employ canopy management techniques to control and prevent mildew, mold, and insect damage. The immense efforts that take place in the vineyard are directed to producing the best possible grape for the *terroir* and specific weather and other environmental conditions, since the quality of the grape can be improved only while it is actively growing on the vine.

Grapes can be incredibly fussy, and growers face a perpetual struggle against the vagaries of weather and pests. Organic grape farmers, while striving to minimize environmental impact and reduce the amount of pesticides that wine drinkers imbibe, face even greater challenges, although the results are rewarding both for the conscience and the palate.

The majority of the vineyards in Niagara are independently owned by growers,

Grape Varietals in Niagara's Wine Country

Because growers in the Niagara wine region do not have the luxury of generations of experience to draw upon when deciding which grape varieties are best suited for its *terroir,* they experiment, with more than four dozen varieties planted throughout the region. Below is a list of the most prevalent grape varietals found in Niagara's wine country.

RED GRAPE VARIETIES

CABERNET FRANC This is the most widely planted red vinifera grape variety in Niagara. "Cab Franc" is often overshadowed by the better-known cabernet sauvignon, but this French black grape is well-suited to Niagara's *terroir,* being winter-tolerant and high-yielding. In hot growing years, excellent medium- to full-bodied wines are produced. Cabernet Franc tends to be lighter in color and tannins than cabernet sauvignon and matures earlier in the bottle. These wines have a deep purple color with an herbaceous aroma.

CABERNET SAUVIGNON This well-known transplant from Bordeaux has small, deep-colored, thick-skinned berries and is harvested in late October to early November in Niagara. The grape produces complex, medium- to full-bodied red wines that are highly tannic when young and usually require a long aging period to achieve their greatest potential. "Cab," as it is often affectionately called, is frequently blended with other related red varietals such as merlot and Cabernet Franc to produce classic full-flavored Bordeaux-style wines. Cabernet is a good match with red meat dishes and is delightful with a well-constructed cheese board.

MERLOT This varietal is traditionally used as a blending wine to smooth the rough edges of other grapes due to its soft and fruity nature and lower tannin levels. The merlot grape is a relative of cabernet sauvignon, but it tends to be less complex, with a black cherry bouquet. Merlots are drinkable at an earlier age than cabernet sauvignons, though they will still gain complexity with age. Merlot may be paired with any dish that a "Cab" would complement.

PINOT NOIR Made famous by the film *Sideways,* pinot noir is a difficult grape to grow. Even in their native Burgundy, the wines are excellent only a few years out of every decade, and they are a challenge for winemakers to master. During good years, pinot noir produces light- to medium-bodied red wines with low tannins and silky textures, making some of Niagara's most elegant and expensive table wines. Pinots are fuller and softer than cabernets and can be drinkable at 2 to 5 years of age, though the best improve with additional aging. Pinot noir is versatile at the dinner table, but it goes best with lamb, duck, turkey, game birds, semisoft cheeses, and even fish.

BACO NOIR & MARECHAL FOCH These French hybrids were developed in the early 1900s to suit the climate of northeastern North America. Strawberry can be detected in these wines, which are often made from older vines and aged in oak barrels.

WHITE GRAPE VARIETIES

CHARDONNAY Chardonnay is the most widely planted white vinifera grape variety in Niagara (and, interestingly, also in California). The grape is relatively winter-hardy and one of the earliest-ripening Niagara varieties, typically harvested toward the end of September. It produces exceptional medium- to full-bodied dry white wines. Chardonnays range from delicate, crisp wines that are clear and light in color to fruity, buttery, oaky wines that tend to have deeper golden hues as they increase in richness. No other wine benefits more from the oak-barrel aging process than chardonnay. This highly complex and aromatic grape is one of the few grapes in the world that doesn't require blending—it is also the principal grape in sparkling wine. Chardonnay goes well with a variety of dishes, from seafood to poultry, pork, veal, and pasta with cream- or butter-based sauces.

RIESLING The grape from which most of Germany's great wines are made, Riesling is a consistent performer and was one of the first commercially planted vinifera grapes in Niagara. This versatile grape produces some outstanding sparkling, dry, off-dry, semi-sweet, and icewine styles. Well-made Riesling wines have a vivid fruitiness and lively balancing acidity, leaving the palate refreshed, even when made into late-harvest dessert wine. Suggested food pairings include crab, pork, sweet-and-sour dishes, and anything with a pronounced citrus flavor. Asian-influenced cuisine also pairs well with Riesling.

SAUVIGNON BLANC This varietal produces crisp, dry whites and has become increasing popular in the region. Its predominant notes are grassy, fruity, and herbaceous when grown in a cool climate. The plant is a vigorous grower and is typically harvested during mild to late October. Because of its acidity, sauvignon blanc pairs well with shellfish, seafood, and salads.

VIDAL This varietal is the most favored for the creation of Niagara's famous icewine and late-harvest wines, since it produces large bunches of thick-skinned grapes and maintains its acidity throughout the winter months.

GEWÜRZTRAMINER This grape produces white wines with a distinctive, powerful floral aroma, often described as rosewater. Slightly sweet yet spicy, its flavor is reminiscent of lychee nuts. The varietal is particularly appreciated for its ability to complement Asian foods; its sweet character stands up to flavors that would diminish a drier wine's flavors and make it seem more tart. The vine is somewhat labor-intensive to grow in Niagara since it produces abundant foliage that must be controlled in order to prevent mildew problems.

with about 16,000 acres under vine, a number that is increasing yearly. Most growers live on their property, farm the land themselves, and sell their grapes to nearby wineries under contract.

THE WINEMAKING PROCESS

Production facilities in the Niagara region rank among the world's best in terms of technology and allow the area to compete with other cool-climate wine regions around the globe. Increasingly, the area is attracting knowledgeable and respected international winemakers, who work alongside the region's established vintners to bring innovation and experience to Niagara's wine industry.

During the winemaking process, many decisions must be made by the winemakers in order to craft wines that are unique to their winery. When to pick the grapes, whether to pick by hand or machine, whether to sort, destem, and crush the grapes, the duration of skin contact, which method to use to press the grapes or pulp, which type of yeast to implement, which sort of container to use for fermentation and whether to use a warm or cool fermentation process, how much exposure to air should be allowed, and which methods of stabilization and filtration to use are all critical decisions that contribute to the personality of the wine. There are many more variables to consider during the winemaking process, many of them specific to certain styles and types of wine. It's no wonder that today's winemakers attend educational programs in oenology and viticulture in addition to hands-on acquisition of knowledge in the wineries themselves. Modern wines truly are a blend of art and science.

WHITE WINES   For white wines, the winemaker wants only the juice from the grapes. (For red wines, both the juice and skins of the grapes are essential—see below.) Grapes are picked either by hand or machine and brought to the winery as quickly as possible. Just as the cut surface of an apple turns brown when left open to the air, grapes oxidize—and can even start fermenting—if they are not processed quickly. At some wineries, the clusters go through a "destemmer–crusher," which pops the berries off their stems and breaks them open (not really crushing them). The resulting mixture of juices, pulp, and seeds—called *must*—is pumped into a press (a widely used technique called, logically, *whole-cluster pressing*).

Most presses these days use an inflatable membrane, like a balloon, and gently use air pressure to separate the skins from the juice, which is then pumped into fermenting vessels. In the recent past, most white wines were fermented in stainless-steel tanks fitted with cooling jackets. Cool, even cold, fermentations preserve the natural fruitiness of white grapes. Wooden barrels are sometimes used for fermentation of white wines, especially chardonnay. This practice reverts to old-style French winemaking techniques and is believed to capture fragrances, flavors, and textures not possible in stainless steel. However, barrel fermentation is labor-intensive and the barrels themselves are expensive.

After white wines are fermented, they are clarified, aged (if appropriate), and bottled, usually before the next harvest. Simpler white wines—Riesling and sauvignon blanc, for example—are bottled first. A small number of white wines, usually chardonnays, undergo 15 to 18 months of barrel aging, producing richly flavored, complex, and expensive wines.

RED WINES   The chief difference between white wines and red wines lies simply in the red pigment that's lodged in the skins of the wine grapes. So while for white wines the juice is quickly pressed away from the skins, for roses and reds the pressing happens after the right amount of "skin contact." That can be anywhere from 6 hours—yielding a rose or very light red—to 6 weeks, producing a red that has extracted all the pigment from the skins and additionally refined the tannin that naturally occurs in grape skins and seeds.

Almost all red wines are aged in barrels or casks for at least several months, occasionally for as long as 3 years. Most wooden containers—collectively called *cooperage*—are barrels now made of American or French oak.

The aging of red wines plays an important role in their eventual style because several aspects of the wine change while in wood. First, the wine picks up oak fragrances and flavors. Second, the wine, which leaves the fermenter in a somewhat murky condition, complete with suspended yeast cells and bits of skin, clarifies as the particulate matter settles to the bottom of the barrel. Third, the texture of the wine changes as the tannins interact and begin to make the wine more supple. Deciding just when each wine in the cellar is ready to bottle challenges the winemaker every year. And, to make the whole process even more challenging, every year is different.

Unlike white wines, which are usually ready to drink shortly after bottling, many of the best red wines improve with aging in the bottle. Red wines generally have a "plateau" of several years when they are at their best condition for consumption, rather than a peak. There are no rigid rules surrounding when it's time to pop the cork. Only by consistently practicing the art of tasting will you find your own sense of when a wine is ready to drink by your standards.

2 The Art of Wine Tasting

At its simplest, all you need to become a wine taster is a glass and the willingness to focus your attention fully on the wine with your senses of **sight, smell, and taste.** To an expert, such details as the time of day and amount of humidity in the room can affect how a wine is perceived, but for the vast majority of wine drinkers, such subtleties are irrelevant.

PREPARING FOR TASTING

What is important is to have a **clean palate** before you begin. During your wine tour, **don't chew gum** or suck on minty sweets as they will interfere with the taste of the wine. Water is always available in a jug on tasting room counters; it is a good idea to **take a sip or two of water** before beginning your tasting session, but not necessary in between samples. Some people like to chew a **small piece of bread** or a few plain, unsalted **nuts** (walnuts are favored) prior to tasting to **neutralize the palate.**

To **clear the olfactory area** at the top of your nose before or between tastings, wine experts often favor a sniff of coffee beans—don't ask me how or why it works, but apparently it does the job. The untrained nose in particular can suffer from sensory overload if too many wines are nosed in too short a time, so take it easy in order to gain full enjoyment of the experience.

You are now ready to approach the glass. About **an ounce of wine** is sufficient for a tasting, although a more generous serving is perfectly acceptable. **Pick up the glass by the stem** (or the base if that feels more comfortable for you) but never cradle the bowl of the glass in your hand, as it will change the temperature of the wine.

SIGHT

Your first assessment is **visual.** Although this is the least important (and less enjoyable than smelling and tasting), it nonetheless can give you significant clues about the characteristics of a wine. Tilt the glass away from you and hold it against a neutral background—white if possible. Check its **clarity.** For the most part, wines ought to be clear, even brilliant, although a few unfiltered wines bear a slight haze. Filtration for clarification is, however, standard practice. Next, observe the **shades of color,** especially at the rim where the age of a wine tends to show itself. The browner a wine is, whether red or white, usually the older it is. Red wines range from purple (often a sign of young wine) through to ruby, garnet, and tawny. The depth of color of red wines lightens as they age, but in order to assess that accurately you would need to know what to expect of that particular wine at a younger age, since lighter shades are also specific to certain grape varietals. White wines vary in hue from pale greenish yellow to straw to deep gold. Better-quality wines seem to show a luster, or sheen, while those at the opposite end of the scale may appear dull and monochromatic.

SMELL

Smelling the wine is the next step, and is vital to enjoyment of a glass of wine. Indeed, to take full pleasure of a wine that speaks to you, we encourage you to "swirl and sniff" before every sip. That may feel pretentious at first, but it makes perfect sense. The olfactory bulb at the top of the nose can detect several thousand scents, but the tongue can discern only four tastes: sweet, sour, bitter, and salty.

The reason why many wine drinkers who do not take the time to smell their wine still reckon they get quite a lot of satisfaction from their wine is twofold. First, wine naturally vaporizes quite easily, so molecules drift up your nose as you drink from a glass whether you encourage them or not. Second, aromas reach the olfactory area via the *retro-nasal passage* at the back of the mouth as you swallow.

A decently shaped wineglass with a bowl that slopes toward the rim will help to direct the heady aromas to your nose (not to mention helping the wine to stay in the glass as you swirl it). Inhale the aroma, then pause for a moment. Take a second sniff, and this time try to identify distinctive scents. Don't worry if you have difficulty trying to describe what your nose smells. The best you can do is find descriptive words that remind you of the smell, although often they are woefully inadequate and sometimes are downright amusing. The **aroma wheel,** a ground-breaking graphic developed by Professor Ann. C. Noble and colleagues at the University of California, contains a battery of terms commonly used to describe a wine's aroma, bouquet, and flavor and can nudge you toward a wider vocabulary when propping up a tasting bar.

The basic aromas include floral, spicy, fruity, caramel, woody, earthy, mineral, and vegetal, among others. These descriptions can be further subdivided, which often then begins to identify particular grape varietals. For example, chocolate and Shiraz, raspberry and young pinot noir, and green apple and chardonnay.

One final point on smell—the words *aroma* and *bouquet* possess widely recognized, distinct meanings when used to describe wine, although they are commonly used almost interchangeably in normal conversation. **Aroma** refers to the characteristic simple, often fruity smell or flavor of a young wine, often a single varietal, for example the distinctive "gooseberry and cat's pee" of sauvignon blanc. **Bouquet** is used to describe the complex, multilayered smells or flavors that develop with aging and therefore from sources other than the grapes, such as the characteristic vanilla fragrance of French oak barrels.

TASTE

Now, it's finally time to **taste.** Take a mouthful of wine and try to cover your entire palate. If you are able to **draw a little air into your mouth** while it's full of wine, without dribbling or otherwise making a spectacle of yourself (some people pick this technique up fairly quickly; for others it's a bit messy), then you will intensify the flavor and encourage the vapor to rise up the retro-nasal passage at the back of your mouth. This is particularly useful if you are going to spit out the wine rather than swallow it.

While the wine is in your mouth, notice its qualities of **sweetness, acidity, and alcohol** and whether any bitterness, tannin, or gassiness is present. Do you find the balance of these elements pleasing? If you are swallowing, note the **"finish."** How long did the impact of the wine last after you swallowed it? Did you notice further scents and flavors during or after swallowing?

It's up to you how seriously you want to take the practice of wine tasting. There are no right or wrong feelings toward a particular bottle of wine. No one other than you can ever understand exactly how a wine will excite your senses. What you *will* find after conducting several wine tastings is that you quickly acquire a sense of the types of wine that appeal to your palate. So let that be your goal and your guide as you travel the quiet country roads of Niagara's wine country.

Index

See also Accommodations and Restaurant indexes, below.